The Latin
of Science

MARCELO EPSTEIN
and
RUTH SPIVAK

Bolchazy-Carducci Publishers, Inc.
Mundelein, Illinois USA

Editor: Donald E. Sprague
Contributing Editors: Laurel Draper and Amelia Wallace
Design & Layout: Adam Phillip Velez
Cover Image: Spain / Al-Andalus: A Muslim and a Christian practicing geometry together, from a fifteenth century illuminated manuscript / Pictures from History / Bridgeman Images

The Latin of Science

Marcelo Epstein and Ruth Spivak

Bolchazy-Carducci Publishers, Inc.
1570 Baskin Road
Mundelein, Illinois 60060
www.bolchazy.com

Printed in the United States of America
2019
by Publishers' Graphics

ISBN 978-0-86516-860-2

Library of Congress Cataloging-in-Publication Data

Names: Epstein, M. (Marcelo), editor. | Spivak, Ruth, editor.
Title: The Latin of science / [edited by] Marcelo Epstein and Ruth Spivak.
Description: Mundelein, Illinois : Bolchazy-Carducci Publishers, Inc., 2019.
Identifiers: LCCN 2019015080 | ISBN 9780865168602 (pbk.)
Subjects: LCSH: Latin language--Readers--Science. | LCGFT: Readers
  (Publications)
Classification: LCC PA2095 .L347 2019 | DDC 478.6/421--dc23

To Noa, Ariana, Solomon, Josephine,
Emilia, Elliot, and Penelope

Contents

List of Illustrations

Facsmiles

Figures

Preface

πάντες ἄνθρωποι τοῦ εἰδέναι ὀρέγονται φύσει
Omnes homines natura scire desiderant. (Aristotle)

For over twenty years the University of Calgary has been offering a two-term course through the Department of Classics entitled The Latin of Science. The main purpose of this course is to attract non-Classics majors to an active awareness of one of the most important components of human culture, namely, the vast literary output of scientific works written in Latin over a period of twenty centuries. The course consists of two parts, each extending over one academic term. The first part is devoted to a fast-paced comprehensive introduction to Latin grammar. Because of the intended application to scientific literature, some of the minutiae of Latin grammar can happily be avoided without detriment to the original aim. Moreover, because of the kind of students interested in this course—mostly, but not only, science and engineering majors—it has been possible to follow in some cases a non-standard route of presentation, one that emphasizes the similarities rather than the differences in patterns of conjugation and declension.

It was when starting with the second part of the course, the one devoted to the reading and translating of actual scientific texts, that we were confronted with the reality that there did not seem to exist in the market an anthology of this kind. Unbelievable as it may sound, a corpus of thousands of works written over a period of more than two millennia does not seem to have deserved so far a panoramic view for the beginner and expert alike. Many of these works are pivotal to the development of civilization as we know it, and many volumes could be filled even by just sticking to these pivotal works and neglecting all the rest. It is true that the quality of Latin in these works varies from the exquisite to the mundane, just as in today's scientific literature written in English. It is precisely the malleability of Latin, its expressive plasticity in spite of the strictness of its rules, its ability to describe with great precision in spite of the relative poverty of its basic vocabulary, that make its study such a joy.

The sense of achievement of our students, deriving from the miraculous quality of the process of going from complete ignorance to a reasonable mastery of a language within such a short period of time, has been conveyed to us time and again in explicit terms, and some of them (now lawyers, engineers, zoologists, physicists, philosophers, and, yes, even classicists) still keep in contact with us and with each other. The sheer intellectual brilliance and curiosity of our two-term students was consistently so high that we feel no reason to despair about the fate of the job of transmitting the traditions of the past to the future generations, one of the pillars of the university ideal.

In publishing this book it is not necessarily our intention to spur the offering of similar courses at other institutions. Instead, we wish to fill to a limited extent the anthological vacuum that we found, so that selections from scientific literature may be incorporated into regular Latin course offerings. We have tried, therefore, to include selections from as many periods and as many sciences as possible. It is hard to imagine that students will not appreciate such gems as William Harvey's comparison of the pumping cycle of the heart to the shooting of a rifle or Maimonides's proto-psychiatric treatise on depression. Nor should one deprive Latin students of the emotion of reading the original formulation of Isaac Newton's laws in his own words—he never actually said that force equals mass times acceleration. We believe that by not including these works in the Latin curriculum, our universities are missing a golden opportunity to demonstrate in palpable terms the relevance of the humanities to the attainment not only of the cultural values but also of the very scientific foundations of our contemporary technologically minded society.

To render the book as self-contained as possible, we have included a grammatical compendium (appendix II) that covers most, if not all, of the fundamental tools necessary to analyze and translate a text. Exercises and answer keys are provided online for each grammar chapter, thereby allowing readers to check their own progress. It is often the case that in scientific texts the science is more difficult than the Latin. Our notes and commentaries on the selections try, therefore, to address both the linguistic and the scientific difficulties that may arise. Isidore of Seville is certainly much easier to read than Newton on both counts. The selections, however, have been arranged by topic, not by level of difficulty. To enhance the intellectual experience, we have chosen to display facsimiles of first editions or even manuscripts, whenever available.[1] This is in the same spirit as playing period music on the corresponding period instruments. To facilitate the task, we have included a modern transliteration of each text. We have, in addition to the grammatical appendix, included an appendix on the pronunciation of Latin and on the contractions and combinations of vowels and consonants, and a Latin to English glossary.

Our expectations will be fulfilled if the publication of this book stimulates the inclusion of selections from Latin scientific literature in current course offerings. Our hopes will overflow of satisfaction if more universities decide to offer courses on the Latin of science, such as the one at the University of Calgary. Finally, all vessels of containment and contentment will break if the appearance of this modest anthology spurs the publication of other works of this kind, but of greater weight.

M.E. and R.S.
Calgary
December 2018

---

1   Digital versions of the facsimiles are provided on the book website for those who prefer to read them online or print them on separate sheets of paper.

Acknowledgements

We are grateful to the University of Calgary for facilitating this unusual blending of the scientific and humanistic cultures represented by the Schulich School of Engineering and the Faculty of Arts. We would especially like to acknowledge the Department of Classics at the University of Calgary, which has consistently supported the Latin of Science course since its inception over twenty years ago. Many students from the departments of engineering, biosciences, neuroscience, mathematics, chemistry, psychology, and classics have provided us with inspiration and encouragement. Without their enthusiasm for Latin and their sense of humor this work would not have come to fruition.

We would like to thank Bolchazy-Carducci Publishers and Bridget Dean, president, for their unwavering support and encouragement of this project and, in particular, Don Sprague and his colleagues—editors Laurel Draper and Amelia Wallace, designer Adam Velez and production manager Jody Cull—for their thorough revision of the manuscript and their suggestions for improvement.

Last but not least, we would like to thank our spouses Nareeza Khan and Mitchell Spivak for their love and patience.

How to Use This Book

The texts are arranged thematically, rather than by level of difficulty. Within each thematic unit, the selections are arranged chronologically. For convenience, a comprehensive glossary has been included at the end of the book. For more detailed explanations a good dictionary should be consulted. A succinct, but comprehensive, grammar of the Latin language is provided as an appendix.

As mentioned in the Preface, we encourage the reader to attempt reading directly from the facsimiles provided. Digital versions of the facsimiles are provided on the book website for those who prefer to read them online or print them on separate sheets of paper. Appendix III: Manuscript and Original Source Quirks explains abbreviations and other symbols often used in early printed editions of Latin texts and not found in classical Latin. Each selection also contains a complete modern transliteration of the Latin text in which all these "quirks" have been resolved, including spelling out abbreviated words and replacing symbols with words. The transliterations faithfully reproduce the headings and their punctuation as found in the facsimile of the Latin text.

Accompanying each selection a detailed set of grammatical, historical, and thematic notes can be found. In these notes, we have attempted to provide a reasonable balance between adequate support and excessive annotation. We hope this balanced approach will facilitate a first reading of the text. The level of annotation is fairly consistent so readers and instructors can pick and choose as they wish.

When all else fails, or for purposes of verification, translations can be found in *The Latin of Science Companion Volume*. Except for a few texts, for which well-known translations have been supplied, the translations are pretty literal renditions, trying to follow the original text as literally as possible. The result may sound occasionally awkward, but may be used as a scaffold for a more literary translation.

For ease of use we provide below a classification of the selections into three levels of Latin ability, according to our estimation. In order of increasing difficulty, they are:

1. Isidore of Seville (both texts); Alhazen; Maimonides; Harvey; Euclid; Leibniz; Oresme;

2. Francis Bacon; Cetius Faventinus; Newton (both texts); Galvani; Kepler; Copernicus, Agricola

3. Seneca the Younger; Pliny the Elder; Vitruvius; Alberti; Libavius; de Soto

Within each of these groups the order is arbitrary. In some cases, a low level of difficulty in the language is compensated by a higher level of difficulty in the scientific content, and vice versa. Euclid and Leibniz are good examples of the former, while Alberti provides a good example of the latter. Depending on your point of departure and general interests, you may enjoy or suffer from either case!

Helpful Hints for Translation

Do not panic! Latin translation is at first a slow analytic process. Do not get discouraged. Do not start translating words sequentially. Rather, have a good look at a whole sentence at a time, even a whole paragraph.

Use the glossary or a dictionary if necessary. Keep an open mind as to the shades of meaning of words. Pay great attention to cases—do not just try to glue words together without regard to their function in the sentence, usually quite clearly indicated by the case.

Read your translation and try to see if it makes global sense. Adjust some of the adjectives and adverbs within the permitted ranges of their meanings. Remember that Latin is not as rich a language, in terms of sheer vocabulary, as English. Many words, therefore, must be made to serve what in English appears as a double duty. Moreover, with the passage of time, and with different local influences and liturgical and theological uses, Latin words changed their meanings slightly. The context is always very important.

Having said all that, it is good practice to trust your instinct too, especially as you become more experienced with the language. Finally, and most importantly, the translation must make sense in English. After the translation is complete, again read the original Latin aloud. This exercise builds up the intuition for further readings, particularly if they are by the same author. It is usually the case that the first few sentences of a text are the most difficult to translate.

On the Subjunctive Mood

Latin likes the subjunctive mood, while English is more inclined toward the indicative. Thus where Vergil writes, *Nunc scio quid sit amor,* "now I know what love be," a modern English writer would prefer the indicative "now I know what love is." Recall, moreover, that purpose and result clauses in Latin, introduced by *ut, ut non,* or *ne,* are usually expressed in the subjunctive mood. For specifics, please see p. 310. In scientific Latin the boundaries between purpose and result clauses can be somewhat fuzzy, but this is usually resolved by the context. Scientific Latin frequently uses the subjunctive mood to express an assumption, such as: *sit AC linea,* the English translation for which is the familiar "let AC be a line." Another frequent use of the Latin subjunctive is the combination "*cum* + subjunctive." You will have to decide according to the context whether this is a temporal usage ("when"), a concessive usage ("although"), or any other of the multiple usages described in Latin grammars and in this book's grammar compendium.

On Indirect Speech

Indirect speech (indirect statement/oratio obliqua) in classical Latin is conveyed by means of the accusative with infinitive construction. The corresponding English construction exists, but is used only occasionally. For example: "she thinks him to be good," which corresponds exactly to *ea putat eum bonum esse.* In English, indirect statement is more commonly expressed in the indicative, often but not always accompanied by "that": "she thinks [that] he is good." In later Latin we often find an increased use of the equivalent to the English "she thinks that he is good," where *quia* or *quod* ("that") has been supplied, the accusative *eum* ("him") has been turned into the nominative *is* ("he"), and the infinitive *esse* ("to be") has been replaced by the finite *est* ("is"). This results in the later Latin *ea putat quia is bonus est.*

Introduction

The rich and complex history of spoken and written Latin defies any attempt at a simplistic description. It is, nevertheless, useful to divide the two and a half millennia over which this history extends into three main periods—classical, medieval, and modern—with the understanding that there is an unavoidable degree of fuzziness in their temporal and spatial boundaries. Indeed, whatever features one may choose to characterize a given period in the historical development of Latin, it soon becomes evident that some of those features were already present at an earlier time or will persist in the works of some authors at a much later date. This phenomenon can be explained in part by the incredibly large territorial extent of Latin, first brought about by the Roman legions, but eventually achieved through the virtual monopoly of Latin upon learned communication in all matters philosophical, theological, and scientific during the Middle Ages, the Renaissance, and a considerable portion of the modern era. As the traditional language of the Roman Catholic Church, Latin enjoys to our very day the status of the official language of the Vatican and, as such, its vocabulary is constantly being brought up to date. Part of the explanation for the coexistence of several Latin styles at any given moment is also a deliberately archaizing tendency.

Historical Survey

The Classical Period (From the Beginnings until 476 CE)

The classical period embraces the greatest literary masterpieces of the Romans, when Latin was still the language of everyday life. It is sufficient to mention the names of Cicero, Julius Caesar, Livy, Catullus, Vergil, Horace, Ovid, Seneca, Tacitus, Martial, Juvenal, Plautus, Terence, Petronius, and Apuleius, among many others, to realize the magnitude of the contribution of Rome to the literary and historical patrimony of civilization. Some of the early Christian writers, such as St. Augustine and St. Jerome, belong to this period too, although the latter's Latin translation of the Bible, known as the Vulgate, can already be considered as a transitional work.

By comparison, the scientific literary output of this period is remarkably thin. In fact, the Romans did not distinguish themselves in this realm, nor did they bother to translate into Latin the works of the Greek scientists. This phenomenon is probably not due to lack of interest, but more to the fact that educated Romans were supposed to be fluent in Greek, still the prevailing language throughout the Hellenistic world. The Roman emperor Marcus Aurelius, for example, wrote his celebrated *Meditations* in Greek, not in Latin. It is also important to realize that such Greek scientific giants as Ptolemy, Heron, and Diophantus belong, respectively, to the first, second, and third centuries CE. The Romans simply could not compete. Nevertheless, without any claim to originality, there existed a few classical Latin works of an encyclopedic nature that are worthy of mention. Marcus Terentius Varro (116–25 BCE) composed one such work, of which only the *Res Rusticae* (*Agriculture*), dealing with agriculture and farm animals, has survived. He is also the author of *De Lingua Latina* (*On the Latin Language*), a treatise on Latin grammar and etymology. It is interesting to remark that Varro's understanding of a proper education was framed within the seven liberal arts: grammar, logic, and rhetoric (the "trivium") and arithmetic, geometry, astronomy, and music (the "quadrivium"). These basic disciplines were supplemented by the practical arts of medicine and architecture. This framework constitutes the basis for the curricula of all universities, from the Middle Ages to our own day. Another work of encyclopedic nature is that of Seneca the Younger (Lucius Annaeus Seneca, 4 BCE–65 CE), who wrote a scientific book entitled *Quaestiones Naturales* (*Natural Questions*), dealing mainly with meteorological and astronomical phenomena. The most celebrated and influential work along these lines was written by Pliny the Elder (Gaius Plinius Secundus, 23–79 CE) under the title *Historia Naturalis* (*Natural History*). Impressive in its scope, it can hardly be considered a purely scientific work, particularly after the centuries-old legacy of Aristotle. A work of great originality is *De Rerum Natura* (*On the Nature of Things*) by Lucretius (Titus Lucretius Carus, 99–55 BCE), a long philosophical poem that adheres to a strict atomistic viewpoint, borrowed from Democritus and Epicurus, to explain everything in the material, spiritual, and social domains.

The classical period did slightly better in the applied sciences of architecture and medicine. Vitruvius (Marcus Vitruvius Pollio, first century BCE) is the author of what can be considered the first comprehensive architectural treatise, *De Architectura* (*On Architecture*). This remarkably modern work had an immense impact on the architects of the Italian Renaissance. Medicine during this period was the exclusive realm of Greek doctors (e.g., Galen) and was generally taught in Greek. One Latin treatise, however, stands out as a masterpiece: *De Medicina* (*On Medicine*), by Aurelius Cornelius Celsus. Written about 30 CE, it was part of a greater encyclopedic work now lost. Its style was considered of a quality comparable to that of Cicero, and Celsus was sometimes called *Cicero medicorum*. Worthy of mention too is the work of Flavius Vegetius (383–450 CE) entitled *Digestorum Artis Mulomedicinae Libri* (*Books of Digests on the Art of Veterinary Medicine*), which can be considered as the first book on veterinary science.

The Middle Ages

Even before the fall of Rome (476 CE), Latin had not been a uniform and rigid language. Side by side with the polished literary form of Cicero, there existed a multitude of vernacular variants, regarded by the purists as barbarian, which manifested themselves not only in considerable regional differences in pronunciation but also in a natural tendency to simplify the grammatical structure in the day-to-day use of the language. These regional and cultural differences were exacerbated with the fall of the central political authority in 476 CE, leaving the Christian Church as the single unifying power in western Europe to preserve at least some aspects of the Latin heritage. In particular, Latin became the language of the learned classes and was used all over western and central Europe for almost all forms of written and oral communication in matters pertaining to politics, science, philosophy, arts, commerce, and even personal life. Thus, Latin remained a living language throughout the Middle Ages and, to a lesser extent, well into the nineteenth century. Although essentially the same as classical Latin, medieval Latin enriched the relatively poor word arsenal of classical Latin by incorporating a myriad of new terms suited to a more precise description and transmission of knowledge. It also allowed for a less rigid adherence to the minute details of Latin grammatical rules. Prepositions were used more often, word order was rendered less artificial, and orthographic freedom was widely exercised.

During most of the Middle Ages, western Europe remained virtually ignorant of the great works of the Greek mathematicians and scientists. Many of these works, as well as a wealth of scientific treatises from India, Persia, and China, had been preserved in Arabic translations made during the eighth and ninth centuries. Original contributions to mathematics and science abounded during this veritable Golden Age of Islamic civilization. But these important developments had to wait some three hundred years before making a revolutionary impact in Western European science through a renewed movement of translations into Latin. We can say, therefore, that, as far as the scientific literature is concerned, the medieval period of Latin is not particularly rich, at least until the twelfth century.

One of the most important figures in this period appears at its very beginning. Boethius (476–524) was born into an aristocratic Roman family and educated in the best schools of the day. Perhaps because he saw and lamented the decline of classical culture, he determined to preserve whatever he could by translating and summarizing the works of its greatest exponents. Some of his books would become required textbooks in the medieval educational system for several centuries. His major extant work, *De Consolatione Philosophiae* (*On the Consolation of Philosophy*), is philosophical-theological in nature, but some of his scientific treatises have also survived. They deal with the seven liberal arts—the trivium and the quadrivium described above. We have complete versions of *De Institutione Arithmetica* (*On Arithmetical Principles*) and *De Institutione Musica* (*On Musical Principles*), which contain no original results, but provide a good summary of the knowledge of the time. Of great significance also are his works on logic, many of them translations or commentaries of classical Greek works.

Apart from Boethius's works, there were a number of encyclopedias of the seven liberal arts written in the Middle Ages, mostly based on the Greek models. The oldest among them was compiled by Cassiodorus (Flavius Magnus Aurelius Cassiodorus Senator, 495–585), also a member of an aristocratic family, under the title of *Institutiones Divinarum et Saecularium Litterarum* (*Institutions of Divine and Secular Literature*). The second part of this work contains an introduction to the seven liberal arts for the edification of Christian monks. Borrowing partially from Cassiodorus, Isidore of Seville (590–636) composed his *Etymologiarum sive Originum Libri XX* (known in English simply as the *Etymologies*), an encyclopedia of the liberal and applied arts, and *De Rerum Natura* (*On the Nature of Things*), a work specialized in astronomy and meteorology. These works enjoyed great popularity as medieval university textbooks. More important than that of his predecessors is the contribution to science of the Venerable Bede (673–735), who was able to add to Isidore's material his direct knowledge of Pliny's *Historia Naturalis*, probably not available to Isidore. Written in straightforward and clear Latin, Bede's encyclopedia was also called *De Rerum Natura* (*On the Nature of Things*). More important still are his original contributions to the exact determination of the calendar, exposed in great detail in *De Temporum Ratione* (*On the Reckoning of Time*). Bede shows a remarkable understanding of the connection between the tides and the phases of the moon, and an acute sense of reliance on the observation of natural phenomena rather than mere speculation.

The twelfth century witnessed the phenomenon of renewed scientific activity stirred by the proliferation of Latin translations, mainly from Arabic versions, of the works of Aristotle, Euclid, Ptolemy, Archimedes, and other exponents of Greek and Hellenistic thought, as well as of original mathematical works written in Arabic. One of the great centers of translating activity was Toledo, reconquered from the Arabs in 1085, the capital of Castile and later of Spain (until 1560). Toledo was a cultural and intellectual melting pot of the Christian, Muslim, and Jewish traditions. By the thirteenth century, King Alfonso X, "the Wise," established there a School of Translators, thus giving official recognition to a century-old reality. Nor was Toledo the only place where translations were being commissioned. Among the most influential translators, we can cite Adelard of Bath (fl. early twelfth century), Gerard of Cremona (1114–1187), and Michael Scot (d. 1235). William of Moerbeke (fl. second half of the thirteenth century) translated directly from the Greek originals.

It was only a matter of time before original scientific works would be written in Latin. Adelard of Bath himself was influential not only as a translator but also as a staunch defender of the scientific method, which he presented in his book *Quaestiones Naturales* (*Natural Questions*), crafted in the attractive style of a dialogue, a popular pedagogical device at that time. Perhaps the first original scientific writer of this period is Fibonacci (Leonardo di Pisa, 1170–1230). Through his extensive travels, he had become familiar with the Hindu-Arabic numerals, and in his *Liber Abaci (The Book of Calculation)* he introduced the decimal system to the West. He was also a pioneer of the use of algebraic methods and algebraic notation. His second major work is *Practica Geometriae (The Practice of Geometry)*, published in 1220. An important contemporary of Fibonacci is Robert Grosseteste (1168–1253), chancellor of the University of Oxford. Apart from performing or commissioning the translation of scientific works from the Greek originals, he made important contributions to optics. He wrote commentaries on the works of Aristotle and a scientific manual called *Compendium Scientiarum (Compendium of the Sciences)*. At about the same time, in the field of rational mechanics, Jordanus Nemorarius (fl. thirteenth century?) made important contributions that foreshadowed the work of Galileo Galilei and Newton. His two masterpieces are *Elementa super Demonstrationem Ponderis (Elements on the Proof of Weight)* and *De Ratione Ponderis (On the Reckoning of Weight)*. Jean Buridan (fl. first half of the fourteenth century), following some ideas of Arabic science, proposed the so-called impetus theory, a sort of forerunner of the concepts of inertia and momentum. His main works in this field are *Quaestiones super Octo Physicorum Libros Aristotelis (Questions on the Eight Books of Aristotle's Physics)* and *Quaestiones de Caelo et Mundo (Questions on the Sky and Earth)*. Further progress in mechanics is associated with Merton College, at Oxford, whose two main exponents are William Heytesbury (*Regula Solvendi Sophismata* [*Rules for Solving Sophisms*]) and Richard Swineshead (*De Motu* [*On Motion*] and *Liber Calculationum* [*Book of Calculations*]). Working in the period 1325 to 1350, they correctly described the kinematics of uniformly accelerated motion, long before Galileo Galilei. Following in their footsteps, Nicole Oresme (1320–1382), a man of remarkable breadth of knowledge ranging from economics to theology, gave a geometric representation of continuous variables and their applications to mechanics in a manner somewhat suggestive of the analytic geometry of René Descartes. These ideas appear in his *Tractatus de Configurationibus Qualitatum et Motuum (Treatise on the Configurations of Qualities and Motions)*, one of his many works. An interesting aspect of Oresme's activity is that he undertook the translations of classical works into French, thus inaugurating a multilingual modus operandi that would become typical of later centuries. Reading the works of Buridan, Heytesbury, and Oresme is essential for anyone wishing to identify some of those giants on whose proverbial shoulders Newton is supposed to have stood.

Medicine in the Middle Ages is often associated with Muslim and Jewish practitioners, the most famous of whom are Avicenna (Ibn Sina, 980–1037) and Maimonides (Moshe ben Maimon, 1135–1204). Avicenna's *Al-Qanun fi-l Tibb* (*The Canon of Medicine*) was translated into Latin in the twelfth century. The first school of medicine in western Europe was that of Salerno in Italy. An important work to come out of this school is a collective effort known as *Regimen Sanitatis Salernitatum* (*The Salernitan Rule of Health*), a handbook of medicine written in verse probably in the early thirteenth century. Important advances were taking place at that time in the field of surgery. Roger of Salernum (fl. second half of the twelfth century) wrote the first surgical treatise, *Practica Chirurgiae* (*The Practice of Surgery*), in the West. Guy de Chauliac (1300–1368) is the author of the influential treatise *Chirurgia Magna* (*Great [Text on] Surgery*).

To close this rather incomplete account of medieval scientific literature in Latin, we mention two important figures for the development of science. Albertus Magnus (Albert the Great, or Albert of Cologne, 1200–1280) was instrumental in the dissemination of Aristotle's works on the natural sciences and made original contributions to botany and zoology. These original works appear within his Aristotelian commentaries *De Vegetalibus* (*On Plants*) and *De Animalibus* (*On Animals*). More relevant than Albertus Magnus is his younger contemporary Roger Bacon (1220–1292). A disciple of Grosseteste, Bacon was an indefatigable student of languages, including Hebrew and Greek, and of mathematics and physics. Through his omnivorous studies, he developed a rather atypical unprejudiced view of human civilizations, expressing it in his recognition that pagan, Muslim, and Jewish thinkers like their Christian counterparts must also have been inspired by God. His contributions to science itself, mainly in the field of optics, are less important than his unyielding defense of the experimental method and the use of mathematics to express physical thoughts. Most of these ideas can be found in his *Opus Maius* (*Greater Work*), consisting of seven parts written in a lively style.

The rise of Italian Humanism and of the wider European movement known as the Renaissance marks the transition into the third period of Latin literature. The humanists advocated and practiced a return to the Greek and Roman sources and the grammatical purification of Latin. Paradoxically perhaps, this humanistic point of view seems to have delayed the development of science for a good hundred years. The impetus of original scholastic medieval science was halted as attention was fixed on the achievements of classical antiquity. Even when the scientific revolution finally took shape in the sixteenth century, the debt to scholastic science often went unrecognized, although many of the important scientific writings of the thirteenth and fourteenth centuries had been committed to print and were used by the new scientists. An example of this borrowing is quite evident in the kinematics of Galileo, inspired no doubt by the legacy of the Merton school, from whose works he sometimes quotes verbatim. Be that as it may, the center of gravity of Latin scientific literature moves drastically and justifiably toward the modern era, while the classical and early medieval periods are virtually dwarfed by the new achievements.

The Modern Era

Some experts use the term "Neo-Latin" to encompass "all writings in Latin since the dawn of humanism in Italy from about 1300 CE, viz. the age of Dante and Petrarch, down to our own time."[2] It would be impossible to do justice in this brief introduction to the hundreds of contributors to Latin scientific literature in this seven-hundred-year period. What follows, therefore, is a selection of authors in chronological order, indicating their fields of activity and, in many cases, the title of their most significant works. It is worth noting that many of these authors wrote both in Latin and in their mother or national tongue, and some even in three or four European languages. The criterion for an author to enter this list, however, is simply to have written at least one book or scientific article in Latin.

Martin Waldseemueller (1470–1518), *Cosmographiae Introductio* (*Introduction to Cosmography*). Geography.

Nicolaus Copernicus (Mikolaj Kopernik, 1473–1543), *De Revolutionibus Orbium Coelestium* (*On the Revolutions of the Heavenly Spheres*). Astronomy.

Juan Luis Vives (1492–1540), *De Anima et Vita Libri Tres* (*Three Books on the Soul and Life*). Psychology.

Georgius Agricola (Georg Bauer, 1494–1555), *De Re Metallica* (*On Metallurgy*). Mineralogy.

---

2 Jozef IJsewin, *Companion to Neo-Latin Studies, part I*, 2nd ed. (Louvain, Belgium: Leuven University Press, 1990), v. See also the first edition (Amsterdam: North-Holland Publ. Co., 1977).

Geronimo (Girolamo) Cardano (1501–1576), *De Malo Recentiorum Medicorum Medendi Usu Libellus (On Medicine)*; *Liber Artis Magnae sive Regulis Algebraicis (Ars Magna or the Rules of Algebra)*; *Liber de Ludo Aleae (The Book on Games of Chance)*. Medicine, Mathematics.

Gerardus Mercator (Gerhard von Kremer, 1512–1594), *Atlas sive Cosmographicae Meditationes de Fabrica Mundi et Fabricati Figura (Atlas or Cosmographical Meditations on the Fabric of the World)*. Geography, Cartography.

Andreas Vesalius (1514–1564), *De Humani Corporis Fabrica Libri Septem (Seven Books on the Fabric of the Human Body)*. Anatomy.

William Gilbert (1540–1603), *De Magnete Magnetisque Corporibus et de Magno Magnete Tellure (On the Lodestone and Magnetic Bodies and on the Great Magnet, the Earth)*. Physics, Magnetism.

Tycho Brahe (1546–1601), *Astronomiae Instauratae Progymnasmata (Introductory Exercises for a Renewed Astronomy)*; *Astronomiae Instauratae Mechanica (Instruments for the Renewed Astronomy)*. Astronomy.

Andreas Libavius (1550–1616), *Alchemia (Alchemy)*. Chemistry.

John Napier (1550–1617), *Mirifici Logarithmorum Canonis Descriptio (A Description of the Marvelous Law of Logarithms)*; *Mirifici Logarithmorum Canonis Constructio (A Construction of the Marvelous Law of Logarithms)*. Mathematics.

Galileo Galilei (1564–1642), *Nuncius Sidereus (Sidereal Messenger)*. Astronomy, Physics.

Johannes Kepler (1571–1630), *Mysterium Cosmographicum (The Cosmographic Mystery)*; *Astronomia Nova (New Astronomy)*; *Harmonices Mundi Liber V (On the Harmony of the World)*; *Epitome Astronomiae Copernicanae (An Epitome of Copernican Astronomy)*; *Apologia pro Tychone contra Ursum (A Defense on behalf of Tycho against Ursus)*; *Somnium (Dream)*; *Dioptrice (Optics)*. Astronomy, Optics.

Jan Baptista van Helmont (1577–1644), *Ortus Medicinae vel Opera et Opuscula Omnia (The Origin of Medicine or Complete Works)*. Chemistry, Medicine.

William Harvey (1578–1657), *Exercitatio Anatomica de Motu Cordis et Sanguinis in Animalibus* (*An Anatomical Exercise on the Motion of the Heart and Blood in Living Beings*). Medicine.

René Descartes (1596–1650), *Regulae ad Directionem Ingenii* (*Rules for the Direction of the Mind*). Philosophy, Mathematics, Physics.

Otto von Guericke (1602–1686), *Experimenta Nova Magdeburgica* (*New Madgeburg Experiments*). Physics.

Bernardus Varenius (1622–1655), *Geographia Generalis* (*A General Geography*). Geography.

Christiaan Huygens (1629–1695), *Horologium Oscillatorium* (*The Pendulum Clock*). Physics.

Isaac Barrow (1630–1677), *Lectiones Opticae et Geometricae* (*Optical and Geometrical Lectures*). Mathematics.

Isaac Newton (1642–1727), *Philosophiae Naturalis Principia Mathematica* (*The Mathematical Principles of Natural Philosophy*). Mathematics, Physics.

Gottfried Wilhelm Leibniz (1646–1716), *Hypothesis Physica Nova* (*A New Physical Hypothesis*); *Historia et Origo Calculi Differentialis* (*The History and Origin of Differential Calculus*). Mathematics, Philosophy.

Jakob (1655–1705) and Johann (1667–1748) Bernoulli. Much of their work was written in Latin and collected in their *Opera Omnia* (*Complete Works*). Mathematics, Physics.

Hermann Boerhaave (1668–1738), *Institutiones Medicae* (*Medical Principles*); *Atrocis nec Descriptii Prius Morbi Historia* (*An Account of a Horrible Disease not Described Before*); *Aphorismi de Cognoscendis et Curandis Morbis* (*Aphorisms on Recognizing and Treating Diseases*). Medicine.

Giovanni Battista Morgagni (1682–1771), *De Sedibus et Causis Morborum per Anatomen Indagatis* (*On the Seats and Causes of Diseases Investigated through Anatomy*). Anatomy, Pathology.

Carolus Linnaeus (Carl von Linné, 1707–1778), *Species Plantarum* (*Species of Plants*); *Systema Naturae* (*A System of Nature*); *Genera Plantarum* (*Genera of Plants*); *Philosophia Botanica* (*Botanical Philosophy*). Botany.

Leonhard Euler (1707–1783), *Introductio in Analysin Infinitorum* (*An Introduction to the Analysis of the Infinite*); *Institutiones Calculi Differentialis* (*The Foundations of Differential Calculus*); *Institutiones Calculi Integralis* (*The Foundations of Integral Calculus*). Mathematics.

Albert von Haller (1708–1777), *Elementa Physiologiae Corporis Humani* (*The Elements of the Physiology of the Human Body*). Physiology, Medicine.

Luigi Aloisio Galvani (1737–1798), *De Viribus Electricitatis in Motu Musculari Commentarius* (*A Commentary on the Effects of Electricity in Muscular Motion*). Physiology, Physics.

Alessandro Volta (1745–1827), *De Vi Attractiva Ignis Electricis* (*On the Attractive Force of Electric Fire*). Physics.

Carl Friedrich Gauss (1777–1855), many articles in Latin. Mathematics, Physics.

Leopold Kronecker (1823–1891), some articles in Latin. Mathematics.

General Knowledge

Seneca the Younger

L ucius Annaeus Seneca (4 BCE–65 CE) was born in Cordoba (*Corduba* in Latin), in the province of Hispania, far from the center of the Roman Empire. His father, Marcus Annaeus Seneca, or Seneca the Elder, a teacher of rhetoric, had considerable wealth and connections in Rome. The young Seneca, known simply as Seneca on account of his greater fame, was educated in Rome, where he absorbed the ideas of Stoicism. Moving in the high circles of Roman society, Seneca was subjected to the vicissitudes of fortune in the ever-changing games of favoritism in the eyes of the ruling family. Thus, on the accession of the teenaged Nero to the throne, Seneca found himself in the powerful position of adviser to the emperor. He was not just Nero's speechwriter, but actually played an important role in decision-making and amassed a considerable fortune. After his forced retirement in the year 62, he had a few years left to muse, and write profusely, on how to reconcile one's life circumstances with the principles of Stoic philosophy. Seneca's *Epistulae Morales ad Lucilium* (*Moral Letters to Lucilius*), written to his friend Lucilius Junior, are perhaps his most enchanting work and can be read today, as in his own time, as some of the most morally edifying thoughts of all time. He was also the author of nine tragedies, based on classical Greek themes, which exercised a lasting influence on the development of modern European drama. He also found the time to write an encyclopedic quasi-scientific work entitled *Quaestiones Naturales* (*Natural Questions*). It may have served as inspiration for the much more comprehensive *Historia Naturalis* (*Natural History*), written a few years later by his younger contemporary Pliny the Elder. Accused of conspiring to murder the emperor, Seneca was forced to commit suicide in the year 65.

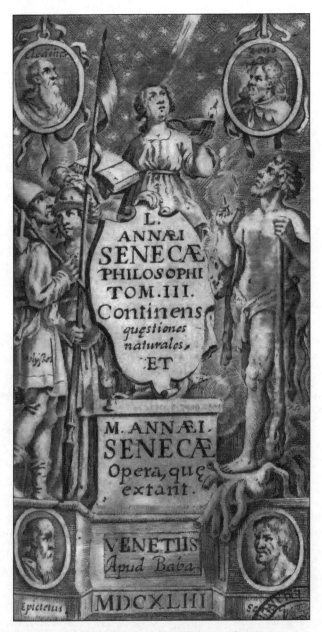

L. Annaei Senecae philosophi Opera tribus tomis distincta, apud Baba, Venice, 1643. Property of the Naples Library Collection. Facsimile courtesy of archive.org.

NATVR. QVÆST. Lib. VI. 107
posse extenuatis sustineri , quod integris
ferebatur . Potest terram mouere impres-
sio spiritus . Fortasse enim aer extrinse-
cus aliò intrante aere agitatur . Fortasse
aliqua parte subitò decidente percutitur ,
& inde motum capit. Fortasse aliqua parte terræ velut columnis quibusdam ac pi-
lis sustinetur : quibus vitiatis ac rece-
dentibus , tremit pondus impositum .
Fortasse calida vis spiritus in ignem versa , & fulmini similis , cum magna strage
obstantium fertur . Fortasse palustres &
iacentes aquas aliquis flatus impellit , &
inde aut ictus terram quatit , aut spiritus
agitatio , ipso motu crescens , & se inci-
tans , ab imo in summa vsque perfertur :
nullam tamen illi placet caussam motus
esse maiorem , quàm spiritum.

CAP. XXI. Nobis quoque placet ,
hunc spiritum esse , qui tanta possit cona-
ri , quo nihil est in rerum natura poten-
tius , nihil acrius , sine quo nec illa quidem, quæ vehementissima sunt , valent .
Ignem spiritus concitat: aquæ, si ventum
detrahas, inertes sunt. Tunc demum im-
petum sumunt , cùm illas agit flatus : qui
potest dissipare magna spatia terrarum,&
nouos montes subrectos extollere ; & in-
sulas non antè visas, in medio mari po-
nere . Therasiam nostræ ætatis insulam,
spectantibus nautis in Ægæo mari ena-
tam , quis dubitat , quin in lucem spiritus
vexerit ? Duo genera sunt (vt Posidonio
placet)

208 L. ANNÆI SENECÆ:
placet) quibus mouetur terra: vtrique nomen est proprium. Altera succussio est ,
cùm terra quatitur , & sursum ac deorsum mouetur: altera inclinatio, qua in
latera nutat nauigij more. Ego & tertium illud existimo, quod nostro vocabulo signatum est: non enim sine caussa
tremorem terræ dixere maiores , qui vtrique dissimilis est. nam nec succutiuntur
tunc omnia , nec inclinantur, sed vibrantur. Res minimè in hüiusmodi casu noxia , sicut longè perniciosior est inclinatio concussione. Nam nisi celeriter ex
altera parte properabit motus , qui inclinata restituat , ruina necessariò sequitur.
Cùm dissimiles ij motus inter se sint ,
caussæ eorum diuersæ sunt.

CAP. XXII. Priùs ergo de motu
quatiente dicamus. Si quando magna
onera per vices vehiculorum plurium
tracta sunt , & rotæ maiore nisu in salebras inciderunt , terram concuti senties.
Asclepiodotus tradit , cùm petra è latere
montis abrupta cecidisset , ædificia vicina
tremore collapsa. Idem sub terris fieri
potest , vt ex his quæ impendent rupibus
aliqua resoluta , magno pondere ac sono
in subiacentem cauernam cadat , eò ve-
hementiùs , quò aut plus ponderis habuit , aut venit altiùs. Et sic commoue-
tur omne tectum cauatæ vallis. Nec tantùm pondere suo abscindi saxa credibile
est, sed cùm flumina suprà ferantur , assi-
                                        duus

NATVR. QVÆST. Lib. VI. 109
duus humor commiſſuras lapidis extenuat, & quotidie his ad quæ religatus eſt
aufert, & illam (vt ita dicam) cutem qua
continetur, abradit. Deinde longa per
æuum diminutio vſque eò infirmat illa,
quæ quotidie attriuit, vt deſinant eſſe
oneri ferendo. Tunc ſaxa vaſti ponderis
decidunt, tunc illa præcipitata rupes,
quidquid ab imo repercuſſit, non paſſura
conſiſtere, ſuccutit:
——*Et ruere omnia viſa repentè* :
vt ait Virgilius noſter. Huius motus ſuc-
cutientis terras hæc erit cauſſa. Ad alte-
ram tranſeo.
  CAP. XXIII. Rara terræ natura
eſt, multumque habens vacui: per has ra-
ritates ſpiritus fertur: qui vbi maior in-
fluxit, nec emittitur, concutit terram.
Hæc placet & aliis, vt paullò antè retu-
li, cauſſa : ſi quid apud te profectura te-
ſtium turba eſt. Hanc etiam Calliſthe-
nes probat non contemptus vir. Fuit
enim illi nobile ingenium, & furibundi
regis impatiens. Hoc eſt Alexandri cri-
men æternum, quod nulla virtus, nulla
bellorum felicitas redimet. Nam quotiens
quis dixerit: Occidit Perſarum multa
millia: opponetur, Et Calliſthenem. Quotiens dictum erit, Occidit Darium, penes
quem tunc magnum regnum erat : opponetur, Et Calliſthenem. Quotiens dictum
erit, Omnia oceano tenus vicit, ipſum quoque tentauit nouis claſſibus, & imperium
  Tom. III.   K   ex

Quaestiones Naturales

Liber Sextus, Caput XXI.

. . .

Duo genera sunt (ut Posidonio placet) quibus movetur terra: utrique
nomen est proprium. Altera succussio est, cum terra quatitur, et
sursum ac deorsum movetur: altera inclinatio, qua in latera nutat
5   navigij more. Ego et tertium illud existimo, quod nostro vocabulo
signatum est: non enim sine caussa tremorem terrae dixere maiores,
qui utrique dissimilis est. Nam nec succutiuntur tunc omnia, nec
inclinantur, sed vibrantur. Res minime in huiusmodi casu noxia,
sicut longe perniciosior est inclinatio concussione. Nam nisi celeriter
10   ex altera parte properabit motus, qui inclinata restituat, ruina
necessario sequitur. Cum dissimiles ij motus inter se sint, caussae
eorum diversae sunt.

Caput XXII.

Prius ergo de motu quatiente dicamus. Si quando magna onera per
15   vices vehiculorum plurium tracta sunt, et rotae maiore nisu in
salebras inciderunt, terram concuti senties. Asclepiodotus tradit,
cum petra e latere montis abrupta cecidisset, aedificia vicina tremore
collapsa. Idem sub terris fieri potest, ut ex his quae impendent
rupibus aliqua resoluta, magno pondere ac sono in subiacentem
20   cavernam cadat, eo vehementius, quo aut plus ponderis habuit, aut
venit altius. Et sic commovetur omne tectum cavatae vallis.

    Nec tantum pondere suo abscindi saxa credibile est, sed cum
flumina supra ferantur, assiduus humor commissuras lapidis
extenuat, et quotidie his ad quae religatus est aufert, et illam (ut
25   ita dicam) cutem qua continetur, abradit. Deinde longa per aevum
diminutio usque eo infirmat illa, quae quotidie attrivit, ut desinant
esse oneri ferendo.

• Notes •

Caput XXI.

2 **Posidonio:** Posidonius (135–51 BCE) was, like Seneca, a Stoic philosopher who flourished in the Hellenistic world. The range of his contributions was as vast as Aristotle's.

placet: Often used as an impersonal verb with **ut** + dative. **Ut placet tibi:** *as it pleases you.* Or, **placeret mihi ut librum legeres:** *it would please me that you (may) read the book.*

utrique: uterque, utraque, utrumque, *each of two*; dative of possession.

3 **Altera . . . altera . . .:** *One . . . the other . . . .*

cum . . .: The use of **cum** + indicative (rather than subjunctive) to mean *when* is permitted.

4 **latera:** latus, lateris (n).

5 **more:** mos, moris (m). In the ablative, followed by the genitive, it means *in the style of, in the way of.*

et: *also, moreover.*

nostro vocabulo: ablative of means. Seneca reserves a special term (**vocabulum**) to the third kind of motion.

6 **caussae:** causae.

dixere: Not to be confused with an infinitive, this is an alternative form of **dixerunt.**

maiores: from comparative of **magnus**; *forefathers, ancestors,* i.e., "those greater [in age]."

8 **sed vibrantur:** Seneca considers this third mode of motion to be his original contribution. To the two conventional types of motion **succussio** and **inclinatio** he adds **vibratio**: *vibration.*

Res minime . . . noxia: Literally, *a thing minimally hurtful.*

9 **perniciosior:** comparative adjective that sets up the ablative of comparison **concussione** (in place of **quam concussio**).

11 **necessario:** adverb.

Cum . . . sint: Construe as causal: *Since they are . . .*

Caput XXII.

14   **onera: onus, oneris** (n).

14–15   **per vices:** *alternately, by turns.*

15   **plurium: plus, pluris,** comparative of **multus.**

tracta sunt: traho, trahere, traxi, tractum. Technically **tracta sunt** is a perfect passive. Nevertheless, as happened later in Romance languages, it can often be understood in the present passive.

nisu: The noun **nisus, -us** (m) means *a strain, a pressure.* It is related to the verb **nitor, niti, nisus sum.**

16   **inciderunt: inciderint** would also have been correct, to indicate possibility rather than certainty.

senties: Seneca uses the second person here, perhaps to make the story more dramatic. Recall that the whole work is addressed to his friend Lucilius. Note the indirect statement/oratio obliqua with the infinitive **concuti.**

Asclepiodotus: Asclepiodotus Tacticus was a disciple of Posidonius.

16–18   **tradit . . . aedificia . . . collapsa:** Supply the infinitive **esse** for the accusative with the infinitive construction governed by **tradit.**

17   **cum . . . cecidisset:** Asclepiodotus is here alluding to a particular event that he witnessed or was told about.

cecidisset: cado, cadere, cecidi, casum.

tremore: ablative of cause.

18–20   **ut . . . cadat:** *that . . . it may fall.*

19   **aliqua resoluta:** Supply **rupes** in the nominative. **resoluta: resolvo, resolvere, resolvi, resolutum** *to untie, to loosen.*

20   **eo . . . quo . . . :** *the more . . . the more . . . ;* Seneca is here giving an intuitive notion of potential and kinetic energies.

vehementius: comparative adverb.

21   **cavatae: cavo, cavare.** Note that **vallis** is feminine.

22 **abscindi saxa credibile est:** indirect statement/oratio obliqua.

22–23 **cum flumina supra ferantur:** *when rivers are carried above* [*the rocks*].

23 **commisuras:** This is derived from **committo, committere, commīsī, commissum.** A **commissura, -ae** (f) is *a joint.*

26 **usque eo . . . ut . . .:** *to such an extent that . . .*; result clause.

attrivit: attero, atterere, attrivi, attritum. This awareness of the large time scale of geological events is also expressed in Roman lore by the adage **Gutta cavat lapidem,** *a water drop hollows the stone,* used by several classical authors (Lucretius, *De Rerum Natura* [*On the Nature of Things*] 1.365; Ovid, *Epistulae Ex Ponto* [*Letters from Pontus*] 4.10.5; Tibullus, *Carmina* [*Poems*] 1.4.18) including Seneca himself in Book 4, Chapter 3, of *Quaestiones Naturales.*

27 **oneri ferendo:** gerundive construction, dative of purpose. *They cease to be* [*apt*] *for the carrying of weight.*

Pliny the Elder

Gaius Plinius Secundus (23–79 CE), known as Pliny the Elder to differentiate him from his nephew Gaius Plinius Caecilius Secundus, was a Roman aristocrat with many intellectual talents and interests. Having studied the law, he entered the military service, where he stayed keeping a low profile until the end of Nero's reign in the year 68. On the accession of Vespasian to the throne, Pliny's fortunes improved and he was made procurator. As such, he had the opportunity to travel to several "exotic" areas of the empire. Always a keen observer of nature, Pliny accumulated a wealth of information about minerals, plants, and animals. These observations, as well as experience accumulated during his early years in the military, served as the basis for his magnum opus, the *Historia Naturalis* (*Natural History*). It can be considered the first encyclopedia and a model for all those that came after. The work has survived in its entirety. Pliny, who was serving as commander of the fleet stationed at Misenum or the Bay of Naples, died during the eruption of Vesuvius in the year 79 while trying to help in the rescue of a friend caught in the catastrophe. The tale is told in moving detail by his nephew and adopted son Pliny the Younger in a letter to the Roman historian Tacitus.

C. Plinii Secundi Naturalis Historia, Tom. I, ex officina Hackiana, Rotterdam 1669. By permission of the HathiTrust.

486

C. PLINII SECUNDI

NATURALIS
HISTORIÆ

LIBER OCTAVUS.

CAP. I.

De animalibus terreſtribus, elephantorum commen-
datio, & de ſenſu eorum.

AD reliqua tranſeamus animalia, & primum terreſtria. Maximum eſt elephas,
proximumque humanis ſenſibus: [a] quippe intellectus illis ſermonis patrii, &
[1] imperiorum [2] obedientia, officiorumque, quæ
didicere, memoria, amoris & gloriæ voluptas : imo
vero (quæ etiam in homine rara) probitas, prudentia, æquitas : religio quoque ſiderum, Soliſque ac
Lunæ veneratio. Auctores ſunt, in Mauritaniæ
ſaltibus ad quendam amnem, cui nomen eſt [b] Amilo, niteſcente Luna nova, greges eorum deſcende-
re : ibique ſe purificantes ſolenniter aqua circum-
ſpergi, [c] atque ita ſalutato ſidere in ſilvas reverti,
· vitu-

[1] Impri-
is. M.
[2] obe-
dientia. Ch.

[a] *Quippe intellectus illis ſermonis, &c.*]
Legend. *Quippe intellectus illis ſermonis*
patrii, & in priorum obedientia officii, eo-
rum quæ didicere memoria, amoris & gloria
voluptas. Intellectus, inquit, illis ſermonis patrii & officii in priorum obedientia, ᾗ καθυπετ@ co τῇ ὑπακύειν
τοῖς πρεσβυτέροις. Priores ætate elephantos intelligit, quibus minores obe-
dientiam præſtant, officii intelligentes
ſunt in priorum obedientia. *Salm.* 305.b
[b] *Amila.*] Dion ait pergere ἐπὶ ὕδωρ ἀέναον perennem ſquam. Vetuſti
codices habent *Annulo,* quæ vox à Græcâ
ἀέναος fortaſſis depravata eſt. Rhodig.
cap. 18. lib. 10. Primus ex Europæ regi-
bus Indis dictis elephantos Alexander
habuit : plurimos Antigonus : multos
Pyrrhus in prœlio captos ſuperato De-
metrio, quos Romanis objecit. Idem
Rhod. cap. 20. lib. 22. *Dalec.*

[c] *Atque ita ſalutato ſidere in ſilvas*
reverti.] Id eſt, ſalutata luna. *Salmaſ.*
p. 306. a.

[2] *Arma*

Liber VIII. Cap. II.   487

vitulorum fatigatos præ se ferentes. Alienæ quoque [1] religionis intellectu, creduntur maria transituri non ante naves conscendere, quam invitati recto-ris jurejurando de reditu. Visique sunt fessi ægritu-dine (quando & illas moles infestant morbi) [2] her-bas supini in cœlum jacientes, veluti tellure preci-bus [3] allegata. Nam quod ad docilitatem attinet, regem adorant, genua submittunt, coronas porri-gunt. [4] Indis arant minores, quos appellant no-thos.

Cap. II. *Quando primum juncti.*

ROmæ juncti primum subiere currum Pompeji Magni Africano triumpho: quod prius India victa triumphante Libero patre memoratur. Proci-lius negat potuisse Pompeji triumpho junctos [5] in-gredi portam. Germanici Cæsaris munere gladia-torio, [6] quosdam inconditos motus edidere, saltan-tium modo. Vulgare erat, per auras [7] arma jacere non auferentibus ventis, atque inter se gladiatorios congressus edere, [8] aut lasciviente? pyrrhiche [9] col-ludere: postea & per funes incessere, [10] lecticis et-jam ferentes quaterni singulos puerperas imitantes: [11] plenisque [12] hominum tricliniis [13] accubitu, iere per lectos ita libratis vestigiis, ne quis [14] potantium attingeretur.

Cap. III. *De docilitate eorum.*

CErtum est, unum tardioris ingenii in accipien-dis quæ tradebantur, sæpius castigatum verbe-ribus, eadem illa meditantem noctu repertum. Mirum

Sidenotes:
1 regionis. V.
2 per herbas supini in cœlum jacentes. V. jacentes ba-ber & Ch.
3 alligata. M ablegata. V Sabellicus.
4 Indi ararunt mino-ribus, quos, Indicis Ara-bici mino-res, quos. Parmense.
5 egredi porta. M. & Ch. ingredi porta. V.
6 quosdam etiam in-conditos. Gal. & Ch.
7 pernici-tate. M. V.
8 collide-re. Tul.
9 lecticæ e. f. q. fin-gulas. M. modo, lecti-cis e. f q. singulas, ut intelligamus elephantes feminas.
10 plerif-que. M.
11 homi-ne. Ch.
12 accubi-tum. M. & Ch.
13 portan-tium. M. structorum, ministro-rum fercula & epulas ferentium.

a *Arma jacere non auferentibus ventis.*] Velut quadam prælusione, more pila-riorum & ventilatorum ea quæ emise-sant, ut scribit Quintilianus lib. 10. ita librantium, ut venire in manus vide-rentur, & qua juberent, decurrere. Rho-

dig. cap. 8. Vide quæ adnotata sunt infra ad finem libri 36. *Daiec.*

b *Aut lasciviente pyrrhiche colludere.*] Est autem πυῤῥίχη saltationis genus Cretensibus imprimis familiare. *Gele-nius.*

Hb 4   a *Funi-*

Historia Naturalis

Liber Octavus.

Cap. I.
De animalibus terrestribus, elephantorum commendatio, et de sensu eorum.

Ad reliqua transeamus animalia, et primum terrestria. Maximum
5 est elephas, proximumque humanis sensibus: quippe intellectus
illis sermonis patrii, et imperiorum obedientia, officiorumque,
quae didicere, memoria, amoris et gloriae voluptas: immo vero (quae
etiam in homine rara) probitas, prudentia, aequitas: religio quoque
siderum, Solisque ac Lunae veneratio. Auctores sunt, in Mauritaniae
10 saltibus ad quendam amnem, cui nomen est Amilo, nitescente Luna
nova, greges eorum descendere: ibique se purificantes solenniter aqua
circumspergi, atque ita salutato sidere in silvas reverti, vitulorum
fatigatos prae se ferentes. Alienae quoque religionis intellectu,
creduntur maria transituri non ante naves conscendere, quam
15 invitati rectoris jurejurando de reditu. Visique sunt fessi aegritudine
(quando et illas moles infestant morbi) herbas supini in coelum
jacientes, veluti tellure precibus allegata. Nam quod ad docilitatem
attinet, regem adorant, genua submittunt, coronas porrigunt. Indis
arant minores, quos appellant nothos.

20 ### Cap. II. *Quando primum juncti.*
Romae juncti primum subiere currum Pompeji Magni Africano
triumpho: quod prius India victa triumphante Libero patre
memoratur. Procilius negat potuisse Pompeji triumpho junctos
ingredi portam. Germanici Caesaris munere gladiatorio, quosdam
25 inconditos motus edidere, saltantium modo. Vulgare erat, per auras
arma jacere non auferentibus ventis, atque inter se gladiatorios
congressus edere, aut lasciviente pyrrhiche colludere: postea et per

funes incessere, lecticis etiam ferentes quaterni singulos puerperas
imitantes: plenisque hominum tricliniis accubitu, iere per lectos ita
30   libratis vestigiis, ne quis potantium attingeretur.

• Notes •

Cap. I.

2–3   **De animalibus . . . eorum:** The title of chapters may not be
original, but a later editorial addition.

3   **sensu: sensus, -us** (m) is both *sensation* and *perception*.

4   **Ad reliqua:** In the previous chapter, Pliny dealt with human
beings. Now he deals with the rest of animals. There is no irony
here.

5–6   **intellectus illis:** Supply **est**. This can be construed as a dative
of possession: *The understanding is to them*, namely, *they have
the understanding*. In short, the elephants understand the native
tongue of the place where they live.

6   **patrii: patrius, -a, -um** *pertaining to the father, native.*

imperiorum: imperium, -ii (n) is a *command*. The footnote in
the seventeenth-century printing suggests an alternative reading
as **in priorum**.

7   **quae:** Construe as the neuter plural accusative referring back to
officiorum and **imperiorum**.

didicere: Not to be confused with an infinitive, this is an
alternative form of **didicerunt**.

memoria: Since punctuation is not original, this can be
construed in the ablative *by memory*. **Memoria discere** can
be translated *to learn by heart*. If one follows the provided
punctuation, it can be construed in the nominative, in which
case memory is one of the things possessed by elephants.

voluptas: The [est] illis still governs the nominatives **obedientia**
and **voluptas**.

immo vero: *nay, indeed.*

8   **probitas:** This and the other nominative words that follow are also governed by [**est**] **illis.**

    religio: *worship.*

9   **siderum: sidus, sideris** (n).

    Auctores sunt: Perhaps one could supply **qui dicunt**, so that various infinitives and accusatives in the following lines can be construed as indirect statement/oratio obliqua.

10   **saltibus: saltus, -us** (m).

    amnem: amnis, -is (m).

    cui nomen est: dative of possession.

10–11 **nitescente Luna nova:** ablative absolute.

11   **greges: grex, gregis** (m). This is the accusative subject of the indirect statement/oratio obliqua [**qui dicunt**] **greges descendere.** It is also the subject of **circumspergi.**

12   **circumspergi:** From **circum + spargo, spargere, sparsi, sparsum** *to sprinkle around.* Notice the **-i** ending, indicating an infinitive passive.

    ita salutato sidere: ablative absolute. The footnote in the facsimile suggests that the intent is **ita salutata luna**, which makes sense, since the moon is also a **sidus.** [Facsmile footnote c: **Atque ita salutato sidere in silvas reverti. Id est, salutata luna.**]

13   **prae se ferentes:** probably with their trunks, so that the calves are indeed in front.

    Alienae . . . religionis intellectu: literally, *by the understanding of another religion.* This does not make much sense. The marginal note suggests replacing **religionis** with **regionis,** which is somewhat better. Both can be forced into the translation.

14–15 **creduntur . . . reditu:** The logical sequence is **transituri maria, creduntur non conscendere naves antequam invitati (sint) jurejurando rectoris de reditu.**

15   **fessi: fessus, -a, -um** *tired, exhausted.*

    aegritudine: ablative of cause.

16   **moles:** an allusion to the elephants' large mass.

17   **jacientes: iacio, iacere, ieci, iactum** *to throw.* Do not confuse with **jacentes** from **iaceo, iacere, iacui** *to lie down.* The two verbs are connected, since to lie down one has to throw one's body down. **Herbas** is the direct object of **jacientes.**

     veluti tellure precibus allegata: Literally, *as if the earth had been bound by prayers.* This is a difficult passage that defies literal translation.

     Nam: Usually, the conjunction **nam** has a consecutive value *for, because, indeed.* In this case, it is just a connective meaning.

17–18   **quod . . . attinet . . . :** *as far as . . . is concerned . . .* In Latin, **attineo** is active: *what pertains to . . .*

18   **genua: genu, -us** (n).

18–19   **Indis arant minores:** *The smaller ones plow for the Indians.* (As opposed to the larger African elephant.)

19   **nothos: nothus, -a, -um** *mixed breed, hybrid.*

Cap. II.

21   **Romae:** For names of cities, Latin still preserves the locative case, *at Rome.*

     juncti: iungo, iungere, iunxi, iunctum *to yoke, to harness.* From the Proto-Indo-European root *ieu-*, which gives rise to the English *yoke* and *join* and the Latin **iugum, iuvare,** and **iungo,** and the Sanskrit **yoga.**

     subiere: subierunt. Subeo can be used as a transitive verb. **Currum** is the direct object.

22–23   **quod prius . . . memoratur:** *which is mentioned earlier.*

22   **India victa:** ablative absolute.

     Libero patre: Liber Pater *free father* was another name for Bacchus, the Roman deity of freedom and wine. According to legend, he conquered India.

23   **negat potuisse . . . junctos:** *says that when harnessed they were not able . . .* Note the indirect statement/oratio obliqua.

24   **Germanici:** Germanicus was the adopted son of Tiberius and the father of Caligula. The son and father of emperors, he died too young to become an emperor himself.

25   **edidere: ediderunt.** From **edo, edere, edidi, editum** *to give out, to bring about, to produce.* **Quosdam motus** is the direct object.

     saltantium modo: *in the style of dancers.*

     Vulgare erat: *It was common* [for the elephants]. This phrase sets up the series of complementary infinitives that follow.

27   **lasciviente: lascivio, lascivire, lascivivi, lascivitum** *to play, to sport, to behave playfully.*

     pyrrhiche: Pyrrhicios is an ancient Greek war dance.

     colludere: conludere = cum + ludo, ludere, lusi, lusum *to play with, to play together at.*

28   **funes: funis, -is** (m) *a rope.*

     incessere: frequentative form of **incedo, incedere, incessi, incessum** *to walk.*

     lecticis: lectica, -ae (f) *a litter* (normally carried by slaves).

     quaterni: *four;* modified by **ferentes.**

     puerperas: puerpera, -ae (f) *a woman at childbirth.*

29   **iere:** This is probably a misprint, or a manuscript error in earlier copies, for **ire.** Otherwise, one can also construe **iere = ierunt** as most translators do. This would be strange, since the previous lines are all tied to **vulgare erat** by means of an infinitive.

30   **libratis: libro, librare,** *to balance.*

     vestigiis: vestigium, -ii (n) *footstep.*

Isidore of Seville
(Isidorus Hispaliensis)

I sidore (Isidorus Hispaliensis, 560–636 CE), the patron saint of the
Internet,[3] is one of the most singular figures in Visigothic Spain. The
province of Hispania had been an integral part of the Roman Empire since the fall of Carthage after the Second Punic War, which
ended in 201 BCE. Hispania produced Roman emperors, poets, and
philosophers. A crucial period in Spanish history started in the year 409
CE when the Romans were driven out from the peninsula by several Ger-
manic tribes crossing the Pyrenees. The Spanish population was by and
large Christian. Although the invaders completely destroyed the political
institutions, they preserved the organization of the Church. The invaders
were Christian as well, but not all of them adhered to the Nicaean credo.
The Visigoths, in particular, practiced the creed known as Arianism, named
after Arius (256–336 CE), the founder of a doctrine that differed from the
official (Catholic) doctrine in respect to the divine nature of Jesus. The First
Council of Nicaea (325 CE) declared Arianism a heresy and asserted the
doctrine of the Trinity. Although small in number, the Visigoths domi-
nated the other tribes and by 550 CE established their capital in Toledo.
In 589 the Visigothic king Recaredo, a convert to Catholicism, established
Catholicism as the official religion. In this historical context, Isidore was
born into a wealthy noble family whose members had played a role in the
conversion of the Visigothic nobility to the Catholic faith. His older broth-
er Leander (534–600 CE) preceded him as bishop of Seville. Isidore and his
siblings (two brothers and a sister, all members of the Church hierarchy)
received a first-class education in the trivium and the quadrivium and had
an unusual command of classical Latin and of Roman and Greek culture.

The *Etymologiae* (*Etymologies*) constitutes an encyclopedic work. In an
era preceding the printing press and the internet, Isidore saw as his educational mission the preservation and transmission of a culture in political
decline. Encyclopedic works had already existed, most notably Pliny the Elder's (23–79 CE) *Historia Naturalis* and the Spaniard Seneca the Younger's
(4 BCE–65 CE) *Quaestiones Naturales*. Nevertheless, the work of Isidore is
peculiar in style, content, and intent. There is a sense of urgency in Isidore's

---

3   Isidore was nominated by Pope John Paul II precisely on account of the *Etymologiae*,
which are the medieval equivalent of Wikipedia.

work, as if it were necessary to record everything that a highly educated man of the past could transmit to an uncertain future world. A glance at the index of the work reveals how comprehensive Isidore wanted to be, venturing even into fields of which he was no master. The title *Etymologiae* (also known as *Origines* [*Origins*]) alludes to a presupposition on the author's part that an investigation of the origin and meaning of the name of a discipline is the key to understanding the discipline itself. Isidore's etymologies are not always precise, but neither are those of more recent thinkers such as Martin Heidegger (1889–1976). These authors, as different as they are, are not interested in philology or linguistics. They believe, rather, that there is much to be learned from deconstructing words, however arbitrarily.[4] The *Etymologiae* remained an important reference work for many centuries. Its first printed edition appeared as early as 1472.

Our selection consists of the first two, very short, chapters of the first book. After analyzing the meaning of the terms *discipline* and *art*, Isidore enumerates and defines the seven liberal arts, which were (and still are) the basis of the classical academic curriculum. The term "liberal" refers to the quality of a person being free. Education in Greece and Rome was meant for free people only, who were not necessarily motivated by practical considerations, but by the attainment of moral excellence and knowledge for its own sake. In Rome it was not unusual to refer to children of free families simply as *liberi*. By the early Middle Ages, the educational curriculum was formally divided into a basic cycle called the trivium and a more advanced cycle known as the quadrivium, to be taken after the trivium had been completed. The former consisted of the three humanistic disciplines: grammar, dialectics (logic), and rhetoric; the latter was composed of the four scientific disciplines: music, geometry, arithmetic, and astronomy. A university curriculum would normally add some specializations, such as medicine and law.

Isidore's Latin is grammatically accurate, while at the same time quite simple and straightforward. It hardly needs any explanation.

---

4   For examples of Heidegger's use of etymologies, see his *The Anaximander Fragment*, where both Greek and German are subjected to a somewhat extreme treatment. (*Anaximander in Holzwege* 4th ed. Frankfurt, Vittorio Klostermann (1963) pp. 296–343. Isidore, with a more modest agenda than Heidegger's search after the meaning of Being, derives, for instance, the word *art* from the Greek *areté*, which may not be a bad guess (from the possibly common Proto-Indo-European root *ar-*; cf. J. Pokorny, online *P-I-E Etymological Dictionary*, 2007). J. Pokorny, *P-I-E Etymological Dictionary*, Vol. 2, p. 705. German original: J. Pokorny, *Indogermanisches Etymologisches Woerterbuch*, Bern: Francke Verlag (1959).

⫶

☞DE DISCIPLINA · ET · ARTE ☞Ca· ·I·

**ISCIPLINA · A DISCENDO·
NOMEN · ACCEPIT · VNDE·
ET SCIENTIA DICI POTEST**
Nam & ſcire dictum a diſcere·quia nemo
noſtrum ſcit niſi quod diſcit. Aliter dicta
diſciplina·quia diſcitur plena.☞Ars vero
dicta é·q̃ artis p̃ceptis reguliſq̃ conſiſtat.
Alii dicunt a graecis hoc tractum eſſe vocabulum a poteſartes-
id eſt a virtute quam ſcientiam vocauerút.Inter artem & diſci/
plinam Plato &.Areſtoteles hanc differentiam eſſe voluerunt-
dicentes artem eſſe in his que ſe & aliter habere poſſunt. Diſci/
plina vero eſt que de his agit que aliter euenire nõ poſſunt.Nã
quando veris diſputationibus aliquid differitur·diſciplina erit·
q̃n aliquid veriſimile atq̃ oppinabile tractat nomé artis habet

☞De.Septem liberalibus diſciplinis. ☞Ca· ·II·

Iſcipline liberalium artium. Septem ſunt.☞Prima
Grammatica id eſt loquendi peritia☞Secunda.Rhe
thorica·que propter nitorem & copiam eloquétie ſue
maxie in ciuilibus queſtionibus neceſſaria exiſtimat.☞Tercia
Dualectica·cognomento logica·q̃ diſputationibus ſubtiliſſimis
vera ſecernit a falſis.☞Quarta.Arithmetica·que cótinet nume/
rorum cauſas et diuiſiones☞Quinta.Muſica·que i carminibus
cantibuſq̃ conſiſtit. ☞Sexta.Geometrica·que menſuras dimen
ſioneſq̃ coplectit☞Septia.Aſtronomia·q̃ cótinet legé aſtrorú

☞De.Litteris communibus· ☞Ca· ·III·

Rimordia grammatice artis littere ɔmunes exiſtunt
quae librarii & calculatores ſequunt.☞Quarú diſci/
plina velut quedam grammatice artis infantia eſt.
Vnde & eam.Varro litterationem vocat.Littere autem ſunt in/
dices rerum· ſigna verború· quibus tanta vis eſt·ut nobis dicta
abſentium ſine voce loquantur ☞Vſus litterarum repertus eſt
propter memoriam rerum. Nam ne obliuione fugiant· litteris

Isidorus <Hispaliensis>: Etymologiae, [Augsburg], 1472. By permission of the Bayerische Staatsbibliothek München. 2 Inc. c.a. 129, fol. 16v.

Etymologiae

De Disciplina et Arte Ca. I

Disciplina a discendo nomen accepit unde et scientia dici potest.
Nam et scire dictum a discere, quia nemo nostrum scit nisi quod
discit. Aliter dicta disciplina, quia discitur plena. Ars vero dicta est
5   quia artis praeceptis regulisque consistat. Alii dicunt a graecis hoc
tractum esse vocabulum a potesartes, id est a virtute quam scientiam
vocaverunt. Inter artem et disciplinam Plato et Aristoteles hanc
differentiam esse voluerunt, dicentes artem esse in his quae se et
aliter habere possunt. Disciplina vero est quae de his agit quae aliter
10 evenire non possunt. Nam quando veris disputationibus aliquid
disseritur, disciplina erit, quando aliquid verisimile atque oppinabile
tractatur nomen artis habet.

De Septem Liberalibus Disciplinis Ca. II

Disciplinae liberalium artium. Septem sunt. Prima Grammatica
15 id est loquendi peritia. Secunda. Rhetorica, quae propter nitorem
et copiam eloquentiae suae maxime in civilibus questionibus
necessaria existimatur. Tertia Dialectica, cognomento logica,
quae disputationibus subtilissimis vera secernit a falsis. Quarta.
Arithmetica, quae continet numerorum causas et divisiones.
20 Quinta. Musica, quae in carminibus cantibusque consistit. Sexta.
Geometrica, quae mensuras dimensionesque complectitur. Septima.
Astronomia, quae continet legem astrorum.

• Notes •

Ca. I

1   **Ca.: Caput.** A *head* in a book is a chapter.

2   **a discendo:** gerund *from learning*. Notice how Isidore connects
the common stem *disc-* in both **disciplina** and **discendo**.

unde: *whence.*

et: *also.*

3   **nemo nostrum:** *no one of us,* partitive genitive.

3–4   **scit … discit …:** This is a typical Isidorean pun. It serves the purpose of connecting two ideas.

4   **Aliter:** *otherwise, on the other hand, alternatively.* If you are not quite convinced with the previous analysis (that did not explain the *-plina* part of the word), here is another explanation.

5   **artis:** artus, -a, -um.

6   **tractum:** traho, trahere, traxi, tractum.

     a potesartes: misprint for **apo tes aretes**, latinized transliteration of the Greek ἀπὸ τῆς ἀρετῆς, *from a virtue.*

6–7   **quam scientiam vocaverunt:** Contrary to the later Christian doctrine of original sin, Socrates and Plato believed that ignorance is the only cause of evil. In Plato's dialogue *Meno* (89a), Socrates asks rhetorically φρόνησιν ἄρα φαμὲν ἀρετὴν εἶναι, ἤτοι σύμπασαν ἢ μέρος τι; (*Is it not true that we say that virtue is knowledge, either wholly or in part?*)

8–9   **se … habere:** *to be or to find oneself in a situation.* Almost synonymous with **esse**.

9   **de … agit:** *treats, deals with.*

11   **disseritur:** *is being discussed, expounded.*

     oppinabile: opinabile.

Ca. II

15   **nitorem:** nitor, -oris (m).

16   **civilibus questionibus:** *in civil litigations.* Note variant spelling for **quaestio**.

17   **cognomento:** *surname,* or just a *name* or a *nickname.*

18   **vera:** plural neuter accusative.

21   **complectitur:** complector, complecti, complexus sum.

Francis Bacon

Francis Bacon (1561–1626), Baron of Verulam, occupies a prominent place in the history of science not for any great particular discovery, but for his pioneering advocacy of the experimental method and of the primacy of empirical induction over theoretical speculation. An important cultural and political figure in Elizabethan and Jacobean England, after his death he became an inspiration to the founders of the Royal Society of London and to the French Enlightenment. Many of his ideas on the proper method in natural science were published in 1620 in the form of a collection of aphorisms under the title *Novum Organum Scientiarum* (*The New Instrument of the Sciences*). This collection of concise sayings was part of a more ambitious unfinished work entitled *Instauratio Magna* (*The Great Restoration*). Perhaps the most celebrated of the aphorisms are those dealing with what Bacon called "The Four Kinds of Idols." These represent intellectual obstacles to the impartial and objective appreciation of the phenomena. The Idols of the Tribe are those that tie the human mind to the intuitive explanations of complex phenomena by means of everyday experience. The Earth appears to be flat and at rest; forces appear to be proportional to velocities; the orbits of the planets appear to be perfect circles. The Idols of the Cave represent the personal prejudices that each individual derives from personal experience and educational background. The Idols of the Marketplace represent the conventional truths developed by individuals through their social intercourse, the conventional lies of society, and the limitations of language. Finally, the Idols of the Theater represent the acceptance of past or present ideologies and systems of thought.

Francisci de Verulamio Instauratio Magna, Londini, Apud J. Billium, 1620. By permission of the University of Toronto Libraries. Facsimile courtesy of archive.org.

PARS SECVNDA OPERIS,

QVAE DICITVR

NOVVM ORGANVM,

SIVE

INDICIA VERA

DE INTERPRETATIONE NATVRÆ.

*tus difficilis pateat ; sed etiam dato & concesso aditu,
illa rursùs in ipsâ instauratione Scientiarum occurrent,
& molesta erunt; nisi homines præmoniti, aduersùs ea
se, quantum fieri potest, muniant.*

XXXIX.

Q *Vatuor sunt genera* Idolorum *quæ mentes humanas obsident.* Iis (*docendi gratiâ*) *nomina imposuimus; vt primum genus,* Idola Tribûs; *secundum,*
Idola Specûs ; *tertium,* Idola Fori; *quartum,* Idola
Theatri *vocentur.*

XL.

E *Xcitatio Notionum & Axiomatum per* Inductionem *veram, est certè proprium remedium ad*
Idola *arcenda & summouenda ; Sed tamen indicatio*
Idolorum *magni est vsûs. Doctrina enim de* Idolis
similitèr se habet ad Interpretationem Naturæ, *sicut
doctrina de Sophisticis Elenchis ad Dialecticam vulgarem.*

XLI.

I Dola Tribûs *sunt fundata in ipsâ Naturâ huma-
nâ, atque in ipsâ Tribu seu gente hominum. Falsò
enim asseritur, Sensum humanum esse Mensuram
rerum ; Quin contrà, omnes Perceptiones tàm Sensûs
quàm Mentis sunt ex analogiâ hominis, non ex analogiâ
Vniuersi. Estque Intellectus humanus instar speculi inæ-
qualis ad radios rerum, qui suam naturam Naturæ
rerum immiscet, eamque distorquet & inficit.*

Idola

XLII.

IDola Specûs *sunt* Idola *hominis indiuidui. Habet enim vnusquisque (præter aberrationes* Naturæ *humanæ in genere*) Specum *siue cauernam quandam induiduam, quæ lumen* Naturæ *frangit & corrumpit; vel propter naturam cujusque propriam & singularem, vel propter educationem & conuersationem cum aliis; vel propter lectionem librorum, & authoritates eorum quos quisque colit & miratur, vel propter differentias Impreßionum prout occurrunt in animo præoccupato & prædisposito, aut in animo æquo & sedato, vel ejusmodi; vt planè spiritus humanus (prout disponitur in hominibus singulis*) *sit res varia, & omninò perturbata, & quasi fortuita : Unde benè* Heraclitus, *homines Scientias quærere in minoribus Mundis, & non in maiore siue communi.*

XLIII.

SUnt etiam Idola *tanquàm ex contractu & societate humani generis ad inuicem, quæ* Idola Fori *propter hominum commercium, & consortium, appellamus. Homines enim per sermones sociantur; At verba ex captu vulgi imponuntur. Itaque mala & inepta verborum impositio, miris modis intellectum obsidet.* Neque definitiones *aut explicationes, quibus homines docti se munire & vindicare in nonnullis consueuerunt, rem vllo modo restituunt. Sed verba planè vim faciunt intellectui, & omnia turbant; & homines ad inanes, & innumeras* Controuersias, *& commenta, deducunt.*   Sunt

XLIV.

S Vnt denique Idola *quæ immigrárunt in animos hominum ex diuerſis* Dogmatibus *Philoſophiarum,
ac etiam ex peruerſis legibus* Demonſtrationum ; *quæ*
Idola Theatri *nominamus; quia quot* Philoſophiæ *re-
ceptæ aut inuentæ ſunt, tot fabulas productas & actas
cenſemus, quæ* Mundos *effecerunt fictitios & ſce-
nicos.* Neque de his quæ jam habentur, aut etiam de
veteribus *Philoſophiis & Sectis tantùm loquimur,cùm
complures aliæ ejuſmodi fabulæ componi & concinnari poſſint ; quandoquidem errorum prorſus diuerſorum
cauſæ ſint nihilominùs ferè communes.* Neque rursùs
de Philoſophiis *vniuerſalibus tantùm hoc intelligimus,
ſed etiam de* Principiis *& Axiomatibus compluribus*
Scientiarum, *quæ ex traditione & fide & neglectu in-
ualuerunt:* Verùm de ſingulis iſtis generibus Idolorum,
fuſiùs & diſtinctiùs dicendum eſt, vt Intellectui humano cautum ſit.

XLV.

I Ntellectus humanus *ex proprietate ſuâ facilè ſup-
ponit maiorem ordinem, & æqualitatem in rebus,
quàm inuenit:* Et cùm multa ſint in Naturâ mono-
dica, *& plena imparitatis, tamèn affingit* Parallela,
& Correſpondentia, & Relatiua *quæ non ſunt. Hinc*
Commenta illa, In cœleſtibus omnia moueri per
circulos perfectos, *lineis ſpiralibus & draconibus
(niſi nomine tenus)* prorſus reiectis. *Hinc elementum* Ignis cum Orbe ſuo *introductum eſt ad conſtituen-
dam*

Novum Organum Scientiarum

Pars Secunda Operis, Quae Dicitur Novum Organum, Sive Indicia Vera De Interpretatione Naturae.

XXXIX.

Quatuor sunt genera Idolorum quae mentes humanas obsident. Iis (docendi gratia) nomina imposuimus; ut primum genus, Idola Tribus; secundum Idola Specus; tertium, Idola Fori; quartum, Idola Theatri vocentur.

XL.

5 Excitatio Notionum et Axiomatum per Inductionem veram, est certe proprium remedium ad Idola arcenda et summovenda; Sed tamen indicatio Idolorum magni est usus. Doctrina enim de Idolis similiter se habet ad Interpretationem Naturae, sicut doctrina de Sophisticis Elenchis ad Dialecticam vulgarem.

XLI.

10 Idola Tribus sunt fundata in ipsa Natura humana, atque in ipsa Tribu seu gente hominum. Falso enim asseritur, Sensum humanum esse Mensuram rerum; Quin contra, omnes Perceptiones tam Sensus quam Mentis sunt ex analogia hominis, non ex analogia Universi. Estque Intellectus humanus instar speculi inaequalis ad 15 radios rerum, qui suam naturam Naturae rerum immiscet, eamque distorquet et inficit.

XLII.

Idola Specus sunt Idola hominis individui. Habet enim unusquisque (praeter aberrationes Naturae humanae in genere) Specum sive cavernam quandam individuam, quae lumen Naturae frangit et 20 corrumpit; vel propter naturam cujusque propriam et singularem, vel propter educationem et conversationem cum aliis; vel propter lectionem librorum, et authoritates eorum quos quisque colit et miratur, vel propter differentias Impressionum prout occurrunt in animo praeoccupato et praedisposito, aut in animo aequo et sedato, vel ejusmodi; ut plane spiritus humanus (prout disponitur

25 in hominibus singulis) sit res varia, et omnino perturbata, et quasi fortuita: Unde bene Heraclitus, homines Scientias quaerere in minoribus Mundis, et non in maiore sive communi.

XLIII.

Sunt etiam Idola tanquam ex contractu et societate humani generis ad invicem, quae Idola Fori propter hominum commercium, et

30 consortium, appellamus. Homines enim per sermones sociantur; At verba ex captu vulgi imponuntur. Itaque mala et inepta verborum impositio, miris modis intellectum obsidet. Neque definitiones aut explicationes, quibus homines docti se munire et vindicare in nonnullis consueverunt, rem ullo modo restituunt. Sed verba plane

35 vim faciunt intellectui, et omnia turbant; et homines ad inanes, et innumeras Controversias, et commenta, deducunt.

XLIV.

Sunt denique Idola quae immigrarunt in animos hominum ex diversis Dogmatibus Philosophiarum, ac etiam ex perversis legibus Demonstrationum; quae Idola Theatri nominamus; quia quot

40 Philosophiae receptae aut inventae sunt, tot fabulas productas et actas censemus, quae Mundos effecerunt fictitios et scenicos. Neque de his quae jam habentur, aut etiam de veteribus Philosophiis et Sectis tantum loquimur, cum complures aliae ejusmodi fabulae componi et concinnari possint; quandoquidem errorum prorsus

45 diversorum causae sint nihilominus fere communes. Neque rursus de Philosophiis universalibus tantum hoc intelligimus, sed etiam de Principiis et Axiomatibus compluribus Scientiarum, quae ex traditione et fide et neglectu invaluerunt: Verum de singulis istis generibus Idolorum, fusius et distinctius dicendum est, ut Intellectui

50 humano cautum sit.

• Notes •

XXXIX.

1   **quatuor: quattuor**

obsident: obsideo, obsidere, obsedi, obsessum. The main meaning (from **ob + sedeo**) is *to sit beside*. But it is mostly used in a transitive way in the sense of *to block, to beset*. The English word *obsession* derives from the fourth principal part. English prefers to derive words, including verbs, from Latin by using the fourth principal part.

2   **docendi gratia: Gratia** in the ablative can be understood as *for the sake of*, thus explaining the genitive of **docendi**. Similar expressions that have made it into English are **exempli gratia**, abbreviated as *e.g., for example, for the sake of an example* and **honoris causa**, *for the sake of honor*. We encounter another example in the selection on architecture by Cetius Faventinus.

3   **Tribus: Tribus, -us** (f) is a fourth declension noun derived from **tres** (**tribus** being the dative and ablative). Originally it referred to a third part of the population, but eventually it was applied to any subset or tribe.

XL.

6   **ad Idola arcenda et summovenda: ad** + gerundive expresses purpose. Here **arceo, arcere, arcui** is used in the sense of *to contain*.

7   **magni est usus: usus, -us** (m). Construe in the genitive singular with *magni*.

8   **se habet = est.**

8–9   **doctrina de Sophisticis Elenchis:** The Sophists were professional, usually itinerant, teachers who, for a fee, instructed young Greek aristocrats in the art of rhetoric. Some of the Sophists approached the stature of true philosophers; they were sharply criticized by Plato and Socrates for not seeking the truth but merely wielding philosophical reasoning for material profit. Elenchus is a Greek term to designate a method of inquiry after the truth favored by Socrates and consisting of engaging one or more interlocutors in a series of guided questions and refuting the answers one by one. Here, Bacon is referring to the Latin title of one of Aristotle's treatises *De Sophisticis Elenchis* (*On Sophistical Refutations*), part of his *Organon* (or *Organum* [*Instrument*]), in which he identified thirteen fallacies of common reasoning (*vulgaris dialectica*). Clearly, Bacon is emulating Aristotle (not without some irony, since Bacon's point was precisely a refutation of Aristotelian physics).

XLI.

11 **Falso:** used adverbially.

12 **Quin:** negative particle; *nay, that not.* **Quin contra** means *on the contrary.*

14 **instar:** with genitive: *like, the equivalent of.*

XLII.

17 **Specus:** The choice of this word may be alluding to Plato's myth of the cave.

26 **quaerere:** Supply **dixit** following **Heraclitus.**

XLIII.

29 **ad invicem:** *mutually, reciprocally, to each other.*

32–34 **Neque definitiones aut explicationes . . . rem ullo modo restituunt:** *Nor do the definitions or explanations . . . restore in any way the matter.*

36 **commenta: commentum, -i** (n) *invention, fabrication.*

XLIV.

39–40 **quot Philosophiae:** *how much of philosophy*; partitive genitive. **quot . . . tot . . . :** *as many . . . so many . . .*

41 **censemus: censeo, censere, censui, censum** *to think, to consider. We consider the received and created philosophies as so many stories produced and acted* [*in the theater*].

44 **possint:** subjunctive denotes possibility or uncertainty.

49   **fusius:** neuter comparative of **fusus, -a, -um** *spread out*; adverb: *more amply.*

dicendum est: passive periphrastic.

Intellectui: dative.

50   **cautum sit: caveo, cavere, cavi, cautum** *to guard against, to be aware of, to caution.*

Architecture
and Engineering

Vitruvius

N ot much is known about the life of Vitruvius (Marcus Vitruvius Pollio). From the few extant citations in ancient sources (notably in Pliny's *Historia Naturalis* [*Natural History*]), as well as from internal evidence, it can be inferred that the writing of his treatise dates to about the year 27 BCE, under Emperor Augustus, and that he had been practicing architecture and engineering already during the reign of Julius Caesar. During the Middle Ages, Vitruvius's work was mainly known through a compendium written in the fourth century by Cetius Faventinus and it was from this abridgment that Isidore drew information for the pertinent parts of his *Etymologiae* (*Etymologies*). Rediscovered during the Italian Renaissance, the original work of Vitruvius served as the model for Leon Battista Alberti's influential work, *De Re Aedificatoria* (*On the Art of Building*). Vitruvius's work exerted an unparalleled influence on the architects of the Italian Renaissance, including Bramante and Michelangelo.

Vitruvius's masterpiece, *De Architectura* (*On Architecture*), is divided into ten books or parts. In the following passage from the first book, the author gives a strikingly modern description of the relation between architecture and other areas of knowledge and a characterization of the personality of a good architect.

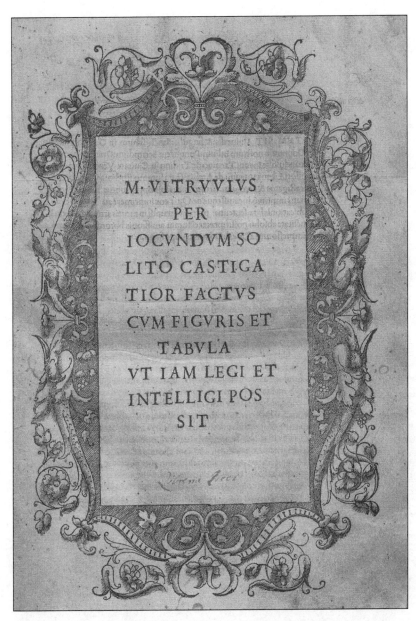

M. Vitruvius per Iocundum solito castigatior factus cum figuris et tabula ut iam legi et intellegi possit, Venetiis: Ioannes de Tridino, 1511. By permission of the Rare Books and Special Collections, McGill University Library.

I

.M. VITRVVII DE ARCHITECTVRA
LIBER   PRIMVS.

VM diuina mens tua & numen imperator Cæ/
far imperio potiretur orbis terrarum, inuictaq;
virtute cunctis hostibus stratis, triumpho vi/
ctoriaq; tua ciues gloriarentur, & gétes omnes
fubactæ tuum spectarét nutum, populufq; ro/
manus & fenatus liberatus timore, ampliffimis
tuis cogitationibus cófiliifq; gubernaretur, nó
audebam tantis occupationibus de architectu/
ra fcripta, & magnis cogitationibus explicata
edere: metuens ne nó apto tempore interpellans, fubirem tui animi of/
fenfionem. Cum vero attenderem te nó folum de vita cómuni omniú
curam, publicæq; rei cóftitutionem habere, fed etiam de opportunitate
publicorum ædificioæ, vt ciuitas per te nó folum prouinciis effet aucta,
verum etiá vt maieftas imperii publicorum ædificioæ egregias haberet
autoritates, non putaui pretermittendum, quin primo quoq; tempore
de his rebus ea tibi ederem. Ideo q; primum paréti tuo de eo fueram no/
'tus, & eius virtutis ftudiofus. Cum autem concilium cœleftium in fe/
dibus imortalitatis eum dedicauiffet, & imperium parentis in tuam po/
teftatem tranftuliffet, idem ftudium meum in eius memoria permanés,
in te contulit fauorem. Itaq; cum M. aurelio, & P. minidio, & Cn. cor/
nelio, ad apparationem baliftarum & fcorpionú, reliquorumq; torme/
torum refectionem, fui prefto, & cú eis cómoda accepifquæ cum primo
mihi tribuifti, recognitionem per fororis cómédationem feruafti. Cú
ergo eo beneficio effem obligatus, vt ad exitum vitæ non haberem ino/
piæ timoré, hæc tibi fcribere cepiq; animaduerti multa te ædificauiffe,
& nunc edificare: reliquo quoq; tempore, & publicorum, & priuatorú
edificiorum, pro amplitudine rerum geftarum, vt pofteris memoriæ tra
derentur, curam habiturum. Cófcripfi perfcriptióes terminatas, vt eas
attendés, & ante facta, & futura qualia fint opera, per te nota poffes ha/
bere: namq; his voluminibus aperui omnes difciplinæ rationes,
Quid fit architectura & De architectis inftituendis, Caput. I.

Rchitectura eft fciétia pluribus difciplinis, & va
riis eruditionibus ornata, cuius iudicio proba/
tur omnia quæ ab ceteris artibus pficiútur ope/
ra. Ea nafcitur ex fabrica, & ratiocinatióc. Fa/
brica eft continuata ac trita vfus meditatio, quæ
manibus perficitur e materia cuiufcunq; gene/
ris opus eft ad propofitú deformationis. Ratio/

A

LIBER

einatio autem e.t, quæ res fabricatas solertia a ratione proportiõnis de/
mõstrare atq; explicare põt.Itaq; architecti qui sine litteris contenderũt
vt manibus essent exercitati,nõ potuerũt efficere vt haberēt pro labori/
bus autoritatẽ.Qui autẽ ratiocinationibus & litteris solis confisi fuerũt,
vmbrã,nõ rem persecuti vident. At qui vtrũq; pdidicerũt, (vt omni/
bus armis ornati) citius cum autoritate quod fuit propositum,sũt as/
sequuti. Cum in omnibus enim rebus,tum maxime etiam in archite/
ctura hæc duo insunt,quod significatur,& quod significat. Significatur
proposita res de qua dicitur.Hanc autem significat demonstratio ratio/
nibus doctrinarum explicata ; Quare videtur vtraq; parte exercitatum
esse debere,qui se architectum profiteatur.Itaq; eum & ingeniosum esse
oportet,& ad disciplinam docilem.Neq; enim igenium sine disciplina,
aut disciplina sine ingenio,perfectum artificem potest efficere , & ut lit/
teratus sit,peritus graphidos,eruditus geometria,& optices non igna/
rus,instructus arithmetica,historias complures nouerit, philosophos
diligenter audiuerit,musicam seuerit,medicinæ non sit ignarus,respõ/
sa iuris consultorum nouerit,astrologiam cœliq; rationes cognitas ha/
beat,Quæ cur ita sint,hæ sunt causæ. Litteras architectum scire opor/
tet,vti cõmentariis memoriam firmiorem efficere possit. Deinde gra/
phidos scientiam habere,quo facilius exemplaribus pictis, quam uelit
operis speciem,deformare valeat. Geometria autẽ plura præsidia præ/
stat architecturæ:& primũ ex euthygrammis circini tradit usum:æ quo
maxime facilius edificiorum in areis expediuntur descriptiões:norma/
rumq; & librationum & linearum directiones. Item per opticen , in
edificiis,ab certis regionibus,cœli lumina recte ducũtur. Per arithme/
ticen,sũptus edificiorũ consumantur:mensurarum rationes expli/
cantur:difficilesq; symmetriarum questiones geometricis rationibus &
methodis inueniũtur. Historias autem plures nouisse oportet,q̃ mul/
ta ornamenta sæpe in operibus architecti designant,de quibus,argumẽ/
tis rationem cur fecerint querentibus reddere debent.Quemadmodum
siquis statuas marmoreas muliebres stolatas,& quæ caryatides dicitur,
pro columnis in opere statuerit , & insuper mutilos & coronas collo/
cauerit,percontaribus ita reddet rationẽ. Carya ciuitas Pelopõnesi cum
persis hostibus cõtra græciã cõsensit: postea græci per victoriã gloriose
bello liberati,cõmuni cõsilio caryatibus bellũ indixerunt.Itaq; oppido
capto,uiris interfectis,ciuitate deleta,matronas eorũ in seruitutẽ abdu/
xerunt.Nec sunt passi stolas,neq; ornatus matronales deponere:vti non
vno triumpho ducerent,sed æterno seruitutis exẽplo graui cõtumelia
pressæ,pœnas pendere uiderentur pro ciuitate.Ideo qui tunc architecti
fuerunt,edificiis publicis designauerũt earũ imagines oneri serũdo col/
locatas:ut etiã posteris nota pœna peccati caryatiũ, memoriæ traderet.

PRIMVS.   2

Exemplu eode formal omni m modum
belli atore sustineta louis prescemsti

Pro trophus simulacru.

Negn pro libertate desendenda.

Nō minus Iacones Pausania Agæsipolidos filio duce plataeo ṗlio, pau/
ca manu iḣnitum numerum exercitus persarū cum superauissent , acto
cum gloria triumpho, spoliorū & predæ porticum persicā ex manubiis
laudis, & uirtutis ciuium, indicem uictoriæ, posteris pro tropheo con/
stituerunt : ibiꝗ captiuorum simulacra barbarico uestis ornatu , super/
bia meritis contumeliis punita, substinentia tectum collocauerunt : uti
& hostes horrescerent timore eorum fortitudinis effectus, & ciues id
exemplum uirtutis aspicientes, gloria erecti, ad defendendam libertatē
essent parati. Itaꝗ ex eo multi statuas persicas substinentes, epistylia &
ornamenta eorum collocauerūt : & ita ex eo argumēto, uarietates egre/
gias auxerunt operibus.

A ii

LIBER

Item sunt aliæ eiusdem generis historiæ, quarum noticiam architectos tenere oporteat. Philosophia uero perficit architectū animo magno, & uti nō sit arrogans, sed potius facilis, æquus, & fidelis: sine auaritia, qd́ est maximum. Nullum enim opus uere sine fide & castitate fieri potest. Ne sit cupidus, neqꝫ in muneribus accipiendis habeat animum occupa̅ tum, sed cum grauitate suam tueatur dignitatem bonam famam habē̅ do. Hæc enim philosophia præscribit. Præterea de rerum natura quæ græce φυσιολοσια dicitur, philosophia explicat: quā necesse est studio̅ sius nouisse, cꝗ habet multas & uarias naturales questiones: ut etiam in aquarum ductionibus. In cursibus enim & circuitiōibus, & librata pla̅ nicie, expressiōibus, spiritus naturales aliter atqꝫ aliter fiũt: quorum of̅ fensionibus mederi nemo poterit, nisi qui ex philosophia principia re̅ rum natūræ nouerit. Item qui Thesbiæ aut Archimedis libros, & cæte̅ rorum qui eiusmodi generis præcepta conscripserunt leget, cum iis sen̅ tire non poterit, nisi his rebus a philosophis fuerit istitutus. Musicen autem sciat oportet, uti canonicam rationem, & mathemáticam, notam habeat: præterea balistarum, catapultarū, scorpionum tꝑaturas pos̅ sit recte facere. In capitulis enim dextra ac sinistra, sunt̅ foramina hemi̅

De Architectura

Quid sit Architectura et De Architectis Instituendis.

Architectura est scientia pluribus disciplinis et variis eruditionibus
ornata, cuius iudicio probantur omnia quae ab ceteris artibus
perficiuntur opera. Ea nascitur ex fabrica, et ratiocinatione. Fabrica
5 est continuata ac trita usus meditatio, quae manibus perficitur e
materia cuiuscunque generis opus est ad propositum deformationis.
Ratiocinatio autem est, quae res fabricatas solertia ac ratione
proportionis demonstrare atque explicare potest. Itaque architecti
qui sine litteris contenderunt ut manibus essent exercitati, non
10 potuerunt efficere ut haberent prolaboribus autoritatem. Qui
autem ratiocinationibus et litteris solis confisi fuerunt, umbram
non rem persecuti videntur. At qui utrumque perdidicerunt,
(uti omnibus armis ornati) citius cum autoritate quod fuit
propositum, sunt assecuti. Cum in omnibus enim rebus, tum
15 maxime etiam in architectura haec duo insunt, quod significatur,
et quod significat. Significatur proposita res de qua dicitur. Hanc
autem significat demonstratio rationibus doctrinarum explicata,
quare videtur utraque parte exercitatum esse debere, qui se
architectum profiteatur. Itaque eum et ingenuosum esse oportet,
20 et ad disciplinam docilem. Neque enim ingenium sine disciplina,
aut disciplina sine ingenio, perfectum artificem potest efficere, et
ut litteratus sit, peritus graphidos, eruditus geometria, et optices
non ignarus, instructus arithmetica, historias complures noverit,
philosophos diligenter audiverit, musicam sciverit, medicinae
25 non sit ignarus, responsa iuris consultorum noverit, astrologiam
coelique rationes cognitas habeat, quae cur ita sint, hae sunt causae.
Litteras architectum scire oportet, uti commentariis memoriam
firmiorem efficere possit. Deinde graphidos scientiam habere, quo
facilius exemplaribus pictis, quam velit operis speciem, deformare
30 valeat. Geometria autem plura praesidia praestat architecturae: et
primum ex euthygrammis circini tradit usum: e quo maxime facilius

aedificiorum in areis expediuntur descriptiones: normarumque et
librationum et linearum directiones. Item per opticen, in aedificiis,
ab certis regionibus, coeli lumina recte ducuntur. Per arithmeticen,
35   sumptus aedificiorum consumantur: mensurarum rationes
explicantur: difficilesque symmetriarum quaestiones geometricis
rationibus et methodis inveniuntur.

Historias autem plures novisse oportet, quod multa ornamenta saepe
in operibus architecti designant, de quibus argumentis rationem
40   cur fecerint quaerentibus reddere debent. Quemadmodum siquis
statuas marmoreas muliebres stolatas, et quae caryatides dicuntur,
pro columnis in opere statuerit, et insuper mutilos et coronas
collocaverit, percontantibus ita reddet rationem. Carya civitas
Peloponnensis cum persis hostibus contra graeciam consensit:
45   postea graeci per victoriam gloriose bello liberati, communi consilio
caryatibus bellum indixerunt. Itaque oppido capto, viris interfectis,
civitate deleta, matronas eorum in servitutem abduxerunt. Nec
sunt passi stolas, neque ornatus matronales deponere: uti non
uno triumpho ducerentur, sed aeterno servitutis exemplo gravi
50   contumelia pressae poenas pendere viderentur pro civitate. Ideo
qui tunc architecti fuerunt, aedificiis publicis designaverunt earum
imagines oneri ferundo collocatas: ut etiam posteris nota poena
peccati caryatium, memoriae traderetur . . .

[...]

Philosophia vero perficit architectum animo magno, et uti non sit
55   arrogans, sed potius facilis, aequus, et fidelis: sine avaritia, quod est
maximum. Nullum enim opus vere sine fide et castitate fieri potest.
Ne sit cupidus, neque in muneribus accipiendis habeat animum
occupatum, sed cum gravitate suam tueatur dignitatem bonam
famam habendo. Haec enim philosophia praescribit. Praeterea de

60 rerum natura quae graece *physiologia* dicitur, philosophia explicat:
quam necesse est studiosius novisse, quod habet multas et varias
naturales quaestiones: ut etiam in aquarum ductionibus. In cursibus
enim et in circuitionibus, et librata planicie expressionibus, spiritus
naturales aliter atque aliter fiunt: quorum offensionibus mederi
65 nemo poterit, nisi qui ex philosophia principia rerum naturae
noverit. Item qui Thesbiae aut Archimedis libros, et caeterorum qui
eiusmodi generis praecepta conscripserunt leget, cum iis sentire non
poterit, nisi his rebus a philosophis fuerit institutus.

• Notes •

1 **Instituendis:** note gerundive.

2 **Architectura est scientia:** Manuscripts and earlier editions have
Architecti est Scientia ... *The architect's is a science ...,* thus
emphasizing the necessary knowledge to be mastered by a true
architect.

4 **perficiuntur: perficio, perficere, perfeci, perfectum (per
+ facio).** One of Vitruvius's favorite verbs, whose meaning is
*to carry out, to achieve, to bring to completion, to thoroughly
accomplish, to complete, to make perfect.*

fabrica, et ratiocinatione: literally, *(physical) work and
reasoning* can be rendered as *practice and theory.*

5 **trita usus:** Construe **usus** as genitive. **tero, terere, trivi, tritum:**
to wear away, to grind.

meditatio: not necessarily *meditation* or *contemplation.* It can
also mean *exercise, practice.*

6 **opus est:** *it is necessary.*

11 **confisi: confido, confidere, confisus sum.**

11–12 **umbram non rem persecuti videntur:** Don't miss the poetic
beauty of the passage. Similar expressions are used, among many
others, by Ben Jonson (1572–1637):

Follow a shadow, it still flies you,
Seem to fly it, it will pursue.

Also, William Wordsworth (1770–1850) said: "We all laugh at pursuing a shadow, though the lives of the multitude are devoted to the chase." And Edmund Burke (1729–1797; inspired by Wordsworth) uttered the famous: ". . . what shadows we are, and what shadows we pursue." In *Macbeth*, William Shakespeare (1564–1616) says: "Life's but a walking shadow." Had they all read Vitruvius? Not necessarily, since the shadow theme as a metaphor of ephemeral existence is very old. We find, among many other instances, in Psalm 102:11, "My days are like a shadow that declineth." Also, in Job 14:2, "[Man] fleeth also as a shadow and continueth not." And in I Chronicles 29:15, "Our days on the earth are like a shadow."

14   **Cum . . . tum . . .:** *both . . . and especially . . .*

18   **videtur:** impersonal *it appears that . . .*

esse debere: The first infinitive is governed by the second, and the second is governed by **videtur**.

19   **profiteatur: profiteor, profiteri, professus sum** *to avow, to profess, to declare oneself as being something.* Notice the use of the subjunctive. Why?

oportet: *it is proper that . . .* followed by accusative + infinitive.

21–22   **et ut litteratus sit:** The string of subjunctive conditions in this sentence is still loosely governed by **oportet**. *And it is also necessary that he be . . .*

22   **peritus graphidos:** *expert in technical drawing* (a desirable and rare talent even today!). **Graphis** is a Greek word meaning a stylus for writing on a waxen tablet. **Graphidos** is the Greek genitive singular. In the next paragraph, however, Vitruvius seems to use a latinized third declension form.

27   **commentariis memoriam:** Vitruvius explains why it is necessary for an architect to be literate. Using the old and safe advice of Latin students ("stick as closely as possible to the sound of Latin"), we may as well translate *to effect a firmer memory by means of commentaries*, and (completing the students' advice) let the professor figure out what the author really meant. Otherwise, we may try to decide whether

memoria here means a written record for posterity or just a technical report for the architect's and his helpers' own use about the construction of a particular building.

28–30 **Deinde . . . valeat:** reordered version: **Deinde graphidos scientiam habere, quo facilius valeat deformare (exemplaribus pictis) speciem operis quam velit. Velit** is a subjunctive hypothetical clause, whereas **valeat** is a subjunctive purpose clause governed by **quo facilius**.

29 **operis:** objective genitive.

deformare: *to fashion, to delineate.*

30 **praesidia praestat: praesidium praestare** *to provide assistance or support.*

euthygrammis: a Greek word meaning *a straight line* (possibly also *a straightedge*).

31 **circini: circinus, -i** (m) *a compass for drawing circles.*

32–33 **normarumque et librationum et linearum directiones: Norma** and **libratio** are carpenter's tools (the square and the level, respectively). Geometry helps the architect in correctly tracing straight lines, right angles, and levels. It is clear that even in Vitruvius's time, there was a well-developed technical jargon for the various professions. Some of these words you will not find in standard Latin dictionaries, but they are included in this text's glossary.

35 **sumptus: sumptus, -us** (m) *expense, cost.* Construe in the nominative plural.

consumantur: consummo, consummare, consummavi, consummatum: to sum up, to accomplish, to complete; not to be confused with **consumo, consumere, consumpsi, consumptum**.

38 **quod:** *because.*

39 **architecti:** nominative plural.

argumentis: argumentum, -i (n) *the subject matter of a work of art, an argument.*

40 **cur fecerint:** subjunctive of an indirect question.

Quemadmodum: *just as, for example.*

41–42   **statuas ... muliebres ... statuerit:** two accusatives in apposition.

41   **stolatas: stolatus, -a, -um** *wearing a stola.*

42   **pro:** here, *in place of.*

mutilos et coronas: architectural terms. Specifically, in the Doric style, the **corona** and the **mutulus** are parts of the cornice, namely, the projecting horizontal member that runs on top of the capitals of a row of columns. The **corona** can be identified with the cornice itself or with its projecting underside, to which the **mutuli** are attached as flat projecting blocks. **Corona** comes directly into English.

45   **liberati: libero, -are** + ablative *to release or set free from.*

communi: ablative.

46   **bellum indixerunt: bellum indicere** + dative *to declare war on or against.*

46–47   **oppido capto, viris interfectis, civitate deleta ...:** ablative absolutes.

47   **civitate deleta:** An alternative reading exists as **civitate declarata.**

48   **passi: patior** + accusative + infinitive *to suffer, to tolerate, or to allow someone* (supply **eas**) *to do something* (**deponere**).

50   **poenas pendere:** *to pay a penalty, to suffer a punishment.*

50–53   **Ideo ... ut etiam ... traderetur:** subjunctive result clause.

52   **oneri ferundo = oneri ferendo:** gerundive construction instead of gerund + accusative (**ferendo onus**). **Oneri ferendo esse** = *to be able to carry* is a common Latin expression.

53   **memoriae traderetur: memoriae tradere** *to commit to memory, to write the history of.*

54   **Philosophia:** Vitruvius takes here the term philosophy in its most comprehensive sense, including both the philosophy of morals (ethics) and natural philosophy (physics).

57   **Ne sit:** *lest he be* or *may he not be.*

59   **famam habendo: famam** is direct object of the ablative gerund.

61   **necesse est . . . novisse:** The dative **architecto** is understood.

62   **ut etiam:** In context, this can be translated *as for example.*

62–63   **In cursibus enim et in circuitionibus, et librata planicie expressionibus:** These are technical terms pertaining to different aspects of the transport of water in pipes: *flowing downward, turning, horizontally, or upward.* **Planicies, planiciei** (f) is a fifth-declension alternative form of **planicia, planiciae or planitia, planitiae.**

63–64   **spiritus naturales aliter atque aliter fiunt:** *natural pressures arise in different ways.*

64   **mederi: medeor, mederi** + dative or accusative, *to cure, to remedy, to correct, to repair.*

66   **Thesbiae aut Archimedis:** both in the genitive case. Archimedes (287–212 BCE) was the greatest scientist of the Hellenistic period. **Thesbia** is an incorrect spelling for *Ctesibius* (or *Tesibius*), a third-century BCE Hellenistic physicist in Alexandria. His work was a precursor of modern fluid mechanics and he was a prolific inventor.

68   **institutus: instituo, instituere, institui, institutum** *to place, to build, to instruct, to educate.*

Marcus Cetius Faventinus

Details of the life of Marcus Cetius Faventinus, including the precise dates of his birth and death, are not known except for the attribution to his authorship of a *Manual of Private Architecture*. This manual, which today (without disrespect) may be called "Vitruvius for Dummies," or "Feng Shui for Latinists," served as a model for even further popularizations of the master's work. Written most probably during the fourth century, it concerns itself only with those aspects of architecture that pertain to the private domain, thus achieving a considerable reduction of the original Vitruvian treatise. That the author was satisfied with his objective is, in fact, the subject of his closing paragraph, which reads:

> *Quantum ergo ad privatum usum spectat, necessaria huic libello ordinavimus. Civitatum sane et ceterarum rerum institutiones praestanti sapientiae memorandas reliquimus.*[5]

The authorship of the work was only established definitively in the nineteenth century. Previous editions published it anonymously (first edition, Paris, 1540; second edition, Padova, 1739). Several complete manuscripts are extant.

---

5 Translation: *As far as the private use is concerned, we have set in order the (things) necessary to this little book. We have, of course, left to an eminent authority the instructions of cities and other subjects.* The second sentence of this paragraph does not appear in the printed edition mentioned below. Moreover, that edition includes a thirtieth chapter, not present in some of the manuscripts.

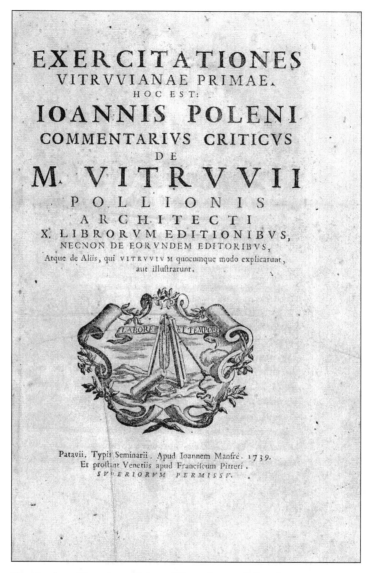

EXERCITATIONES
VITRVVIANAE PRIMAE,
HOC EST:
IOANNIS POLENI
COMMENTARIVS CRITICVS
DE
M. VITRVVII
POLLIONIS
ARCHITECTI
X. LIBRORVM EDITIONIBVS,
NECNON DE EORVNDEM EDITORIBVS,
Atque de Aliis, qui VITRVVIVM quocumque modo explicarunt,
aut illuftrarunt.

LABORE ET TEMPORE

Patavii. Typis Seminarii. Apud Ioannem Manfrè. 1739.
Et proftant Venetiis apud Francifcum Pitteri.
SVPERIORVM PERMISSV.

Exercitationes Vitruvianae Primae. Hoc est Ioannis Poleni Commentarius Criticus de M. Vitruvii Pollionis Architecti, Patavii, apud Ioannem Manfrè, 1739. Getty Library holding. Digital version courtesy of archive.org.

177

ANONYMI
SCRIPTORIS VETERIS
DE
ARCHITECTVRA
COMPENDIVM.

I.

De Principiis Artis Architectonicæ.

DE Artis Architectonicæ peritia multa oratione Vitruvius Pollio, aliique [2] Auctores scripsere . Verum , ne longa eorum diſſertaque [3] facundia humilioribus ingeniis alienum faceret ſtudium , pauca ex his , mediocri licet ſermone , privatis uſibus [4] ornare fuit conſilium . Quæ partes itaque cæli & regiones ventorum ſalubres ædificiis videantur , & qua ſubtilitate nocivi flatus avertantur, adituſque januarum & lumina feneſtris utiliter tribuantur , quibuſque menſuris ædificiorum membra diſponantur , quibus ſignis tenuis abundanſque aqua inveniatur; alia etiam, quæ ædificandi gratia ſcire oportet, brevi ſuccinctaque narratione cognoſces. Primo ergo quæ principia ad Architecturam pertinere debeant ſtudioſe attendere convenit . Omnia enim pulchro decore ac venuſta utilitate fieri poterunt, ſi ante hujus artis [5] peritus ordo diſcatur . Nam architecturæ partes ſunt octo , quæ ſunt ordinatio, diſpoſitio, venuſtas , menſura , diſtributio , ædificatio, conlocatio, machinatio. Ex his Græci, quin-

---

[1] Hujuſmodi titulum hic fecimus (facilitatis gratia) Operi huic ; quamvis in editionis hujuſce fronte eundem illum titulum , qui legitur in Vaſcoſani Editione , maluerimus adhibere.

[2] AVCTORES SCRIPSERE] Cod. R, 2. habet; *Auctores ſcientiſſime ſcripſerunt* .

[3] FACVNDIA] Ita reſtituimus ex Ed. V. & Cod. R. 2. legebatur in Cod. R, 1, *facundiora* ;

[4] ORNARE] Cod. R. 2. *excerpere* ;

[5] PERITVS ORDO DISCATVR] Ita Cod. R. 1. & Ed. V. Verum in Cod. R. 2. legitur , *peritus ordinem diſcat* . Et hæc quidem dictio videretur aptior : neque enim memini a Latinis *peritas* dici res inanimes. Nihilo tamen minus a veteri Codice recedendum, non putavi ;

194   ARCHITECTVRAE

Nitidiorem enim cultum recipiunt si ad lumen attendant. Latitudo XV. pedibus 2 disponatur, & in singulis parietibus 3 VIIII. pedes relinquantur. Equilia 4 calidis locis ordinentur, & obscuriora fiant, ut securi equi pabulentur. Ovilia, & Caprilia pro magnitudine agri componantur. Cella vinaria contra frigidissimas cæli plagas collocetur. Lumen fenestris a Septentrione tribuatur: ut undique frigidus aer vina incolumia servet. Vapore enim omnia corrumpuntur. 5 Torcular hujus in Septentrionem ponatur. Cella autem olearis in meridie constituenda est: fenestræ ab eadem parte tribuantur, ne frigore oleum 6 cum sordibus retineatur, & suavitas saporis pereat. 7 Torcular hujus in meridie statuatur: magnitudo pro abundantia rei fiat. Granaria ad Septentrionem, vel Aquilonem spectent, ut aere gelidiori fruges tutius serventur. Vaporatæ enim regiones curguliones, & alia genera bestiolarum nutriunt. Quæ fruges corrumpunt. Horrea, fenilia, pistrina extra villam sunt constituenda, ut ab ignis periculo villæ sint tutiores. Si quid vero melius, ac nitidius facere volueris, exempla de Vrbanis fabricis sumes.

XIIII.

De dispositione operis Vrbani.

VRbani itaque operis gratiam luminosam esse 1 oportet: præsertim cum nulli vicini parietes impediant. Disponendum erit tamen ante, ut certa genera ædificiorum cæli regiones apte possint spectare. Hiberna ergo hibernum occidentem spectare debent, 2 quoniam vespertino lumine opus est. Nam sol occidens non solum illuminat, sed 3 pro vi caloris tepidas facit regiones. Cubicula & Bibliothecæ ad orientem spectare debent.
                                1 Vi-

---

expectentur, sed proculdubio mendose. Vitruvius f Lib. VI. Cap. 9. in quo de rusticorum ædificiorum rationibus agit) *Conjuncta autem* (culina) *habeat bubilia, quorum præsepia ad focum, & orientis cæli regionem spectent.*

2 DISPONATVR] Sic Cod. R. 2. At Cod. R. 1. *quod ponatur*: & Ed. V. *componatur.*

3 VIIII.] Cod. R. 2. numerum exhibet *VIII.*

4 CALIDIS] Consentit hæc lectio Cod. R. 2. cum Vitruvii præceptis. Cod. R. 1. & Ed. V. habent *cardinis.*

5 TORCVLAR HVIVS] Nimirum *hujus cella vinaria*; quod scilicet usui esset cellæ

vinariæ. In Cod. R. 2. deest pronom. *hujus.*

6 CVM SORDIBVS RETINEATVR, ET SVAVITAS] Ita Cod. R. 2. cujus lectionem, ceu clariorem, præferendam ratus sum. Cod. R. 1. & Ed. V. *cum sordibus & suavitas saporis.*

7 TORCVLAR HVIVS] Hoc est, *hujus cella olearis.*

1 OPORTET] Verbum hoc in Cod. R. 2. retrusum est post verbum, *impediant.*

2 QVONIAM] Legitur in Cod. R. 2. Sed in Cod. R. 1. *quomodo*, & in Ed. V. *quum.*

3 PRO VI] Seu verba hæc in Codice aliquo invenerit is, qui præfuit Vaseosani Editioni, sive ex ingenio emendationem adulerit,
                    cer-

1 Vifus enim matutinum poftulat lumen . Nam quæcumque loca frigida
2 fpectant , humore vitiantur ; quoniam venti humidi , fpirantes madidos
flatus, omnia 3 pallore corrumpunt. Triclinia verna, & autumnalia ad orientem fpectare debent , 4 ut gratiora fint, quod his uti folitum eft. AEfti-
va triclinia ad Septentrionem fpectare debent ; quod ea regio, 5 præter
ceteras, frigidior eft, & folftitiali tempore jucundam fanitatis voluptatem
corporibus præftat.

XV.

De menfuris AEdificiorum.

TRicliniorum , & conclavium quanta latitudo & longitudo fuerit 6 in
uno computata menfura, ex ea medietas altitudini tribuatur . Si autem exedræ, 7 aut oeci quadrati fuerint, media pars menfuræ in altitudinem ftruatur. Pinacothecæ & Plumariorum officinæ in parte feptentrionali
funt conftituendæ; ut colores, & purpuræ fine vitio referventur . De va-
poratis enim regionibus corruptelæ nafcuntur .

XVI.

De Fabrica Balnearum.

BAlneis locus eligendus eft contra occafum hibernum , aut partem
meridianam ; ut fole decedente 8 vaporetur 9 ufque ad vefperum ,
quod

certe apta vifa funt. In Codicibus legitur ,
proximi .

1 VISVS ENIM &c.] vocabulum , Vifus,
defcriptum eft in Cod. R 1. & in Ed. V.:
at in Cod. R 2. vocabulum ufus vel defcri-
pferunt, vel fcripferunt permoti auctoritate
Vitruvii , qui (Libro VI. Cap. VII. quo
variæ partes hujufce noftri Articuli continentur) Vfus enim , ait, matutinum poftulat lumen .

2 SPECTANT, HVMORE VITIANTVR;
QVONIAM] Ita Cod. R 2. cui hoc quoque loco parere placuit . Mendofa enim
haud dubie funt quæ habet Cod. R 1. fpectantur umorem , videntur, quomodo . Ed. V.
fpectantur umore , vitentur , quoniam .

3 PALLORE] Vocem hanc , in qua con-
fentiunt Cod. R 1. & Ed. V. non reperies
in Cod. R 2.

4 VT GRATIORA SINT, QVOD HIS
VTI SOLITVM EST . AESTIVA TRICLI-
NIA AD SEPTENTRIONEM SPECTA-

RE DEBENT] Omnia verba hæc , quæ leguntur in Cod. R 2. & in Ed. V. & quæ
ipfo Vitruvii (Cap. cit.) textu probantur,
defunt in Cod. R 1. prætermiffa haud dubie Amanuenfis incuria .

5 PRAETER CETERAS] Cod. R 2.
præ ceteris.

6 IN VNO COMPVTATA MENSVRA]
Cod. R 2. in unam computa menfuram .

7 AVT OECI QVADRATI] Cod. R 1.
aut tycii quadrati : Ed. V. aut nifi quadrati : Cod. R 2. aut quadrati . Sed oeci effe
legendum plane credidi , cum Vitruvius
(Lib. VI. Cap. 6.) agat de oecis, ubi præ-
cipit, ut altitudines eorum dimidia latitudinis
addita conftituantur .

8 VAPORETVR] Nempe , calore tem-
peretur . Horatius (Lib. I. Ep. 16. v. 7.)
afpiciat Sol :

Lævum difcedens curru fugiente vaporet .

9 VSQVE AD VESPERVM , QVOD]
Ita

De Architectura Compendium

De principiis artis Architectonicae. Caput I.

De artis Architectonicae peritia, multa oratione Vitruvius Pollio
aliique auctores scripsere: verum ne longa eorum disertaque
facundia humilioribus ingeniis alienum faceret studium, pauca ex
5   his, mediocri licet sermone, privatis usibus ornare fuit consilium.
Quae partes itaque caeli, et regiones ventorum salubres aedificiis
videantur, et qua subtilitate nocivi flatus avertantur, aditusque
ianuarum, et lumina fenestris utiliter tribuantur, quibusve
mensuris aedificiorum membra disponantur, quibus signis tenuis
10   abundansque aqua inveniatur; alia etiam quae aedificandi gratia
scire oportet, brevi succinctaque narratione cognosces.

    Primo ergo quae principia ad architecturam pertinere debeant,
studiose attendere convenit. Omnia enim pulchro decore ac venusta
utilitate fieri poterunt, si ante huius artis peritus ordo discatur.
15   Nam architecturae partes sunt octo, quae sunt, ordinatio, dispositio,
venustas, mensura, distributio, aedificatio, collocatio, machinatio.

De dispositione operis urbani. Cap. XIIII.

Urbani itaque operis gratiam luminosam esse oportet, praesertim cum
nulli vicini parietes impediant. Disponendum tamen erit ante, ut certa
20   genera aedificiorum caeli regiones apte possint spectare. Hyberna ergo
hybernum occidentem spectare debent, quoniam vespertino lumine
opus est. Nam sol occidens non solum illuminat, sed pro vi caloris
tepidas facit regiones. Cubicula et bibliothecae ad orientem spectare
debent. Visus enim matutinum postulat lumen. Nam quaecunque
25   loca frigida spectant humore vitiantur, quoniam venti humidi
spirantes madidos flatus, omnia pallore corrumpunt. Triclinia verna
et autumnalia ad orientem spectare debent, ut gratiora sint: quod his
uti solitum. Aestiva triclinia ad septentrionem spectare debent, quod
ea regio praeter caeteras frigidior est, et solstitiali tempore iucundam
30   sanitatis voluptatem corporibus praestat.

• Notes •

Caput I.

3   **scripsere: scripserunt.**

           verum: sed.

3–5   **ne . . . consilium:** negative purpose clause, *lest . . .* The sentence
           could be reorganized as **Ne eorum longa disertaque facundia**
           faceret studium alienum humilioribus ingeniis, consilium
           fuit [mihi] ornare pauca ex his licet mediocri sermone privatis
           usibus. Humilioribus ingeniis, in the dative, is a reference to us,
           common mortals, who are baffled by the expert language **longa**
           disertaque facundia used by Vitruvius and others. Instead, Cetius
           Faventinus intends to express himself by **mediocri sermone** to
           convey a few of these ideas for private applications.

5   **mediocri: mediocris, mediocre:** Avoid the English pejorative
           connotation of **mediocris**. See glossary.

           ornare: An alternative version has **ordinare**, which is more
           logical and more compatible with the closing sentence mentioned
           above in the introduction to this selection (**ordinavimus**).

6–8   **Quae . . . qua . . . quibusve . . .:** All these are interrogative
           adjectives in a series of indirect questions, hence the
           subjunctives, governed by the final **cognosces**, addressed
           directly to the reader.

6   **partes . . . caeli . . . regiones ventorum:** These are "poetic" ways
           to refer to the cardinal orientations and the directions of the
           winds. *By means of* **subtilitate** [of design] the **nocivi flatus** *may*
           be averted.

9   **tenuis:** This is a third declension adjective and, therefore, it
           cannot be construed with **signis** (in the ablative plural). It must
           be taken together with **abundans**.

10   **aedificandi gratia: Gratia**, in the ablative, can be understood
           as *for the sake of*, thus explaining the genitive of the gerund
           aedificandi. Similar expressions (which have made it into
           English) are **exempli gratia** (*e.g., for* [*the sake of*] *example*) and
           honoris causa (*for the sake of honor*).

11   **oportet:** impersonal verb followed by accusative with an infinitive.

14   **fieri: facta esse.**

        poterunt . . . discatur: Cetius Faventinus mixes a subjunctive verb in the condition and an indicative in the conclusion.

        ante: used here adverbially, *beforehand.*

15   **architecturae partes sunt octo:** Notice how Cetius Faventinus skips all of the talk of Vitruvius about the relation of architecture with other disciplines. The eight parts of architecture mentioned by Cetius Faventinus are indeed found in Vitruvius, Chapters II and III of Book I. They are not precisely the same nor are they all presented at the same level. Cetius Faventinus tries to present what in his mind is the distillation of Vitruvian thought. We now abandon this introductory part and move to Chapter XIV, dealing with the design of a city dwelling.

Cap. XIIII.

18   **esse oportet: Oportet** is an impersonal verb that can be used to introduce an indirect statement/oratio obliqua. *It is fitting that a luminous grace* (**gratiam luminosam**) *be* [*a feature*] *of an urban building.*

19   **Disponendum erit:** passive periphrastic.

20   **Hyberna:** alternative spelling of **hiberna.** The noun **hiems, hiemis** (f) is *winter.* **Hibernus, -a, -um** is the adjective *wintry, of winter.* The plural noun **hiberna, -orum** (n pl) is used for *winter quarters.* **Hybernum occidentem** refers to the direction of sunset during the winter months.

22   **opus est:** an expression meaning *it is necessary.* The thing needed goes in the ablative case.

24   **quaecunque:** From **quicumque, quaecumque, quodcumque** *every.* Here, in the nominative neuter plural. The whole sentence has been considered by some experts as having a dubious logical meaning and alternative readings have been suggested. See the critical edition and French translation by Marie-Thérèse Cam in *Cetius Faventinus: Abrégé d'Architecture Privée* (Paris: Les Belles

Lettres, 2001). This is one of the merits of looking at the original manuscripts and early printed editions. Translators, of necessity, must choose one of several possible interpretations.

26 **triclinia: triclinium, -ii** (n): Roman dining room where they reclined on three sides as they dined. **Triclinia verna et autumnalia** are the dining rooms used in spring and autumn (as opposed to the **hyberna**). These are obviously dwellings for the wealthy.

27–28 **quod his uti solitum: Quod** here means *because* or *since*. **Uti** is the infinitive of the deponent **utor, uti, usus sum**, which takes an ablative object. Supply **est** after **solitum**. **Soleo, solere, solitus sum** is semi-deponent. **solitum, -i** (n) *a habitual, customary thing.*

30 **praestat: Praesto, -are** has the primary sense of *to stand before, to be outstanding, to be preferable.* As a transitive verb, however, it can also mean *to show* and *to confer, to grant, to lend.*

Leon Battista Alberti

A s befits a Renaissance man, Leon Battista Alberti (1404–1472) made significant contributions to more than one field, including cryptography and painting. His treatise *De Pictura* (*On Painting*) seems to have been the first to explain and apply the theory of perspective to art that had been anticipated in practice by Filippo Brunelleschi (1377–1446), the great Renaissance architect. But it is as an architect that Alberti is mostly remembered, both through his many buildings and monuments and through his treatise *De Re Aedificatoria* (*On the Art of Building*), written in Latin and dealing (like his great predecessor Vitruvius fifteen centuries earlier) with both the theory and the practice of architecture. As a humanist, Alberti went beyond Vitruvius in emphasizing holistic concepts such as the harmony of the individual with the environment, the use of musically inspired proportions, and, more generally, the theory of architecture. *De Re Aedificatoria* was the first architectural treatise to ever be printed. It had an enormous influence on the architecture of the following two centuries.

We have chosen the opening of the first book. Alberti's Latin is very sophisticated and demands a slow and careful reading. Nevertheless, it is very rewarding, since some of his ideas are equally sophisticated. The Platonic notion that the mental conception of a building is on par with, or perhaps above, the actual material building is worthy of consideration. To put it in mundane terms, not all estate is necessarily real estate.

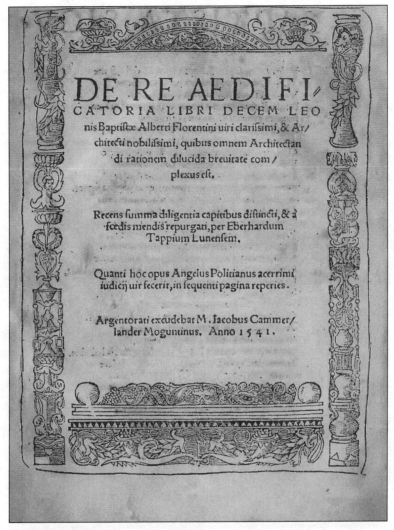

De re aedificatoria libri decem Leonis Baptistae Alberti, Argentorati [Strasbourg]: excudebat M. Iacobus Cammerlander Moguntinus, 1541. By permission of the Getty Research Institute. Facsimile courtesy of archive.org.

DE RE AEDIFICATORIA LIB. I. 3

to Singulorum opus. Sexto ornamentum. Septimo Sacrorum or/
namentum. Octauo Publici profani ornamentum. Nono Priuatori
um ornamentum. Decimo operum inftauratio, additi na
uis, æraria hiftoria, numeri & linearum, quid
conferat architectus in negotio.

LEONIS BAPTI-
STAE ALBERTI, DE RE AEDIFICATORIA
Liber primus, qui de Lineamentis infcribitur.

De Lineamentis, & eorum ui ac ratione.   Caput I.

E LINEAMENTIS AEDIFI
ciorum confcripturi optima, & elegan/
tiſſima quæcß à peritiſſimis maioribus
fuiſſe literis tradita, & quæ in ipſis operi
bus faciundis eſſe obſeruata animaduer
terimus, colligemus, noftrumcß hoc in
opus transferemus. His etiam addemus
fi quid noftro ingenio, & peruestigandi
cura, & labore adinuenerimus, quòd q/
dem ufui futurum putemus. Sed cum hu
iufmodi rebus alioquin duris & aſperis,
atcß multa ex parte obſcuriſſimis confcribendis me cupiam eſſe aper
tiſſimum, & quoad fieri poſſit, facilem, & expedinſſimũ, noftro pro
more explicabimus quid nam fit quod aggrediar. Nam hinc nõ ne/
gligendi rerum dicendarum fontes patebunt, unde cætera æquabili/
ore oratione dicantur. Rem igitur fic ordiemur. Tota res ædificato
ria lineamentis, & ftructura cõftituta eft. Lineamêtorum omnis uis
& ratio confumitur, ut recta, abfolutacß habeatur uia, coaptandi, iũ/
A 3 gen/

Quibus ar/
chitectura cõ
ftituatur.

LEONIS BAPTISTAE ALBERTI

gendi'q; lineas, & angulos, quibus ædificij facies comprehendatur,
atq; concludatur. Atqui est quidem lineamenti munus & officium,
præscribere ædificijs, & partibus ædificiorum aptum locum, & cer
tum numerum, dignumq; modũ, & gratum ordinem, ut iam tota
ædificij forma, & figura ipsis in lineamentis conquiescat. Neq; habet
lineamentum in se ut materiã sequatur, sed est huiusmodi, ut eadem
plurimis in ædificijs esse lineamẽta sentiamus, ubi una, atq; eadem in
illis spectetur forma. Hoc est, ubi eorum partes, & partium singula/
rum situs, atq; ordines inter se conueniant totis angulis, totisq; line/
is. Et licebit integras formas præscribere animo, & mente, seclusâ o/
mni materia. Quam rem assequemur adnotando, & præfiniendo an
gulos, & lineas certa directione, & connexione. Hæc cũ ita sint, erit
ergo lineamentũ certa, constans'q; præscriptio, concepta animo, fa/
Liniamẽtum . cta lineis, & angulis, perfecta'q; animo & ingenio erudito . Quod si
uelimus inuestigare quidnam ipsum ædificium, rota'q; structura per
se sit, fortassis faciet ad rẽ, si consyderabimus quibus primordijs, qui
busue progressibus inhabitandi sedes, quas ædificia nuncupât, olim
cœperint, atq; excreuerint. Qui, si recte opinor, de tota hac re sic sta/
tuisse possumus.

De occasione constituendarum ædium. Quot partibus
tota ædificandi ratio constet, quæq; cuiq; harum
partium conferant.   Cap. II .

Condendorũ   **P**Rincipio genus hominum in aliqua tuta regione sibi quæsiuisse
ædificiorũ pri quiescendi spacia, & illic inuenta area usui commoda & grata cõ
mi ortus. stitisse, atq; situm ipsum occupauisse, ut non eodem loco fieri dome/
stica omnia, & priuata uoluerit, sed alibi accubari, alibi focum habe
ri, alibi alia ad usum collocari. Hinc adeo cepisse mediarius ut tecta po
nerent, quò essent à sole & imbribus operti, idq; ut facerent, adiecisse
deinde parietum latera, quibus tecta imponerentur. Sic enim à geli/
dis tempestatibus & pruinosis uentis se futuros tutiores intelligebãt.
Demum parietibus aperuisse à solo in sublimi uias, & fenestras, qui
bus cum aditus, & congressus darentur, tum & lumina, & aurç aper
tis temporibus exciperentur, & concepta fortassis intra lares aqua,
uaporesq; expurgarentur. Ita quicumq; ille fuit seu Vesta dea Satur/
ni filia, seu Euryalus, Hyperbiusq; fratres, seu Gellio , aut Thrason ,
Cyclops'ue Tiphrinchius, qui ista principio instituerit, tandem sic pu

                                             to

De Re Aedificatoria
Liber primus, qui de Lineamentis inscribitur.

De lineamentis, et eorum vi ac ratione. Caput I.

De lineamentis aedificiorum conscripturi optima, et elegantissima
quaeque a peritissimis maioribus fuisse literis tradita, et quae in ipsis
operibus faciundis esse observata animadverterimus, colligemus,
5   nostrumque hoc in opus transferemus. His etiam addemus si quid
nostro ingenio, et pervestigandi cura, et labore adinvenerimus, quod
quidem usui futurum putemus. Sed cum huiusmodi rebus alioquin
duris at asperis, atque multa ex parte obscurissimis conscribendis
me cupiam esse apertissimum, et quoad fieri possit, facilem, et
10   expeditissimum, nostro pro more explicabimus quid nam sit quod
aggrediar. Nam hinc non negligendi rerum dicendarum fontes
patebunt, unde caetera aequabiliore oratione dicantur. Rem igitur
sic ordiemur. Tota res aedificatoria lineamentis, et structura
constituta est, Lineamentorum omnis vis et ratio consumitur, ut
15   recta, absolutaque habeatur via coaptandi, iungendique lineas, et
angulos, quibus aedificii facies comprehendatur, atque concludatur.
Atqui est quidem lineamenti munus et officium praescribere
aedificiis, et partibus aedificiorum aptum locum, et certum
numerum, dignumque modum, et gratum ordinem, ut iam tota
20   aedificii forma, et figura ipsis in lineamentis conquiescat. Neque
habet lineamentum in se ut materiam sequatur, sed est huiusmodi,
ut eadem plurimis in aedificiis esse lineamenta sentiamus, ubi una,
atque eadem in illis spectetur forma. Hoc est, ubi eorum partes,
et partium singularum situs, atque ordines inter se conveniant
25   totis angulis, totisque lineis. Et licebit integras formas praescribere
animo, et mente, seclusa omni materia. Quam rem assequemur
adnotando, et praefiniendo angulos, et lineas certa directione,
et connexione. Haec cum ita sint, erit ergo lineamentum certa,
constansque praescriptio, concepta animo, facta lineis, et angulis,

30 perfectaque animo et ingenio erudito. Quod si velimus investigare
    quidnam ipsum aedificium, totaque structura per se sit, fortassis
    faciet ad rem, si consyderabimus quibus primordiis, quibusve
    progressibus inhabitandi sedes, quas aedificia nuncupant, olim
    coeperint, atque excreverint. Qui, si recte opinor, de tota hac re sic
35 statuisse possumus.

• Notes •

lineamentis: Lineamentum, when used in the plural, means *a
drawing*. Alberti's view is that nothing can be accomplished in
practice without a careful mental design of what it is that one
is trying to build. In Aristotelian terms, the planning and the
drawings are the "formal cause" of the building. One can go as
far as saying that the mere conception of a building in the right
proportions and ideal location is already a work of architecture.

1–5 **De lineamentis . . . transferemus:** Alberti's Latin is more
convoluted than that of Vitruvius and, at times, even than that of
Cicero. Notice that Alberti is using the royal "we" of self-reference,
a practice not uncommon in our own day in scientific papers.
With this in mind, we observe that **conscripturi** is a future active
participle in the nominative plural and that it means *we who are
about to write*. The bare bones of the sentence can be written as
**Conscripturi de lineamentis aedificiorum, animadverterimus,
colligemus et transferemus in hoc opus nostrum quae tradita
fuisse et quae observata esse a maioribus.**

3 **maioribus: maior, maioris,** the comparative of **magnus, -a,
-um.** As a noun in the plural, *ancestors*.

5–7 **His . . . putemus:** The bare bones version of this sentence can be
written as **His addemus si adinvenerimus quid quod putemus
futurum usui. Futurum** is a future active participle of **sum, esse.**

7–11 **Sed cum . . . aggrediar:** Here, the bare bones version can be
written as **Sed cum cupiam me esse apertissimum et, quoad
fieri possit, facilem et expeditissimum rebus huiusmodi
alioquin duris et asperis atque ex multa parte obscurissimis
conscribendis, explicabimus pro more nostro quid (nam) sit
quod aggrediar.** Alberti uses both the royal "we" and the modest

"I" in this sentence. Since he wants to be very open-minded and, inasmuch as possible, easy and expeditious while writing things of this kind and otherwise hard and rough and very obscure from many aspects, he shall explain, following his own custom, what it is that he will undertake.

7   **alioquin:** *in another way, otherwise.*

9   **quoad fieri possit:** *to the extent that it may be possible.*

11–12   **Nam . . . dicantur:** reordered version: **Nam hinc patebunt fontes non negligendi rerum dicendarum, unde caetera dicantur aequabiliore oratione.** It is ironic how Alberti is telling us that his style is going to be more balanced and fair.

11   **fontes: fons, fontis** (m) *source.*

13   **ordiemur: ordior, ordiri, orsus sum** *to begin.*

13–14   **Tota . . . constituta est:** Alberti uses the term **lineamenta** sometimes not only as *drawing* but more like *design, conception.* Here, he is referring specifically to the plans of the building. Correspondingly, the term **structura** refers to the actual physical building. There is a ring here of Aristotle's causes.

14–15   **ut . . . habeatur:** The subject is **recta via**. The objective of the drawing is to represent the views of the building accurately, by means of properly drawn lines and angles.

15   **coaptandi: Coapto, -are** is a strengthened form of **apto, -are** or **adapto, -are.**

17–20   **Atqui . . . conquiescat:** The specialists in the theory of architecture may have something to say about the choice and exact meaning of the terms. In plain language, however, Alberti seems to be simply saying that the duty and function of design (drawing) is to outline for the buildings and their parts a proper location, a precise number (or quantity), a worthy (dignified) style, and an agreeable order (harmony) so that the whole form and figure of the building may already reside in the drawings themselves. For Alberti, the aesthetic of the conception is as important as the aesthetic of the actual building.

20–23   **Neque . . . forma:** Alberti seems here to be under the influence of Plato's "Ideas." A drawing of a building functions as such an Idea, which then materializes (albeit imperfectly) in particular buildings that can be built according to the same plan. This philosophical tack may be literally lost in translation (into any modern language), but it is certainly present in the Latin original. Notice, in particular, the use of the (reordered) expression **ut eadem lineamenta sentiamus esse in multiplis aedificiis**. The actual buildings participate in the Idea delineated in the plan, but not one of the buildings is identical to it. On looking at a real triangular shape, as Plato would have it, we feel the Idea of a perfect triangle.

25   **licebit:** impersonal, *it will be permitted, it may be possible.*

26   **seclusa: secludo, secludere, seclusi, seclusum** *to be separate from.*

       assequemur: alternative spelling of **adsequemur**, from the deponent verb **adsequor, adsequi, adsecutus sum** *to attain (by striving), to reach (after following).*

27   **adnotando, et praefiniendo:** ablative gerunds, *by noting (making notes, annotations)* and *by prescribing (predefining, stipulating).*

28   **Haec cum ita sint:** an expression meaning *things being as they are,* or *when/since things are this way, if this is the case.* Now Alberti is ready to provide a more precise definition of "design" or "plan."

30   **velimus:** present subjunctive of **volo, velle, volui**.

30–32   **velimus . . . faciet ad rem:** Alberti is mixing a subjunctive mood in the condition with the indicative mood in the conclusion. **faciet ad rem:** *it will matter.*

33   **sedes, quas aedificia nuncupant:** *habitations that they call buildings.*

Medicine

Isidore of Seville (Isidorus Hispaliensis)

Although not himself a physician, Isidore of Seville (ca. 560–636) was well acquainted with the Hippocratic-Galenic tradition of medicine. His treatise on medicine (Book 4 of the ever popular *Etymologiarum sive Originum Libri XX* [*Twenty Books on Etymologies or Origins*], known also by the shorter Latin title *Etymologiae* and by the English title *Etymologies*) had, therefore, a considerable influence on the transmission and perpetuation of this tradition. It is perhaps interesting to note that Maimonides (who lived about five centuries later), the famous Cordobese rabbi and court physician, was also a follower of the same tradition. Isidore, on the other hand, was a virulent attacker of Judaism and, among other things, advocated (in his treatise *De fide Catholica contra Iudaeos* [*On the Catholic Faith against the Jews*]) the removal and baptizing of Jewish children by force. Had he been successful, there would have been no Maimonides. The following selection from the *Etymologiae* gives a nice account of the history and methods of the medical discipline, always in terms of the origins of the words used to describe its various parts. Isidore's style is always clear and flows naturally, making the reading experience a pleasurable one.

Isidorus <Hispaliensis>: Etymologiae, [Augsburg], 1472. By permission of the Bayerische Staatsbibliothek München. 2 Inc. c.a. 129, fol 64v.

Etymologiae

Incipit Liber Quartus de Medicina

Medicina est quae corporis vel tuetur vel restaurat salutem cuius materia versatur in morbis et vulneribus. Ad hanc itaque pertinent non ea tantum quae ars eorum exhibet, qui proprie medici nominantur, sed etiam cibus et potus, tegmen et tegimen. Defensio denique omnis atque munitio, qua sanum corpus nostrum adversus externos ictus casusque servatur.

De Nomine Medicinae Ca. II

Nomen autem medicinae a modo id est temperamento impositum aestimatur, ut non satis, sed paulatim adhibeatur. Nam in multo contristatur natura, mediocriter autem gaudet. Unde et qui pigmenta et antidota satis vel assidue biberint vexantur. Inmoderatio enim omnis non salutem sed periculum affert.

De Inventoribus Eius Ca. III

Medicinae autem artis auctor ac repertor apud graecos perhibetur Appollo. Hanc filius eius Aescolapius laude vel opere ampliavit, sed postquam fulminis ictu Aescolapius interiit, interdicta fertur medendi cura, et ars simul cum auctore periit, latuitque per annos paene quingentos, usque ad tempus Artaxerxis regis persarum. Tunc eam revocavit ad lucem Ipocrates Asclepio patre genitus in insula Choo.

De Tribus Haeresibus Medicorum Ca. IIII

Hi itaque tres viri totidem haereses invenerunt. Prima metodica inventa est ab Appolline, quae remedia sectatur et carmina. Secunda empherica id est experientissima inventa est ab Aescolapio, quae non indiciorum signis, sed solis constat experimentis. Tertia logica id est rationalis inventa ab Ippocrate. Iste enim discussis aetatum, regionum, vel infirmitatum qualitatibus, artis curam rationabiliter perscrutatus est. Empirici enim experientiam solam sectantur.

30   Logici experientiae rationem adiungunt. Metodici nec elementorum
      rationem observant, nec tempora, nec aetates, nec causas, sed solas
      morborum substantias.

• Notes •

2   **tuetur: tueor, tueri, tutus sum** *to look at, to look after, to protect.*

4–5   **non ... tantum ... sed etiam ...:** *not only ... but also ...*

        ars eorum ... nominantur: The subject of **exhibet** is **ars**, while
        the direct object is the preceding **quae**, referring back to **ea** (*those
        things*). The subject of **nominantur** is **qui**, referring back to
        eorum (*those people*). **Proprie** is an adverb, *properly.*

5   **tegmen et tegimen:** In fact, **tegmen** and **tegimen** (or **tegumen**)
        are two alternative spellings of the same word, namely, *a cover.*
        Isidore never misses an opportunity to play with words. Perhaps
        tegmen is intended to refer to *clothing* and **tegimen** to *shelter.*

6   **adversus:** used as a preposition + accusative.

Ca. II

        Ca. II: The book is divided into small **capita** or **capitula**,
        numbered in this abridged form. The chapter number is placed
        after the title.

9   **a modo:** According to Isidore, the word **medicina** derives from
        modus, -i (m) *measure* or from its adjectival form **modicus, -a,
        -um,** which means *moderate, temperate.*

10   **aestimatur:** Supply **esse** after **impositum.**

        non satis, sed paulatim: Satis usually means *enough.* Here,
        it can be understood as *all at once, in excess,* as opposed to
        paulatim, which means *little by little.*

10–11   **Nam in multo contristatur natura, mediocriter autem
        gaudet:** a beautiful Latin adage crafted by Isidore probably on
        the basis of the ancient doctrine of moderation in all things.
        Arthur Schopenhauer (1788–1860) took this saying as the basis
        for his own (though completely different) *natura non contristatur,*
        in the sense that nature has no feelings but follows its own
        inexorable path.

12   **pigmenta et antidota:** This is a curious choice of words to describe medicinal substances in general, but the intention is clear.

Ca. III

15   **perhibetur:** *is considered.*

16   **Appollo: Apollo, Apollinis** (m).

    Aescolapius: Aesculapius or Asklepios, the son of Apollo. He developed medicine **laude vel opere** *with prestige and in deed.* **Laude vel opere** could also be rendered as *with praiseworthy work.* Note that Isidore seems to use two spellings, both **Aescolapius** and **Ascolapius,** interchangeably.

17   **postquam fulminis ictu Aescolapius interiit:** Aesculapius is said to have been killed by a stroke of lightning, sent by an angry Zeus. The verb **intereo, interire, interii, interitum** means *to perish,* derived from the Latin verb **pereo.** In English too we can express dying by means of going, such as in "passing away." The verb **obeo** gives rise to the English "obituary."

    fertur: *It is told that.* It can introduce indirect statement/oratio obliqua. The verb **fero, ferre, tuli, latum** (linguistic cognate of the English *to bear*) has the basic meaning of *to carry.* Notice that with the prefix **re-** it acquires the connotation of referring. Moreover, note the perfect passive participle **relatum** (*brought back*), whence we get the English *to relate.*

17–18   **interdicta fertur medendi cura: cura medendi fertur interdicta esse.** The prohibition is thus associated with Aesculapius's death. It is not clear whether this is an actual prohibition or merely a consequence, since Isidore adds **ars simul cum auctore periit.**

18   **medendi: medeor, mederi,** *to heal, to remedy.* Since, as the experts affirm, this verb derives from the Proto-Indo-European root ***med-***, which means *to measure,* it appears that Isidore's derivation of **medicina** from **modus** is correct. See, for example, J. Pokorny, *P-I-E Etymological Dictionary,* Vol. 2, p. 705. German original: J. Pokorny, *Indogermanisches Etymologisches Woerterbuch,* Bern: Francke Verlag (1959). Available in archive.org.

latuit: lateo, latere, latui from which we derive the English "latency."

19   **Artaxerxis:** Artaxerxes I, king of Persia from 465 to 424 BCE, is the same king mentioned in the biblical books of Ezra and Nehemiah. Since, according to Isidore, medicine remained hidden for about five hundred years, we conclude that the (imagined) death of Aesculapius took place sometime during the tenth century BCE.

20–21   **Ipocrates Asclepio patre genitus in insula Choo:** Hippocrates of Kos is a historical character. He was a contemporary of Socrates. Because of his larger than life personality, the Greeks considered him to be actually descended from Asklepios (**genitus Asclepio patre**).

Ca. IIII

22   **Tribus Heresibus:** While most numerals in Latin are indeclinable, the number three (**tres**) in Latin is declined. **Haeresis, haeresis** (f) is an imported Greek word that means *sect, school of thought*. Only later it adopted the pejorative meaning encountered in *heretic*, that is, *sectarian*.

23   **totidem:** *as many*. Each of the aforementioned characters (Apollo, Aesculapius, and Hippocrates) gave rise to (or invented) a separate school of medical thought.

24   **quae remedia sectatur: Sector, sectari, sectatus sum**, a frequentative form of **sequor**, means *to follow assiduously*. Literally, therefore, Isidore is saying that the first school, called methodical, was invented by Apollo. It follows remedies and songs, that is, medications and invocations.

25   **empherica:** empirica. The *h* after the *p* is incorrect, showing perhaps that Isidore's (or the copyist's) Greek was not as good as his Latin. The error is avoided a few lines below. The **empiricus** was a physician whose art was exclusively based on **experientia** and averted any theoretical considerations. It does not attribute great importance to the analysis of symptoms (**signa indiciorum**). Recall that empirical science relies solely on observation and experimentation. The Greek word **empeiria** conveys precisely this meaning.

27–28   **discussis . . . qualitatibus:** ablative absolute. Hippocrates, after considering the details of age (**aetas**), location, and diseases of the patient, thoroughly investigated (**perscrutatus est**) by means of reason the cure of his art (or, perhaps, just the appropriate cure, since the word **artis** seems superfluous).

30   **experientiae:** Construe as dative with **adiungunt**.

31–32   **solas morborum substantias:** The methodical school did not take into consideration either theoretical considerations or empirical knowledge. It just concentrated on the underlying existence of the diseases themselves.

Maimonides
(Rabbi Moshe ben Maimon)

A mong the earliest *incunabula*,[6] we find a remarkable document. This is an anonymous Latin translation, under the title *De Regimine Sanitatis* (*On the Regimen of Health*), from the original Arabic of the *Maqalah Fi Tadbir as-Sihhah* or Hebrew (*Hanhagat Habriuth*) of Maimonides (1135–1204), known in Hebrew as the Rambam, an acronym for Rabbi Moshe ben Maimon.[7] The first reason for considering this document as remarkable is the early date of its printing, the year 1481, at the Monastery of Sanctus Jacobus de Ripoli in Florence. Among the authors published there we find Pliny the Elder and Petrarch. The second reason is that a treatise on medicine written by a Jewish philosopher, doctor, and rabbi in the twelfth century should be considered as worthy of printing three centuries after its composition. Maimonides, regarded as the greatest philosophical and religious mind produced by Judaism in the Middle Ages, had a not inconsiderable influence on scholastic philosophy. His works are mentioned, among others, by Thomas Aquinas. In style and compass he is comparable to his slightly older contemporary Averroes. Both tried to reconcile divine revelation with Greek philosophy. Both were interested in mathematics, physics, astronomy, and medicine. Maimonides was equally fluent in Hebrew and Arabic and he wrote in both languages. His most influential work, *Dalalat al-Hayrin* (*The Guide of the Perplexed*),[8] was written in Arabic using Hebrew characters, a practice of many other Jewish sages of the period. Maimonides was considered one of the best physicians of his time and was

---

6   An *incunabulum* is any book printed in Europe before the year 1501. The earliest incunabulum printed with movable type is considered to be the Gutenberg Bible, printed in 1455.

7   A detailed discussion, translation, and source analysis can be found in A. Bar-Sela, E. F. Hoff, and E. M. D. Faris, "Moses Maimonides' Two Treatises on the Regimen of Health," *Transactions of the American Philosophical Society* 54, no. 4 (1964): 1–50.

8   The book was originally written by Maimonides in Judeo-Arabic, that is, Arabic spelled in Hebrew characters. It was translated into Hebrew during Maimonides's lifetime as *Moreh Nevukhim*. The first Latin translation, under the title *Dux seu Director Dubitantium aut Perplexorum* was published in 1520. Partial Latin translations of the book must have existed earlier, since Thomas Aquinas (1225–1274) quotes from it.

consulted by important political personalities on issues of health. He was chief medical adviser to the famous Saladin (1137–1193), Sultan of Syria and Egypt. One of Saladin's many sons, Al-Afdal, who had been victorious at the battle of Cresson (1187) against the Crusaders and who later became the ruler in Damascus, was beset by chronic depression. The treatise *Fi Tadbir as-Sihhah* was written perhaps in 1193, possibly at the request of Saladin just before his death. This gave an opportunity for Maimonides to expose his views on the interaction between physical and mental health, thus becoming a pioneer in the field of psychiatry.

Comments on the text

On the first page of the 1481 Latin edition, the name of the author is given as Rabi Moysi, and further described as Cordubenus. Maimonides's reputation was such that there was no need to say anything else. Thomas Aquinas himself refers to Maimonides as The Rabbi or Rabbi Moyse. The Arabic (thirteenth century) manuscript copy starts with the usual *Bismillah* invocation.[9] The second line of the Arabic manuscript contains the name *Musa bin Abdu-l-lah al-Israili al-Kurtubi*.[10] It also mentions the name of *al-Afdal*, the king to whom the book is addressed. The four large titles in the Arabic manuscript correspond exactly to the description of the four chapters of the book on the second page of the Latin edition. The last page of the Latin edition contains the information about the printing house and an invocation *Laus deo et Marie virgini*, which would not have appeared in the original Arabic nor in the Hebrew translation, produced by Moses ibn Tibbon in Provence in 1244.

The language in the Latin translation is straightforward and the grammar is uncomplicated.

---

9   "Bismillah," literally "in the name of Allah," is the opening sentence of the Qur'an. This expression is used by Muslims as an invocation at the beginning of a work.

10   The usual translation of Maimonides into Arabic is "Musa bin-Maymun." For some reason this version uses this alternative name, which means "Moses son of Abdullah the Israelite from Cordoba."

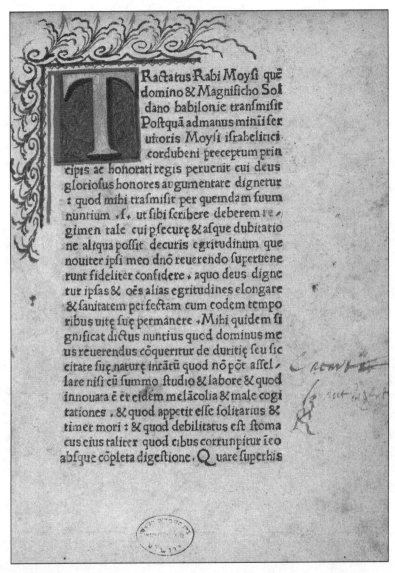

Tractatus Rabi Moyfi que domino & Magnificho Soldano babilonie tranfmifit Poftquá admanus minii feruitoris Moyfi ifrahelitici cordubeni preceptum principis ac honorati regis peruenit cui deus gloriofus honores augumentare dignetur : quod mihi trafmifit per quemdam fuum nuntium .f. ut fibi fcribere deberem regimen tale cui pfecurę & afque dubitatione altqua poffit decuris egritudinum que nouiter ipfi meo dnō reuerendo fuperueneunt fideliter confidere . aquo deus dignetur ipfas & oēs alias egritudines elongare & fanitatem perfectam cum eodem temporibus uitę fuę permanere . Mihi quidem fignificat dictus nuntius quod dominus meus reuerendus cōqueritur de duritie feu ficcitate fuę naturę intātū quod nō pōt affellare nifi cū fummo ftudio & labore & quod innouata ē et eifdem melācolia & male cogitationes . & quod appetit effe folitarius & timet mori : & quod debilitatus eft ftomacus eius taliter quod cibus corrunpitur ieo abfque cōpleta digeftione . Quare fuperhis

Moshe ben Maymon De regimine sanitatis ad Soldanum Babyloniae. Florentie: Apud Sanctum Jacobum de Ripolis [ca. 1481]. Courtesy of the National Library of Israel.

dere adcelebrum & corroborat senſus & aü
fert eorum ſtuporem & iuuat coytū & dila
tat aīam Cuius conpoſitio eſt ut accipiatur
mirab. kebuloꝝ yndoꝝ & bellic. añ ōcia. i.
roſarū rūbeaꝝ lingue auis feñ marini feīs
ſparagi feīs carotarū feīs eruce ābarū ſpe
tierū ben anici maſticiſ corticiſ belſen. añ
oncia media cubebe cardāomi gariofilorū
aneti galāge piperis lōgi zīziberiſ. dorōi
ce. ligni aloesboni. añ octauā pte ūius ūcie
pioꝝ mūdatorū oncie. iii. terāt medicine
ſicce & cribellent & terant ſemina & pini
ut ſint bene lenia & fricentur mirab. cum
qnq̃ libris olei amigdalaꝝ uel olei ſiſtico
rum rem poſt rem. deinde miſceantur cīa
cūtribus libris mellis diſpumati & reponat
in uaſe & doſis eius erit a iiii. dragmas uſ
que adquinque tepefacto cum aqua calida
inqua coctum ſit aniſum. ſed in aere tem
perato ſumat exea minimā ſorbitiōem nec
ſumat exea temporibus intenſe caliditatis
nec aliis temporibus utatur ea frequet. ſed
ſumenda eſt ſemel inſeptimana. hii ſyrupi
& elletuaria quos prouidit ſeruus debent
eſſe feꝑ ithesauro regis. Et notū ē apud do

minum meum regem quod paſſiones aníe
mutant corpora mutatóibus magnis & ma
nifeſtis omnibus & teſtatio huius eſt quod
aliqua hora tu uidebis aliquē hominē con ⸗
buſte conpoſitionis & fortem habentem uo
cem et cum uigoroſa fame et cum ſuper ue.
nerit ei aliquod dequo timet tunc uidebis ip
ſum mutatū colore et uigore faciei perdito
et in curuata ſtatura et uocē raucam qui etiā
ſi uoluerit eleuare uocē ſuā toto poſſe nō
poterit et de bilitabit eius uirtus et forſitā
arripit eū trēor exdebilitate niia & euis pul
ſ9 míorabit et eius oculi p̄ ſūdāt et palpe
bre grauāt amotu et iſrigidāt corporis ſu
perficies eiusq̄ cibi appetitus cadit et cauſa
quidem omnium harum paſſionum eſt re ⸗
uocatio caloris naturalis et ſanguis ad cor ⸗
dis interiora ✦ Contrarium horum quoque
pre lictorum eſſe poterit ut aliquis erit de
bilis corpore et pallidus coloris faciei et uo
cem habet planā perceperit aliquodq̄d letifi
cat ipſum grandi letificationē ſtatim uide ⸗
bis ipſum robuſtum corpore et eleuata uo ⸗
ce et ſplendida facie et accelerātur eius mo
tus et pulſus eius magnificabitur et ipſius
corporis ſuperficies caleſiet et appa ⸗. c ii

rebit exultatio & letitia inipso quę nō pote
rit occultari' Et caufa quidem iftorū affe
ctuum eft motus naturalis carnis & fangui
nis admāifestas partes corporis ficcp accide
tia pterritorū & timidotum qui uicti funt
& similiter uictorum qui optinuerunt ma
nifesta funt . quādocp possibile eft uictū ni
hil posse uidere exdefectu uirtutis uifiue
eiusqp segregatiōe Victoris aūt quafi auge
tur splendor faciei augumentatione mani
festa ita quod uidetur ei lumen aeris augu
mentatum & magnificatū abeo quod erat
hoc aūt patet maifeste & non eget prolixita
redeclaratiōis et ideo iubere debet medici
ut abeat follicitudo īmotibus animalibus
& ipforū uifitatiēe quotidie & puideat in
ipforum certificatione tempore fanitatis &
egritudiis nec aliud . r̃ debet hic pcedere
aliquomodo & oportet medicum hic habere
in eius extimatione f quod oīs eger habe
at aīam aut cāufā & ōnis fāus latā uel āplā
& ideo intendit medicus inhis que aufe
rant animales passiones quę faciunt ipfam
aggregari Nām cum hoc fanitas confer
uatur & id eft magis primum & precipuum

clmſaʒ +

in egrotū sāatiōe. & maxime eum egritu
do sua fuerit aīalis sicut pleuresis & sicut stu
pefactio melīcōica ī quibus solicitudo aīalı
um motuū maior uel fortior debet esse. Si
militer cuicūq̃ superuenerit lōga cogitatio
& sollicitudo debis quibus mos nō erat hoc
facere uel dicas ipsā extensionem. nam in
huius non presumit peritus medicus rectisī
care motus animarū ipsarum ihillis passio
nibus remouendis. Medicus uero in quā
tum medicus cuius ratio nō est scire inge
nium tales passiones excludere. Verunta
men hec omnia pernotescunt aspeculatiua
phylosofia & doctrinis legū. philosofi eim
quemadmodum ediderūt libros degeneri
bus scientiarum sic fecerunt plures libros
inrectificatiōne morum & doctrinis anime
ad querendum mores nobiles exquibus nō
resultet nisi operatio bona et prohibēt adese
ctu & docent modū auferendi abaia qdcūq̃
uitium in ipsa inuenerit donec deleat ille ha
bitus inducens defectum similiter quidem
doctrine legū & iuriū accepte exppheta⅊
ppheriis & natura et scientia bonorum regi
minum etiam iuuant ad rectificationem
uirtutū anime ut eius bone disposi

c iii

Regimen Sanitatis

Et notum est apud dominum meum regem quod passiones animae
mutant corpora mutationibus magnis et manifestis omnibus et
testatio huius est quod aliqua hora tu videbis aliquem hominem
combustae compositionis et fortem habentem vocem et cum
5   vigorosa fame et cum super venerit ei aliquod de quo timet
tunc videbis ipsum mutatum colore et vigore faciei perdito et
in curvata statura et vocem raucam qui etiam si voluerit elevare
vocem suam toto posse non poterit et debilitabitur eius virtus
et forsitan arripit eum tremor ex debilitate nimia et eius pulsus
10   minorabitur et eius oculi perfundatur et palpebre gravantur a motu
et infrigidatur corporis superficies eiusque cibi appetitus cadit
et causa quidem omnium harum passionum est revocatio caloris
naturalis et sanguinis ad cordis interiora. Contrarium horum
quoque praedictorum esse poterit ut aliquis erit debilis corpore et
15   pallidus coloris faciei et vocem habet planam perceperit aliquod
quod laetificat ipsum grandi laetificatione statim videbis ipsum
robustum corpore et elevata voce et splendida facie et accelerantur
eius motus et pulsus eius magnificabitur et ipsius corporis superficies
calefiet et apparebit exultatio et laetitia in ipso quae non poterit
20   occultari. Et causa quidem istorum affectuum est motus naturalis
carnis et sanguinis ad manifestas partes corporis sicque accidentia
perterritorum et timidorum qui victi sunt et similiter victorum qui
optinuerunt manifesta sunt. Quandoque possibile est victum nihil
posse videre ex defectu virtutis visivae eiusque segregatione; Victoris
25   autem quasi augetur splendor faciei augumentatione manifesta ita
quod videtur ei lumen aeris augumentatum et magnificatum ab
eo quod erat. Hoc autem patet manifeste et non eget prolixitate
declarationis. Et ideo iubere debent medici ut habeatur sollicitudo
in motibus animalibus et ipsorum visitatione quotidie et provideatur
30   in ipsorum certificatione tempore sanitatis et aegritudinis nec aliud
Rx debet hic praecedere aliquomodo et oportet medicum hic habere

in eius existimatione. Scilicet quod omnis aeger habeat animam
aut causam et omnis sanus latam vel amplam, et ideo intendit
medicus in his quae auferant animales passiones quae faciunt ipsam
35 aggregari. Nam cum hoc sanitas conservatur et id est magis primum
et praecipuum in aegrorum sanatione. Et maxime cum aegritudo
sua fuerit animalis sicut pleuresis et sicut stupefactio melinconica
in quibus sollicitudo animalium motuum maior vel fortior debet
esse. Similiter cuicumque supervenerit longa cogitatio et sollicitudo
40 de his quibus mos non erat hoc facere vel dicas ipsam extensionem.
Nam in huiusmodi non praesumit peritus medicus rectificare motus
animarum ipsarum in illis passionibus removendis.

• Notes •

1   **Et notum est apud dominum meum regem:** Maimonides
addresses the king respectfully, as if he could assume that the
king naturally knows about these issues.

quod: The translator does not use indirect statement/oratio
obliqua.

passiones animae: Passio, -onis (f) is, literally, *a suffering.*
Maimonides refers here to psychological illness.

2   **manifestis omnibus:** *obvious to all people.*

5   **cum super venerit ei aliquod de quo timet:** *when something
(about which) he fears should overcome (or suddenly come upon, or
suddenly reach) him.*

7   **voluerit: volo, velle, volui.**

8   **toto posse:** abbreviated form for **pro toto posse suo,** which
literally means *to his entire power,* namely, *to the utmost of his
power.* This is a legal expression appearing, for example, in the
Magna Carta. Notice that the infinitive **posse** can be used as a
noun. It gives rise to the English term *posse* as a group of people
empowered by the sheriff.

9   **arripit: adripit,** from **adripio, adripere, adripui, adreptum
(ad + rapio).**

10   **perfundantur: perfundo, perfundere, perfudi, perfusum** *to fill.*

      gravantur a motu: *They are made heavy and prevented from motion.*

11   **infrigidatur:** *becomes cold.* Nonclassical verb derived from **in** + **frigidus.**

12–13 **revocatio . . . sanguinis ad cordis interiora:** literally: *The recalling of blood toward the interior parts of the heart.* An alternative reading could be **corporis** instead of **cordis.**

13–14 **horum . . . praedictorum:** *of the aforementioned things.*

14   **debilis corpore:** *weak with respect to* [*his*] *body,* ablative of respect.

19   **calefiet:** The active verb is **calefacio, calefacere, calefeci, calefactus.** In the passive voice, **facio** is replaced by **fio.** Thus, **calefiet** means *it will become warm.*

21   **sicque:** This is the beginning of a new sentence.

21–22 **accidentia perterritorum:** *the things that happen to terrified people.*

23   **optinuerunt:** *they obtained victory.*

23–24 **nihil posse . . . visivae . . . segregatione:** *not to be able to see anything from* [*on account of*] *the lessening of the visual virtue and its removal.* Bar-Sela et al. ("Moses Maimonides' Two Treatises on the Regimen of Health," p. 25) remark that according to Galen (whom Maimonides follows) the ability to see resided in a substance or "virtue" carried by the nerves.

27   **non eget prolixitate: Egeo, egere, egui** takes the ablative.

28   **sollicitudo in motibus animalibus:** *care in the animic motions.* Here, **animalibus** is used as an adjective, *pertaining to the soul or to the psyche.*

29   **provideatur:** *that precautions be taken,* purpose clause.

30   **certificatione:** from **certum facere.**

      tempore sanitatis et aegritudinis: *in time of health and sickness.*

nec aliud: *and no other way.* The alternative printed edition reads **Nec aliud recipe**, where the symbol Rx has been decoded as the symbol still in use to indicate a medical prescription. This interpretation, however, is not borne out by the Hebrew translation.

32   **quod omnis aeger habeat animam:** *that every sick person should have a [healthy] soul.*

33   **et omnis sanus latam vel amplam:** *and every healthy person, a broad and ample [soul, cheer].*

33–34 **ideo intendit medicus in his quae auferant animales passiones:** *So does the physician strive in those things that remove the sufferings of the psyche.*

35   **aggregari:** passive infinitive of **aggrego, aggregare**, literally, *to be assembled.* We could perhaps say *to become constricted.*

36   **praecipuum in aegrorum sanatione:** *preeminent (special) for the cure of the sick.*

37   **animalis:** *of the soul.*

      stupefactio melinconica: *melancholic numbness (depression).*

39   **cuicumque:** from **quicumque, quaecumque, quodcumque** *whoever, whatever.*

41   **in huiusmodi:** *namely, in cases of this kind.*

42   **passionibus removendis:** gerundive construction. *By passions that must be removed.*

William Harvey

Willliam Harvey (1578–1657) received his medical degree in 1602 from the University of Padua in Italy. Returning to his native England, he obtained a doctoral degree in medicine from the University of Cambridge. He became both a practicing physician and an academic. He was appointed physician to the king and as such was a witness to important historical events. His scientific output is not limited to the definitive proof of the role of the heart in the circulation of blood. Nor is this a completely original discovery. Nevertheless, it was Harvey who first formulated it in precise and unequivocal terms and, moreover, made it public in a manner that would be assured of immediate and ample diffusion. The precise, enthusiastic, and almost poetic style of Harvey is clearly displayed in the two pages that we have chosen from his book *Exercitatio Anatomica de Motu Cordis et Sanguinis in Animalibus* (*An Anatomical Exercise on the Motion of the Heart and Blood in Living Things*). The circulation of blood is precisely described at the beginning of chapter 5. Harvey's Latin is impeccable. Apart from this work, Harvey published a treatise on animal generation, in which he proved the implausibility of the classical theory of spontaneous generation, asserting instead that all life has a definite beginning, which he called the egg.

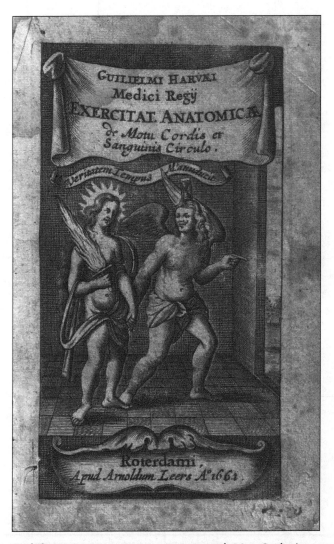

Guilielmi Harveji Exercitationes Anatomicae, de Motu Cordis &
Sanguinis Circulatione, ex officina Arnoldi Leers, Roterodami,
1661. Property of the National Library of Naples. Facsimile courtesy of archive.org.

48   *Exercitatio Anatomica I.*

ut, inter ipfum videri & non videri,
quafi inter effe & non effe, palpitatio-
nem & vitæ principium ageret.

C A P. V.

Cordis motus actio, & functio.

EGo ex his tandem & hujufmo-
di obfervationibus repertum iri
confido, motum cordis ad hunc modum fieri.

Primum fefe contrahit auricula, &
in illâ contractione fanguinem contentum, quo abundat, (tanquam venarum caput, & fanguinis promptuarium & cifterna) in ventriculum cordis conjicit; quo repleto cor fefe erigens, continuo omnes nervos tendit,
contrahit ventriculos, & pulfum facit, quo pulfu immiffum ab auricula
fanguinem continenter protrudit in
arterias; dextet ventriculus in pulmones per vas illud, quod vena arte-
riofa nominatur, fed revera, & con-
                                        ftitu-

ſtitutione & officio , & in omnibus
arteria eſt ; ſiniſter ventriculus in aortam, & per arterias in univerſum corpus.

Iſti duo motus , auricularum unus,
alter ventriculorum , ita per conſecu-
tionem fiunt , ſervata quaſi harmonia
& rhytmo, ut ambo ſimul fieri,& unicus tantum motus eſſe appareat, præ-
ſertim in calidioribus animalibus, dum
illa celeri agitantur motu.

Nec aliâ ratione id fit , quam cùm
in machinis, una rota aliam movente,
omnes ſimul moveri videantur ; & in
mechanico illo artificio, quod ſclo-
petis adaptant; ubi compreſſione alicujus ligulæ, cadit ſilex, percutit chalybem & propellit , ignis elicitur, qui
dum in pulverem cadit , ignitur pulvis, interius prorepit,diſploditur,evo-
lat globulus, metam penetrat, & omnes iſti motus, propter celeritatem,
quaſi in nictu oculi ſimul fieri apparent.

C   Sic

50   *Exercitatio Anatomica* I.

Sic etiam in deglutitione, radicis linguæ elevatione, & oris compreſ-ſione, cibus vel potus in fauces detur-batur, larinx à muſculis ſuis & epi-glottide clauditur, elevatur & ape-ritur ſummitas gulæ à muſculis ſuis, (haud aliter quam ſaccus ad implen-dum attollitur, & ad recipiendum di-latatur) & cibum, vel potum accep-tum tranſverſis muſculis deprimit, & longioribus attrahit : & tamen omnes iſti motus, à diverſis & contradiſtin-ctis organis facti, cum harmoniâ & ordine dum fiunt, unum efficere mo-tum videntur, & actionem unam, quam deglutitionem vocamus. Sic contingit planè in motione & actio-ne cordis; quæ deglutitio quædam eſt, & transfuſio ſanguinis è venis in arterias.

Si quis (dum hæc habuerit in ani-mo) cordis motum diligenter in vivâ diſſectione animadverterit, videbit non ſolum, quòd dixi, cor ſeſe eri-gere,

gere, & motum unum facere, cum
auriculis continuum, fed undationem
quandam & lateralem inclinationem
obfcuram, fecundum ductum ventriculi dextri, & quafi fefe leviter
contorquere, & hoc opus peragere:
quemadmodum cernere licet, cùm
equus potat, & aquam deglutit, fin-
gulis gulæ tractibus abforberi aquam,
& in ventriculum demitti; qui motus
fonitum & pulfum quendam, aufcul-
tantibus & tangentibus exhibet; ita
dum iftis cordis motibus, fit portionis
fanguinis è venis in arterias traductio,
pulfum fieri & exaudiri in pectore
contingit.

    Motus itaque cordis omnino ad
hunc fe habet modum, & una actio
cordis eft ipfa fanguinis transfufio, &
in extremâ ufque, mediantibus arteriis, propulfio; ut pulfus, quem nos
fentimus in arteriis, nil nifi fanguinis
à corde impulfus fit.

    An verò cor fanguini, præter trans-
           C 2   pofi-

Exercitatio Anatomica de Motu Cordis et Sanguinis in Animalibus

Cap. V.

Cordis motus, actio, et functio.

Ego vero ex his tandem et hujusmodi observationibus repertum iri confido, motum cordis ad hunc modum fieri.

Primum sese contrahit auricula, et in illa contractione
5 sanguinem contentum, quo abundant, (tanquam venarum caput, et sanguinis promptuarium, et cisterna) in ventriculum cordis conjicit; quo repleto cor sese erigens, continuo omnes nervos tendit, contrahit ventriculos, et pulsum facit, quo pulsu immissum ab auricula sanguinem continenter protrudit in arterias; dexter ventriculus
10 in pulmones per vas illud, quod vena arteriosa nominatur, sed re vera, et constitutione, et officio, et in omnibus arteria est: sinister ventriculus in aortam, et per arterias in universum corpus.

Isti duo motus, auricularum unus, alter ventriculorum, ita per consecutionem fiunt, servata quasi harmonia et rhytmo, ut ambo
15 simul fieri, et unicus tantum motus esse appareat, praesertim in calidioribus animalibus, dum illa celeri agitantur motu.

Nec alia ratione id fit quam cum in machinis, una rota aliam movente, omnes simul moveri videantur; et in mechanico illo artificio, quod sclopetis adaptant; ubi compressione alicujus ligulae,
20 cadit silex, percutit chalybem et propellit, ignis elicitur, qui dum in pulverem cadit, ignitur pulvis, interius prorepit, disploditur, evolat globulus, metam penetrat, et omnes isti motus, propter celeritatem, quasi in nictu oculi simul fieri apparent.

Sic etiam in deglutitione, radices linguae elevatione, et oris
25 compressione, cibus vel potus in fauces deturbatur, larinx a musculis suis et epiglottide clauditur, elevatur et aperitur summitas gulae a musculis suis, (haud aliter quam saccus ad implendum attollitur, et ad recipiendum dilatatur) et cibum, vel potum acceptum transversis

musculis deprimit, et longioribus attrahit: Et tamen omnes isti

30 motus, a diversis et contradistinctis organis facti, cum harmonia et ordine dum fiunt, unum efficere motum videntur, et actionem unam, quam deglutitionem vocamus.

Sic contingit plane in motione et actione cordis; quae deglutitio quaedam est, et transfusio sanguinis e venis in arterias.

35 Si quis (dum haec habuerit in animo) cordis motum diligenter in viva dissectione animadverterit, videbit non solum, quod dixi, cor sese erigere, et motum unum facere, cum auriculis continuum, sed undationem quandam et lateralem inclinationem obscuram, secundum ductum ventriculi dextri, et quasi sese leviter contorquere,

40 et hoc opus peragere: quemadmodum cernere licet, cum equus potat, et aquam deglutit, singulis gulae tractibus absorberi aquam, et in ventriculum demitti; qui motus sonitum et pulsum quendam, auscultantibus et tangentibus exhibet; ita dum istis cordis motibus, fit portionis sanguinis e venis in arterias traductio, pulsum fieri et

45 exaudiri in pectore contingit.

Motus itaque cordis omnino ad hunc se habet modum, et una actio cordis est ipsa sanguinis transfusio, et in extrema usque, mediantibus arteriis, propulsio; ut pulsus, quem nos sentimus in arteriis, nil nisi sanguinis a corde impulsus sit.

• Notes •

1 **motus:** May be construed either as genitive singular or nominative singular. Both interpretations, *of the motion of the heart* or *the motion of the heart*, are plausible, and in fact, various editions do not agree on one or the other. In the original, the title is in the nominative case. The translation of **functio** as *office*, while correct, is not consistent with modern terminology. We speak, indeed, of the function of the heart, and in this case also of its *functioning* or *performance*.

2 **Ego:** emphatic but not usual in Latin writing.

repertum iri: future passive infinitive, used here in an accusative in the indirect statement/oratio obliqua governed by **confido**. *I trust that it will be found.*

3 **ad hunc modum:** *in this way, in the following way.*

4 **Primum:** Translate as an adverb.

sese: emphatic form of **se**.

auricula: In Harvey's time, the atria used to be called auricles, a term now applied to appendages of the atria.

5 **abundant: abundo, -are** *to abound in, to overflow with* + ablative.

tanquam: *as, in its capacity of.* Alternative spelling of **tamquam**.

6 **promptuarium:** *promptuary, storehouse, repository.*

conjicit: = **conicit** = **con** + **iacio, -iacere, -ieci, -iactum** *to throw, to hurl.* Its appearance at the very end of the sentence reminds us to look for the main verb and not translate sequentially as the words appear.

7 **quo repleto:** ablative absolute.

continuo: *and then.*

8 **quo pulsu:** ablative of means.

9 **continenter:** *immediately.*

protrudit: pro + **trudo, -trudere, -trusi, -trusum** *to push forward.*

dexter ventriculus: another subject of **protrudit**. At this point, Harvey seems to be so excited that he cannot stop the enumeration of all the various processes taking place in rapid succession. He sounds like a child telling an exciting story, with the grammar barely holding all the pieces of the story together.

10 **vas:** neuter accusative singular.

10–11 **sed re vera:** *but in truth.*

11 **et . . . et . . . et . . .:** *both . . . and . . . and . . .*

in omnibus: *in all other matters* or literally *in all things.*

11–12 **sinister ventriculus:** another subject of **protrudit**.

13–14   **ita . . . ut . . . :** *in such a way . . . that . . .*; result clause.

15   **tantum:** adverbial use, *only.*

        appareat: subjunctive; why?

16   **illa:** referring back to its antecedent **animalibus.**

17–18   **una rota aliam movente:** ablative absolute; best rendered as concessive with *although.*

19   **sclopetis: sclopetum, -i** (n) is *a firearm* or, more specifically, *a rifle.* Compare with Spanish *escopeta* and Italian *schioppo.* The etymology is uncertain, but some derive it from the onomatopoeic classical Latin term **stloppus,** which is the sound produced by slapping the inflated cheeks. What follows is a masterful comparison of the action of the heart with the action of the discharge of a rifle. In both cases, the naïve view is that many processes occur simultaneously. A careful observation, however, reveals that they take place by means of a rigorous causal chain of events.

        adaptant: The third person plural is sometimes used as an impersonal *people adapt* and it is correct to render it as the English passive voice *is adapted.*

        alicujus: genitive singular of **aliquis.**

        ligulae: also **lingula,** diminutives of **lingua.** In this case, it denotes *the trigger*, which looks like a little tongue.

20   **silex: silex, silicis** (m) *flint.*

        chalybem: chalybs, chalybis (m) *a steel piece.*

22   **globulus:** diminutive of **globus.** Here, *bullet.*

24–25   **elevatione, compressione:** ablatives of means.

27   **haud: non, nec.**

33   **contingit:** here used as intransitive and impersonal, *it happens.*

        plane: adverb, *certainly, obviously.*

35   **Si quis:** *if someone.*

        habuerit: Notice the ambiguity between the future perfect active indicative and the perfect active subjunctive: *if someone might have.*

36–38   **non solum . . . sed (etiam) . . .:** *not only . . . but (also) . . .*

40   **quemadmodum:** *in whatever manner.*

cernere licet: literally, *it is permitted to perceive*; namely, *one may see.*

cum: here, *when.* The use of **cum** + subjunctive would be more appropriate.

41–45   **absorberi, demitti, exaudiri:** passive infinitives.

46–48   **itaque . . . ut . . .:** *and in such a way . . . that . . .*

46   **se habet:** *behaves, is, keeps itself.*

49   **nil nisi:** *nothing but, nothing if not.*

sit: subjunctive; why?

Luigi Aloisio Galvani

L uigi Aloisio Galvani (1737–1798) is credited with the discovery of animal electricity or, more precisely, the relationship between electricity and muscular innervation. Galvani's discovery was truly revolutionary. He hypothesized that the origin of the electrical energy was itself biological. His colleague Alessandro Volta (1745–1827), initially an admirer and supporter of Galvani's views, maintained that the nerve was merely a conductor and that the electrical source was of external origin. Eventually, after the invention of the "voltaic" battery, the views of Volta prevailed. Modern science, however, vindicated Galvani's point of view, at least in part.[11] An interesting point for us to note is that, as late as the last part of the eighteenth century, both Galvani's and Volta's works were written and published originally in Latin. Galvani's Latin is quite elaborate.

Although propounding different views, Galvani and Volta respected each other and kept a lifelong friendship. Galvani's wife, Lucia Galeazzi Galvani (1743–1788), was an active scientific assistant in Luigi's experiments, including the famous one reported in our selection, as well as in his surgical practice. They also shared a deep religious devotion. Her premature death was a devastating event in Galvani's life. As a professor at the University of Bologna, Galvani was required to declare his allegiance to Napoleon's vassal state in northern Italy, known as the Cisalpine Republic, established in 1797. After his refusal to do so, Galvani lost the professorship he had held. He died only a year later.

The term "galvanism," apparently created by Volta to honor his colleague, is used today to describe the production of an electrical current by a chemical reaction. Mary Shelley (1797–1851), influenced in part by the belief that galvanism could be used to reanimate a corpse, mentions this idea explicitly in her literary masterpiece *Frankenstein*.[12]

---

11   A detailed presentation of the Galvani-Volta dispute and its modern repercussions can be found in M. Piccolino, "Animal Electricity and the Birth of Electrophysiology: The Legacy of Luigi Galvani," *Brain Research Bulletin* 46, no. 5 (1998): 381–407.

12   The third edition (1831) of Mary Shelley's *Frankenstein* contains two references to galvanism. In the introduction she writes: "Perhaps a corpse would be re-animated; galvanism had given token of such things." The second mention appears in chapter II of the same edition, where the main character and narrator says: "Before this I was not unacquainted with the more obvious laws of electricity. On this occasion a man of great research in natural philosophy was with us, and, excited by this catastrophe, he entered on the explanation of a theory which he had formed on the subject of electricity and galvanism, which was at once new and astonishing to me."

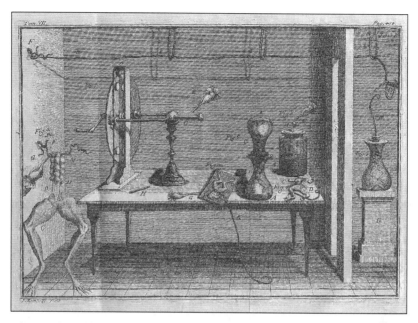

Aloysii Galvani de Viribus Electricitatis in Motu Musculari, Bononiae: Ex Typographia Instituti Scientiarium, 1791. Property of the Smithsonian Libraries. Facsimile courtesy of archive.org.

ALOYSII GALVANI

DE

VIRIBUS ELECTRICITATIS

IN

MOTU MUSCULARI.

COMMENTARIUS.

BONONIÆ

Ex Typographia Instituti Scientiarum. 1791.

CUM APPROBATIONE.

3

PARS PRIMA

De viribus electricitatis artificialis in motu musculari.

Optanti mihi, quæ laboribus non levibus post multa experimenta detegere in nervis, ac musculis contigit, ad eam utilitatem perducere, ut & occultæ eorum facultates in apertum, si fieri posset, ponerentur, & eorumdem morbis tutius mederi possemus, nihil ad hujusmodi desiderium explendum idoneum magis visum est, quam si hæc ipsa qualiacumque inventa publici tandem juris facerem. Docti enim præstantesque viri poterunt nostra legendo, suis meditationibus suisque experimentis non solum hæc ipsa majora efficere, sed etiam illa assequi, quæ nos conati quidem sumus, sed fortasse minime consecuti.

Equidem in votis erat, sin minus perfectum, & absolutum, quod numquam forte potuissem, non rude saltem, atque vix inchoatum opus in publicam lucem proferre; at cum neque tempus, neque otium, neque ingenii vires ita mihi suppetere intelligerem, ut illud absolverem, malui sane æquissimo huic desiderio meo deesse, quam rei utilitati.

Operæ itaque pretium facturum me esse existimavi, si brevem, & accuratam inventorum historiam afferrem eo ordine, & ratione, qua mihi illa partim casus, & fortuna obtulit, partim industria, & diligentia detexit; non tantum ne plus mihi, quam fortunæ, aut plus fortunæ, quam mihi tribuatur, sed ut vel iis, qui hanc ipsam experiendi viam inire voluissent, facem præferremus aliquam, vel saltem honesto doctorum hominum desiderio satisfaceremus, qui solent rerum, quæ novitatem in se recondunt aliquam, vel origine ipsa principioque delectari.

Experimentorum vero narrationi corollaria nonnulla, nonnullasque conjecturas, & hypotheses adjungam eo maxime con-

A 2

si-

4

silio, ut novis capiendis experimentis viam sternamus aliquam,
qua sin minus ad veritatem pervenire possimus, novus saltem
ad eamdem aditus aperiatur.

Res autem ab hujusmodi profecta initio est. Ranam dissecui, atque præparavi ut in *Fig. Ω. Tab.* 1., eamque in tabula, omnia mihi alia proponens, in qua erat machina electrica
Fig. 1. *Tab.* 1., collocavi ab ejus conductore penitus sejunctam, atque haud brevi intervallo dissitam; dum scalpelli cuspidem unus ex iis, qui mihi operam dabant, cruralibus hujus ranæ internis nervis D D casu vel leviter admoveret, continuo omnes artuum musculi ita contrahi visi sunt, ut in vehementiores incidisse tonicas convulsiones viderentur. Eorum
vero alter, qui nobis electricitatem tentantibus præsto erat,
animadvertere sibi visus est, rem contingere dum ex conductore machinæ scintilla extorqueretur *Fig.* 1. B . Rei novitatem ille admiratus de eadem statim me alia omnino molientem, ac mecum ipso cogitantem admonuit. Hic ego incredibili sum studio, & cupiditate incensus idem experiundi, &
quod occultum in re esset in lucem proferendi. Admovi propterea & ipse scalpelli cuspidem uni vel alteri crurali nervo,
quo tempore unus aliquis ex iis, qui aderant, scintillam eliceret . Phænomenon eadem omnino ratione contigit; vehementes nimirum contractiones in singulos artuum musculos,
perinde ac si tetano præparatum animal esset correptum, eodem ipso temporis momento inducebantur, quo scintillæ extorquerentur.

At metuens, ne ii ipsi motus a cuspidis potius contactu,
qui pro stimulo forte esset, quam a scintilla orirentur, eosdem nervos iterum eadem ratione in aliis ranis cuspide tentavi, & quidem gravius, quin ulla tamen scintilla tunc temporis ab aliquo eliceretur; at nulli omnino visi sunt motus. Hinc
mecum ipse putavi, forte ad phænomenon inducendum & contactum alicujus corporis, & scintillæ jactum una requiri. Quamobrem scalpelli aciem iterum nervis apposui immotamque detinui, tum quo tempore scintilla extraheretur, tum quo tempore machina perfecte quiesceret. At phænomenon educta dumtaxat scintilla prodiit.

Experimentum iteravimus eodem semper scalpello adhibito: verum non sine nostra admiratione interdum educta scintilla recensiti motus contigebant, interdum deficiebant.

De Viribus Electricitatis in Motu Musculari

Pars Prima

De viribus electricitatis artificialis in motu musculari.

Optanti mihi, quae laboribus non levibus post multa experimenta detegere in nervis, ac musculis contigit, ad eam utilitatem
5 perducere, ut et occultae eorum facultates in apertum, si fieri posset, ponerentur, et eorumdem morbis tutius mederi possemus, nihil ad hujusmodi desiderium explendum idoneum magis visum est, quam si haec ipsa qualiacumque inventa publici tandem juris facerem. Docti enim praestantesque viri poterunt nostra legendo, suis
10 meditationibus suisque experimentis non solum haec ipsa majora efficere, sed etiam illa assequi, quae nos conati quidem sumus, sed fortasse minime consecuti.

Equidem in votis erat, sin minus perfectum, et absolutum, quod numquam forte potuissem, non rude saltem, atque vix inchoatum
15 opus in publicam lucem proferre; at cum neque tempus, neque otium, neque ingenii vires ita mihi suppetere intelligerem, ut illud absolverem, malui sane aequissimo huic desiderio meo deesse, quam rei utilitati.

Operae itaque pretium facturum me esse existimavi, si brevem,
20 et accuratam inventorum historiam afferrem eo ordine, et ratione, qua mihi illa partim casus, et fortuna obtulit, partim industria, et diligentia detexit; non tantum ne plus mihi, quam fortunae, aut plus fortunae, quam mihi tribuatur, sed ut vel iis, qui hanc ipsam experiendi viam inire voluissent, facem praeferremus aliquam, vel
25 saltem honesto doctorum hominum desiderio satisfaceremus, qui solent rerum, quae novitatem in se recondunt aliquam, vel origine ipsa principioque delectari.

Experimentorum vero narrationi corollaria nonnulla, nonnullasque conjecturas, et hypotheses adjungam eo maxime
30 consilio, ut novis capiendis experimentis viam sternamus aliquam,

qua sin minus ad veritatem pervenire possimus, novus saltem ad
eamdem aditus aperiatur.

Res autem ab hujusmodi profecta initio est. Ranam dissecui,
atque praeparavi ut in *Fig. Ω Tab. I.*, eamque in tabula, omnia
35 mihi alia proponens, in qua erat machina electrica *Fig. I., Tab. I.*,
collocavi ab ejus conductore penitus sejunctam, atque haud brevi
intervallo dissitam; dum scalpelli cuspidem unus ex iis, qui mihi
operam dabant, cruralibus hujus ranae internis nervis D D casu vel
leviter admoveret, continuo omnes artuum musculi ita contrahi visi
40 sunt, ut in vehementiores incidisse tonicas convulsiones viderentur.
Eorum vero alter, qui nobis electricitatem tentantibus praesto erat,
animadvertere sibi visus est, rem contingere dum ex conductore
machinae scintilla extorqueretur *Fig.* I. B. Rei novitatem ille
admiratus de eadem statim me alia omnino molientem, ac mecum
45 ipso cogitantem admonuit. Hic ego incredibili sum studio, et
cupiditate incensus idem experiundi, et quod occultum in re esset in
lucem proferendi. Admovi propterea et ipse scalpelli cuspidem uni
vel alteri crurali nervo, quo tempore unus aliquis ex iis, qui aderant,
scintillam eliceret. Phaenomenon eadem omnino ratione contigit;
50 vehementes nimirum contractiones in singulos artuum musculos,
perinde ac si tetano praeparatum animal esset correptum, eodem
ipso temporis momento inducebantur, quo scintillae extorquerentur.

At metuens, ne ii ipsi motus a cuspidis potius contactu, qui
pro stimulo forte esset, quam a scintilla orirentur, eosdem nervos
55 iterum eadem ratione in aliis ranis cuspide tentavi, et quidem
gravius, quin ulla tamen scintilla tunc temporis ab aliquo eliceretur;
at nulli omnino visi sunt motus. Hinc mecum ipse putavi, forte
ad phaenomenon inducendum et contactum alicujus corporis, et
scintillae jactum una requiri. Quamobrem scalpelli aciem iterum
60 nervis apposui immotamque detinui, tum quo tempore scintilla
extraheretur, tum quo tempore machina perfecte quiesceret. At
phaenomenon educta dumtaxat scintilla prodiit.

Experimentum iteravimus eodem semper scalpello adhibito:
verum non sine nostra admiratione interdum educta scintilla
65   recensiti motus contigebant, interdum deficiebant.

• Notes •

2   **viribus:** When used in the plural, **vis, vis** (f) can often be
        rendered as *strength* or *influence.*

3   **Optanti mihi:** *to me wishing, since I wish.* Construe **optanti** with
        ad eam utilitatem perducere.

4   **detegere in nervis, ac musculis:** *to uncover/reveal in nerves and
        muscles.*

        contigit: used as impersonal. **detegere . . . contigit:** *it befell* [*to
        me*] *to uncover.*

5   **perducere. Quae** is the object of **perducere.**

4–6   **ad eam utilitatem . . . ut . . . in apertum . . . ponerentur:** This
        ut in the purpose clause picks up from **eam utilitatem.**

6   **tutius:** comparative adverb.

        mederi: medeor, mederi *to heal, to cure.* It takes the dative of
        the disease being cured.

6–7   **nihil . . . visum est:** This is a reordered version of the Latin:
        **Nihil visum est magis idoneum ad explendum desiderium
        huiusmodi.** Note the **ad** + gerundive construction to indicate
        purpose.

7   **magis . . . quam . . . :** *more . . . than . . .*

8   **qualiacumque: qualiscumque, qualiscumque, qualecumque**
        of whatever kind.

        publici . . . juris: legal expression, *of public right, of the public
        domain, of common property.*

9   **nostra legendo:** gerund ablative of means, *by means of reading
        our (words).*

10–11   **ipsa majora efficere:** *to render them larger,* that is, *to develop them further.* Although the opening paragraph might sound a mere formality, Galvani was a person of firm moral convictions, great modesty, and utmost sincerity.

11   **assequi:** deponent infinitive.

11–12   **conati . . . consecuti:** deponent perfect participles.

13–15   **Equidem . . . proferre:** This a reordered version of the Latin: **Equidem in votis erat proferre in publicam lucem opus si non perfectum et absolutum, (quod numquam fortasse potuissem) saltem non rude atque vix inchoatum.**

13   **in votis erat:** *it was among* [*my*] *desires.*

16   **ita . . . ut . . .:** *so much . . . that . . . .*

17   **absolverem:** The main meaning of **absolvo, absolvere, absolvi, absolutum** is *to untie, to loosen.* Here, it means *to complete, to accomplish, to absolve oneself of a duty.*

        malui: malo, malle, malui. Malo is a contraction of **magis volo.**

        sane . . . quam . . .: *rather . . . than . . .*

        deesse: Desum, deesse, defui takes the dative.

19   **Operae . . . pretium . . . esse:** *to be worthwhile.* Literally, *to be the reward/value of the work.*

21   **partim . . . partim . . .:** *partly . . . partly . . .*

        obtulit: offero, offerre, obtuli, oblatum. The subject is dual (**casus et fortuna**), so we are in the presence of a synesis. The Greek term synesis, whose Latin equivalent is **constructio ad sensum,** is applied to a justifiable grammatical incongruence, such as a plural subject with a singular verb.

22–23   **non tantum ne plus mihi, quam fortunae, . . . tribuatur, sed ut . . .:** *not so much lest . . . but so that . . .*

        iis: indirect object of **praeferremus.**

24   **facem: fax, facis** (f) *a torch.* Thus, **facem praeferremus aliquam** means *we may shed some light.* Torches were used to show the way in darkness. In other words, for those wishing to **ipsam experiendi viam inire,** Galvani is carrying a torch.

25   **honesto . . . desiderio:** dative object of **satisfaceremus.**

29–30   **eo maxime consilio:** *mainly with the purpose.* The idiom here is **eo maxime consilio ut . . . .**

30   **novis capiendis experimentis:** gerundive, *by means of carrying out new experiments.*

31   **qua:** relative pronoun referring back to **viam.**

    qua sin minus . . . saltem: *but if by means of that path we may not arrive to the truth . . . then at least . . .*

33   **Res . . . initio est:** This is a reordered version of the Latin: **Res profecta est ab hujusmodi initio.** Literally, *the thing (experiment) started from this kind of beginning.* In other words, after a somewhat pompous introduction, Galvani is ready to describe his experiments, and *in much simpler language.* This peculiar way to start the description implies, perhaps, a connotation of "this is the way things actually started." Recall that there was a certain degree of chance in the discovery. This fact is confirmed by the phrase **omnia mihi alia proponens.**

35   **machina electrica:** An electric machine consisted of a rotor operated by hand which, by friction, generated static electricity. The energy was stored in a so-called Leyden jar, which can be clearly seen in the picture.

36   **sejunctam: seiungo, seiungere, seiunxi, seiunctum** *to separate.*

37   **dissitam: dissero, disserere, dissevi, dissitum** *to spread.*

37–38   **mihi operam dabant: Operam dare** means *to pay attention to, to assist.* Tradition has it that it was actually Galvani's wife Lucia who triggered the lucky accident.

41   **tentantibus: temptantibus.**

    praesto: adverb, *near at hand, ready, present.*

42   **animadvertere sibi visus est:** *it appeared to himself to have noticed.* In other words, *he seemed to notice.*

43–45   **Rei . . . admonuit:** This is a reordered version of the Latin: **Ille, admiratus novitatem rei, de eadem (re) statim admonuit me (alia omnino molientem ac mecum ipso cogitantem).**

44   **molientem: molior, moliri, molitus sum** *to toil.*

45–46   **Hic . . . experiundi:** This is a reordered version of the Latin: **Hic ego incensus sum incredibili studio et cupiditate idem experiundi.**

46   **quod occultum . . . esset:** *what might be hidden.* Note the use of subjunctive to express uncertainty.

49   **eliceret: (ut) eliceret.** purpose clause.

51   **perinde ac si:** *just as if.*

53   **metuens, ne:** *fearing lest.*

53–54   **potius . . . quam . . .:** *rather . . . than . . .*

57   **Hinc:** *from this,* namely, from what was just mentioned.

57–59   **putavi . . . requiri:** This is a reordered version of the Latin: **Putavi una** (*at one and the same time*) **requiri ad phaenomenon inducendum et contactum alicujus corporis et jactum scintillae.** He thought that to produce the phenomenon one would require both the contact with some body and, simultaneously, the throwing of a spark.

58   **ad phaenomenon inducendum:** gerundive of purpose.

60–61   **tum quo tempore . . . tum quo tempore . . .:** *once when . . . once when . . .*

64   **verum:** *but.*

64–65   **interdum . . . interdum . . .:** *sometimes . . . other times . . .*

Mathematics

Euclid

Elementa Geometriae

Adelard of Bath (1080?–1152?) traveled extensively from his native England to Europe and the Middle East and acquired an encyclopedic knowledge of all the liberal arts. Having acquired fluency in Arabic, but probably not in Greek, Adelard was the first to produce one or more translations of Euclid's *Elementa Geometriae* (*Elements of Geometry*) from one or more Arabic translations of the original Greek.[13] The attribution to Adelard of Bath has been questioned by many historians, who propose instead Robert of Chester, Adelard's contemporary, as the author of at least one of these translations. A curious aspect of these second-hand translations (attributed to Adelard) is the presence of many transliterated Arabic words, including the term *alkaida* for the base of a triangle. Adelard wrote also original works, the best known of which is his *Questiones Naturales*

---

13 Euclid (ca. 340–ca. 270 BCE) flourished in Alexandria and was associated with its foremost school, known as the Museum, which comprised the famous Library of Alexandria, a repository of ancient culture. His most celebrated work, *The Elements of Geometry*, was the first systematic account of the achievements of Greek mathematics. Its originality consists in the formulation of axioms and definitions out of which results are obtained by a strictly logical argument known as a theorem. The influence of this book on the development of the mathematical method cannot be overstated. It remained the standard manual for teaching geometry for over 2,200 years.

(*Natural Questions*), consisting of a dialogue between himself and his nephew, who conveniently asks questions on natural science for which Adelard has a ready answer based on his learnings from Arabic science.[14]

Our Latin version of Euclid's *Elements* is organized in three parts: (i) the statement of the proposition; (ii) an example via a figure with letters to indicate particular points; and (iii) the rational justification (or proof) of the theorem.[15] Most proofs end with a statement of the fact that we have achieved our objective, later fossilized into our own QED (**quod erat demonstrandum**). In this version, as in many medieval Latin mansucripts and books, the diphthong *ae* is usually collapsed into the single vowel *e*. Thus **aequales** becomes **equales** and **lineae** becomes **linee**. One has to be constantly mindful of this feature, particularly when it comes to the identification of singular genitive and dative or plural nominative of nouns and adjectives of the first declension. Otherwise, the grammar is quite straightforward and conveys the typical dry style of mathematics from antiquity all the way to our own days. We have enough to worry about from the technical difficulties of the subject to care too much about grammar! The verb **est** is often omitted. Notice that the classical accusative-infinitive construction for indirect speech is cavalierly replaced by the use of **quia** with an indicative verb. Thus, for instance, **dico eum esse** is rendered as **dico quia is est**, just as in modern Romance languages.

---

14 The dialogue, a common pedagogical practice, was also a literary genre. Peter Abelard's famous dialogue about philosophy *Dialogus inter Philosophum, Iudaeum, et Christianum* (*Dialogue between a Philosopher, a Jew, and a Christian*) involved a priest, a rabbi, and an imam in conversation.

15 As reported in H. L. L. Busard, *The First Latin Translation of Euclid's Elements commonly ascribed to Adelard of Bath* (Toronto: Pontifical Institute of Mediaeval Studies, 1983).

First printing of the thirteenth-century Arabic translation by Nasir al-Din al-Tusi of Euclid's *Elements*. The picture shows part of the statement and proof of the theorem of Pythagoras. Reproduced by permission of the Master and Fellows of St. John's College, Cambridge. Translators of the *Elements* took a large degree of freedom in their translations, perhaps because they also assumed the role of clarifiers and commentators. Nevertheless, this particular Arabic version corresponds quite closely (at least at the start) with Adelard's version, as given below. Recall that the theorem of Pythagoras states that, in a right-angled triangle, the square built upon the longer side is equal in area to the sum of the squares built upon the other two sides. The above sample page of this Arabic translation starts with the end of the statement of the theorem as: "... the sum of the squares of the sides that surround it." Then the proof commences (on the second line) as follows: "Let the angle *bag* from the triangle *abg* be right, then I say that the square of *bg* is equal to the sum of the squares of *ab* and *ag*. Its proof: We draw on the sides of the triangle *abg* the squares *bdhg, agyt* (and) *abcr* in the preceding manner. Let us draw out from point *a* the line *al* parallel to the line *bd* ... " It is interesting to notice that the Arabic version makes explicit reference to previous propositions, mentioning them by number. Thus, the preceding "manner" refers to the previously proved proposition, but there are also references to propositions 31 and 29 in the next couple of lines. Our Latin version is not that helpful, and the reader is supposed to remember how to draw a square or a line parallel to a given one through a given point. The first printed edition, however, does include such cross references.

Adelard's Version
The Theorem of Pythagoras[16]
Proposition 46, Book I

Omnis trianguli rectanguli latus recto angulo oppositum si ductum
in seipsum quadratum constituerit, erit quadratum illud sicut duo
quadrata ex duobus reliquis lateribus in seipsa ductis.

Exempli gratia: Sit triangulus *a b g* angulusque rectus *b a g*. Dico
5   quia quadratum quod constiterit ex latere *b g* in seipsum ducto sicut
duo quadrata que sunt ex ductu duorum laterum *b a* et *a g* in seipsa.

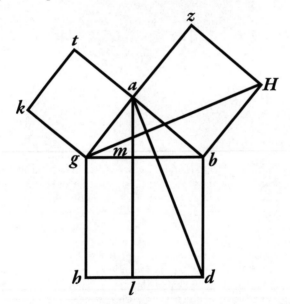

Figure 1: Theorem of Pythagoras

Rationis causa: Fiat enim supra lineam *b g* superficies quadrata
supra quam *b g d h*. Itemque supra duas lineas *b a* et *a g* due

---

16   Pythagoras (ca. 570– ca. 495 BCE) was a Greek mathematician, philosopher, and mystic. Among his important contributions to science, we can mention his discovery of
the mathematical basis of musical harmony. He is credited with the first rigorous
proof of the theorem that bears his name.

superficies quadrate supra unam quarum *a z H b* atque supra aliam
a t k g. Extrahaturque de puncto *a* linea usque ad *l* lineis *b d* et *g h*
equidistans. Iungaturque *a* cum *d* et *H* cum *g*. Anguli autem *b a g* et
z a b recti. Cum ergo extracte fuerint de *a* puncto linee *a b* linee *a z*
et *a g* in duas partes oppositas supra duos angulos rectos, scilicet, *z a*
b et *b a g*, erunt due linee *z a* et *a g* directe iuncte linea una. Anguli
item *H b a* et *g b d* recti sibi equales, sitque angulus *a b g* communis.
Totus ergo angulus *H b g* sicut totus angulus *a b d*. Linea autem *H*
b sicut linea *b a* et *b g* sicut *b d*. Linee ergo *b H* et *b g* sicut linee *a b*
et *b d* unaqueque sibi opposite equales. At vero angulus *H b g* sicut
angulus *a b d*. Basis itaque *H g* sicut basis *a d*. Triangulusque *H b g*
sicut triangulus *a b d*. Atqui superficies *a z H b* dupla triangulo *H*
b g. Eorum enim basis una que est *H b*. Suntque inter duas lineas
equidistantes *H b* et *z g*. Superficies vero *b d l m* dupla triangulo *a b*
d. Basis enim eorum *b d* una. Suntque inter duas lineas equidistantes
b d et *a l*. Omnium autem duplorum alicui uni unumquodque erit
equale alteri. Ostensum itaque est quia superficies *a z H b* superficiei
b d l m equalis. Eodemque modo superficies *l m h g* superficiei *t a*
k g equalis. Tota quoque superficies *g b d h* duabus superficiebus *a*
b H z et *a g k t* equalis. Atqui superficies *g d b h* est quadratum ex
latere *b g* in seipsum ducto constitutum. Superficies vero *a b H z*
et *a g k t* sunt quadrata ex ductu duum laterum *b a* et *a g* utriusque
in seipsum constituta. Manifestum igitur est quia quadratum ex
ductu *b g* in seipsum existens est sicut duo quadrata que ex ductu *b*
a et *a g* utriusque in seipsum existunt. Et hoc est quod in hac figura
demonstrare intendimus.

• Notes •

Notice that the gist of this proof is to divide the square over the
hypotenuse into two rectangles (*g m l h* and *m b d l*), each of
which is shown to have an area equal to that of the square over
one of the sides. Other proofs use only triangle similarity, but
they require the use of algebraic formulas. Euclid tacitly assumes

the additivity property of the measure of area (the sum of the areas of two essentially disjoint figures is equal to the area of the compound figure). Proofs that do not invoke this property generally assume that the rules of algebra (opening brackets in a product) can be applied. That these two different procedures are interconnected (each one requiring its own assumptions) is clear from the fact that in Islamic and Renaissance mathematics the rules were used interchangeably. Thus, the solution of a quadratic equation was obtained by literally "completing the square."

1   **recto angulo**: dative with **oppositum**.

1–2   **si ductum in seipsum: lineam ducere** means to draw a line. Thus, **latus in seipsum ductum** means a side drawn perpendicularly to itself (so as to form a square).

2   **seipsum: se + ipsum.**

    erit sicut: literally, *it will be like*. In this case, interpret it as *it will be equal to the sum of.*

4   **exempli gratia**: literally, *for the sake of an example*. This expression gives rise to the abbreviation *e.g.*

4–5   **Dico quia**: Notice the abandonment of the classical indirect statement/oratio obliqua construction using the accusative with the infinitive and in its place the (classically incorrect) use of **quia.**

6   **que sunt: quae sunt.**

    ex ductu: supine in the ablative case.

10   **lineis**: dative case with **equidistans.**

18   **unaqueque: unaquaeque** from **unus + quisque** = *each one.* Notice that the form **unaquaeque** can only be in the feminine singular nominative case (consider why this is the case). **Equales** is in the nominative plural. Adelard uses this set phrase in many instances, including a few lines further down in this passage, sometimes at the expense of grammar. *The segments* b H *and* b g *(are) in the same ratio as* a b *and* b d, *each segment [being] equal to its opposite* (i.e., the corresponding one in the pair).

Campanus of Novara's Version

As early as 1482, the first printed edition of Euclid's *Elementa* was published by Erhard Ratdolt in Venice. It was based on Campanus of Novara's Latin version. Campanus (1220–1296) was an Italian mathematician, who based his text in part on Adelard's (or Robert of Chester's) translation from the Arabic. Ratdolt himself explained that the reason for not having had any important mathematical books printed before his edition lies in the fact that figures were difficult to print. He claimed to have discovered a method to print figures, which he placed on the wide margins of each printed page.[17]

As a translation exercise, we propose the following facsimile of Ratdolt's edition. The three propositions therein, from Euclid's book III, are particularly interesting in that they show the great sophistication of the Greek mathematical achievements. In these propositions the task is neither to prove a mathematical relation nor to propose a method of geometrical construction. Rather, these propositions assert the impossibility of the existence of certain objects, which could a priori be conceived. Proposition 9 (at the top of the page) asserts that, given a circle, it is not possible to find a point other than the center with the property of being equidistant from three or more points of the circumference.[18] Most striking is Proposition 10 asserting that two different circles can have at most two points in common. The proof proceeds by showing that if two circles have three points in common, then they must necessarily have the same center and radius and, hence, they coincide. The corresponding figure is particularly curious. Since the fact being discussed is impossible, the drawing shows the second circle as an ovate shape! Proposition 11 asserts that in two tangent circles, the point of tangency and the two centers cannot form a triangle.

---

17   See Sir Thomas L. Heath, *The Thirteen Books of Euclid's Elements*, 2nd ed. (Cambridge: Cambridge University Press, 1926).

18   Circle and circumference are often used interchangeably by Campanus.

III

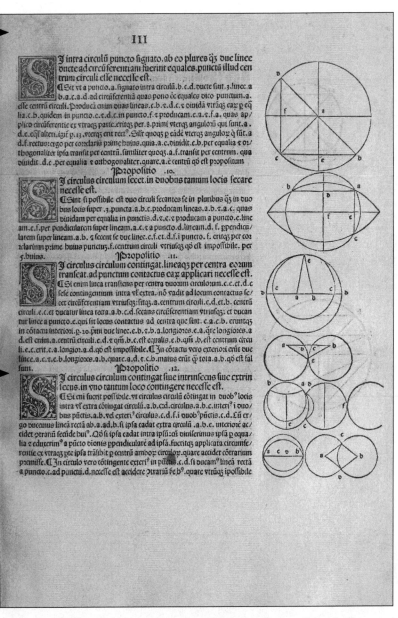

S intra circulũ puncto signato.ab eo plures q̃ due linee
ducte ad circũferentiam fuerint equales.punctũ illud cen
trum circuli esse necesse est.
¶Sit vt a puncto.a.signato intra circulũ.b.c.d.ducte sint.3.linee.a
b.a.c.a.d.ad circũferentiã quas pono ée equales dico punctum.a.
esse centrũ circuli. Produci enim duas lineas.c.b.e.d.c.z divida eaz p eq̃
lia.c.b.quidem in puncto.e.e.d.c.in puncto.f.z producam.e.a.z.f.a. quas ap/
plico circũferentie ex vtraq̃ parte.eritq̃3 per.8.primi vterq̃ angulorũ qui sunt.a.
d.e.eq̃l'alteri.izit p.13.vterq̃3 erit rect'.Silr quoq̃3 p eãde vterq̃3 angulo z q̃ sũt.a
d.f.rectus:ergo per corelariũ prime huius.quia.a.c.dividit.e.b.per equalia z or/
thogonaliter ipsa transit per centrũ.similiter quoq̃3.a.f.transit per centrum. qua
dividit .d.e .per equalia z orthogonaliter.quare.a.é centrũ centri q̃ est propositum
Propositio .10.
S circulus circulum secet.in duobus tantum locis secare
necesse est.
¶Sint si possibile est duo circuli secantes se in pluribus q̃3 in duo
bus locis super.3.puncta.a.b.c.producam lineas.a.b.z.a.c. quas
dividam per equalia in punctis.d.e.e.z producam a puncto.e.line
am.e.f.per pendicularem super lineam.a.c.z a puncto.d.lineam.d. f. ppendicu/
larem super lineam.a.b. z secent se due linee.e.f.et.d.f.i puncto. f. eritq̃3 per cor
relarium prime huius punctuz.f.centrum circuli vtriusq̃3 q̃ est impossibile. per
5.huius. Propositio .11.
S circulus circulum contingat.lineaq̃3 per centra eorum
transeat.ad punctum contactus eaz applicari necesse est.
¶Si enim linea transiens per centra duorum circulorum.c.c.et.d.c
sese contingentium intra vel extra.nõ vadit ad locum contactus se/
et circũferentiam vtriusq̃:sitq̃3.a.centrum circuli.c.d.et.b. centrũ
circuli.e.c.et ducatur linea recta.a.b.c.d.secans circũferentiam vtriusq̃: et ducan
tur linee a puncto.e.qui sit locus contactus ad centra que sunt. e.a.e.b. eruntq̃3
in cõtactu interiori.p.20.primi due linee.e.b.z.b.a.longiores.e.a.q̃re longiores.a
d.est enim.a.centrũ circuli.e.d.z q̃n.b.c.est equalis.e.b.q̃n.b.est centrum circu
li.e.c.erit.c.a.longior.a.d.q̃ est impossibile.¶In cõtactu vero exteriori erit due
linee.a.c.z.c.b.longiores.a.b.quare.a.d.z.e.c.b.maius erũt q̃ tota.a.b.q̃ est fal
sum. Propositio .12.
S circulus circulum contingat sine intrinsecus sive extrin
secus.in vno tantum loco contingere necesse est.
¶Si eni fuerit possibile.vt circulus circulũ cõtingat in duob' locis
intra vel extra cõtingat circulũ.a.b.cd.circulus.a.b.c.interi' i duo/
bus punctis.a.b.vel exteri' circulus.c.d.f.i duob' punctis.c.d.Cũ er/
go ducamus linea rectã ab.a.ad.b.si ipsa cadat extra circuli .a.b.c. interioné ac/
cidet ptrariũ secãde hui'.Q̃ si ipsa cadat intra ipsũ:cũ diviserimus ipsã p equa/
lia z eduxerim' a pũcto divisio z ppendiculare ad ipsã.fueritq̃3 applicata circumfe/
rentie ex vtraq̃3 pte ipsa trãsibit p centrũ amboz circuloz.quare accidet cõtrarium
præmisse.¶In circulo vero cõtingente exteri' in pũctis.c.d.si ducam' lineã rectã
a puncto.c.ad punctũ.d.necesse est accidere ptrariũ se b'.quare vtriũq̃3 ipossibile

---

Image in the Folger Shakespeare Library Digital Image Collection. From the first
printed edition under the title: *Preclarissimus liber elementorum Euclidis perspicacis-*
simi, in artem geometrie incipit qua[m]foelicissime. Erhardus Ratdolt Augustensis
impressor solertissimus Venetijs impressit Anno 1482.

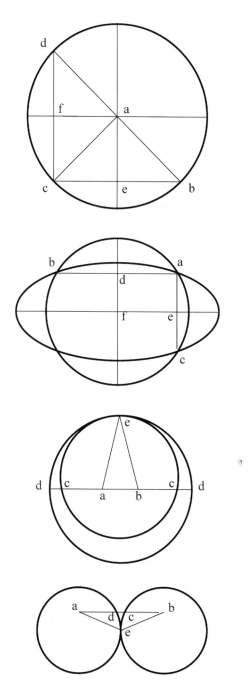

Figure 2: An enlargement of figures on p. 112

III

Si intra circulum puncto signato ab eo plures quam duae lineae
ductae ad circumferentiam fuerint aequales punctum illud centrum
circuli esse necesse est.

Sit ut a puncto *a* signato intra circulum *bcd* ductae sint tres lineae
5   *ab,ac, ad* ad circumferentiam quas pono *ec* aequales dico punctum *a*
esse centrum circuli. Producam enim duas lineas *cb* et *dc* et dividam
utramque earum per aequalia, *cb* quidem in puncto *e* et *dc* in puncto
f et producam *ea* et *fa,* quas applico circumferentiae ex utraque parte.
Eritque per 8 primi uterque angulorum qui sunt ad *e* aequales alteri.
10   Igitur per 13 uterque erit rectus. Sit quoque per eandem uterque
angulorum qui sunt ad *f* rectus: ergo per correlarium primae huius
quia *ae* dividit *cb* per aequalia et orthogonaliter ipsa transit per
centrum. Similiter quoque *af* transit per centrum. Qua dividit *dc* per
aequalia et orthogonaliter quare *ae* centrum quod est propositum.

15   **Propositio 10**
Si circulus circulum secet in duobus tantum locis secare necesse est.

Sint si possibile est duo circuli secantes se in pluribus quam
in duobus locis super 3 puncta *abc* producam lineas *ab* et *ac* quas
dividam per aequalia in punctis *d* et *e* et producam a puncto *e* lineam
20   *ef* perpendicularem super lineam *ac* et a puncto *d* lineam *df*
perpendicularem super lineam *ab* et secent se duae lineae *ef* et *df*
in puncto *f* eritque per correlarium primae huius punctumque *f*
centrum circuli utriusque quod est impossibile. Per 5 huius.

  Propositio 11
25   Si circulus circulum contingat lineaque per centra eorum transeat
ad punctum contactus earum applicari necesse est.

Si enim linea transiens per centra duorum circulorum *ce*
et *dc* sese contingentium intra vel extra. non vadit ad locum
contactus secet circumferentiam utriusque: sitque a centrum
30   circuli *ed* et *b* centrum circuli *ec* et ducatur linea recta *abcd* secans

circumferentiam utriusque: et ducantur lineae *a* puncto *e* qui sit locus contactus ad centra quae sint *eacb* eruntque in contactu interiori. Per 20 primi duae lineae *eb* et *ba* longiores *ea* quare longiores *ad*. Est enim *a* centrum circuli *ed* et quoniam *bc* est

35   aequalis *eb* quoniam *b* est centrum circuli *ec* erit *ca* longior ad quod est impossibile.

In contactu vero exteriori erunt duae lineae *ae* et *eb* longiores *ab* quare *ad* et *cb* maius erunt quam tota *ab* quod est falsum.

• Notes •

III

1   **signato: adsignato.**

        plures quam duae: Plures is the nominative feminine plural of **plus, pluris**, which is the comparative form of **multus, -a, -um**. The indeclinable relative conjunction **quam** corresponds to the English *than*. The two terms of the comparison (before and after **quam**) agree in case, gender, and number.

3   **necesse:** indeclinable adjective meaning *necessary* used mostly with the verbs **esse** and **habere**. The typical construction is **necesse est** + dative + infinitive, such as **necesse est mihi legere** = *It is necessary for me to read.* The alternative construction used here employs the accusative with the infinitive construction.

4   **Sit ut:** *let it be that.* Jussive subjunctive but it is not a classical expression.

5–6   **pono . . . aequales . . . esse:** *I assume to be equal.*

        dico . . . esse . . . : Notice that this version is more careful than that of Abelard with the use of the accusative with the infinitive construction for indirect statement/oratio obliqua. Adelard tends to use unclassical **dico quia . . . sunt.**

7   **utramque:** recall **uter** + **que**, *each one of two.*

8   **circumferentiae:** dative.

9   **per 8 primi:** In our context, this must mean *according to Proposition 8 of the first book.*

qui sunt ad *e*: Namely, the two angles at point *e* must be equal since, according to Proposition 8 of the first book, the two triangles *aec* and *aeb* are congruent, the corresponding sides being respectively equal by construction.

10 **per 13:** Again, this is a reference to Proposition 13 of the first book. It essentially states that when a straight line stands upon another straight line, the sum of the adjacent angles is equal to two right angles. In this case, therefore, each of the two angles is right.

11 **per corollarium primae huius:** *by the corollary of the first (proposition) of this (book).* This proposition shows how to find the center of a given circle by drawing the perpendicular to a chord at its midpoint.

Propositio 10

16 **tantum:** *only.*

Propositio 11

25 **circulum contingat: Contingo, contingere, contigi, contactum** is used here in the technical term of *to be tangent to.* In fact, the English word *tangent* derives directly from the present participle. Notice carefully that the letters *c* and *e* on the inner circle are not clearly distinguished in the figure. Point *e* is the point of contact between the mutually tangent circles, while *c* denotes a couple of points on the inner circumference.

26 **earum:** this should probably be **eorum,** *of the circles.*

applicari: Applico, -are is not deponent. Its meaning is *to place, to apply, to attach.* It can be used in the passive *to be placed* to mean *to reach,* just like **pervenire.**

28 **sese:** intensive form of **se.**

contingentium: Apply to **circulorum.**

intra vel extra: This remark alludes to the fact that, in the figure, it has been assumed that one circle is inside the other ("interior contact"). The case in which the circles touch from outside ("exterior contact") is dealt with in the corollary.

29   **contactus:** genitive singular. A comma should be understood
      after **contactus** to avoid running out of breath and to signify
      where the contrary-to-fact condition ends.

33   **Per 20 primi:** *by Proposition 20 of the first book.* This proposition
      states that the sum of the lengths of two sides of a triangle is
      always more than the length of the third side. This important
      feature of Euclidean geometry is known, in modern mathematics,
      as the triangle inequality (for the distance function in a metric
      space).

      duae lineae *eb* et *ba* longiores *ea*: In Euclid's mind the
      expression "the two quantities x and y are greater than z" means
      that *the sum* of the first two quantities is larger than the third.
      The comparative (in this instance, **longior, longioris**) can be
      used either with the particle **quam**, as we saw above, or without
      any intermediary particle. In the second construction, the second
      term of the comparison must go in the ablative case. Here,
      it is not apparent since the name of the line (*ea*) is obviously
      indeclinable.

38   **quare: qua + re** *for which reason.*

Comparison with Adelard's version

It may not be a bad idea to compare Campanus's version of the passage
just studied with Adelard's version of the same passage.[19] Proposition 9, for
example, reads as follows:

> Si puncto in circulo assignato linee plures ab eo usque ad
> circumferentiam extracte fuerint equales, punctum illum centrum
> circuli esse necesse est.
>
>   Exempli gratia: Sit punctus in circulo *a b* assignatus *g*.
> 5 Extrahanturque ab eo usque ad circumferentiam linee plures *g d* et *g*
> *b* et *g h*. Sintque equales. Dico quia *g* centrum circuli esse necesse est.

---

19   As reported in Busard, ibid.

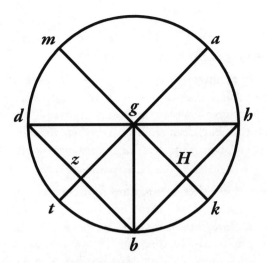

Figure 3: Circle based on Euclid

Rationis causa: Si enim iungatur *d* cum *b* et *b* cum *h* dividanturque
due linee in duo media *d b* et *b h* supra puncta *H* et *z*. Iungaturque
z cum *g* et *H* cum *g* protrahanturque *g z* et *g H* in duas partes
10 diversas usque ad circumferentiam, erit *d z* sicut *z b* et *z g* communis.
Due itaque linee *d z* et *z g* sicut due linee *g z* et *z b* unaqueque
sicut respiciens se. Basis autem *g d* sicut alkaida *g b*. Angulus ergo
d z g sicut angulus *b z g*. Cum autem linea supra lineam ceciderit
fuerintque anguli utrobique equales, rectos esse necesse est. Duo
15 itaque anguli *d z g* et *b z g* recti. Sicque cadet línea *a t* in circulo *a b*
dividetque *b d* in duo media supra duos angulos rectos. Erit itaque
centrum circuli supra lineam *a t*. Itemque circuli centrum supra
lineam *k m* factum est eritque divisio illa duabus lineis *t a* et *k m*
communis. Supra eandem igitur centrum circuli esse necesse est.
20 Estque punctus *g*. Et hoc est quod demonstrare proposuimus.

Gottfried Wilhelm Leibniz

Gottfried Wilhelm Leibniz (1646–1716) was one of the greatest philosophers and mathematicians of all times. His most important mathematical contribution was his invention, or discovery, of infinitesimal calculus. His article on this topic *Nova Methodus pro Maximis et Minimis* (*A New Method for the Maxima and Minima*) published in the *Acta Eruditorum* in 1684 is the first publication in this field.

The first page of this short paper should be enough to convey the general impression of this momentous contribution. One of the most striking features of Leibniz's paper is its notation and its almost modernistic style, whereby the rules governing the differential operator "d" are introduced axiomatically at the beginning of the treatment and then systematically exploited to derive conclusions. As a philosopher, Leibniz was interested in the creation of a symbolic system capable of expressing any thought independently of the usual human languages. For him, therefore, calculus was a first important step in this direction. Isaac Newton reacted immediately. Almost twenty years earlier, he had developed, but not published, his own version of calculus, though not as elegant in its notation as Leibniz's. The dispute between the two great men constitutes one of the ugliest incidents in the history of science. Newton exercised his considerable power within the Royal Society to claim originality and accused Leibniz of plagiarism. A supposed exchange of letters to prove this point was published in Latin under the title of *Commercium Epistolicum*. In turn, Leibniz produced a booklet, also in Latin, entitled *Historia et Origo Calculi Infinitesimalii* (*The History and Origin of Infinitesimal Calculus*). It is easy to imagine how Leibniz's fundamental philosophical optimism and belief that we live in the best of all possible worlds, a belief unfairly ridiculed by Voltaire in his play *Candide*, may have been shaken by what he saw as a great injustice perpetrated against him. The dispute was indeed a major source of grief for Leibniz during the last years of his life.

ACTA
ERUDITORUM
ANNO M DC L XXXIV

publicata,

ac

SERENISSIMO FRATRUM PARI,

DN. JOHANNI
GEORGIO IV,

Electoratus Saxonici Hæredi,

&

DN. FRIDERICO
AUGUSTO,

Ducibus Saxoniæ &c.&c.&c.

PRINCIPIBUS JUVENTUTIS

dicata.

Cum S.Cæsareæ Majestatis & Potentissimi Ele-
ctoris Saxoniæ Privilegiis.

LIPSIÆ,

Prostant apud J. GROSSIUM & J. F. GLETITSCHIUM.
Typis CHRISTOPHORI GüNTHERI.
Anno M DCLXXXIV.

Leibniz, "*Nova Methodus pro Maximis et Minimis*," *Acta Eruditorum, Lipsiae,* 1684.
Property of the Complutense University of Madrid. Facsimile courtesy of archive.org.

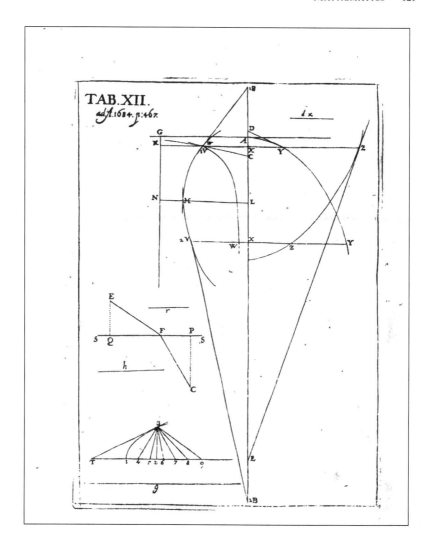

NOVA METHODUS PRO MAXIMIS ET MI-
nimis, itemque tangentibus, quæ nec fractas, nec irrationales
quantitates moratur, & singulare pro illis calculi
genus, per G. G. L.

SIt axis AX, & curvæ plures, ut V V, W W, Y Y, Z Z, quatum ordi- TAB.XII.
natæ, ad axem normales, V X, W X, Y X, Z X, quæ vocentur respective, v, w, y, z; & ipsa A X abscissa ab axe, vocetur x. Tangentes sint
V B, W C, Y D, Z E axi occurrentes respective in punctis B, C, D, E.
Jam recta aliqua pro arbitrio assumta vocetur dx, & recta quæ sit ad
dx, ut v (vel w, vel y, vel z) est ad V B (vel W C, vel Y D, vel Z E) vocetur d v (vel d w, vel dy vel dz) sive differentia ipsarum v (vel ipsarum w, aut y, aut z) His positis calculi regulæ erunt tales:

Sit a quantitas data constans, erit da æqualis o, & d ax erit æqu-
a dx: si sit y æqu v (seu ordinata quævis curvæ Y Y, æqualis cuivis ordinatæ respondenti curvæ V V) erit dy æqu. dv . Jam *Additio & Subtractio*: si sit z — y + w + x æqu. v, erit d z — y + w + x seu d v, æqu
d z — d y + d w + d x. *Multiplicatio*, d x v æqu. x d v + v d x, seu posito
y æqu. x v, fiet d y æqu x d v + v d x. In arbitrio enim est vel formulam,
ut x v, vel compendio pro ea literam, ut y, adhibere.   Notandum & x
& d x eodem modo in hoc calculo tractari, ut y & dy, vel aliam literam
indeterminatam cum sua differentiali.   Notandum etiam non dari
semper regressum a differentiali Æquatione, nisi cum quadam cautio-
ne, de quo alibi.   Porro *Diviso*, d $\frac{v}{y}$ vel (posito z æqu. $\frac{v}{y}$) dz æqu.
$\frac{\pm v dy \mp y dv}{yy}$

Quoad *Signa* hoc probe notandum, cum in calculo pro litera
substituitur simpliciter ejus differentialis, servari quidem eadem signa,
& pro + z scribi + dz, pro — z scribi - d z, ut ex additione & subtra-
ctione paulo ante posita apparet; sed quando ad exegesin valorum
venitur, seu cum consideratur ipsius z relatio ad x, tunc apparere, an
valor ipsius d z sit quantitas affirmativa, an nihilo minor seu negativa:
quod posterius cum fit, tunc tangens Z E ducitur a puncto Z non versus A, sed in partes contrarias seu infra X, id est tunc cum ipsæ ordinatæ
Nnn 3   z decre-

Nova methodus pro maximis et minimis

Nova methodus pro maximis et minimis, itemque tangentibus, quae nec fractas, nec irrationales quantitates moratur, et singulare pro illis calculi genus, per G.G.L.

Sit axis AX, et curvae plures, ut VV, WW, YY, ZZ, quarum
5 ordinatae ad axem normales, VX, WX, YX, ZX, quae vocentur
respective, v, w, y, z; et ipsa AX abscissa ab axe, vocetur x. Tangentes
sint VB, WC, YD, ZE axi occurrentes respective in punctis
B,C,D,E. Jam recta aliqua pro arbitrio assumta vocetur dx, et recta
quae sit ad dx, ut v (vel w, vel y, vel z) est ad VB (vel WC, vel YD, vel
10 ZE) vocetur dv (vel dw, vel dy vel dz) sive differentia ipsarum v (vel
ipsarum w, aut y, aut z). His positis calculi regulae erunt tales:

Sit a quantitas data constans, erit da aequalis o, et d $\overline{ax}$ erit
aequalis a dx: si sit y aequalis v (seu ordinata quaevis curvae YY,
aequalis cuivis ordinatae respondenti curvae VV) erit dy aequalis dv.
15 Jam *Additio et Subtractio:* si sit z−y+w+x aequalis v, erit d $\overline{z-y+w+x}$
seu dv, aequalis dz−dy +dw+dx. *Multiplicatio,* d $\overline{xv}$ aequalis x dv +
v dx, seu posito y aequalis xv, fiet d y aequalis x d v + v d x. In arbitrio
enim est vel formulam, ut x v, vel compendio pro ea literam, ut y,
adhibere. Notandum et x et d x eodem modo in hoc calculo tractati,
20 ut y et dy, vel aliam literam indeterminatam cum sua differentiali.
Notandum etiam non dari semper regressum a differentiali
Aequatione, nisi cum quadam cautione, de quo alibi. Porro *divisio,*
$d\frac{v}{y}$ vel (posito z aequalis $\frac{v}{y}$) dz aequalis $\frac{\pm vdy \mp ydv}{yy}$

• Notes •

1   **methodus:** Because of its derivation from Greek, this word
preserves in Latin the Greek feminine gender. This is true also in
modern French, though not in Spanish or Italian.

itemque: *and likewise.*

2   **quae . . . moratur:** To understand what it is that Leibniz has in mind, it is important to know that Pierre de Fermat (1601–1665) had already adumbrated the techniques of calculus (such as finding maxima, minima, and tangents to certain curves). But Fermat's method was stumped by the fact that it seemed to work only for polynomials. Fermat could not have known how to deal with general functions, since a precise definition of limit did not exist. Leibniz, therefore, bowing to Fermat in recognition of his insight, refers to this obstacle in the very title of his paper.

       moratur: moror, morari, moratus sum: *to delay, to hinder, to stay.* The subject is **methodus.**

3   **singulare pro illis calculi genus:** *a singular (remarkable, unique) kind of calculus for them.* The word "calculus" (a pebble) was already in use in Roman times to indicate a counting and, thus, a calculation. Leibniz's use of this word in the title of his paper, however, established the use of the term "calculus" without any qualification almost exclusively for the differential and integral calculus as conceived by Leibniz and Newton. Newton himself, however, did not use "calculus" to refer to his own work.

       per G.G.L.: Leibniz's name in Latin is **Godofredus Guilelmus Leibnitius.** In classical Latin an authorship is indicated by **a(b),** as in **liber a Leibnitio.**

4   **Sit:** jussive subjunctive but used as a "mathematical subjunctive" throughout the passage to mean *suppose* or *let.*

       Sit axis AX: Notice that Leibniz draws the x-axis, or line of abscissas, vertically in contrast to the modern convention of drawing it horizontally. Leibniz places what we call the abscissas on a vertical axis, while the ordinates are measured horizontally. Notice that the word **abscissa** comes from **abscindere,** *to tear off, to cut away.* Leibniz uses it in this sense at the end of the sentence.

7   **axi occurrentes: Occurro, ocurrere, ocucurri, occursum** is *to meet.* It takes the dative of the thing or person met.

8   **Jam recta . . .:** Leibniz is just defining the notation. Given any straight-line segment, he calls dx the difference of the abscissas of its end points, while he calls dy (or dw, dz . . .) the difference of the corresponding ordinates. In the next paragraph, he refers to

the operator *d* as the differential. Here there is a misprint: Where it says **ut *v* . . . est ad *VB***, it should actually say: **ut *v* est . . . ad *XB***. In other words, the ratio between the increments of the two variables is equal to the ratio of the corresponding side, not the hypotenuse, of the characteristic triangle. For more about this and other interesting details, see S. Roero, "Gottfried Wilhelm Leibniz, First Three Papers on the Calculus," in *Landmark Writings in Western Mathematics 1640–1940*, ed. I. Grattan-Guinness (Amsterdam: Elsevier, 2005), 46–58.

assumta: assumpta.

11   **His positis:** ablative absolute: *these things having been established/posited . . .*

12   **Sit . . .:** Leibniz proceeds now to enumerate his rules in an axiomatic fashion. Notice that the use of brackets had not been standardized. Instead, Leibniz uses an "overbar" to essentially bracket an expression. Thus, he writes $\overline{z - y + w + x}$ in place of our usual $(z - y + w + x)$. The number zero he writes as the letter *o*. Paraphrasing Leibniz, the rules are as follows: (1) The differential of a constant is zero; (2) The differential of a sum is the sum of the corresponding differentials; (3) The differential of a product of two objects x and y abides by what we now call Leibniz's rule, namely, $d(xy) = x(dy) + (dx)y$. He remarks that the symbols x, y are themselves immaterial.

18   **ut:** *such as, like, as.*

21   **Notandum:** Supply **est** for the passive periphrastic construction.

21–22   **non dari semper regressum a differentiali Aequatione:** Literally, *that not always a way back is given from a differential equality.* The meaning is that two equal objects necessarily have the same differential. But, if two objects have the same differential, they are not necessarily equal.

22   **de quo alibi:** *about which (we will talk) elsewhere.*

       Porro *divisio* . . .: If Leibniz had taken his own axioms more seriously (that is, as axioms), the rule for division could have been obtained directly as a consequence of the previous rules. It is, therefore, disappointing to see Leibniz including an ambiguity of sign in the division rule. The concept of "function" had not been formalized yet and the reasoning was mostly based on the geometric idea of a curve as representative of the function. This is most probably the source of the incorrect ambiguity. Indeed, following Leibniz, if we denote $z = \frac{v}{y}$ then it follows that $v = yz$. Using the product rule (just postulated by Leibniz) we must have $dv = y\, dz + z\, dy$. From here we read off: $dz = \frac{dv}{y} - z\frac{dy}{y} = \frac{dv}{y} - \left(\frac{v}{y}\right)\frac{dy}{y} = \frac{y\,dv - v\,dy}{y^2}$. From the merely formal point of view, the inconsistency of the alternative sign in the numerator should have warned Leibniz that his ambiguous formula was problematic. In fact, the great merit of Leibniz's notation (as opposed to Newton's) is the ability to manipulate the symbols in this formal way.

Astronomy and Rational Mechanics

Nicolaus Copernicus

The Copernican revolution had its antecedents in ancient Greece, where the heliocentric theory had been propounded, among others, by Aristarchus of Samos (310?–230? BCE), a true pioneer in the field of theoretical astronomy. Nevertheless, the acceptance of the Ptolemaic geocentric model was only finally shaken by the Polish Dominican priest Nicolaus Copernicus (Mikolaj Kopernik, 1473–1543) in his seminal work *De Revolutionibus Orbium Coelestium* (*On the Revolutions of Heavenly Spheres*), published in 1543, the year of his death. Copernicus was reluctant to have his work published, but his ideas had spread far and wide even before the appearance of the book in print and enjoyed a considerable degree of serious attention, in spite of his own apprehensions. The book is not merely a proposal of the idea of heliocentrism in general terms, but a rather rigorous and mathematically formulated system of the universe.

An interesting feature of the book is the short introduction written not by Copernicus himself but by his friend Andreas Osiander (1498–1552), a Lutheran theologian, who was in charge of the printing of the book while Copernicus lay in his deathbed. This unauthorized and unsigned introduction, considered by many as a cowardly interference in scientific affairs designed only to preempt religious criticism, is actually a remarkable document. It posits explicitly a point of view in the philosophy of natural science, anticipated by William of Ockham (1287–1347), and amply entrenched in the modern philosophy of science. You will be able to judge for yourself when translating the introduction.

The opening of the book itself finds Copernicus arguing for a preliminary necessary point in his theory, namely, that the universe is spherical and so is the Earth. The perfection of the circle and the sphere was an essential component of ancient physics leading, as it turned out, to incorrect conclusions. Not only the shape of the celestial bodies was necessarily spherical, but also the orbits were necessarily circular or, at the very least, made up of combinations of circular motions. It was only a few years later that Johannes Kepler (1571–1630) arrived at the painful observational conclusion that, in the heliocentric system, the planets actually moved along elliptical trajectories. Just a few years after this disappointing discovery, Isaac Newton (1642–1727) proved that under a central force field the motion of a body must necessarily abide by Kepler's so-called second law (equal areas swept in equal times) and that, in particular, the gravitational field only requires the orbits to be quadrics, not necessarily circular. The Copernican revolution, however, opened the doors for these more refined and more logically based theories. The irony of it all is that Osiander's politically correct preface may not have been so cowardly after all.

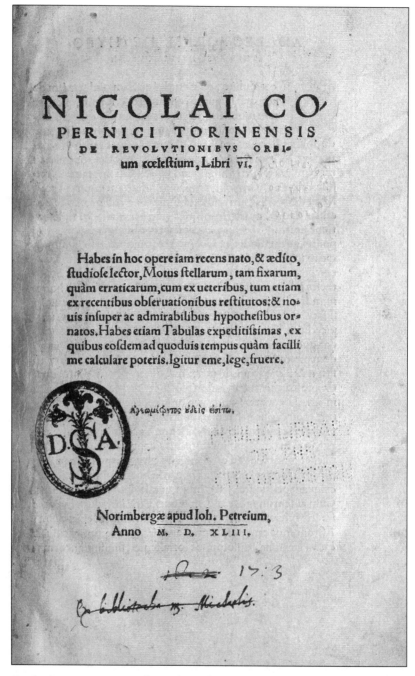

NICOLAI CO-
PERNICI TORINENSIS
DE REVOLVTIONIBVS ORBI-
um cœleſtium, Libri VI.

Habes in hoc opere iam recens nato, & ædito,
ſtudioſe lector, Motus ſtellarum, tam fixarum,
quàm erraticarum, cum ex ueteribus, tum etiam
ex recentibus obſeruationibus reſtitutos: & nouis inſuper ac admirabilibus hypotheſibus or-
natos. Habes etiam Tabulas expeditiſsimas, ex
quibus eoſdem ad quoduis tempus quàm facilli
me calculare poteris. Igitur eme, lege, fruere.

Ἀγεωμέτρητος οὐδεὶς εἰσίτω.

Norimbergæ apud Ioh. Petreium,
Anno M. D. XLIII.

Nicolai Copernici Torinensis de Revolutionibus Orbium Coelestium. Property of the
Boston Public Library. Facsimile courtesy of archive.org.

AD LECTOREM DE HYPO:
THESIBVS HVIVS OPERIS.

 on dubito, quin eruditi quidam, uulgata iam de nouitate hypothefeon huius operis fama, quòd terram mobilem, Solem uero in medio uniuerfi immobilē conftituit, uehementer fint offenfi, putētæ difciplinas liberales recte iam olim conftitutas, turbari nō oportere. Verum fi rem exacte perpendere uolent, inueniēt authorem huius operis, nihil quod reprehendi mereatur cōmififfe. Eft enim Aftronomi proprium, hiftoriam motuum cœleftium diligenti & artificiofa obferuatione colligere. Deinde caufas earundem, feu hypothefes, cum ueras affequi nulla ratione poffit, qualefcunqʒ excogitare & confingere, quibus fuppofitis, ĳdem motus, ex Geometriæ principĳs, tam in futurū, quàm in præteritū recte poffint calculari. Horū autē utruncʒ egregie præftitit hic artifex. Necʒ enim neceffe eft, eas hypothefes effe ueras, imò ne uerifimiles quidem, fed fufficit hoc unum, fi calculum obferuationibus congruentem exhibeant. ni fi forte quis Geometriæ & Optices ufcʒadeo fit ignarus, ut epicyclium Veneris pro uerifimili habeat, feu in caufa effe credat, quod ea quadraginta partibus, & eo amplius, Solē interdum præcedat, interdū fequatur. Quis enim nō uidet, hoc pofito, neceffario fequi, diametrum ftellæ in ασογείω plufcʒ quadruplo, corpus autem ipfum plufcʒ fedecuplo, maiora, quàm in ἀπογείω apparere, cui tamen omnis æui experientia refragatur? Sunt & alia in hac difciplina non minus abfurda, quæ in præfentiarum excutere nihil eft neceffe. Satis enim patet, apparentiū inæqualium mótuū caufas, hanc arte penitus & fimpliciter ignorare. Et fi quas fingēdo excogitat, ut certe quãplurimas excogitat, nequaquã tamen in hoc excogitat, ut ita effe cuiquam perfuadeat, fed tantum, ut calculum recte inftituant. Cum autem unus & eiufdem motus, uarie interdum hypothefes fefe offerant (ut in motu Solis, eccentricitas, & epicyclium) Aftronomus eam potifsimum arripiet, quæ compræhenfu fit quàm facillima, Philofophus fortaffe, ueri fimilitudinem magis re:

gis requiret,neuter tamen quicquam certi compræhedet, aut
tradet,nisi diuinitus illi reuelatum fuerit. Sinamus igitur &
has nouas hypotheses,inter ueteres,nihilo uerisimiliores inno
rescere,præsertim cum admirabiles simul,& faciles sint.ingen
teniœ thesaurum, doctisimarum obseruationum secum ad-
uehant.Necœ quisquam,quod ad hypotheses attinet,quicquã
certi ab Astronomia expectet,cum ipsa nihil tale præstare que
at,ne si in alium usum conficta pro ueris arripiat , stultior ab-
hac disciplina discedat, quàm accesserit. Vale.

NICOLAVS SCHONBERGIVS CAR
dinalis Capuanus , Nicolao Copernico, S.

Vm mihi de uirtute tua,cõstanti omniũ sermone
ante annos aliquot allatũ esset,cœpi tum maiorem
in modũ te animo cõplecti , atcœ gratulari etiã no-
stris hominibus,apud œs tãta gloria floreres.Intellexerã enim
te nõ modo ueterũ Mathematicorũ inuẽta egregie callere,sed
etiã nouã Mũdi rationẽ cõstituisse.Qua doceas terrã moueri:
Solem imũ mũdi , adeoœ mediũ locũ obtinere:Cœlũ octauũ
immotũ,atcœ fixũ ppetuo manere:Lunã se unã cũ inclusis suæ
sphæræ elementis,inter Martis & Veneris cœlũ sitam,anni-
uersario cursu circũ Solem cõuertere.Atcœ de hac tota Astronomiæ ratione cõmentarios à te cõfectos esse, ac erraticarum
stellarũ motus calculis subductos in tabulas te cõtulisse,maxi
ma omniũ cum admiratione.Quamobrem uir doctisime,ni
si tibi molestus sum,te etiã atcœ etiã oro uehementer , ut hoc
tuũ inuentũ studiosis cõmunices,& tuas de mundi sphæra lu
cubrationes unã cũ Tabulis,& si quid habes præterea , œd ad
eandem rem pertineat , primo quocœ tempore ad me mittas.
Dedi autem negotiũ Theodorico à Reden ,ut istic meis sum-
ptibus omnia describantur,atcœ ad me transferantur.Quod si
mihi morem in hac re gesseris,intelliges te cum homine no-
minis tui studioso,& tantæ uirtuti satisfacere cupiente rem ha
buisse. Vale, Romæ, Calend. Nouembris,anno M.D.XXXVI.

ij

De Revolutionibus
Orbium Coelestium

Ad Lectorem de Hypothesibus Huius Operis.

Non dubito, quin eruditi quidam, vulgata iam de novitate
hypotheseon huius operis fama, quod terram mobilem, Solem
vero in medio universi immobile constituit, vehementer sint
5   offensi, putentque disciplinas liberales recte iam olim constitutas,
turbari non oportere. Verum si rem exacte perpendere volent,
invenient authorem huius operis, nihil quod reprehendi mereatur
commisisse. Est enim Astronomi proprium, historiam motuum
coelestium diligenti et artificiosa observatione colligere. Deinde
10   causas earundem, seu hypotheses, cum veras assequi nulla ratione
possit, qualescunque excogitare et confingere, quibus suppositis,
iidem motus, ex Geometriae principiis, tam in futurum quam in
praeteritum recte possint calculari. Horum autem utrunque egregie
praestitit hic artifex. Neque enim necesse est, eas hypotheses
15   esse veras, immo ne verisimiles quidem, sed sufficit hoc unum,
si calculum observationibus congruentem exhibeant. Nisi forte
quis Geometriae et Optices usqueadeo sit ignarus, ut epicyclium
Veneris pro verisimili habeat, seu in causa esse credat, quod ea
quadraginta partibus, et eo amplius, Solem interdum praecedat,
20   interdum sequatur. Quis enim non videt, hoc posito, necessario
sequi, diametrum stellae in περιγείῳ plusquam quadruplo, corpus
autem ipsum plusquam sedecuplo, maiora, quam in ἀπογείῳ apparere,
cui tamen omnis aevi experientia refragatur. Sunt et alia in hac
disciplina non minus absurda, quae in praesentiarum excutere, nihil
25   est necesse. Satis enim patet, apparentium inaequalium motuum
causas, hanc artem penitus et simpliciter ignorare. Et si quas
fingendo excogitat, ut certe quamplurimas excogitat, nequaquam
tamen in hoc excogitat, ut ita esse cuiquam persuadeat, sed
tantum, ut calculum recte instituant. Cum autem unius et eiusdem

30   motus, variae interdum hypotheses sese offerant (ut in motu Solis,
eccentricitas, et epicyclium) Astronomus eam potissimum arripiet,
quae compraehensu sit quam facillima.

Philosophus fortasse, veri similitudinem magis regis requiret,
neuter tamen quicquam certi compraehendet, aut tradet, nisi
35   divinitus illi revelatum fuerit. Sinamus igitur et has novas
hypotheses, inter veteres, nihilo verisimiliores innotescere
praesertim cum admirabiles simul, et faciles sint, ingentemque
thesaurum, doctissimarum observationum secum advehant.
Neque quisquam, quod ad hypotheses attinet, quicquam certi ab
40   Astronomia expectet, cum ipsa nihil tale praestare queat, ne si in
alium usum conficta pro veris arripiat, stultior ab hac disciplina
discedat, quam accesserit. Vale.

• Notes •

Ad Lectorem de Hypothesibus Huius Operis.

2   **quin:** Arising as it does from the combination **qui + ne**, this
particle is a kind of negative relative. With verbs of doubting it
can be translated as *but that.*

2–3   **vulgata . . . fama:** ablative absolute.

3   **hypotheseon:** Greek genitive plural.

3–4   **quod terram mobile . . . constituit:** explaining the novelty of
the hypothesis alluded to above.

4   **sint:** The subject is **eruditi quidam.**

5   **putent:** potential subjunctive, *may think.* The potential
subjunctive appears quite frequently in the subsequent text.

5–6   **putentque disciplinas . . . turbari non oportere:** The infinitive
oportere is governed by **putent** in the typical accusative with
the infinitive construction for indirect statement/oratio obliqua.
The infinitive **turbari** is governed by **oportere**, which is an
impersonal verb translated as *it is appropriate, it behooves.* The
accusative of the indirect statement/oratio obliqua, therefore,
is not **disciplinas** but the understood **id.** As for the use of

    oportere, in English we may say *It is appropriate for her to read* or *It behooves her to read*. In the first sentence *for her* is in the dative case, while in the second sentence *her* is in the accusative. Accordingly, in Latin too we find both constructions: **opportet ei legere** or **opportet eam legere**.

6   **Verum:** *but.*

    exacte: adverb.

7   **authorem:** This is a solecism for **auctorem**. The confusion (entrenched in the English term "author") arises from the belief that it is an originally Greek word. On the contrary, **auctor** derives from the Latin verb **augeo, augere, auxi, auctum**, whose meaning is *to increase*. Thus an **auctor** is one who causes something to increase, an originator.

    mereatur: subjunctive form of **mereor, mereri, meritus sum** *to deserve, to merit*. The verb exists also in the active form **mereo, merere, merui, meritus**, but both forms can be active in meaning.

8   **commisisse:** infinitive active perfect of **committo, committere, commisi, commissum** *to commit*. The main clause is the indirect statement/oratio obliqua: **invenient authorem . . . nihil . . . commisisse**.

    Est enim Astronomi proprium: The implicit subject is the impersonal "it."

8–9   **historiam . . . colligere:** an expression that can mean *to study carefully the facts*.

10   **hypotheses:** nominative plural.

10–11   **cum . . . nulla ratione possit: cum** + subjunctive construction. In this case, we can choose the translation: *Since by means of no reasoning is he able to*. The subject **Astronomus** is understood from the previous sentence.

11   **excogitare et confingere:** We may attach these infinitives to **Est . . . proprium**. *Since the astronomer cannot attain the true causes of the phenomena it is proper for the astronomer to devise and to fabricate some hypotheses whatever.*

quibus suppositis: One way to translate this phrase is as an ablative absolute: *(by means of) which having been laid down.*

12   **tam . . . quam . . .:** *as much . . . as . . .*

13   **possint calculari:** The subject is **iidem motus.**

        utrunque: utrumque. Accusative masculine singular of **uterque, uter + que,** *each one of two, either, both.*

        egregie: adverb. The adjective **egregius, -a, -um** derives from **ex** and **grex, gregis** (m) *a flock.* Thus "egregius" is one that stands out from the flock, someone outstanding, extraordinary.

14   **praestitit: praesto, praestare, praestiti, praestitum,** two of whose meanings are *to exhibit* and *to execute.*

15   **immo:** *nay, on the contrary.*

        ne . . . quidem: *not even.* This sentence is central to the argument. The hypotheses need not be true or even probable (likely to be true). It is enough that they produce a calculation congruent with the observations.

16   **Nisi forte:** *unless perhaps.*

17   **usqueadeo: usque + adeo** = *up to such a point, so much* balanced by **ut** *that.*

        sit: subjunctive because of **forte.** The subject is **quis,** not the interrogative pronoun, but rather the indefinite pronoun **quis, quae, quid,** used mainly after **ne, nisi, num,** and **si,** signifying *anyone, anything.*

17–18   **epicyclium Veneris:** The epicycle of (the planet) Venus. In the geocentric (Ptolemaic) system, the motions of the planets, relative to the Earth, exhibit partial retrograde motion. To account for this phenomenon, while at the same time keeping the Aristotelian obsession with uniform circular motion, Ptolemy assumes that the trajectories have an epicycloidal shape. This shape is obtained by following the trajectory of a point rigidly attached to a wheel that rolls, like a gear, around another circle, resulting in small loop-like portions— epicycles. Each planet has a specific number of epicycles. In the case of Venus, there is just one epicycle. In the heliocentric

(Copernican) model, the trajectories of the planets, with respect to the sun, show no epicycles at all. Which model is correct? From the vantage point of modern understanding, both models are (or can be made to be) in fact equivalent, the trajectory of an object depending on the chosen frame of reference. The Copernican frame, however, is closer to what in Newtonian mechanics is regarded as an inertial frame, where Newton's laws apply. But as far as kinematics is concerned, the Ptolemaic system is, in principle, as good as its Copernican counterpart. The epicycle of Venus, therefore, is literally in the eyes of the beholder. But Osiander goes further to show an internal contradiction in the Ptolemaic account of the epicycle of Venus.

18   **ea:** antecedent is Venus.

19   **quadraginta partibus:** *by forty degrees.* A **pars** is clearly one degree. The division of the circumference into 360 parts is found already in Babylonia and India and is in use to this day. The Napoleonic attempt at dividing the circle into 400 equal parts was doomed to failure. The point here is that, according to Ptolemaic theory, the epicycle of Venus is so large that the apparent diameters of Venus, as seen from the Earth, should vary in a ratio as large as 4, which is not the case in actual observations.

    eo amplius: *more than that.*

20–22   **Quis . . . apparere:** The bare skeleton of the whole sentence is **quis non videt sequi necessario diametrum apparere.** *Who does not see that it necessarily follows that the diameter appears . . . ?* These are two enchained indirect statements/orationes obliquae.

20   **Quis:** here, interrogative pronoun.

    hoc posito: concessive ablative absolute.

    necessario: adverbial sense.

21   **stellae:** Stella may refer to any celestial body, including the planets. Here it refers to Venus.

περιγείῳ: *perigee*, namely, the closest position of the planet's orbit to the Earth. Osiander correctly places the word in the Greek dative case as Greek has no ablative case. The farthest position in the orbit is the apogee (appearing below in the Greek dative as ἀπογείῳ).

plusquam: plus + quam *more than.*

corpus: What does Osiander mean by **corpus** *body?* If it is the volume, then to a diameter four times larger there corresponds a volume 64 times larger. But the text says **sedecuplo** *sixteenfold.* He must, therefore, be referring to the surface area or, most likely, the area of the (flat) visible disk. This point is not clear (or terribly important) in most translations, that simply render *body.*

23   **cui:** dative case with **refragatur** from **refragor, refragari, refractus sum** *to be opposed to.* The subject is **experientia.**

24   **in praesentiarum:** solecism for **in praesentarium,** from the adjective **praesentarius, -a, -um,** meaning *at hand;* here *at the present time, at this moment.*

25   **Satis . . . patet:** *It is sufficiently clear* sets up indirect statement/ oratio obliqua.

26   **hanc artem . . . ignorare:** indirect statement/oratio obliqua depending on **patet.** The *art* here, the subject of **ignorare,** refers to Ptolemaic astronomy.

      penitus: *deeply, wholly.*

      quas: indefinite pronoun **quis, quae, quid** referring back to **causas.**

27   **fingendo:** gerund from **fingo, fingere, finxi, fictum** *to imagine, to fabricate.*

      excogitat: The subject must be **ars.**

      quamplurimas: Plurimus, -a, -um is the superlative of **multus, -a, -um.** Thus, **quam plurimas** means *as many (causes) as possible, very many (causes).* **quam** + superlative = *as much . . . as possible.*

      nequaquam: *by no means.*

28   **cuiquam:** form of the indefinite pronoun **quisquam, quaequam, quicquam**, namely, *anybody, somebody*. The use of the dative here is dictated by the verb **persuadeat**.

29   **instituant:** The plural subject is understood. It must be **causae** or possibly the old astronomers. The point in this sentence is that the various devices are invented as tricks to obtain the right results in the calculations rather than from a desire to persuade anyone that these assumptions are actually true in any sense whatever.

29–30   **Cum . . . variae hypotheses sese offerant: cum** + subjunctive construction. *Since . . . various hypotheses offer themselves.*

30   **hypotheses:** nominative plural feminine.

    ut in motu Solis: some translators have wrongly assumed that this phrase is dependent on **eccentricitas, et epicyclium**. This is not correct. The verb **est** should be supplied after **Solis**. In other words, the author enumerates three separate hypotheses that astronomers adopt from time to time, namely, eccentricity (of the orbits), epicycle (of a planet), and that the sun is in motion.

31–32   **eam . . . quae:** *that (hypothesis) . . . which.*

31   **potissimum:** superlative of **potis** *able, possible*. Here used as an adverb, *most preferably*.

    arripiet: adripiet from **adripio, adripere, adripui, adreptum**. Derived from **ad** + **rapio**. What is the tense of **adripiet**?

32   **compraehensu:** This is a supine ablative form. For example, **facile dictu** means *easy to say*. The supine is a verbal noun of the fourth declension and it is used exclusively in the accusative or ablative singular. It is easily obtained from the fourth principal part of a verb with the endings -*um* (accusative) or -*u* (ablative).

    quam facillima: quam + superlative = *as much . . . as possible*. **Facillimus, -a, -um** is the superlative of **facilis**.

33   **veri similitudinem:** Construe as a single word: *probability, likelihood to be true*. Alternatively, one may consider it as two separate words, in which case it can be translated as *a closeness to the truth*.

34   **neuter: ne** + **uter** = *neither*.

certi: partitive genitive. Thus **quicquam certi** = *something (of) certain.*

35 **divinitus:** adverb.

et: *also.*

36 **nihilo:** *in no way.*

38 **secum: se + cum = cum se.**

39–40 **Neque quisquam . . . expectet:** *and let no one . . . expect.*

40–42 **ne . . . discedat:** *lest . . . he may go away.* It is best to understand the clause **si in alium usum . . . arripiat** as parenthetical.

41 **conficta:** perfect passive participle of **confingo, confingere, confinxi, confictum.** Consider as an accusative neuter plural noun: *things that have been fashioned.*

NICOLAI COPER'
NICI REVOLVTIONVM
LIBER PRIMVS.

Quòd mundus fit fphæricus.   Cap. I.

 R I N C I P I O aduertendum nobis eſt, glo
boſum eſſe mundum, ſiue quòd ipſa for=
ma perfectiſſima ſit omnium, nulla indi=
gens compagine, tota integra : ſiue quòd
ipſa capaciſsima ſit figurarum, quæ com
præhenſurũ omnia, & conſeruaturũ maxi
me decet: ſiue etiam quòd abſolutiſsimæ
quæcp mundi partes, Solem dico, Lunam & ſtellas, tali forma
conſpiciantur: ſiue quòd hac uniuerſa appetãt terminari. quod
in aquæ guttis cæteriſcp liquidis corporibus apparet, dum per
ſe terminari cupiunt. Quo minus talem formam cœleſtibus cor
poribus attributam quiſquam dubitauerit.

Quòd terra quocp ſphærica ſit.   Cap. II.

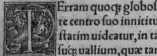Erram quocp globoſam eſſe, quoniam ab omni par=
te centro ſuo innititur. Tametſi abſolutus orbis non
ſtatim uideatur, in tanta montiũ excelſitate, deſcen=
ſucp uallium, quæ tamen uniuerſam terræ rotundita
tem minime uariant. Quod ita manifeſtũ eſt. Nam ad Septen=
trionem undequacp commeantibus, uertex ille diurnæ reuolu=
tionis paulatim attollitur, altero tantundem ex aduerſo ſubeun
te, plurescp ſtellæ circum Septentriones uidentur nõ occidere,
& in Auſtro quædam amplius non oriri. Ita Canopum non cer
nit Italia, Ægypto patentem, Et Italia poſtremam fluuij ſtellam
uidet, quam regio noſtra plagæ rigentioris ignorat. E contra=
rio in Auſtrum tranſeuntibus attolluntur illa, reſidentibus ijs,
quæ nobis excelſa ſunt. Interea & ipſ̨ polorum inclinationes ad
emenſa terrarum ſpacia eandem ubicp rationem habent, quod

                                        a   in

Nicolai Copernici Revolutionum
Liber Primus.

Quod mundus sit sphaericus. Cap. I.

Principio advertendum nobis est, globosum esse mundum,
sive quod ipsa forma perfectissima sit omnium, nulla indigens
compagine, tota integra: sive quod ipsa capacissima sit figurarum,
5   quae compraehensurum omnia, et conservaturum maxime decet:
sive etiam quod absolutissimae quaeque mundi partes, Solem dico,
Lunam et stellas, tali forma conspiciantur: sive quod hac universa
appetant terminari. Quod in aquae guttis caeterisque liquidis
corporibus apparet, dum per se terminari cupiunt. Quo minus talem
10   formam coelestibus corporibus attributam quisquam dubitaverit.

Quod terra quoque sphaerica sit. Cap. II.

Terram quoque globosam esse, quoniam ab omni parte centro suo
innititur. Tametsi absolutus orbis non statim videatur, in tanta
montium excelsitate, descensumque vallium, quae tamen universam
15   terrae rotunditatem minime variant. Quod ita manifestum est. Nam
ad Septentrionem undequaque commeantibus, vertex ille diurnae
revolutionis paulatim attollitur, altero tantundem ex adverso
subeunte, pluresque stellae circum Septentriones videntur non
occidere, et in Austro quaedam amplius non oriri. Ita Canopum non
20   cernit Italia, Aegypto patentem. Et Italia postremam fluvij stellam
videt, quam regio nostra plagae rigentioris ignorat. E contrario in
Austrum transeuntibus attolluntur illa, residentibus iis, quae nobis
excelsa sunt.

• Notes •

Cap. I.

Nicolai Copernici Revolutionum: Notice the genitive case,
both for Copernicus's name and for **revolutionum**. This is the
first book of the *Revolutions of Copernicus*.

1   **sit:** The use of the subjunctive is common in titles of chapters. One may imagine an unwritten part of the title such as: [*This chapter claims*] *that the world be spherical*. The use of the English subjunctive has been in decline for a long time, so today we would say *that the world is spherical*. Copernicus translates this thought (essentially an indirect statement/oratio obliqua) by means of **quod** *that*, whereas Newton might have written it with the more classical accusative with the infinitive construction, as **mundum sphaericum esse**, as he did in the axioms and theorems of his *Principia*. In his *Lectiones Opticae*, however, he sometimes uses the same style as Copernicus. Harvey (in his *Exercitatio Anatomica de Motu Cordis et Sanguinis in Animalibus*), for example, uses the subjunctive in the titles of some of his chapters, without the relative **quod**. Other chapter titles are just verbless phrases and still others are in classical indirect statement/oratio obliqua.

2   **Principio:** ablative of time or space, *in the beginning, to begin with, at the outset*.

     advertendum nobis est: classic passive periphrastic.

     esse: infinitive because of the indirect statement/oratio obliqua introduced by **advertendum**.

3–6   **sive … sive … sive …:** *whether … or … or …*

3   **quod:** *because*.

     sit: The use of the subjunctive is logically implied by the fact that a variety of possible, hence, subjunctive, alternative causes is attributed to the sphericity of the world.

     indigens: indigeo, indigere, indigui *to be in need of* takes the ablative of the thing needed.

4   **capacissima:** superlative of **capax**. This is an allusion to the so-called isoperimetric problem, namely, given a fixed perimeter, to find the figure enclosing the maximum area. This problem is similar to Dido's problem, immortalized in Vergil's *Aeneid* 1.365–368. The solution is, of course, the circle. But a rigorous proof of this fact was only obtained in the nineteenth century by Jakob Steiner, and even this proof has been subjected to mathematical criticism.

5   **compraehensurum, conservaturum:** future active neuter singular participles used as nouns, *the thing that will embrace and conserve.*

decet: decet, decere, decuit *to be fitting, be suited for.* It can be used as an impersonal verb similar to **oportere.** But it can also be used personally, with a subject, as is the case here. The subject is **quae,** referring to **ipsa forma.** A classical example of the personal use of **decet** is **parvum parva decent** (Horace, *Epistulae* [*Letters*] 1.7:44): *Small things befit a small person.*

6   **absolutissimae:** Here **absolutus, -a, -um** is understood as *separate* or *perfect.*

quaeque: quisque, quaeque, quodque *each.*

7   **tali forma:** ablative.

hac: ablative, referring back to **forma.**

universa: *all things.*

9   **Quo minus:** literally, *by which the less.* Thus, the sentence **Quo minus . . . quisquam dubitaverit** can be rendered as *for which reason no one would doubt.*

Cap. II.

12   **globosam esse:** Here Copernicus reverts to the use of the indirect statement/oratio obliqua governed by some unspecified verb, e.g., **dico.**

13   **innititur: innitor, inniti, innixus sum** takes the ablative of the thing on which the subject supports itself. Here Copernicus is being poetic rather than scientific. This is basically an argument of symmetry.

16   **undequaque:** *from anywhere.*

commeantibus: present active plural dative participle of **commeo, commeare** *to come and go,* dative of reference.

vertex ille: *that vertex,* that is, the celestial North Pole.

17–18   **altero . . . subeunte:** ablative absolute. Someone walking northward in the southern hemisphere would observe the celestial South Pole going down.

17   **tantundem: tantusdem, tantadem, tantundem** *just as much.*

19   **Canopum:** Canopus is the second brightest star in the sky (after Sirius). It is visible in the southern hemisphere and only partially in the northern hemisphere, up to the northern latitude of about 37 degrees. Since Italy, the subject of the sentence, excluding Sicily, extends between 38 and 47 degrees, Copernicus is right in his assertion. Notice that Egypt's extreme latitudes are 22 and 32 degrees.

20   **fluvij: fluvii** genitive singular of **fluvius** *river.* This is another name of the southern constellation Eridanus, the name of the river Po in Greek. Its last (southernmost) and brightest star is Alpha-Eridanus or Achernar (from Arabic: *the end of the river*), with a declination of 57 degrees, almost 4 degrees larger than Canopus and, thus, less visible from the northern hemisphere. In earlier days, however, the last star of the constellation was supposed to be Acamar (Theta- Eridanus) with a declination of about 40 degrees and thus visible from the northern hemisphere at latitudes of up to 50 degrees. With latitudes from 50 to 54 degrees at Copernicus's time, it would not have been visible from Poland, located, as he says, in the region of the colder zone.

Johannes Kepler

I n the history of astronomy, Johannes Kepler (1571–1630) is regarded as having provided the link between Nicolaus Copernicus and Isaac Newton. By placing a reference frame at the sun, rather than the earth, Copernicus achieved a considerable simplification of the kinematic description of the planetary system. Nevertheless, the Copernican system was still confidently relying on the Aristotelian-Ptolemaic bias toward circular orbits (or compositions thereof). More significantly, the Copernican system did not provide any causal (dynamic) explanation for the motion of the planets. Kepler tackled both these issues, achieving success only on the first. In an early work, Kepler had expressed his belief in a geometrical arrangement of the universe based on a nested set of the five Platonic solids. The long road from this view to his portentous contributions in *Astronomia Nova* (*New Astronomy*, 1609) is one of the great adventures in the history of science.[20] Without a clear notion of the gravitational force, Kepler, who had by then become convinced, against his own intuition, that the orbits were not circular but elliptical, understood that this force or "virtue" waned with the distance to the sun. On this basis, Kepler assumed that the transversal component of the velocity of a planet was inversely proportional to this distance, an assumption consistent with the elliptical shape. He thus arrived at his celebrated law of the equality of areas swept in equal times. A more definitive formulation of his laws was published a decade later as the *Epitome Astronomiae Copernicanae* (*An Epitome of Copernican Astronomy*), from which we selected our two selections from books 1 and 5.

---

20 A fascinating account of this adventure, based on Kepler's diaries, is given in A. Koestler, *The Sleepwalkers* (New York: MacMillan, 1959). (Other editions exist.)

EPITOME
ASTRONOMIAE
Copernicanæ

Usitatâ formâ Quæſtionum & Reſpon-
ſionum conſcripta, inq; VII. Libros digeſta, quorum TRES hi priores ſunt de

Doctrina Sphærica.

*HABES, AMICE LECTOR, HAC PRIMA
parte, præter phyſicam accuratam explicationem Motus
Terræ diurni, ortuq; ex eo circulorum Sphæra, totam do-
ctrinam Sphæricam noVa & concinniori METHODO,
auctiorem, additis Exemplis omnis generis Computatio-
num Aſtronomicarum & Geographicarum;quæ in-
tegrarum præceptionum Vim ſuut com-
plexa.*

AVTHORE

JOANNE KEPPLERO IMP: CÆS:
MATTHIÆ, Ordd: q; Illium Archiduca-
tus Auſtriæ ſupra Onaſum, Ma-
thematico.

Cum Privilegio Cæſareo ad Annos XV.

Lentijs ad Danubium, excudebat
Johannes Plancus.

ANNO MDCXVIII.

*Epitome astronomiae copernicanae, usitatâ formâ quaestionum & respon-
sionum*, Lentiis ad Danubium, 1618. Property of the Fisher Library at the
University of Toronto. Facsimile courtesy of archive.org.

EPITOMES
ASTRONOMIAE
Copernicanæ

LIBER PRIMVS.

De principiis Astro-
nomiæ in genere, doctrinæq́;
SPHÆRICÆ in specie.

QVid est ASTRONOMIA?

EST scientia, causas tradens eorum,
quæ nobis in Terra versantibus de cœlo & stellis
apparent, Temporumq́; vicissitudines pariunt : quibus
perceptis, cœli faciem, hoc est, Apparentias cœlestes in
futurum prædicere, præteritarumq́; certa tempora assignare possimus,

Vnde dicta est Astronomia?

Ab Astrorum, id est motuum, quibus astra moventur, lege seu regimine, ut Oeconomia à regenda re
domestica, Pædonomus à regendis pueris.

Quæ est cognatio hujus Scientiæ cum cæteris?

1. Est pars Physices, quia inquirit causas rerum & e-
ventuum naturalium : & quia inter ejus subjecta sunt
motus corporum cœlestium : & quia vnus finis ejus est,
conformationem ædificij mundani partiumq́; ejus indagare.

A   2. Geo-

2 EPITOMES ASTRONOMIÆ,

2. Geographiæ & Hydrographiæ feu Rei Nauticæ
anima est Astronomia. Quæ enim diversis Terrarum
Oceaniq; locis & plagis diversa cœlitus eveniunt, ex sola Astronomia dijudicantur.

3. Subordinatam habet Chronologiam, quia motus
cœlestes disponunt tempora annosq; politicos, & signant historias.

4. Subordinatam habet Meteorologiam. Astra enim
movent & incitant Naturam sublunarem & homines
ipsos quodammodò.

5. Complectitur magnam partem Optices, quia cō-
mune cum ipsa subjectum habet, Lucem corporum
cœlestium: & quia multas visus deceptiones circa mundi motuumq; formas detegit.

6. Subest tamen generi Mathematicarum disciplinarum, & Geometria atq; Arithmetica pro duabus alis
vtitur; quantitates & figuras considerans corporum
motuumq; mundanorum, & tempora dinumerans,
perq; hæc demonstrationes suas expediens : & totam
speculationem ad vsum seu praxin deducens.

Quotuplex est igitur Astronomi
cura munusq; ?

Partes muneris Astronomici potissimùm quinque sunt, Historica de Observationibus, Optica de Hypothesibus, Physica de causis Hypothesium, Arithmetica de Tabulis & Calculo, Mechanica de Instrumentis.

Quomodo inter se differunt ?

Etsi nulla earum potest carere demonstrationibus Geometricis, quæ ad Theoriam faciunt, Numerisque, qui ad Praxin, cum sint quidam quasi sermo Geometrarum : tres tamen priores magis ad Theoriam pertinent, duæ vltimæ magis ad Praxin.

De

Epitomes Astronomiae Copernicae
Epitomes Astronomiae Copernicae Liber Primus.

De principiis Astronomiae in genere, doctrinaeque Sphaericae in specie.

Quid est Astronomia?

    Est scientia, causas tradens eorum, quae nobis in Terra
5 versantibus de coelo et stellis apparent, Temporumque vicissitudines
pariunt: quibus perceptis, coeli faciem, hoc est, Apparentias coelestes
in futurum praedicere, praeteritarumque certa tempora assignare
possimus.

Unde dicta est Astronomia?

10   Ab Astrorum, id est motuum, quibus astra moventur, lege seu
regimine, ut Oeconomia a regenda re domestica, Paedonomus a
regendis pueris.

Quae est cognatio hujus Scientiae cum ceteris?

    1. Est pars Physices, quia inquirit causas rerum et eventuum
15 naturalium: et quia inter ejus subjecta sunt motus corporum
coelestium: et quia unus finis ejus est, conformationem aedificij
mundani partiumque eius indagare.

    2. Geographiae et Hydrographiae seu Rei Nauticae anima est
Astronomia. Quae enim diversis Terrarum Oceanique locis et plagis
20 diversa coelitus eveniunt, ex sola Astronomia dijudicantur.

    3. Subordinatam habet Chronologiam, quia motus coelestes
disponunt tempora annosque politicos, et signant historias.

    4. Subordinatam habet Meteorologiam. Astra enim movent et
incitant Naturam sublunarem et homines ipsos quodammodo.

25   5. Complectitur magnam partem Optices, quia commune cum
ipsa subjectum habet, Lucem corporum coelestium: et quia multas
visus deceptiones circa mundi motuumque formas detegit.

6. Subest tamen generi Mathematicarum disciplinarum, et
Geometria atque Arithmetica pro duabus alis utitur; quantitates
30   et figuras considerans corporum motuumque mundanorum, et
tempora dinumerans, perque haec demonstrationes suas expediens:
et totam speculationem ad usum seu praxin deducens.

Quotuplex est igitur Astronomi cura munusque?

Partes muneris Astronomici potissimum quinque sunt, Historica
35   de Observationibus, Optica de Hypothesibus, Physica de causis
Hypothesium, Arithmetica de Tabulis et Calculo, Mechanica de
Instrumentis.

Quomodo inter se differunt?

Etsi nulla earum potest carere demonstrationibus Geometricis,
40   quae ad Theoriam faciunt, Numerisque, qui ad Praxin, cum sint
quidam quasi sermo Geometrarum: tres tamen priores magis ad
Theoriam pertinent, duae ultimae magis ad Praxin.

• Notes •

Liber Primus.

Epitomes: a Greek word meaning *abridgment*. May be Latinized
as **epitome, -ae** (f) or left in the Greek form **epitome, -es**,
which form Kepler uses here, as also in the opening of the first
book. This long book was intended by Kepler as some kind of
textbook of modern astronomy. He had already published his
Astronomia Nova a decade earlier. Kepler attempts to be as
didactic as possible, while framing his arguments as responses to
hypothetical questions. This selection is the opening of the first
volume.

1–2   **in genere . . . in specie:** *in general . . . in particular.* This is
neither the only nor the most classical use of these expressions,
but the intention is clear here from the context.

4   **eorum, quae:** Construe as *of those things which.*

in Terra: *on Earth.* It is common in Latin, as well as in the Romance languages, not to distinguish always between *in* and *on.*

5   **versantibus:** dative with **nobis,** induced by **apparent.**

6   **pariunt: pario, parere, peperi, partum** *to bring forth, to bear.* The subject is still **quae.**

        quibus perceptis: ablative absolute.

6–8   **coeli . . . possimus:** This long sentence may be rearranged as **Possimus praedicere faciem coeli (hoc est, apparentias coelestes in futurum) et assignare certa tempora praeteritarum (apparentiarum).**

10   **Ab Astrorum:** Reminder: the preposition **ab** takes the ablative case. It follows that **astrorum** is not governed by **ab**! Understand the order as **ab lege seu regimine astrorum, id est motuum, quibus astra moventur.**

        moventur: In English the verb *to move* can be understood as transitive (she moves something) or intransitive (she moves from one place to another). In Latin, the verb **moveo, movere, movi, motum** is exclusively transitive. To express the intransitive action of moving, Latin employs either the reflexive **se movet** or the passive **movetur.**

11   **Oeconomia . . . Paedonomus . . . :** Here Kepler is following in the footsteps of Isidore of Seville, trying to explain the etymology of **Astronomia.** His point is that in Greek the word **nomos** means *law.* Thus, economics is the discipline that deals with the laws of the house (Greek **oikos**), and Paidonomos (from the Greek **paidos,** *child*) was a Spartan official whose duties involved the military training of children and youngsters. Other similar examples are agronomy and gastronomy.

11–12   **a regendis pueris:** Notice the stylistic use of the gerundive instead of the gerund, **a regendo pueros,** namely, *from ruling children.*

13   **cognatio: cognatio, -onis** (f), *relationship, kinship.* Notice how these introductory paragraphs follow, in some measure, the pattern set by Vitruvius in *De Architectura.* The discipline is defined and related to other disciplines.

14   **Physices:** Just as with **epitomes**, Latin has both the Latinized **physica, -ae** (f) and the original Greek form **physice, -es** (f). We can, therefore, understand **Physices** as genitive. *It is part of physics.*

18   **Geographiae ... anima est Astronomia ...: Astronomia est anima Geographiae ...**

19   **Quae:** neuter plural nominative. This is a new sentence and **quae** does not refer to anything previously said. It just starts with **Quae ... diversa ... eveniunt** *Those various things that happen ...*

20   **coelitus:** alternative spelling for **caelitus**, an indeclinable adverb meaning *heavenly, from the heavens, divinely.*

     dijudicantur: diiudico, -are *to decide, to judge between.*

24   **homines ipsos quodammodo:** In spite of his scientific mind, Kepler was also a believer in astrology.

25   **Optices:** Compare **epitomes** and **physices.**

26   **ipsa:** feminine because it refers back to **Optices.**

27   **visus deceptiones: visus, -us** (m), genitive here, *deceptions of vision,* i.e., *optical illusions.*

28   **Subest: subsum, subesse, subfui** with dative, *to be close to.*

29   **alis:** ablative plural of **ala, -ae** (f) *a wing.* Kepler sometimes waxes poetic.

     utitur: utor, uti, usus sum takes the ablative, *to make use of.* It follows that the subject is still the implied **Astronomia,** while **Arithmetica** and **Geometria** must be in the ablative case.

31   **perque ... expediens:** It may be useful to reorder the Latin as follows: **Et expediens per haec (id est, per haec supradicta) suas demonstrationes.** Thus, Astronomy uses Mathematics to facilitate the demonstration of its laws.

32   **praxin:** Greek accusative of **praxis, praxeos** (f).

     deducens: deduco, deducere, deduxi, deductum does not necessarily mean *to deduce.* Its primary meaning is *to lead down* and *to take away, to deduct, to reduce.* Kepler was, first and foremost, an outstanding mathematician.

33 **Quotuplex: quotuplex, quotuplicis**, derived from **quot +
multiplex**, *how manifold.*

est: The verb is singular, while the subject is plural, **cura
munusque**. This apparent grammatical incongruence is
an example of what is called in Greek *synesis* and in Latin
constructio ad sensum. It appears quite frequently both in
classical and in later Latin.

34 **potissimum:** used adverbially, *chiefly.*

Historica: The term **historia** does not necessarily refer to
history, but rather to the gathering of data for an inquiry into any
matter.

39 **Etsi:** *even if.* When followed by the correlative **tamen**, it is
rendered as **etsi . . . tamen . . .** *although . . . nevertheless . . .*

carere: careo, carere, carui, (caritum) *to be lacking in* takes the
ablative.

40 **faciunt: facere** + **ad** + accusative can be rendered as *to be suited to.*

40–41 **cum . . . Geometrarum:** This is a parenthetical remark. **Cum
sint** is probably best translated in this case as *although they
are . . .* Even those parts of astronomy pertaining to practical
applications sound sometimes as if they were the parlance of
geometers!

EPITOMES
ASTRONOMIÆ
Copernicanæ,
Vsitata formâ Quæstionum & Responsio-
num conscriptæ,

LIBER QUARTUS,
Doctrinæ THEORICÆ Primus:

QVO

Physica Cœlestis,

HOC EST,
OMNIVM IN COELO MAGNITVDI=
num, motuum, proportionumq́, causæ vel Naturales vel Archetypicæ explicantur,

ET SIC
PRINCIPIA DOCTRINÆ
Theoricæ demonstrantur,

QVI QVOD VICE SVPPLEMENTI LIBRO-
rum Aristotelis de Cælo esset, certo consilio seor-
sim est editus.

AUTHORE
IOANNE KEPPLERO,
Cum Privilegio Cæsareo ad Annos XV.

Lentiis ad Danubium, impensis Gode=
fridi Tampachii excudebat Iohannes
Plancus.

ANNO M. DC. XXII.

LIBER QVINTVS. 665

appropinquat proportioni graduum PG. Vergit tamen ver-
ſus D. quidem ad proportionem ſinuum DB. ad GF. at ver-
ſus P. ad proportionem ſagittarum BP. ad FP.

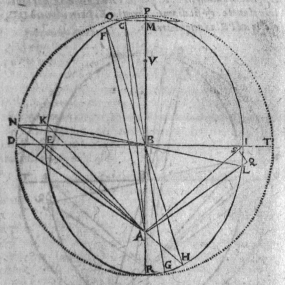

IV·
DE MENSVRA TEMPORIS, SEV MO-
RÆ PLANETÆ IN QVOLIBET ARCV
orbitæ.

Qua ratione planum Elliptici ſegmenti fit aptum ad
menſurandam planetæ moram in illius
ſegmenti arcu?

NOn aliter, quàm ſi diuiſione circuli in partes æ-
quales, conſtituantur arcus ellipſeos inæquales,
& parui circa Apſidas, maiuſculi circa longitudines
medias, in hunc modum.

Centro B. interuallo BP. ſcribatur circulus PDPT. cu-
ius diameter PBR. & in eo, vt in lineâ Apſidum, A. Sol,

Bbbb 5 *ſont*

666 EPITOMES ASTRONOMIÆ

fons motus versus R. AB. Eccentricitas, eique æqualis BV.
versus P. ut P. R. sint Apsides.

Iam punctis A V. focis existentibus, scribatur Ellipsis,
tangens circulum in P. R. quæ sit PERI. repræsentans orbi-
tam planetæ: & sit diameter breuior E. I. circuli verò DT.
erecta ad P R. ad angulos rectos.

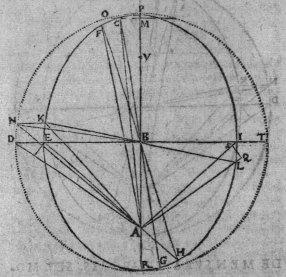

Diuidatur iam semicirculus PDR. in partes æquales
minutas, & sint P. O. N. D. R. T. signa inter diuisiones, ex
quibus ducantur ipsi lineæ apsidum PR. perpendiculares, ut
OM. NK. secantes Ellipsin in C.K. punctis. Connexis igitur
punctis C. K. E. I. sectionum cum A. Sole, dico moram Pla-
netæ in arcu PC. mensurari ab areâ PCA. sic mora in arcu
PCK. mensuram esse penes aream PCKA. & mora in PE.
mensuram penes aream PEA. denique mora in PER. se-
misse Orbitæ ab Apside P. ad apsidem R. mensuram esse a-
ream PERP. quæ itidem semissis est areæ totius Ellipsis
PERIP.

                                                    Ostende

LIBER QVINTVS. 667

*Oftende quanam in proportione per hanc fectionem orbitæ
planetæ partes mediæ fiant maiores partibus circa apfidas?*

In proportione femidiametri longioris ad breuiorem.

Sint enim in circulo partes æquales PO. *&* ND. *illa a-
pud Apfidem* P. *hæc apud longitudinem mediam* D. *Cum
igitur iu refpondeant de fecta ellipfi, arcus* PC. KE. *iam fupra dictum eft,* KE. *effe æqualem ipfi* ND (*fuppofita diuifio-
ne minutiffima)erit igitur* KE. *etiam æqualis ipfi* PO. *Amplius dictum eft,ficut fe habeat* OM. *ad* MC. *hoc eft* DB. *ad*
BE. *feu femidiameter logior* PB. *ad breuiorem* BE *fic fe habere* PO, *arcum circuli, ad* PC. *arcum ellipfis: vt igitur* PB.
ad BE. *fic etiam erit* KE. *arcus ellipfis in mediâ longitudine
ad* PC. *arcum in Apfide.*

*Quid fequitur ad hanc fectionem orbitæ ellipticæ in
arcus inæquales?*

Hoc fequitur, vt arcubus orbitæ circa ambas Apfidas fimul fumptis, minoribus exiftentibus, & arcubus
circa vtramque longitudinem mediam fimul fumptis, maioribus exiftentibus, attribuantur pro menfu-
ris morarum in iis, areæ æquales : cùm tamen illi fimul fumpti diftent æqualiter à fole cum his fimul
fcriptis.

Sint enim æquales vt fupra, PC. *&* RG. *erunt etiam æ-
quales areæ* PCB. *&* RGB. *Sint iterum æquales* KE. *&* LI.
*inter fe, maiores verò prioribus vt iam demonftratum eft:
erunt etiam æquales areæ* KEB. *&* LIB.

Iam verò demonftratum eft, vt fe habet PB. *ad* BE. *fic fe
habere (in traditâ fectione orbitæ)* KE *ad* PC. *Sunt igitur
triangula* BPC. *&* BEK. *(rectilinea vel quafi: cuiuſvis pó-
tæ, quia vt altitudo vnius* BP. *ad altitudinem alterius* BE.
fic bafis huius KE. *ad bafin illius* PC. *Quare areæ* BEK. *&
BPC. *funt inter fe æquales. Igitur & iunctorum* BEK BIL.
areæ funt æquales arcu iunctorum BPC. BRG. *Sed* BPC.
BRG. *iuncta funt æquales iunctis* APC. ARG. *quia altitu-*
dines

dines BP. BR. æquales sunt iunctæ, altitudinibus iunctis
AP. AR. Et BEK. BIL. iunctæ area sunt æquales iunctis
AEK AIL; quia super basibus EK IL. seu earum contin-
gentibus in E I. triangula BEK AEK item BIL AIL. ha-
bent easdem altitudines BE. BI. & bases easdem, illa EK.
hac IL. Igitur hic area E AK I AL. tribuuntur longis arcu-
bus KE. LI. iisque æquales area APC. ARG. tribuuntur
breuioribus arcubus PC. RG. iunctis: cum tamen illorum
distantiæ à Sole EA. AI. iunctæ, sint æquales iunctis horum
PA. AR. vt prius est demonstratum.

Si inæqualibus æqualiter à Sole distantibus assignantur æ-
quales area: tempora vero seu moræ inæqualium, æqua-
liter à Sole distantium etiam inæqualia esse debent, per axi-
oma superius vsurpatum: quomodo igitur area æ-
quales metientur moras inæqua
les?

Etsi hoc pacto bigæ arcuum sunt inter se reuerâ in-
quales, æquipollent tamen æqualibus in participan-
do tempore periodico.

Dictum quidem est in superioribus, diuisâ orbitâ
in particulas minutissimas æquales: accrescere iis moras planetæ per eas, in proportione interuallorum inter eas & Solem. Id verò intelligendum est non de omnimoda portionum æqualitate, sed de iis potissimum,
quæ rectâ obiiciuntur soli, vt de PC. RG. vbi recti sunt
anguli APC. ARG. in cæteris verò obliquè obiectis intelligendum est hoc de eo solùm, quod de qualibet illarum portionum competit motui circa Solem. Nam
quia orbita planetæ est eccentrica, miscentur igitur ad
eam efformandam duo motûs elementa, vt hactenus
fuit demonstratum, alterum est circumlationis circa
Solem virtute Solis, vna reliquum librationis versus
Solem virtute Solis alia distinctâ à priori. Vt in IL. termini I. & L. inæquales habent distantias ab A. fonte motus, continuata igitur AL. in Q. vt AQ. sit
quantitate media inter AL. & AI. & centro A. interuallo

LIBER QVINTVS. 669

lo AQ.ſcripto arcu QS.ſecante longiorem AI.in S.ar-
cus quidem QS. eſt de priore motus compoſiti elemento,differentia verò inter AL.AI.ſeu LQ.& SI.iun-
ctæ portiones, ſunt de poſteriore motus elemento,
quod iam mente ſeparandum eſt:nihil enim ei debetur de tempore periodico, cum iam in ſuperioribus
ſuam portionem acceperit, vbi de libratione agebatur,legibus aliis. Atqui nõ aliâ viâ ſeparari poteſt hoc
alterum motus elementum,quàm ſectione illa orbitæ
in partes inæquales,quam ſupra tradidimus. Quantum enim excedunt iunctæ KE.LI.iunctasPC.RG.to-
tum, id eſt, de poſteriori motus elemento ; & illo ex-
ceſſu ſeparato, relinquitur de priori elemento aliquid
quod eſt æquale iunctis PC. RG. quod ſic demon-
ſtro.

Quia enim AE. AI.per ſuperius demonſtrata ſunt æqua-
les ipſis BP. BR. quare ſcriptis arcubus per E.I ſigna,quorũ
ill de areâ AEK.tantundem abſecat & excludit verſus K.
quantum iſte ad AIL. adſciſcit ſupra L. vt ita triangula
(ſectores verius) nouas has baſes rectas nanciſcantur loco
baſium obliquarum KE.LI. fiet vt areâ, iunctis PCB.RGB.
æquali, ad AE. AI.applicata, baſes etiam ſeu arcus per E.I.
ſcripti, fiant æquales baſibus per PR. ſcriptis. Atqui prius
eſt demonſtratum iunctas areas KEA. LIA. eſſe æquales
iunctis PCB.RGB. Quod igitur de obliquis baſibus KE.LI.
pertinet ad circumlationem circa Solem, id æquale eſt ar-
cubus PC.RG. iunctis , vbi nulla fere miſcetur ei libratio
verſus Solem , quia AP. AC.ſunt in differentia inſenſibili,
ſic & AR.AG.

Eadem demonſtrabuntur etiam de aliis particulis orbi-
tæ:vt ſi ſumatur CF. & continuatis CB.FB.in G.& H.ad-
iungatur reſpondens ei GH.punctaq̃ quatuor cum A fonte
motus connectantur Nam demonſtratũ eſt in ſuperioribus,
iunctas CA. AG. necnon & iunctas FA. AH. æquales eſſe
iũctis PA. AR.ſeu PR diametro lõgiori;quare etiã, vt prius
area ACF. AGH iuncta erũt æquales iunctis BCF.BGH.&
per has, iũctis APC. ARG quæuis CF per inſtitutã ſectionis
rationem

Liber Quintus.
De Mensura Temporis, Seu Morae Planetae in Quolibet Arcu Orbitae.

Dictum quidem est in superioribus, divisam orbitam in particulas minutissimas aequales: accrescere iis moras planetae per eas, in proportione intervallorum inter eas et Solem. Id vero intelligendum est non de omnimoda portionum aequalitate, sed de iis potissimum,

5   quae recta obiiciuntur soli, ut de PC.RG. ubi recti sunt anguli APC. ARG. in caeteris vero oblique obiectis intelligendum est hoc de eo solum, quod de qualibet illarum portionum competit motui circa Solem. Nam quia orbita planetae est eccentrica, miscentur igitur ad eam efformandam duo motus elementa, ut hactenus fuit

10 demonstratum, alterum est circulationis circa Solem virtute Solis, una reliquum librationis versus Solem virtute Solis alia distincta a priori. Ut in IL. termini I. et L. inaequales habent distantias ab A. fonte motus, continuata igitur AL. in Q. ut AQ. sit quantitate media inter AL. et AI. et centro A. intervallo AQ. scripto arcu QS.

15 secante longiorem AI. in S. arcus quidem QS. est de priore motus compositi elemento, differentia vero inter AL. AI. seu LQ. et SI. iunctae portiones, sunt de posteriore motus elemento, quod iam mente separandum est: nihil enim ei debetur de tempore periodico, cum iam in superioribus suam portionem acceperit, ubi de libratione

20 agebatur, legibus aliis.

• Notes •

The previous excerpt from Kepler's *Epitome* may have conveyed the impression that Kepler is a "friendly" author, addressing his book to the general public. Nothing is farther from the truth. Kepler writes page after page of sometimes awkward mathematical reasoning. Kepler's genius manifests itself in his scientific honesty, having recognized that his point of departure was actually contradicted by the results of his own observations, and in the precise formulation of his remarkable laws. Lacking a dynamic theory, his laws were not actually demonstrable mathematically from first principles. This task was left to Newton. One of the most astounding aspects of Newton's *Principia* is that, almost at the very beginning of his magnum opus, Newton produces a magnificent and incredibly simple geometric proof of a generalized version of Kepler's Second Law of planetary motion. For the sake of comparison, we reproduce here Kepler's own formulation of this law followed later by Newton's proof.

Liber Quintus.

1   **in superioribus:** *in the above.*

divisam: Supply **esse** to complete the indirect statement/oratio obliqua introduced by **Dictum . . . est.**

Particula is the diminutive of **pars.**

1–2   **particulas minutissimas:** Kepler is in desperate need of the infinitesimal calculus, which he is trying to invent as he goes.

2   **moras: mora, -ae** (f). The main meaning of **mora** is *delay* (as in "moratorium"), but it can also mean *the lapse of time.*

per eas: referring to **particulas.**

2–3   **in proportione intervallorum:** Kepler has somehow arrived at the conclusion that the times elapsed on equal (and small) lengths of arcs of the orbit of a planet are proportional to the respective distances to the sun.

3–4   **Id vero intelligendum est: vero** = *but.* **intelligendum est:** passive periphrastic. He still has to fix the argument, because his conclusion holds only for arcs that happen to be perpendicular to the "radius vector" (the line joining the instantaneous position of the planet with the sun). In the figure of facsimile page 666, Kepler points at the small arcs PC and RG, which happen to be at the two extremes of the ellipse, where the tangent is indeed perpendicular to the radius. The expression **quae recta obiiciuntur soli** literally means *which are thrown to the sun in a straight line,* but Kepler immediately clarifies this expression by pointing out that the angles APC and ARG are right angles, while in other portions, **oblique**

obiectis, *obliquely thrown*, that proportionality is to be understood *only* (**solum**) *about that which matches* or *pertains to* (**competit** + dative) the motion around the sun. Clearly, if Kepler knew about angular momentum or, more generally, about the cross product of vectors, he would have an easier time expressing himself. *That which pertains to the motion around the sun* simply means the transversal component of the velocity. The next few lines address this issue.

8–12   **Nam ... priori:** Kepler attempts to propose some kind of gravitational theory. The sun exerts some kind of forces, **virtutes**, which are the ultimate cause of the motion of the planets.

8   **orbita planetae est eccentrica:** Even in Ptolemaic and Copernican astronomy, where the orbits are circular, with or without epicycles, the motions are eccentric. This feature was needed to account for observations. Kepler discovered that the orbits are actually ellipses and that the sun occupies one of the foci—which is his First Law of planetary motion.

9   **ad ... efformandam: efformo, -are** *to form, to shape*; **ad** + gerundive expresses purpose.

    motus: genitive.

11–12   **distincta a priori:** *different from the previous one.* Kepler naively considers that the sun exerts two different forces, one pulling toward it and the other taking care of pushing the planet along its path. By discarding the second "virtue" and replacing it with the principle of inertia, Newton solved the problem.

12–18   **Ut ... separandum est:** passive periphrastic. This very long sentence is relatively clear, particularly when looking at the drawing. What Kepler achieves here is a decomposition of the instantaneous motion along the "oblique" arc IL into two components: the first (transverse) component is perpendicular to the radius AL, while the second component is made up of the sum of LQ and IS. This second (radial) motion must be separated out in the reader's mind.

18   **nihil enim ei debetur de tempore periodico:** *for nothing relating to the periodic time is owed to it.*

19 **cum iam . . . acceperit:** *since it has already received.* The "libration," radial motion, has already been accounted for by other laws.

From here on, we don't really need to follow Kepler's argument. If we assume that the proportionality law enunciated above applies not to the arcs themselves but to their transverse components, we obtain Kepler's Second Law. At any rate, this is not an actual proof, but nothing more or less than an assumption ad hoc.

This valiant effort, quite apart from demonstrating Kepler's genius, shows that the advent of Newton was absolutely necessary to place motions of the heavens within the larger compass of a rational science of mechanics that would subsume all possible motions, from the mundane proverbial fall of an apple to the celestial harmony of the spheres. The unparalleled genius of Newton succeeded to achieve this goal by means of a small number of laws general enough to be up to the grand unifying task and simple enough to pass the test of Occam's razor. As demonstrated in the next section, Kepler's Second Law is a mere consequence of Newton's laws when applied to a central force field. The proof is rather elementary and almost purely geometric, written in a style that would have been comprehensible to Eudoxus of Cnidus (ca. 395) or Archimedes.

Isaac Newton

A mong all the works of the Western scientific canon none has a better claim to occupy the first place than Sir Isaac Newton's (1642–1727) *Philosophiae Naturalis Principia Mathematica* (*The Mathematical Principles of Natural Philosophy*). Published in 1687, this book was, and still is, revolutionary in its aims, nothing less than the rigorous accounting of the laws of motion of material bodies, and in its method. It inaugurates modern physical science by establishing rational mechanics as a mathematical discipline based upon a set of axioms from which experimentally verifiable conclusions can be deduced logically. Before this magnum opus, Newton had created calculus, a tool that was indispensable to implement his physical ideas. For the modern reader, accustomed to the current formulations and notations, based mainly on Gottfried Wilhelm Leibniz's competing approach, it is perhaps surprising to realize that in the *Principia* Newton limited the analytic use of derivatives while adhering more to the old Greek, Eudoxian-Archimedean tradition based on geometrically clear limits. Perhaps aware of the importance of his new physics, he wanted, first and foremost, to be understood by as many people as possible.

Within the *Principia*, there are two pages that stand out as the distillation of the basic principles underlying the whole book, just as the Decalogue (the Ten Commandments) in the Bible. Our first selection, therefore, consists precisely of these two pages.

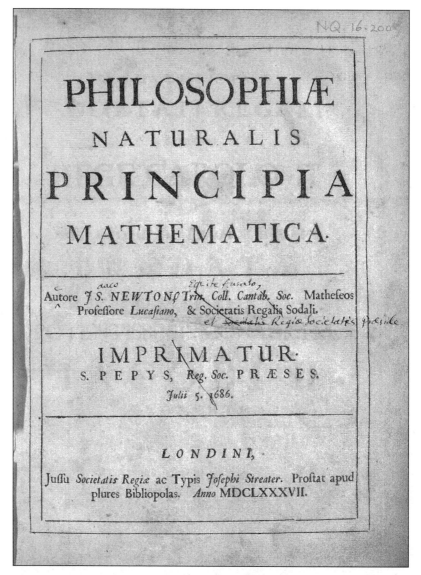

Newton, *Principia*: Facsmile of a 1687 printing. Master and Fellows of Trinity College Cambridge

Lib. 1. Axiomata

[12]

AXIOMATA
SIVE
LEGES MOTUS

Lex. I.

*Corpus omne perseverare in statu suo quiescendi vel movendi unifor-
miter in directum, nisi quatenus a viribus impressis cogitur statum
illum mutare.*

Rojectilia perseverant in motibus suis nisi quatenus a resistentia aeris retardantur & vi gravitatis impelluntur deorsum.
Trochus, cujus partes cohærendo perpetuo retrahunt sese
a motibus rectilineis, non cessat rotari nisi quatenus ab aere retardatur. Majora autem Planetarum & Cometarum corpora motus suos & progressivos & circulares in spatiis minus resistentibus
factos conservant diutius.

Lex. II.

*Mutationem motus proportionalem esse vi motrici impressæ, & fieri se-
cundum lineam rectam qua vis illa imprimitur.*

Si vis aliqua motum quemvis generet, dupla duplum, tripla triplum generabit, sive simul & semel, sive gradatim & successive impressa fuerit; Et hic motus quoniam in eandem semper plagam
cum vi generatrice determinatur, si corpus antea movebatur, motui ejus vel conspiranti additur, vel contrario subducitur, vel obliquo oblique adjicitur, & cum eo secundum utriusq; determinationem componitur. Lex. III.

Lib. I. Axiomata

[13]
Lex. III.

*Actioni contrariam semper & æqualem esse reactionem : sive Corporum
duorum actiones in se mutuo semper esse æquales & in partes contrarias dirigi.*

Quicquid premit vel trahit alterum, tantundem ab eo premitur
vel trahitur. Siquis lapidem digito premit, premitur & hujus
digitus a lapide. Si equus lapidem funi alligatum trahit, retrahetur etiam & equus æqualiter in lapidem : nam funis utrinq; distentus
eodem relaxandi se conatu urgebit Equum versus lapidem, ac lapidem versus equum, tantumq; impediet progressum unius quantum promovet progressum alterius. Si corpus aliquod in corpus
aliud impingens, motum ejus vi sua quomodocunq: mutaverit, i-
dem quoque vicissim in motu proprio eandem mutationem in partem contrariam vi alterius (ob æqualitatem pressionis mutuæ)
subibit. His actionibus æquales fiunt mutationes non velocitatum
sed motuum, (scilicet in corporibus non aliunde impeditis :) Mutationes enim velocitatum, in contrarias itidem partes factæ, quia
motus æqualiter mutantur, sunt corporibus reciproce proportionales.

Corol. I.

*Corpus viribus conjunctis diagonalem parallelogrammi eodem tempore
describere, quo latera separatis.*

Si corpus dato tempore, vi sola M,
ferretur ab *A* ad *B*, & vi sola *N*, ab
A ad *C*, compleatur parallelogram-
mum *ABDC*, & vi utraq; feretur id
eodem tempore ab *A* ad *D*. Nam
quoniam vis *N* agit secundum lineam
AC ipsi *BD* parallelam, hæc vis nihil mutabit velocitatem acce-
dendi ad lineam illam *B D* a vi altera genitam. Accedet igitur
corpus eodem tempore ad lineam *B D* sive vis *N* imprimatur, sive
non, atq; adeo in fine illius temporis reperietur alicubi in linea
illa

Principia

Axiomata Sive Leges Motus

Lex. I.

Corpus omne perseverare in statu suo quiescendi vel movendi
uniformiter in directum, nisi quatenus a viribus impressis cogitur
5 *statum illum mutare.*

Projectilia perseverant in motibus suis nisi quatenus a resistentia
aeris retardantur et vi gravitatis impelluntur deorsum. Trochus,
cujus partes cohaerendo perpetuo retrahunt sese a motibus
rectilineis, non cessat rotari nisi quatenus ab aere retardatur.
10 Majora autem Planetarum et Cometarum corpora motus suos
et progressivos et circulares in spatiis minus resistentibus factos
conservant diutius.

Lex. II.

Mutationem motus proportionalem esse vi motrici impressae, et fieri
15 *secundum lineam rectam qua vis illa imprimitur.*

Si vis aliqua motum quemvis generet, dupla duplum, tripla triplum
generabit, sive simul et semel, sive gradatim et successive impressa
fuerit; Et hic motus quoniam in eandem semper plagam cum
vi generatrice determinatur, si corpus antea movebatur, motui
20 ejus vel conspiranti additur, vel contrario subducitur, vel obliquo
oblique adjicitur, et cum eo secundum utriusque determinationem
componitur.

Lex III.

Actioni contrariam semper et aequalem esse reactionem: sive corporum
25 *duorum actiones in se mutuo semper esse aequales et in partes*
contrarias dirigi.

Quicquid premit vel trahit alterum, tantundem ab eo premitur vel
trahitur. Siquis lapidem digito premit, premitur et hujus digitus a

30 lapide. Si equus lapidem funi allegatum trahit, retrahetur etiam et equus aequaliter in lapidem: nam funis utrinque distentus eodem relaxandi se conatu urgebit equum versus lapidem, ac lapidem versus equum, tantumque impediet progressum unius quantum promovet progressum alterius. Si corpus aliquod in corpus aliud impingens, motus ejus vi sua quomodocunque mutaverit, idem quoque vicissim
35 in motu proprio eandem mutationem in partem contrariam vi alterius (ob aequalitatem pressionis mutuae) subibit. His actionibus aequales fiunt mutationes non velocitatum sed motuum, (scilicet in corporibus non aliunde impeditis:) Mutationes enim velocitatum, in contrarias itidem partes factae, quia motus aequaliter mutantur,
40 sunt corporibus reciproce proportionales.

• Notes •

Axiomata

1 **Axiomata:** Greek form. Neuter nominative plural.

Motus: genitive.

Lex. I.

2 **Lex. I:** Read **Lex prima**.

3 **Corpus omne perseverare:** common use of the accusative with the infinitive without a governing verb (such as **dico**). Equivalent to our English phrase *That every body persists.*

4 **in directum:** *directly, in a straight line.*

nisi quatenus: *unless and until.* **Nisi** alone would have been sufficient. The combination is a feature of scholastic and later Latin.

6 **Projectilia:** Newton feels it necessary to clarify each of his three axioms to anticipate, as it were, objections that may arise in the mind of the reader. One of the great lessons to be learned from Newton is that science is, more often than not, counterintuitive.

7 **vi: vis, vis** (f) ablative singular.

Trochus: trochus, -i (m) *hoop.* One may object, Newton anticipates, that a hoop set in perpetual circular motion seems to contradict the axiom. Newton notes, however, that it is the cohesive forces acting between the particles that cause the motion to deviate from a straight line. It would have been wiser for Newton to talk about a single (infinitesimally small) material particle in the formulation of his axioms and to leave the theory of extended bodies for later treatment.

8   **perpetuo:** adverb.

        sese: intensive form of **se**.

9   **rotari:** The use of the passive voice is necessary, since **roto** literally means *I cause [something] to rotate.* The same reasoning would apply to **moveo**.

13   **Lex. II:** Read **Lex secunda**.

14   **Mutationem . . . esse:** accusative with the infinitive construction, just as in the previous law.

        motus: genitive. Notice that Newton uses the term **motus** both to describe a motion in general and, more specifically, to refer to the momentum, that is, mass times velocity. In many languages, the mechanical momentum is known as "quantity of motion."

        vi motrici impressae: dative with **proportionalem**.

        fieri: fio, fieri, factus sum *to occur, to take place, to become.*

15   **secundum:** + accusative, *according to, following* (Spanish: *según,* Italian: *secondo*).

16   **generet:** subjunctive. Why?

        dupla duplum . . . generabit: This is a slightly reordered version of the Latin with understood direct objects supplied: **dupla [vis] generabit duplum [motum]**. Note that **generabit** has a double set of subjects and direct objects: **dupla/duplum** and **tripla/ triplum**. Note Newton's clever arrangement of words here.

17   **sive . . . sive . . . :** *whether . . . or whether . . .*

        simul et semel: *all at once.* Emphatic style reminiscent of **nisi quatenus** above, line 4.

18   **fuerit:** Note that this third person singular active form can be construed, in principle, either as the future perfect indicative or as the perfect subjunctive. The combination of either with a perfect passive participle does not correspond to any formal tense. Nevertheless, the use of the perfect subjunctive in this construction is perfectly legitimate and quite common. A possible rendering is *whether it might have been applied all at once or gradually.*

18–20   **Et hic motus . . . motui ejus . . . conspiranti additur:** *And this momentum is added to its harmonizing momentum.* Newton is here at pains to explain in words the parallelogram rule of addition of vectors. If the change of momentum (**hic motus**) is in the same line and in the same sense (**conspiranti**) of the original momentum, then it is simply added. On the other hand, if this change of momentum is in the same line but in the opposite sense, then it is subtracted (**subducitur**). Finally, if it is not on the same line, namely, oblique, then it is composed as it is determined according to both contributors, that is, according to the parallelogram rule to be clarified on the next page.

18   **quoniam:** *since.* It is best to understand the whole clause **quoniam . . . determinatur** as parenthetical. A comma before **quoniam** is warranted.

       in eandem semper plagam: The change of momentum (**hic motus**) always occurs (**determinatur**) in the same region (**plaga**) with the force. Here Newton is telling us that the proportionality is not one of scalars but of vectors. The two vectors, force and change of momentum, are proportional and the constant of proportionality is actually positive, so that they both point in the same direction (into the same region).

23   **Lex. III:** Read **Lex tertia**.

24   **esse reactionem:** accusative with the infinitive. The reaction is equal and contrary to the action. It is interesting to note that in Newton's own copy of the first edition he crossed out the first line up to and including **sive** and, correspondingly, capitalized **Corporum**. Most probably, Newton did not like the word "reaction," since it had not been introduced previously. Nevertheless, this correction was not implemented in later

editions and the first line has become a classic statement not only in physics but also in the social sciences and in everyday life, where it is used rather carelessly.

26 **dirigi: dirigo, dirigere, direxi, directum** *to direct, to arrange, to aim,* passive infinitive.

29 **funi: funis, funis** (m) *rope, cord*; dative dependent on **allegatum**.

30 **funis utrinque distentus:** Here Newton attempts to explain the concept of internal force in a deformable medium. The rope is extended or stretched (**distentus**) from both sides (**utrinque**) and in trying (**conatu**) to relax the elastic internal force pulls both the stone and the horse toward each other.

34 **mutaverit:** Note again the ambiguity between the future perfect active indicative and the perfect active subjunctive.

36 **subibit: subeo, subire, subivi, subitum** *to undergo.*

37 **non velocitatum sed motuum:** Newton emphasizes here that when two bodies collide, since the forces during the collision are of the kind being discussed—action and reaction—the changes (**mutationes**) of momenta (**motuum**) are equal in value and opposite in sense, but the changes in velocity depend on the respective masses. Newton does not use the word *mass* in this case but just the word *body.* In his words, the changes in velocity are inversely proportional (**reciproce proportionales**) to the bodies (**corporibus**).

Lib 1. Sect II Prop 1

[37]

SECT. II.

De Inventione Virium Centripetarum.

Prop. I. Theorema. I.

Areas quas corpora in gyros acta radiis ad immobile centrum virium ductis describunt, & in planis immobilibus consistere, & esse temporibus proportionales.

Dividatur tempus in partes æquales, & prima temporis parte describat corpus vi insita rectam *A B.* Idem secunda temporis parte, si nil impediret, recta pergeret ad *c,* (per Leg. 1) describens lineam *B c* æqualem ipsi *A* B, adeo ut radiis *A S,* B S, *c S* ad centrum actis, confectæ forent æquales areæ *A S* B, B *Sc.* Verum ubi corpus venit ad B, agat vis centripeta impulsu unico sed magno, faciatq; corpus a recta B *c* deflectere & pergere in recta B *C.* Ipsi B *S* parallela agatur *c C* occurrens B *C* in

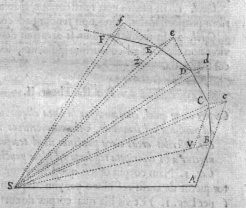

C, & completa secunda temporis parte, corpus (per Legum Corol. 1) reperietur in *C,* in eodem plano cum triangulo A *S B.* Junge *S C,* & triangulum *S B C,* ob parallelas S B, C *c,* æquale erit triangulo *S B c,* atq; adeo etiam triangulo *S A B.* Simili argumento si

vis

Let us now look at Newton's proof. Newton's second law of motion states that, in an inertial frame of reference, the force applied to a material point (a planet, say) is proportional to the instantaneous change of momentum. As Newton points out, this equation is what in modern language is called a vector equation. We are now merely on page 37 of the *Principia*. The three famous axioms have been introduced on pages 12 and 13 and nothing much else has been done, except a bit of what today we call vector algebra, the parallelogram rule for vector addition. To prove Kepler's Second Law, Newton does not even need a theory of gravitation. He only needs to assume that the attractive force is along the line joining the planet with the sun (assumed to be fixed). Ellipses are not involved at all.

Sect. II.

De Inventione Virium Centripetarum. (Kepler's Second Law)
Prop. I. Theorema I.

Areas quas corpora in gyros acta radiis ad immobile centrum
virium ductis describunt, et in planis immobilibus consistere, et esse
5 *temporibus proportionales.*

     Dividatur tempus in partes aequales, et prima temporis parte describat corpus vi insita rectam AB. Idem secunda temporis parte, si nil impediret, recta pergeret ad c, (per Leg. I) describens lineam Bc aequalem ipsi AB, adeo ut radiis AS, BS, cS ad centrum actis,
10 confectae forent aequales areae ASB, BSc. Verum ubi corpus venit ad B, agat vis centripeta impulsu unico sed magno, faciatque corpus a recta Bc deflectere et pergere in recta BC. Ipsi BS parallela agatur cC occurrens BC in C, et completa secunda temporis parte, corpus (per Legum Corol. I) reperietur in C, in eodem plano cum triangulo
15 ASB. Junge SC, et triangulum SBC, ob parallelas SB, Cc, aequale erit triangulo SBc, atque adeo etiam triangulo SAB.

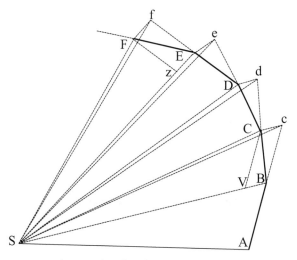

Figure 4: Image based on figure in *Principia* facsmile.

• Notes •

1 **Inventione: inventio, -onis** (f) *a finding, an invention.* Thus, the title can be translated as *On the finding of centripetal forces.*

3–5 **Areas . . . proportionales:** Note that Newton states all his axioms, propositions, and theorems in indirect statement/oratio obliqua, as if there were an implied **dico**. In the *Principia*, moreover, Newton does not compromise with the use of **quod** or **quia** for indirect statement/oratio obliqua, so that he uses the accusative with the infinitive construction. So, we must construe the main sentence skeleton as **Areas . . . et consistere et proportionales esse . . .,** that is, *That the areas . . . both fall upon and are proportional . . .* The secondary clause **quas . . . describunt** has as its subject **corpora**. But these are not arbitrary bodies. They are **corpora acta radiis ductis ad immobile centrum virium.** This is all Newton needs to assume, namely, that the forces are directed along radii traced toward a fixed point or center of forces. Notice that Newton does not assume any particular shape, such as an ellipse. The shape, in fact, will depend on the particular nature of this central force. Notice, too, that Kepler was wrong in attributing two "virtues" to the gravitational force. There is just what Kepler would call the "libration" force. The other "virtue" is just the property of inertia.

6   **Dividatur tempus:** Newton divides the arc into parts of equal duration, since he is considering time, rather than length, as the independent variable. What is striking about Newton's proof is that he does not quite use the more sophisticated methods of calculus, which he had invented, but proceeds with a proof that would have been understood by the Greeks Eudoxus or Archimedes. Newton does not quite write differential equations. He proceeds geometrically, in a style not unlike Kepler's.

7   **vi insita:** ablative. **Insitus, -a, -um** can be rendered as *innate* or *intrinsic*. Newton is here referring to inertia. Newton's idea here is the following: Assume that you could switch the force of gravity on and off, and that you do that as pulses acting at small equal intervals of time. Then, during the time between pulses, the body would move, by its own inertia, along a straight segment AB. This is a straightforward application of Newton's First Law. Now, as you switch on the pulse, the Second Law kicks in.

9   **adeo ut:** *so that*.

10   **forent:** alternate form for imperfect subjunctive of **sum**. Notice that the areas of the two triangles are exactly equal since they have respectively equal bases AB and Bc, by construction, and identical heights, measured from the vertex S perpendicularly to the base. So far, everything is crystal clear.

     Verum: *but*.

12   **Ipsi BS:** dative.

13   **completa . . . parte:** ablative absolute.

14   **per Legum Corol. I: per Legum Corollarium I:** *by the first corollary of the Laws*. This is nothing but the parallelogram law for adding vectors, introduced on page 167.

15   **Junge:** imperative singular.

     ob parallelas: *on account of the two lines being parallel*. The triangles SBC and SBc are equal because they have a common base SB, and equal heights, measured perpendicularly to SB from either C or c, which lie on a line parallel to SB by construction. We are practically done! The only thing remaining is to go to the limit as the time intervals become smaller and smaller.

Newton has proved Kepler's Second Law under the minimal set of assumptions and within slightly more than a printed page. He drives his point further by stating as a corollary that in nondissipative media (say, in vacuo), if the law of equal areas swept in equal times is not satisfied, the only explanation is that the force is not central. In later editions (the last edition during Newton's lifetime was produced in 1723) the corollaries were replaced by stronger statements. For example, that the speed of a body in a central force field is inversely proportional to the distance from the center to the tangent to the trajectory. Kepler would have appreciated this simple formulation of his main assumption.

Optics

Ibn Al-Haytham (Alhazen)

Alhazen (965–1040) is one of the greatest representatives of Islamic science. He was born in Basra (now in Iraq) and can be considered either Arab or Persian. His influence in the development of modern science was immense. His most influential work is *Kitab al Manazir* (*The Book of Optics*). Its anonymous Latin translation dating to the late 1200s (printed in 1572) was widely read and quoted by, among others, Roger Bacon, Leonardo da Vinci, René Descartes, Galileo Galilei, Christiaan Huygens, and Johannes Kepler. An important contribution of this treatise is its assertion, carefully supported by experiments, that light is an important component of vision. It travels in straight lines and, when reflected from an object, it impinges upon the eye to produce a visual image. This was not an entirely original theory, but Alhazen's use of the scientific method lent it credence and helped dispel Ptolemy's assumption that the eye was an emitter of rays and that it initiated the process of vision. An interesting aspect of Alhazen's treatise is the inclusion of the anatomy and physiology of the eye as a crucial component of this process.

Note: The following two pages contain images from the manuscript facsimile. However, for an image of the Latin text, please consult the product page on www.bolchazy.com.

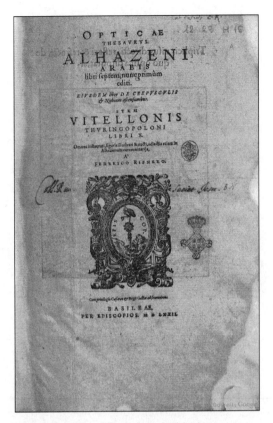

Opticae thesaurus. Alhazeni Arabis libri septem, nunc primùm editi. Eiusdem liber De crepusculis & nubium ascensionibus. Item Vitellonis Thuringolopoli libri 10. Omnes instaurati, figuris illustrati & aucti, adiecti etiam in Alhazenum commentarijs, a Federico Risnero. Basel, 1572. Property of the National Central Library of Rome. Facsimile courtesy of archive.org.

Triplicis uisus, directi, reflexi & refracti, de
quo optica disputat, ar-
gumenta.

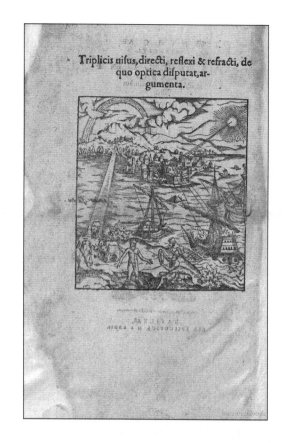

Opticae Thesaurus

Alhazen Filii Alhayzen Opticae
Liber Primus.

Primus liber in septem capita dividitur. Primum est quod lux per
se et colores illuminati operentur in visum aliquam operationem.

5   Secundum quod lux vehemens occultat quaedam visibilia, quae
lux debilis manifestat, et contra. Tertium quod colores corporum
diversificantur apud visum secundum diversitatem lucium orientium
super ipsos. Quartum est de compositione oculi, forma, et situ.
Quintum declarat qualitatem visionis, et dependentia ab illa.

10   Sextum est de officio et utilitate instrumentorum visus. Septimum
de ijs, sine quibus visio non potest compleri.

Quod lux per se, et colores illuminati operentur in visum
aliquam operationem. Cap. I.

1. Lux per se, et color illuminatus feriunt oculos. Vitell. in hypothes.

15   6.16 p 3.

Invenimus quod visus, quando inspexerit luces valde fortes, fortiter
dolebit ex eis, et habebit nocumentum: aspiciens enim quando
aspexerit corpus solis, non potest bene aspicere ipsum, quoniam
visus eius dolebit propter ipsius lucem. Et similiter quando inspexerit

20   speculum tersum, super quod ascendebat lux solis, et fuerit visus
eius in loco, ad quem reflectitur lux ab illo speculo: dolebit iterum
propter lumen reflexum, perveniens ad suum visum a speculo,
et non poterit aperire oculum ad inspiciendum lumen illud. Et
invenimus iterum quando aspiciens intuetur corpus mundum

25   album, super quod ascendebat lux solis, et moretur in aspectu
ipsius: deinde convertat visum suum ab eo ad locum obscurum,
debilis lucis: quod fere non poterit comprehendere res visibiles illius
loci comprehensione vera: et inveniet coopertorium quasi inter
visum et ipsas: deinde paulatim discooperietur, et revertetur visus

30   in suam dispositionem. Et iterum, quando inspiciens inspexerit
ignem fortem: et fuerit intuitus ipsum: et moretur in aspiciendo
longo tempore: deinde declinet visum suum ad locum obscurum,
debilis lucis: inveniet iterum idem in visu suo. Et iterum invenimus,
quando inspiciens inspexerit corpus mundum album, super quod

35   oriebatur lux diei: et fuerit illa lux fortis, quamvis non sit lux solis:
et moretur in aspectu diu: deinde convertat visum suum ad locum
obscurum: inveniet formam lucis illius in loco illo, et inveniet cum
hoc figuram eius: deinde si clauserit visum: inveniet in ipso formam
illius lucis: deinde auferetur hoc, et revertetur oculus in suam

40   dispositionem. Et similiter erit dispositus visus, quando inspexerit
corpus, super quod oriebatur lux solis. Et similiter quando inspexerit
corpus clare album, super quod oriebatur lux ignis, quando lux ignis
fuerit fortis, et moretur in aspiciendo ipsum: deinde recesserit ad
locum obscurum: inveniet iterum in eo idem hoc in suo visu. Et

45   similiter quando aspiciens fuerit in domo, in qua fuerit foramen
amplum discoopertum ad coelum: et aspexerit ex illo loco coelum
in luce diei: et moretur in aspiciendo ipsum: deinde revertatur
visus eius ad locum obscurum in domo: inveniet formam lucis,
quam comprehendebat ex foramine cum figura foraminis in loco

50   obscuro: et si clauserit oculum suum: inveniet iterum in eo formam
illam. Omnia ergo ista significant, quod lux operetur in visum
aliquam operationem. Et invenimus iterum quod, quando aspiciens
inspexerit viridarium multae spissitudinis herbarum, super quod
oriebatur lux solis: et moretur in aspiciendo ipsum: deinde convertat

55   suum visum ad locum obscurum: inveniet in illo loco obscuro
formam coloratam a virore illarum herbarum: deinde si aspexerit
in ista dispositione visibilia alba: et fuerint illa visibilia in umbra,
et loco debilis lucis: inveniet colores istos admixtos cum virore: et
si clauserit oculum suum: iterum inveniet in ipso formam lucis et

60   formam viroris: deinde discooperietur illud, et auferetur. Et similiter
si aspexerit corpus coloratum colore caeruleo vel rubeo, vel alio

colore forti scintillante, super quod oriebatur lux solis: et moretur
in aspiciendo ipsum: deinde auferat visum suum ad visibilia alba in
loco debilis lucis: inveniet colores illos admixtos cum illo colore. Ista
65 ergo significant quod colores illuminati operentur in visum.

• Notes •

1   **Alhazen filii:** The proper name Alhazen is indeclinable. Since
it is followed by the genitive **filii** we understand that Alhazen
here is also in the genitive. Thus we have *of the son of Alhazen.*
This corresponds exactly to the Arabic *ibn-il-Haythami*, which,
with this voweling, is also in the genitive case. It is interesting
that although, following Arabic tradition, the surname of a man
is derived from his father's first name (or, alternatively, from
his oldest son's first name), the **ibn** was eventually dropped in
European translations and he became known simply as *Alhacen,*
Alhazen, or *Alhayzen,* or a number of other orthographic variants.
In fact, the complete Arabic name of Alhazen is Abu Ali al-Hasan
ibn al-Hasan ibn al-Haytham, namely, father of Ali Alhasan,
son of Ali Alhasan the son of Alhaytham. The inconsistency of
spelling does not seem to bother the editor. Thus, the whole title is
The first book of the optics of Alhayzen, the son of Alhazen.

3   **capita: caput, capitis** (n) a *head* in a book is a *chapter.*

Primum est quod: *The first is that* is not exactly a classical
expression, but very common in medieval scholastic writing.

4   **operentur:** Notice the (correct) use of the subjunctive mood.
Why? Notice also that this is a deponent verb, so that its
meaning is active.

visum: visus, -us (m). In this instance, **visum** should be
understood as *the eyes.*

5   **vehemens:** as opposed to **debilis.**

quaedam: Notice that **visibilia**, which **quaedam** modifies, is in
the accusative neuter plural.

6   **et contra:** *and vice versa.* The most common idiomatic use is
e contra = ex + contra, which stands for *on the other hand,*
conversely.

7   **secundum:** here used as a preposition, *according to*, followed by an accusative.

       orientium: oriens, orientis, present participle of **orior**. It is important to bear in mind that deponent verbs exhibit three active participles (present, perfect, and future) and one passive participle, also the gerundive.

11   **ijs: iis = eis.**

14   **feriunt: ferio, ferire, ferivi, feritum** *to strike*.

       Vitell.: Vitellius, Latinized form of Witelo (b. 1230), a Polish theologian and scientist whose work on optics (*Perspectiva* [*Optics*]) is included in the same volume with the present edition of Alhazen's work, as indicated in the title page above. Witelo's work, which had great influence on Renaissance art and science, was largely based on Alhazen's and can be considered a commentary on it. Here the editor refers the reader to the corresponding chapter in Witelo's work.

16   **Invenimus:** Notice that Alhazen does not start with theoretical speculations, but rather with experimental evidence drawn from everyday phenomena.

17   **nocumentum:** a medieval Latin neologism formed from the verb **noceo, nocere** in the same spirit as the word **documentum** is formed from **doceo, docere**, or **monumentum** from **moneo, monere**. It is used in legal contexts to mean *damage* or *nuisance*; here, *injury* or *harm*.

18   **solis: sol, solis** (m) *sun*; not from **solus, -a, -um.**

20   **tersum: tergeo, tergere, tersi, tersum** or **tergo, tergere** *to wipe, to clean, to polish.*

20–21   **visus eius in loco:** *instead of sighting.* Compare with the legal expression **in loco parentis** *in place of a parent.*

24   **mundum:** here used as an adjective *clean.*

25   **moretur: moror, morari, moratus sum** *to delay, to tarry*

26   **convertat: converto, convertere, converti, conversum** *to turn* (*in another direction*), not *to convert.*

27   **comprehendere:** *to perceive.*

28   **coopertorium:** *a cover, a veil,* from **cooperio, cooperire, cooperui, cooperitum** *to cover, to envelop.*

31   **fuerit intuitus:** The deponent verb **intueor, intueri, intuitus sum** gives rise to the future perfect (active) **intuitus erit.** The use of **fuerit** is also acceptable (since **intuitus** by itself is a legitimate active perfect participle = *one that has seen*) and appears in classical Latin (e.g., Quintilian, *Institutio Oratoria* (*The Institute of Oratory*), Liber II, Caput VIII: **quum sagaciter fuerit intuitus** = *once he had cleverly studied* = *once he will have had cleverly studied*). Notice that **fuerit** can serve both as the future perfect indicative and as the perfect subjunctive.

35   **quamvis non sit:** *although it is not, although it not be.*

42   **clare:** adverb from **clarus, -a, -um.**

56   **virore: viror, viroris** (m) *greenness.* The important point in all of the above experiments is the demonstration that the so-called emission theory, proposing that vision was produced by the eye emitting light rays toward the objects, is wrong. He agreed instead with al-Kindi (801–873) in asserting that the objects themselves emit rays that enter the eye to produce vision. Al-Kindi's work also influenced Roger Bacon's (1220–1292) thought on this and other topics.

Isaac Newton

The genius of Isaac Newton was not limited to having revolutionized (or, more accurately, created) the science of rational mechanics. In the years 1670 to 1672 Newton delivered a series of inaugural lectures for his appointment to the Lucasian Chair in Mathematics at Cambridge. Newton chose the topic of optics and made significant contributions to this science as well. His manuscript notes, known as *Lectiones Opticae* (*Optical Lectures*, preserved in Newton's crystal clear handwriting in Latin), served as the basis for his treatise on *Opticks*, written in English and published in 1704. His original notes in Latin were eventually printed and published in 1729.[21] Newton's ideas on optics underwent a process of evolution and many were refuted by the emergence of the wave theory of light. His most lasting contribution, however, was already enunciated at the beginning of the *Lectiones* in the passage proposed for reading. It demonstrates on the basis of experiments that the white light of the sun is in fact a continuous mixture of monochromatic lights and that the individual components can be separated by means of a prism. Moreover, a circular source of white light, when refracted by a prism, results in general in an elliptical image, unless the prism is positioned in a very particular way to counteract the different angles of refraction associated with each individual component.

---

21 A scholarly edition of Newton's optical papers, including Latin and English versions with critical commentaries, can be found in A. E. Shapiro, *The Optical Papers of Isaac Newton, Volume 1, The Optical Lectures 1670-1672* (Cambridge: Cambridge University Press, 1984).

ISAACI NEWTONI, *Eq. Aur.*

IN

Academiâ Cantabrigienfi

Mathefeos olim Profefforis Lucafiani

LECTIONES OPTICÆ,

Annis MDCLXIX, MDCLXX & MDCLXXI,

In Scholis publicis habitæ:

Et nunc primum ex MSS. in lucem editæ.

LONDINI

Apud GUIL. INNYS, Regiæ Societatis Typographum
MDCCXXIX.

*Isaaci Newtoni lectiones opticae annis MDCLXIX, MDCLXX
& MDCLXXI : in scholis publicis habitae ; et nunc primum
ex mss. in lucem editae.* Publisher: G. Innys. London, 1729.
Facsimile courtesy of Echo, Berlin and Max Planck Institute
Library.

4   RADIORUM DIVERSA   Par. I.

II. *Quod omnium radiorum non sit eadem refrangibilitas.*

DE luce itaque compertum habeo, quod radii ejus, quoad quantitatem refractionis, ab invicem differant. Ex iis, qui omnes habent eundem angulum incidentiæ, alii angulum refractionis aliquanto majorem, alii minorem habebunt. Plenioris illuſtrationis gratiâ, fit E F G (fig. 1.) ſuperficies quælibet refringens puta vitrea, & ducatur quævis O F huic occurrens in F, & cum eâ efficiens angulum O F E acutum. Concipe etiam radios ſolares per iſtam lineam O F ſibi continuo ſucceſſivos fluere, ita ut alii poſt alios in punctum F impingant, ibidemque in medium denſius refringantur; vel ſi mavis, finge parallelos radios indefinite parum diſtare ab O.F, & incidere in puncta ipſi F viciniſſima. Jam ex opinione receptâ, hi radii eandem habentes incidentiam eandem quoque refractionem omnes habere debent, puta in lineam F R. At contrarium compertum habeo, ſcilicet, quod poſtquam refringuntur, divergant ab invicem, quaſi quidam refringerentur in lineam F P, alii in lineam F Q, & alii in lineas F R, F S, & F T, ac alii etiam innumeri per ſpatia intermedia, ut & ultra citraque nonnulli pervagantes, prout radius quilibet ad refractionem majorem
mi-

Sect. I. REFRANGIBILITAS. 5

minoremve patiendum fit aptus. Invenio præterea, quod Radii F P maxime refracti colores purpureos producant, & illi F T minime refracti rubros, qui autem hifce intermedii F Q, F R, F S pergunt, colores intermedios, nempe cæruleos, virides & flavos generant : & fic radii, prout apti funt, ut alii aliis magis atque magis refringantur, hos ordine colores, rubrum, flavum, viridem, cæruleum, & purpureum generant, una cum omnibus intermediis, quos in iride liceat confpicere; unde productio colorum prifmatis & iridis facile patebit. Sed his jam perfunctorie notatis, quæ de coloribus dicenda funt, in pofterum differam.

III. *Probatur experimento vulgari per longitudinem imaginis folaris refracta.*

SENTENTIA noftrâ de hâc re fic breviter explicatâ, ne putetis fabulas pro veris enarratas effe, rationes & experimenta, quibus ifthæc innituntur, continuo proferam. Et quoniam experimentum quoddam prifmatis valde obvium mihi primo dedit occafionem excogitandi reliqua, iftud primum explicabo. Sit F (fig. 2.) foramen aliquod in pariete vel feneftrâ cubiculi, per quod radii folares O F trajiciantur, reliquis ubique foraminibus diligenter obturatis, ne lux alibi ingrediatur. Ifta autem obfcuratio cubiculi non eft prorfus neceffaria, fed efficit

6   R A D I O R U M D I V E R S A   Par. I.

efficit tantum, ut experimentum evadat aliquanto
evidentius. Deinde prifma triangulare vitreum
A *a* B *b* C *c* ad foramen istud applicetur, quod radios O F per se trajectos refringat versus P Y T Z, ubi
videbis imaginem valde oblongam efformari, cujus
nempe longitudo P T sit quadruplex latitudinis Y Z
& amplius. Et hinc evinci certo videtur, quod
radiorum æqualiter incidentium alii majorem aliis
refractionem patiuntur. Nam si contrarium esset
verum, prædicta solis imago appareret fere orbicularis, & in quâdam positione prifmatis ad sensum orbicularis conspiceretur, id quod contra omnem experientiam est. Quocunque enim situ prifma disposui,
nunquam tamen potui efficere, quin longitudo
imaginis esset latitudinis plusquam quadrupla; angulo scilicet prifmatis A C B vel *a c b* existente
graduum plus minus sexaginta.

IV. *Casus in quo radii æque refrangibiles*
faciunt imaginem orbicularem.

QUOD autem datur quædam prifmatis positio, in
quâ imago solis ex opinione de refractionibus receptâ appareret orbicularis, sic ostendo. Juxta foramen in fenestrâ cubiculi factum, prifma collocetur
foras; vel, quod eodem recidit, sit E G (fig. 3.)
corpus aliquod opacum citra prifma locatum, in
quo sit F foramen indefinite parvum & orbiculare,
per

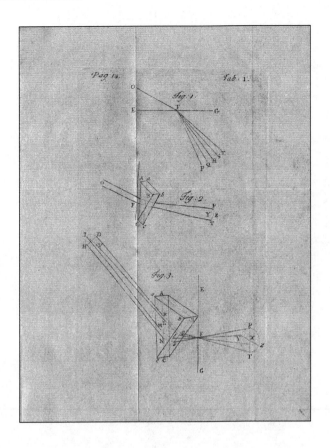

Manuscript with Newton's handwriting: Reproduced by
kind permission of the Syndic of Cambridge University
Library. Lectiones Opticae (MS.Add.4002)

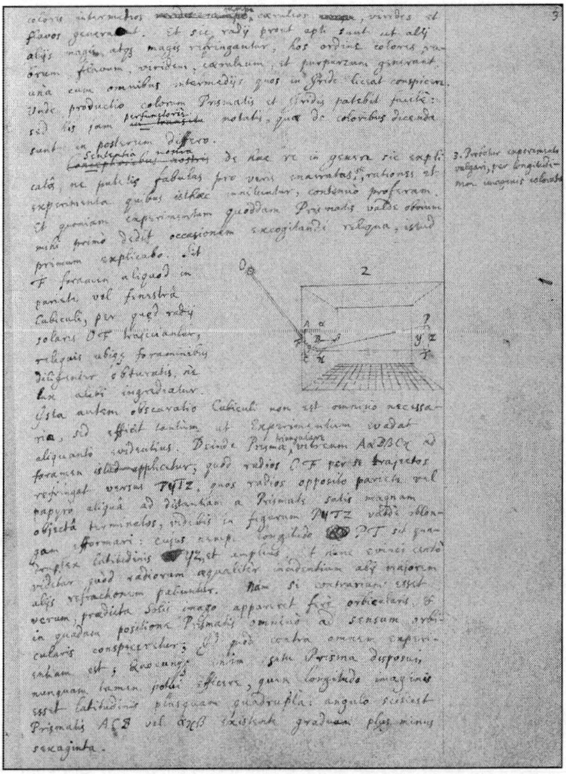

Lectiones Opticae

II. Quod omnium radiorum non sit eadem refrangibilitas.

De luce itaque compertum habeo, quod radii ejus, quoad quantitatem refractionis, ab invicem differant. Ex iis, qui omnes habent eundem angulum incidentiae, alii angulum refractionis
5 aliquanto majorem, alii minorem habebunt. Plenioris illustrationis gratia, sit E F G (fig. I.) superficies quaelibet refringens puta vitrea, et ducatur quaevis O F huic occurrens in F, et cum ea efficiens angulum O F E acutum. Concipe etiam radios solares per istam lineam O F sibi continuo successivos fluere, ita ut alii post alios in
10 punctum F impingant, ibidemque in medium densius refringantur; vel si mavis, finge parallelos radios indefinite parum distare ab O F, et incidere in puncta ipsi F vicinissima. Jam ex opinione recepta, hi radii eandem habentes incidentiam eandem quoque refractionem omnes habere debent, puta in lineam F R. At contrarium
15 compertum habeo, scilicet, quod postquam refringuntur, divergant ab invicem, quasi quidam refringerentur in lineam F P, alii in lineam F Q, et alii in lineas F R, F S, et F T, ac alii etiam innumeri per spatia intermedia, ut et ultra citraque nonnulli pervagantes, prout radius quilibet ad refractionem majorem minoremve patiendum sit
20 aptus. Invenio praeterea, quod Radii F P maxime refracti colores purpureos producant, et illi F T minime refracti rubros, qui autem hisce intermedii F Q, F R, F S pergunt, colores intermedios, nempe caeruleos, virides et flavos generant: et sic radii, prout apti sunt, ut alii aliis magis atque magis refringantur, hos ordine colores, rubrum,
25 flavum, viridem, caeruleum, et purpureum generant, una cum omnibus intermediis, quos in iride liceat conspicere; unde productio colorum prismatis et iridis facile patebit. Sed his jam perfunctorie notatis, quae de coloribus dicenda sunt, in posterum differam.

III. Probatur experimento vulgari per longitudinem imaginis
30 **solaris refractae.**

Sententia nostra de hac re sic breviter explicata, ne putetis
fabulas pro veris enarratas esse, rationes et experimenta, quibus
isthaec innituntur, continuo proferam. Et quoniam experimentum
quoddam prismatis valde obvium mihi primo dedit occasionem
35 excogitandi reliqua, istud primum explicabo. Sit F (fig. 2.) foramen
aliquod in pariete vel fenestra cubiculi, per quod radii solares O F
trajiciantur, reliquis ubique foraminibus diligenter obturatis, ne
lux alibi ingrediatur. Ista autem obscuratio cubiculi non est prorsus
necessaria, sed efficit tantum, ut experimentum evadat aliquanto
40 evidentius. Deinde prisma triangulare vitreum A a B b C c ad foramen
istud applicetur, quod radios O F per se trajectos refringat versus
P Y T Z, ubi videbis imaginem valde oblongam efformari, cujus
nempe longitudo P T sit quadruplex latitudinis Y Z et amplius. Et
hinc evinci certo videtur, quod radiorum aequaliter incidentium
45 alii majorem aliis refractionem patiuntur. Nam si contrarium esset
verum, praedicta solis imago appareret fere orbicularis, et in quadam
positione prismatis ad sensum orbicularis conspiceretur, id quod
contra omnem experientiam est. Quocunque enim situ prisma
disposui, nunquam tamen potui efficere, quin longitudo imaginis
50 esset latitudinis plusquam quadrupla; angulo scilicet prismatis
A C B vel a c b existente graduum plus minus sexaginta.

• Notes •

II.

1   **sit:** For the style of the title of the chapter, see our commentary
on Copernicus's first chapter, p. 141. A satisfactory reading
of this title can be gathered from rearranging it as **Quod
refrangibilitas omnium radiorum non sit eadem**. The use of
quod here is not classical, but rather the equivalent of "that" in
dico quod refrangibilitas omnium radiorum non sit eadem.

The classical expression would have employed an accusative-infinitive construction: **dico refrangibilitatem non esse eandem.**

refrangibilitas: Refrangibility or refractability is the capability of being refracted. The phenomena of reflection (by mirrors) and refraction (by translucent media) were well known since antiquity. Their mathematical modeling was variously developed over many centuries. The word "refraction" is derived from the Latin **refringere** (*to break back*), which is an apt description of the apparent breaking of a stick diagonally inserted in water. It is, of course, the basis for the theory and manufacture of lenses. It can be described by means of geometrical optics. The phenomenon of diffraction, however, necessitated the advent of the wave theory of light. This phenomenon had been named by Francesco Maria Grimaldi (1618–1663), from the same Latin root. Newton's corpuscular theory was unable to tackle this problem convincingly, but he argued vehemently against the wave theory.

2   **compertum habeo:** literally, *I have it as a found fact*, but classically understood as *I know with certainty*. For example, Cicero writes (*Pro Fonteio* [*On Behalf of Fonteius*], 29), **ea dicimus . . . quae comperta habemus.** It is interesting to note also that in the Romance languages the combination **habere** + perfect passive participle became the basis for the perfect tense, just as in English, *we have discovered*. Notice the construction **compertum habeo.** For a scholarly discussion of these nuances, see G. V. M. Haverling, "On the use of *habeo* and the perfect participle in earlier and later Latin," in *Early and Late Latin: Continuity or Change?*, edited by J. N. Adams and N. Vincent (Cambridge: Cambridge University Press, 2016).

quoad: *as far as.*

4–5   **alii . . . alii . . .:** *some . . . others . . .*

6   **gratia:** *for the sake of.*

quaelibet: **quilibet, quaelibet, quodlibet** *anyone or anything you will.*

puta: imperative; Newton talks to the reader.

7   **ducatur:** Notice how Newton is using the language of Euclid (Proposition 11 in Campanus version, lines 30–31): **et ducatur linea recta abcd secans circumferentiam utriusque.**

     quaevis: similar to **quaelibet.**

8   **Concipe:** See **puta.**

9   **sibi:** The reflexive **sibi** indicates that the rays succeed each other continuously.

     fluere: infinitive in indirect statement/oratio obliqua governed by **Concipe. sibi fluere** *to flow on their own, one after the other.*

10   **densius:** Note the neuter comparative.

11   **mavis:** alternative form of **malis** from **malo, malle, malui,** a contraction of **magis + vis,** *to prefer.* Newton again addresses the reader.

     indefinite parum distare: *to be at an infinitely* (or *indefinitely*) *small distance.* This is a typical expression of Newton's infinitesimal calculus of fluxions.

12   **ipsi:** dative singular.

14   **puta in lineam:** an imperative literally meaning "think into the line." In modern English we use "say" instead of "think." We can also translate it as "for example."

     in lineam F. R.: This second imagery (of parallel rays) does not appear in other versions of the lectures. But it is well taken, since it is always wise in geometrical optics to think of a bundle of parallel rays which, when refracted or reflected, will behave slightly differently from each other.

18   **et ultra citraque:** *both beyond and on this side.*

19   **patiendum:** **patior, pati, passus sum** *to suffer, to undergo.* Although Newton uses the gerund form **patiendum,** it would have been more literary to use **patiendam,** construed as a gerundive **ad refractionem patiendam.**

22   **hisce: hice, haece, hoce,** an emphatic form of **hic, haec, hoc.** The use of the ablative (or dative) here may be inferred also upon F Q, F R, and F S. *But those intermediate ones that follow along FQ, FR, and FS . . .*

24   **aliis:** ablative of comparison.

25   **una:** *together.*

26   **iride: iris, iridis** (f) *the rainbow.* Iris was the Roman goddess of the rainbow. To this day, the rainbow is called *arco iris* in Spanish and in Portuguese.

        liceat: This is one of the basic uses of the subjunctive: **liceat conspicere** *that may be possible to observe, that it is possible to observe, that can be seen.*

27   **prismatis: prisma, prismatis** (n) *prism.*

27–28   **his . . . notatis:** ablative absolute.

28   **dicenda sunt:** passive periphrastic. Its subject is **quae.**

III.

31   **Sententia nostra:** *in our opinion.*

31–32   **ne putetis fabulas . . . enarratas esse:** *lest you think that fables have been told.* It is noteworthy that, whereas in his *Principia* Newton attempts to be as axiomatic as possible, the *Lectiones Opticae* are strongly based on experimental evidence. Newton was well aware that the theoretical foundations of his optical theories were rather shaky, as they eventually proved to be.

33   **isthaec: istae.**

        continuo: Construe as an adverb.

34   **obvium: Obvius, -a, -um** can mean *being in the way* or frequently *met.*

37   **trajiciantur: traiciantur.**

        reliquis . . . obturatis: ablative absolute.

39   **evadat: ex + vadat,** *to come out, to proceed.*

44   **hinc:** *hence.*

        evinci: infinitive passive of **evinco, evincere, evici, evictum** with the primary sense of *to conquer utterly*, but also *to prove beyond the shadow of a doubt.*

45   **aliis:** See above, line 24.

48   **Quocunque:** variant of **quocumque** *wherever.*

49   **quin:** *that not.* The particle **quin** is a negative version of **qui.** It is sometimes a source of confusion due to the somewhat different nature of multiple negatives between English and Latin. Newton is in effect saying that he always observed that the length was greater than four times the width. He was never able to observe the contrary.

51   **graduum . . . sexaginta:** **Graduum** is a partitive genitive with **sexaginta.**

Economics

Nicole Oresme

T
he genius of the French scholastic polymath Nicole Oresme (1320–1382), just like that of his contemporary and friend Jean Buridan in Paris or the Calculators of Merton College at Oxford, has been eclipsed by those who, three centuries later, were responsible for the modern scientific revolution. It is, however, fair to say that the fourteenth-century giants, with all their limitations and their attachment to the Aristotelian tradition, more than paved the way for the makers of that revolution. The case of Oresme is particularly interesting in that he foreshadowed advances in several fields of mathematics and science.[22] His *De Configurationibus Qualitatum et Motuum* (*On the Configurations of Qualities and Motions*) foreshadows René Descartes's analytic geometry in that it proposes the representation of an extensive quantity over a linear continuum by means of line segments proportional to that quantity erected perpendicularly to the continuum.

Rather than focusing on this famous work, we propose a reading in a completely different field, namely, the origin and meaning of money. Oresme translated into French and commented on Aristotle's *Politics* and *Economics* (attributed to Aristotle). He was a champion of the use of the local languages and, although he wrote mainly in Latin, he provided translations of his own works into French. In so doing, he coined several technical terms wherever necessary. The chosen selection is taken from his *Tractatus*

---

22   For an excellent appreciation of Oresme's work, see M. Clagett, *Nicole Oresme and the Medieval Geometry of Qualities and Motions* (Madison: University of Wisconsin Press, 1968).

de Origine, Jure et Mutationibus Monetarum (*Treatise on the Origin, Law, and Changes of Money*). Apparently, the above-mentioned translations from Aristotle were written after the Latin version of his own book. Oresme emphasized the deleterious effects on the economy caused by an intentional devaluation of the physical coin through alterations of its weight, shape, or composition. Paper money had not been widely introduced yet and a coin was supposed to be of, rather than just represent, a definite value.

R. P. D.

NICOLAI ORES-
MII, LEXOVIENSIS EPI-
COPI, THEOLOGI PARITER
AC PHILOSOPHI ACVTISSIMI, TRA-
ctatus de Origine & iure, nec non & de
mutationibus Monetarum.

[*Hic fuit praceptor* CAROLI V. *cognomento Sapientis , Regis Gallia, qui regnauit circa Annum* MCCC. *Eiusdemque infectationem Astrologica superstitionis peculiari commentario scriptam, item librum de proportionibus proportionum, alicubi citat Picus Mirandulanus. Nescio an idem, cuius Orationem habitam coram Urbano PP. V. & Cardinalibus Anno* MCCCLXIII. *in Catalogo Testium Veritatis ponit Illyricus.*]

De re monetaria vetervm Romanorvm et hodierni apvd Germanos Imperii, libri duo Marquardi Freheri . . . : accedit Nicolai Oresmii . . ., Lubduni apud Gothardum Voegelinum, 1605. By permission of the Getty Research Institute. Facsimile courtesy of archive.org.

PROLOGVS.

VIBVSDAM videtur, quod aliquis Rex
aut Princeps, auctoritate propria possit
de iure aut priuilegio liberè mutare monetas in suo regno currētes, & de eis ad
libitum ordinare, ac super hoc capere
lucrum aut emolumentum quantumlibet: aliis autem videtur oppositum. Propter quod intendo in præsenti tractatu
de hoc scribere, quod secundum philo-
sophiam Aristotelis principaliter videtur mihi esse dicendum, incipiens ab origine monetarum : nihil temerè asserendo, sed totum submitto correctioni maiorum, qui forsan
ex eis quæ dicturus sum, poterunt excitari ad determinandum veritatē super isto, ita vt omni cessante scrupulo omnes
in vnam possint sententiam pariter conuenire, & circa hoc
inuenire, quod principibus & subiectis, immò toti Reipublicæ proficiat in futurum.

Propter quid Moneta sit inuenta.

CAPVT I.

QVando diuidebat Altissimus gentes, quando separabat
filios Adam, constituit terminos populorum. Inde multiplicati sunt homines super terram, & possessiones pro vt
expediebat diuisæ sunt. Ex hoc autem contigit, quod vnus
habuit de vna re vltra suam necessitatem: alius verò de eadem
re habuit parum aut nihil : & de alia re fuit è contrario. Sicut forsan quis abundauit ouibus, & pane indiguit; & agricola è conuerso. Vna etiam regio superabundauit in vno, & defecit in alio. Cœperunt ergo homines mercari sine moneta,
& dabat vnus alteri ouem pro frumento, & alius de labore
suo panem vel lanam, & sic de aliis rebus: quod adhuc longo

Deutero. 32.

A 2   tempore

NICOLAI ORESMII

tempore postea fuit inftitutum, vt narrat Iuftinus. Sed tamen
in huiufmodi permutatione & transportatione rerum, mul-
tæ difficultates acciderunt. Subtilifati homines vfum mone-
tæ inuenere, quæ effet inftrumentum permutandi ad inuicem naturales diuitias, quibus de per fe fubuenitur naturaliter humanæ neceffitati. Nam ipfæ pecuniæ dicuntur *Ar-*
tificiales diuitiæ: contingit enim his abundantem mori fame,

Midas. ficut exemplificat Ariftoteles de Rege cupido, qui orauit, vt
quidquid ipfe tangeret, aurum effet: quod Dii annuerunt, &
& fic fame periit, vt dicunt Poetæ. Quoniam per pecuniam
non immediatè fuccurritur indigentiæ vitæ, fed eft inftrumentum artificialiter adinuentum pro naturalibus diuitiis
leuiter permutandis. Et abfque alia probatione clarè poteft
patere, quod numifma eft valde vtile bonæ Communitati
ciuili, & Reipublicæ vfibus opportunum, imo neceffarium:
vt dicit Ariftoteles V. Ethicorum. Quanquam de hoc dicat
Ouidius:

Effodiuntur opes irritamenta malorum,
Iamque nocens ferrum ferroque nocentius aurum.

Hoc enim facit peruerfa malorum cupiditas, non ipfa pecunia, quæ eft humano conuictui multum accommodata, &
cuius vfus per fe bonus eft. Inde ait Caffiodorus: *Pecuniæ ipfæ*

1. Variar. 10. *quamuis vfu creberrimo viles effe videantur, animaduertendum eft*
tamen, quanta à veteribus ratione collectæ funt. Et in alio loco dicit,
quod conftat *Monetarios in vfum publicum fpecialiter effe inuentos.*

De qua materia debeat effe Moneta.

CAPVT II.

ET quoniam moneta eft inftrumentum permutandi diuitias naturales, vt patet ex capitulo præcedenti: conue-
niens fuit, quod adhoc tale inftrumentum fuerit aptum:
quod fit, fi fit attrectabile feu palpabile, & leuiter portabile,
& quod pro modica eius portione habeantur diuitiæ naturales in quantitate maiori, cum aliis conditionibus, quæ poft-
ea videbuntur. Oportuit igitur, quod numifma fieret de materia preciofa & cara, cuiufmodi eft aurum. Sed talis materia
debet effe in competenti abundantia. propter quod vbi aurum

Tractatus de Origine, Jure et Mutationibus Monetarum

Prologus.

Quibusdam videtur, quod aliquis Rex aut Princeps, auctoritate propria possit de iure vel privilegio libere mutare monetas in suo regno currentes, et de eis ad libitum ordinare, ac super hoc capere
5 lucrum aut emolumentum quantumlibet: aliis autem videtur oppositum. Propter quod intendo in praesenti tractatu de hoc scribere, quod secundum philosophiam Aristotelis principaliter videtur mihi esse dicendum, incipiens ab origine monetarum: nihil temere asserendo, sed totum submitto correctioni maiorum,
10 qui forsan ex eis quae dicturus sum, poterunt excitari ad determinandum veritatem super isto, ita ut omni cessante scrupulo omnes in unam possint sententiam pariter convenire, et circa hoc invenire, quod principibus et subiectis, immo toti Reipublicae proficiat in futurum.

15 **Propter quid Moneta sit inventa.**
Caput I.

Quando dividebat Altissimus gentes, quando separabat filios Adam, constituit terminos populorum. Inde multiplicati sunt homines super terram, et possessiones pro ut expediebat divisae
20 sunt. Ex hoc autem contigit, quod unus habuit de una re ultra suam necessitatem: alius vero de eadem re habuit parum aut nihil: et de alia re fuit e contrario. Sicut forsan quis abundavit ovibus, et pane indiguit; et agricola e converso. Una etiam regio superabundavit in uno, et defecit in alio. Coeperunt ergo homines mercari sine
25 moneta, et dabat unus alteri ovem pro frumento, et alius de labore suo panem vel lanam, et sic de aliis rebus: quod adhuc longo tempore postea fuit institutum, ut narrat Iustinus. Sed tamen in huiusmodi permutatione et transportatione rerum, multae difficultates

acciderunt. Subtilisati homines usum monetae invenere, quae
30 esset instrumentum permutandi ad invicem naturales divitias,
quibus de per se subvenitur naturaliter humanae necessitati. Nam
ipsae pecuniae dicuntur *Artificiales divitiae*: contingit enim his
abundantem mori fame, sicut exemplificat Aristoteles de Rege
cupido, qui oravit, ut quidquid ipse tangeret, aurum esset: quod
35 Dii annuerunt, et sic fame periit, ut dicunt Poetae. Quoniam per
pecuniam non immediate succurritur indigentiae vitae, sed est
instrumentum artificialiter adinventum pro naturalibus divitiis
leviter permutandis.

• Notes •

Prologus.

2–5 **Quibusdam . . . aliis . . .:** to some . . . to others . . .

2 **videtur:** impersonal.

quod: In typical Renaissance Latin, the indirect statement/
oratio obliqua is avoided and replaced by **quod**.

3 **de iure:** by right (as opposed to **de facto** *in fact*). Used in English
and other modern languages in legal and political contexts.

libere: adverb.

mutare monetas: By the expression *to alter the coins*, Oresme
means literally to alter the shape, the rate of exchange, the
material, the denomination or the weight of the existing coins or
to mint new money to replace the old.

4 **ad libitum:** *at one's pleasure or whim*. In modern musical
terminology, it is used to indicate that the player is encouraged to
interpret a passage freely. In the form "ad-lib" this expression is
used as a modern English verb standing for "to improvise."

5 **quantumlibet:** *as much as he wants*. There is a profit to be made
by the king or the prince deriving from any money alteration.

6 **Propter quod:** *for this reason*.

7   **quod secundum philosphiam Aristotelis:** Oresme had translated the treatise on economics attributed to Aristotle. Oresme modestly claims that he will only reason following Aristotle's footsteps.

9   **temere:** adverb, *audaciously, carelessly.*

        maiorum: maior, maioris, comparative adjective of **magnus, -a, -um**, *greater; elders, ancestors, greater* (with respect to age).

10   **dicturus:** future active participle.

10–11 **ad determinandum:** ad + gerund or gerundive expresses purpose.

11   **ita ut:** *in such a way that,* subjunctive result clause.

        omni cessante scrupulo: ablative absolute.

12   **sententiam:** here, *opinion.*

13   **quod:** direct object of **invenire.**

        immo: *nay.*

15   **quid:** Notice the interrogative pronoun (even if it is not technically a question).

Caput I.

17   **Quando dividebat Altissimus gentes:** a direct quote from Deuteronomy 32:8 (in the Vulgate the whole verse reads **Quando dividebat Altissimus gentes, quando separabat filios Adam, constituit terminus populorum iuxta numerum filiorum Israel.**) Oresme had a doctorate in theology and was also a bishop. We may imagine, however, that there is a teasing quality on Oresme's part when quoting this passage, which has been taken out of context. The end of the verse is: ". . . according to the number of the children of Israel." This biblical song starts with the love of God for the Israelites, their supposed misbehavior and then God's renewed promise of protection. The verse has nothing much to do with economics. But it had been a custom already in classical Roman literature to intersperse poetic quotes, usually out of context, even in scientific treatises, so as

to confer an air of authority. A typical example appears a few lines below the end of our Seneca selection. He is talking about earthquakes, but somehow he manages to quote from the *Aeneid*!

18–19 **multiplicati sunt homines super terram:** This is another direct biblical quotation. Chapter 6 of Genesis starts (in the Vulgate) as follows: **Cumque coepissent homines multiplicari super terram . . . .** It continues: **. . . et filias procreassent, videntes filii Dei filias hominum quod essent pulchras . . .** Oresme, however, does not need to pursue this politically incorrect tack and turns instead to the creation of money.

19 **pro ut expediebat:** *as it was expedient, useful,* or *advantageous.*

divisae: divido, dividere, divisi, divisum *to divide, to separate.*

20 **contigit: contingo, contingere, contigi, contactum** *to happen, to befall.* **Hoc contingit mihi** means *this happens to me.*

22 **e contrario:** *the opposite.*

27 **ut:** The translation of **ut** depends on whether it is followed by an indicative or a subjunctive verb.

Iustinus: Marcus Junianius Justinus (uncertain dates) was a Roman historian. Since in Oresme's time the obsession of exact references and quotes did not exist in academia, it is not clear to what statement from Iustinus he is alluding. Lacking web resources, it is quite probable that Oresme got mixed up with some other author, since he was relying on his prodigious memory anyway.

29 **Subtilisati:** The verb **subtiliso, subtilisare** does not quite exist. On the other hand, it is possible (first in Greek and then in Latin) to form a verb out of a noun or adjective by adding the ending *-izo* or *-iso*, which we often do in English. From **dogma** we obtain *dogmatize.* These are frequentative verbs. For instance, in Latin from **venire** we obtain the perfectly classical **ventitare** *to keep coming.* In other words, **subtilisati** can be actually read as **subtilitati**, which would mean *having been made more subtle, smarter* from so much experience.

invenere: invenerunt.

29–30 **quae esset:** *which would be.*

30   **ad invicem:** *mutually, reciprocally.*

divitias: divitiae, divitiarum (f) *riches, wealth,* used only in the plural.

31   **de per se:** *in and of themselves.*

subvenitur: impersonal, *it becomes of help to* + dative.

33   **mori fame:** *to die of hunger, to starve to death,* ablative of cause; cf. **fame,** line 35 below.

34   **oravit, ut:** indirect command.

35   **Dii: dei.**

annuerunt: adnuerunt.

38   **permutandis:** gerundive.

Domingo de Soto

The name "School of Salamanca" is applied to a group of Renaissance theologians and jurists that, inspired by the personality and works of Francisco de Vitoria (1486–1546) and acting within the Universities of Salamanca and Coimbra, made decisive changes to the European conception of natural law and the Rights of Man. The innovations in economic theory made by some of the members of the group went largely unrecognized in modern times until relatively recently. Domingo de Soto (1494–1560) is considered one of the greatest exponents of the School of Salamanca. His major economic work is *De Iustitia et Iure* (*On Justice and Law*) in ten parts, dealing mainly with the philosophy of law. In this influential treatise he devotes considerable attention to economic issues including the right determination of the price of goods in an organized society. Interesting too, although not included in the chosen selection, are his considerations on the effects of demand and supply on the price of goods.

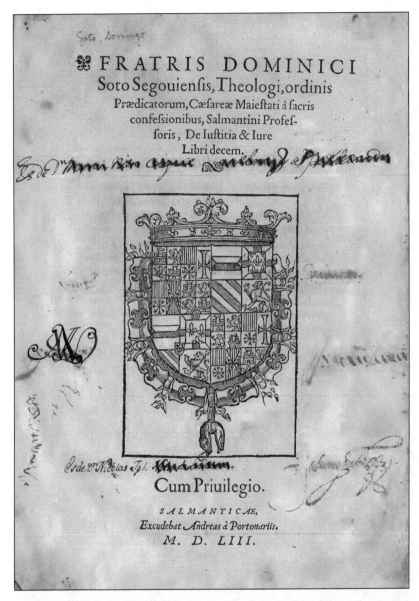

✠ FRATRIS DOMINICI
Soto Segouienſis, Theologi, ordinis
Prædicatorum, Cæſareæ Maieſtati à ſacris
confeſsionibus, Salmantini Profeſ-
ſoris, De Iuſtitia & Iure
Libri decem.

Cum Priuilegio.

SALMANTICAE,
Excudebat Andreas à Portonariis.
M. D. LIII.

Fratris Dominici Soto Segouiensis, theologi De iustitia & iure : libri decem, Salmanticae : Excudebat Andreas à Portonariis, 1553. By permission of The Robbins Collection, University of California, Berkeley School of Law. Facsimile courtesy of archive.org.

546   F. D. Soto, de Iustitia & Iure,

parati funt illa coëmere,quæ pauperes necef
fitate coacti,nec emptores inuenientes,ven
dere volunt:vt veftes,libros,&c.Qui verò an
nónam emunt vt tempore futuro reuendât,
licèt quandoq; vtiles fint,quafi rerum necef
fariarum cuftodes, multò tamê pluries funt
peftiferi:vt pote caufa immodicè augêdi pre
tia:& ideo nifi vbi necefsitas aliud expofcat,
meritifsimò eiufmodi mercatus vetatur.

Ad primum
argumentũ.
PER hæc ergo,argumenta fuprà facta fa
cilimę folutionis fiunt.Ad primum enim
negatur,negotiationem côtra naturã necef
fariæ emptionis pugnare:quin imò illi obfe
quens eft. Minifterio fiquidem mercatorũ,
res funt veluti in penu,fingulis indigentibus
Ad fecundũ
argumentũ.
expofitæ. Illa autem negotiatio quæ me
rum lucrum haberet pro fine, quia infatiabi
lem faceret animum, non folùm neceffaria
non eft,fed eft impendiò peftilens.Attamen
hæc fitis in cuncta mortalium pectora fe in
finuat. Et per hoc refpondetur ad fecundũ
Ad tertium
argumentũ.
argumentum. Tertiò verò côcedimus ne
cetiarium effe hac ratione rerum pretia au
geri:fed tamen ex altera parte maiora fierêt
difpendia fi vnufquilibet deberet longa fa
cere itinera ad quęritandũ quod in fua deeft
Ad quartũ
argumentũ.
ciuitate. Ad quartum refpondet Auguft.
Auguftinus.
fuper Pfal.70.Et refertur eâdem dift.88.can.
quoniam. quòd negotiatorum vitia nô funt
negotij, fed perfonarum. Etenim fi propter
eorum fraudes releganda effent negotia à re
publica, eâdê ratione & agricolas & omnes
pariter artifices atq; opifices, profcribere de
beremus profligareq; ab vrbe. Nam & men
titur quâdoq; agricola vt grana fua vendat,
& opifex vt pretium augeat. Qui autem ne
gotiatores in facris literis malè audiant, de
Caſſiodorus
clarat eâd.dift.Caffiodo.can.quid eft.Nego
tiatores enim illi,inquit,abominabiles exifti
mantur, qui iuftitiam Dei minimè confide
rantes, per immoderatũ pecuniæ ambitum
polluunt merces fuas,plus periurijs oneran
do, quàm pretijs. Veruntamen negare non
poffumus, vt paulò antè declarabam', quin
huic arti multò plus periculorum à dolis &
fraudib' immineat,quàm cæteris.Vnde Ec
clefiaft.26. Duæ fpecies difficiles & periculo
fæ mihi apparuerunt.Difficilè exuitur nego
tians à negligentia,& non iuftificabitur cau
po à peccatis labiorũ. Et cap. fequêti: Sicut
in medio compaginis lapidum palus figi
tur:fic inter medium venditionis & emptio
nis , qui quærit locupletari anguftiabitur

peccatis. Quocircà Prouerb.20. in vniuer
fum ait Sapiens : Malum eft, malum eft, ait
omnis emptor:& cùm recefferit,gloriatur.

ARTICVLVS. III.

Vtrùm rerum pretia, arbitrio merca
torum fint taxanda.

Voniam primum in emptio
ne & venditione fundamentũ
iuftitiæ eft pretiũ,de illo quæ
rendum eft loco tertio,an mer
catorũ æftimatione fit taxan
dum.Et arguitur à parte affirmatiua.Primò, *Primũ ar-*
Axiôma inter iurifconfultos eft & celebrata *gumentum.*
regula ,Tantum valet res,quantũ vendi po
teft:quam videlicet adnotant.l.pretia. ff. ad
legem Falcidian. &.l.1. §. fi hæres. ad fenat.
côfult.Trebellian. & alibi fæpe: ergo fi fraus
modò abfit & dolus, mercatorum erit arbi
trium pretia fuis mercibus ftatuere. Se- *Argumĕ. 2.*
cundò.In vnaquâq; arte eiufdem peritis cre
dendum eft,vti.3.Polit.cap.7.author eft Phi *Ariſtot.*
lofophus:& vt Iurifconfultus ait.l.in re mâ
data. C. mandati . vnufquifque in re fua eft
moderator & arbiter. merciũ autem artifi
ces,funt mercatores:ipfis ergo ipforum iudi
cio deferêdum eft vt pretia ponât. Tertiò: *Argumẽn.3.*
vnufquifque dominium rerum fuarum ha
bet,ac fubinde liberam poteftatem:ergo po
teft quifq; tantum petere ac recipere pretiũ
pro fua re , quantũ extorquere potuerit. id
quod in gemmis & rebus pretiofis vfu fieri
compertum eft. In contrarium autem fa
cit lex, Pretia. citata ad.l. Falci. cuius verba
funt:Pretia rerum non ex affectu neq; vtili
tate fingulorum , fed cômuniter finguntur:
hoc eft communi æftimatione taxantur.

AD hanc quæftionem quatuor conclufio *Prima con-*
nibus refpondetur. Prima: Pretia rerũ *clufio.*
non fecundùm ipfarum naturam æftiman
da funt,fed quatenùs in vfus veniunt huma
nos. Conclufionis huius ratio naturalis eft, *Ratio côcla*
quòd cùm mundus & quæ eo continentur *fionis.*
propter hominem facta fint, tanti ciuiliæfti
matione res valent quantum hominibus in
feruiunt. Quapropter Arift.5.Ethico.cap.5. *Ariſtot.*
ait indigentiam caufam menfuramque effe
humanarum commutationum.Si enim nul
lus alterius re vel opera indigeret,omnis cef
faret commutatio rerum humanarum:ergo
indigentiæ admetiri debemus rerum pretia.

Viuentia

Libri Sexti   Quæstio. II.   547

Viuentia enim genere suo prestantiora sunt
vitæ expertibus:attamen (vt ait Augustin.
lib.11.c.16.de Ciuita.Dei.) mallet homo frumentum domi habere,quàm mures .Et solet
domus plus vænire,quàm equus: & nonun-
quàm equus,quàm seruus:licet cùm natura
hominis nihil in corporalibus conferri ad
æqualitatem valeat. Vbi autem indigentiâ
nominamus,ornatum etiam reipublicæ in-
telligimus:vt cūcta complectamur quæ hominibus præter vitæ necessitatem etiam ad
suam voluptatem & splendorē vsui esse pos-
Secunda con- sunt. ❡ Secunda conclusio. Ad exploran-
clusio. dum iustum rei pretium ex multis ducenda
est ratio,quæ in triplici sunt ordine. Primū
enim attendenda est necessitas rei, mox copia & inopia:deinde negotiationis labor,cu
ra,industria, & pericula .Præterea si merces
vel in melius mutatæ sunt vel in deterius, vē
ditorumq; atque emptorum frequētia, atq;
id genus alia, quæ prudentissimus quisque
speculari potest. ❡ Tertia conclusio. Cùm
Tertia con- pretium rerum iustum,duplex sit,aliud sci-
clusio. licet legitimum, & aliud naturale:iustum legitimum cōsistit in indiuisibili:naturale autem seu arbitrarium minimè: sed in latitudi
ne diuisibili.Iustum legitimū est illud quod
lege principis positum est: arbitrarium autem seu naturale currit quando per legem
non est constitutum. Distinctio est Arist. 5.
Aristo. Ethi.c.7. de iusto naturali & legitimo.❡Ad
huius autem conclusionis intellectū notandum est quòd merita illa & causas statuendi
rerum pretia existimare,per se quidem primùm ad rem publicā & eius gubernatores
spectat:qui scilicet omnibus supradictis pē-
satis deberent sua singulis mercibus statuere pretia. At quia illud in omnibus impossi
bile est,relinquitur vendentium ementiūq;
existimationi. Et illud nunc vocamus natu
rale:quia secundùm rerum naturam vsui ac
commodatam currit . Igitur vbi pretium le
ge positum est:nempe,vt modius aut tritici
aut vini,aut vlna panni vēdatur decem, neq;
vnius oboli accessio licita est:sed est peccatū
mortale si excessus notabilis augeat,obno-
xiumq; restitutioni. Et si excessus sit perexi
guus,erit veniale.Et ideo dicimus in indiuis
bili consistere. Atq; hoc est quod ait loco ci
tato Arist.iustum legitimum esse,quod licet
antequàm positum sit nihil referat,refert ta
men postquàm positum est . Pretium verò
quod non est lege positum,non indiuisibile
est,sed latitudinem habet iustitia:cuius vnū

extremum dicitur rigidum:alterū verò piū: *Pretium rigi*
sed medium,moderatum . Vt quæ res iustè *dū,piū, mo*
vēditur decem, iustè quoq; vendit ,tum vn- *deratum.*
decim,tum etiam nouem.Atqui ratio huius
est quòd prudentia humana,qua per supradictorum considerationes de pretio existimatur,nequit pūctim attingere metam : sed
arbitramento quodam. Sicuti.2. Ethic. c. 6.
de virtute ait Arist. φ consistit in medio , vt
definierit ipse prudens. Atq; adeò dū respu
blica penes quam talis residet autoritas,pun
ctum non indicat,laxior restat iustitia pretij latitudinem habens. ❡Ex quo fit primò *Prima dedu*
cōsequēs vt infra illos extremos limites vēde *ctio.*
re cuicunque liceat cariùs pecunia credita,
quàm numerata:inimico quàm amico: diui
ti deniq; quàm pauperi. ❡ Sequitur secun- *Secunda.*
dò sensum illius legis, In causæ.ff. de minor.
vbi.§.idem Pomponius.habetur licère natu
raliter contrahentibus se decipere, cui simi-
le habetur.l.item si pretio.ff.locati.non esse
(vt Conrad.& aliqui putant) infra latitudinem iusti pretij:quia intra hos carceres nul
lum habet locum deceptio:neque vlla opus
est remissione (vt pdicti doctores autumāt)
sanè cùm tota latitudo iusta sit. Sed (vt. q.
proxima exponetur)intelligitur citra dimi-
dium iusti pretij. Et ideo ait naturaliter , φ
humanum ingenium lucri auidum,in causa
est. Quare,licère,illic non est idem quod sine culpa,sed impunè in humano foro. ❡Se- *Tertia colle-*
quitur tertiò,multò tutiùs,si fieri posset,con *ctio.*
sultum fore , tum coēmptorum negotiato-
rumq; conscientijs,tum etiam communi bo
no,si omnium pretia lege patèrent: vnde.l.
1.ff.de offic.præfect.vrbi.§.cura carnis. inter
alias præfecti curas illa censetur vt rerū pretia statuat iusta. Ob idq; quando in omnibus seruari nequit,quàm fieri posset maxi-
mè,deberent taxari . Enimuerò negotiato-
res,eò præsertim φ (vt suprà dictum est)lu-
cris sitienter inhiant,non solùm præ sua cæ-
citate decipiuntur,verùm etiam propter suā
auaritiam consultò astuq; decipiunt.Quam
ob rem quādo lege nō est signatū pretium,
non est standū vniuscuiuslibet mercatorum
arbitrio,sed prudentium iudicio , eorūq; qui
sunt æquitatis cultores. Est em fallacissima *Fallax regu-*
regula si quis semper quāto emit ptio, quā- *la in taxādis*
tuinq; laboris & periculorum subijt, tāti ve *pretijs.*
lit vendere cum lucri accessione. Enimuerò
si mercator,artis negotiorūq; ignarus pluris
iusto emit,aut sibi fortuna aduersa restlauit:
quia scilicet copia merciū insperata succre-
uit,

De Iustitia et Iure

Articulus III.

Utrum rerum pretia, arbitrio mercatorum sint taxanda.

Quoniam primum in emptione et venditione fundamentum
iustitiae est pretium, de illo quaerendum est loco tertio, an
mercatorum aestimatione sit taxandum. Et arguitur a parte
5   affirmativa. Primo. Axioma inter iurisconsultos est et celebrata
regula: Tantum valet res, quantum vendi potest: quam videlicet
adnotant l. pretia. ff. ad legem Falcidiam. et l. 1. videlicet si haeres.
ad senat. consult. Trebellian. et alibi saepe: ergo si fraus modo absit
et dolus, mercatorum erit arbitrium pretia suis mercibus statuere.
10   Secundo. In unaquaque arte eiusdem peritis credendum est, uti.
3. Polit. cap. 7. author est Philosophus: et ut Iurisconsultus ait. l. in
re mandata. C. mandati. Unusquisque in re sua est moderator et
arbiter. Mercium autem artifices, sunt mercatores: ipsis ergo ipsorum
iudicio deferendum est ut pretia ponant.
15   Tertio. Unusquisque dominium rerum suarum habet, ac subinde
liberam potestatem: ergo potest quisque tantum petere ac recipere
pretium pro sua re, quantum extorquere potuerit. Id quod in
gemmis et rebus pretiosis usu fieri compertum est.
In contrarium autem facit lex, Pretia. citata ad l. Falci. cuius
20   verba sunt: Pretia rerum non ex affectu neque utilitate singulorum,
sed communiter finguntur: hoc est communi aestimatione taxantur.

Ad hanc quaestionem quatuor conclusionibus respondetur.
Prima: Pretia rerum non secundum ipsarum naturam aestimanda
sunt, sed quatenus in usus veniunt humanos. Conclusionis huius
25   ratio naturalis est, quod cum mundus et quae eo continentur
propter hominem facta sint, tanti civili aestimatione res valent
quantum hominibus inserviunt. Quapropter Arist. 5. Ethico.

cap. 5. ait indigentiam causam mensuramque esse humanarum commutationum. Si enim nullus alterius re vel opera indigeret,

30 omnis cessaret commutatio rerum humanarum: ergo indigentiae admetiri debemus rerum pretia. Viventia enim genere suo praestantiora sunt vitae expertibus: attamen (ut ait Augustin. lib. ii. c. 16. de Civita. Dei.) mallet homo frumentum domi habere, quam mures. Et solet domus plus vaenire, quam equus: et nonunquam

35 equus, quam servus: licet cum natura hominis nihil in corporalibus conferri ad aequalitatem valeat. Ubi autem indigentiam nominamus, ornatum etiam reipublicae intelligimus: ut cuncta complectamur quae hominibus praeter vitae necessitatem etiam ad suam voluptatem et splendorem usui esse possunt.

40 Secunda conclusio. Ad explorandum iustum rei pretium ex multis ducenda est ratio, quae in triplici sunt ordine. Primum enim attendenda est necessitas rei, mox copia et inopia: deinde negotiationis labor, cura, industria, et pericula. Praeterea si merces vel in melius mutatae sunt vel in deterius, venditorumque atque

45 emptorum frequentia, atque id genus alia, quae prudentissimus quisque speculari potest.

Tertia conclusio. Cum pretium rerum iustum, duplex sit, aliud scilicet legitimum, et aliud naturale: iustum legitimum consistit in indivisibili: naturale autem seu arbitrarium minime: sed in

50 latitudine divisibili. Iustum legitimum est illud quod lege principis positum est: arbitrarium autem seu naturale currit quando per legem non est constitutum. Distinctio est Arist. 5. Ethi. c. 7. de iusto naturali et legitimo.

Ad huius autem conclusionis intellectum notandum est quod

55 merita illa et causas statuendi rerum pretia existimare, per se quidem primum ad rem publicam et eius gubernatores spectat: qui scilicet omnibus supradictis pensatis deberent sua singulis mercibus statuere pretia. At quia illud in omnibus impossibile est, relinquitur vendentium ementiumque existimationi. Et illud nunc vocamus

60 naturale: quia secundum rerum naturam usui ac commodatam
currit. Igitur ubi pretium lege positum est: nempe, ut modius aut
tritici aut vini, aut ulna panni vendatur decem, neque unius oboli
accessio licita est: sed est peccatum mortale si excessus notabilis
augeatur, obnoxiumque restitutioni. Et si excessus sit perexiguus,
65 erit veniale. Et ideo dicimus in indivisibili consistere. Atque hoc
est quod ait loco citato Arist. iustum legitimum esse, quod licet
antequam positum sit nihil referat, refert tamen postquam positum
est. Pretium vero quod non est lege positum, non indivisibile est,
sed latitudinem habet iustitia: cuius unum extremum dicitur
70 rigidum: alterum vero pium: sed medium, moderatum. Ut quae
res iuste venditur decem, iuste quoque venditur, tum undecim, tum
etiam novem. Atqui ratio huius est quod prudentia humana, qua
per supradictorum considerationes de pretio existimatur, nequit
punctim attingere metam: sed arbitramento quodam. Sicuti. 2.
75 Ethic. c. 6. de virtute ait Arist. quae consistit in medio, ut definierit
ipse prudens. Atque adeo dum respublica penes quam talis
residet autoritas, punctum non indicat, laxior restat iustitia pretij
latitudinem habens.

• Notes •

1 **taxanda: taxo, -are** *to appraise*. It is one of a series of passive
periphrastics that follow.

3 **loco tertio:** *in the third place* (considering that two other
arguments have already been made in previous sections).

an: introducing a question, here an indirect question. Often to
be interpreted as *whether or not*.

4 **sit:** The subject is still **pretium**.

5 **Primo:** *In the first place*. The argument for the affirmative is
based on three separate considerations enumerated as **primo**,
secundo, and **tertio**. The first argument goes back to the dictum
Tantum valet res, quantum vendi potest, entrenched in
Roman law.

6–8   **quam videlicet . . . alibi saepe:** This is just a parenthetical remark indicating where references can be found. The *Lex Falcidia*, later incorporated into the *Institutiones Iustiniani* [(*Justinian Institutes*) sixth century CE], was introduced by Publius Falcidius, a tribune of the plebs. Marcus Trebellius Maximus was consul in the year 55 CE. These references are clearly addressed to a reader who is an expert in Roman law.

8   **modo absit:** *if only there isn't.* Note that the verb is used in the singular, although it refers both to **fraus** and to **dolus.** This apparent grammatical incongruence is an example of what is called *synesis* from the Greek and in Latin **constructio ad sensum.**

10   **unaquaque:** ablative feminine singular of the adjective **unusquisque, unaquaeque, unumquodque** *every.* The two components (**unus, -a, -um,** and **quis, quae, quod**) are declined following their independent patterns.

    credendum est: impersonal passive periphrastic. *One must believe.* Note that **credo** takes the dative.

10–12   **uti . . . mandata:** These are references to Aristotle (**Philosophus**) in his *Politics* and to the prescription (known as **lex in re mandata**) **mandatam sibi jurisdictionem, mandare alteri non posse manifestum est,** which appears in the *Digesta* (*Justinian Digest*) 22. The **Iurisconsultus** is probably the Italian jurist Paulus de Castro (ca. 1360–1440), author of a treatise known as the *Consilia.*

12–13   **unusquisque . . . arbiter:** a well-known principle of Roman law.

18   **compertum est:** impersonal: *it is found.*

19   **citata ad l. Falci.: citata ad legem Falcidii,** *cited by/according to the law of Falcidius.* This law contradicts the previous arguments, since it establishes that prices are set not by the advantage of individuals but artificially by common agreement.

22   **quatuor:** medieval spelling for **quattuor.** De Soto is following the typical scholastic method, as exemplified by Thomas Aquinas: arguments are presented, a counterargument is opposed, and, finally, one or more conclusions are reached.

24   **quatenus:** *inasmuch, insofar as.*

26   **facta sint:** Technically, this is again a case of synesis, since **mundus** is masculine.

res valent: *things have value.*

29–30   **Si . . . indigerit, . . . cessaret:** contrary to fact present condition.

31   **admetiri: admetior, admetiri, admensus sum** *to measure out to.* It takes the accusative of the thing measured and the dative of the thing or person to whom it is measured out. Be careful not to confuse **admetiri** with **admittere** (as some experts have done), which would completely pollute the argument.

Viventia: *living things.* In at least one expert translation, this word was mistakenly rendered as "food," thus completely missing not only the point of the argument but also the humoristic element. Indeed, living things are clearly of great importance to those who know life. Nevertheless (as Augustine points out) a man would rather have wheat than mice in his house!

32   **praestantiora:** comparative of **praestans.**

33   **mallet: malo, malle, malui** *to prefer* (from **magis + volo**).

34   **vaenire: vaenio, vaenire,** a rare form of **venio** and perhaps of **vendo**. The basic meaning is *to be worth* or *to be able to be sold.* Thus, when Ovid says (in his *Ars Amatoria* [*The Art of Love*] 2.278) **plurimos auro venit honos** he may mean that honor is worth a large amount in gold.

nonunquam: *sometimes.* Latin is very precise here, since the negation of "never" is "at least once."

35   **licet:** impersonal verb. Literally *it is permitted, one may, that is.* Often used as *granted that, although.* To make matters worse, the personal verb **liceo, licere, licui, licitum** means *to be on sale* or *to be valued at.* We can then ignore **licet** and construe **cum natura hominis valeat**: *Although the nature of (his being a) man avails (is worth) nothing to be conferred to the corporeal qualities toward equality.* This is a bit forced, so you should try a better solution. The general sense is that the human nature of a slave does not seem to be strong enough to increase his monetary value so as to make it at least equal to that of a horse. In other words, the human nature of the slave does not seem to confer to him a value equal to that of an animal. They are both material objects.

37   **ornatum:** *adornment, equipment.* The intention here is that the term "need" or "want" is relative, since a society has to be granted certain luxuries that may not appear to be really necessary.

39   **usui esse: Usui** is in the dative case, *for the use.*

41   **ducenda est ratio: Rationem ducere** means *to turn one's attention, to consider, to reason.* The first in another set of passive periphrastics.

42   **mox:** The common meaning of **mox** is *soon.* It can also mean *then.*

      inopia: This word derives from **ops, opis** (f) *assistance.* In the plural (**opes**) it means *wealth, means.* **Inopia**, therefore, is *lack of means, scarcity.*

      deinde: We had **primum, mox,** and **deinde,** namely, three stages: *firstly, then,* and *finally* (or *thereafter*).

44   **deterius:** *weaker, poorer* as opposed to **melius**; *are changed for something better or for something worse.*

45   **frequentia:** *large number.* Do not translate as *frequency.*

      id genus alia: One would expect here **alia eius generis** or **alia eiusmodi.** But **id genus alia** is a classic expression imported from a Greek equivalent. *Other things of this kind.*

47–48 **aliud ... aliud ...:** *one ... the other ...*

48   **scilicet:** literally, *it is permitted to know.* It is best translated as *that is.*

49   **indivisibili:** Recall that adjectives of the third declension form the ablative in *–i.*

      minime: adverb: *not at all.*

50   **legitimum:** *imposed by law.* **Legitimus, -a, -um** should not necessarily be rendered as *legitimate,* but more *as according to law* or *lawful.*

54–56 **notandum est ... spectat:** One way to reorder this long sentence can be the following: **notandum est quod existimare illa merita et causas statuendi pretia rerum spectat (per se quidem primum) ad rem publicam et eius gubernatores.** If this is acceptable, then the meaning would be: *It is to be noted that to evaluate the merits and causes of establishing the prices of things is something that pertains (of itself, in the first place) to the state and its rulers.* In the *Nicomachean Ethics*, Chapter 5, Section 7, Aristotle states that justice is of two kinds, one natural and the other conventional. He is not referring to prices at all. Moreover, natural justice has a higher meaning for Aristotle than it has in the present context. It is not clear whether de Soto is strengthening or weakening his conclusion by this allusion to the great philosopher.

75   **definierit: definiverit.** A common elision of the *v* has occurred. Here we have a perfect subjunctive of possibility.

Chemistry

Georgius Agricola

G eorgius Agricola (1494–1555) is the Latin version of the name Georg Bauer.[23] Trained in classical languages and an avid learner by nature, Agricola was an expert in chemistry and medicine. In 1527 he was appointed head physician at Joachimsthal, a mining town in Saxony, today part of Germany. This appointment served as inspiration for his careful observations and systematic analysis of the mining industry and of minerals in general. Transferred to Chemnitz, an important mining center, also in Saxony, he continued his studies in the field. However, these were times of religious strife and as a Catholic, Agricola found himself forced to resign his position as Chemnitz was mostly Protestant. He then devoted most of his time to writing on many subjects. His masterpiece, however, remains the book *De Re Metallica* (*On Metallurgy*), published posthumously. In classical Latin the word *metallum* was used to designate both a metal and a mine. So, at least in principle, the name of the book can be translated most appropriately as "On the Mining Industry" rather than as "On Metallurgy." When he wants to be more specific, Agricola uses the term **fodina, -ae** (f) for a mine. This is not a classical term (although

---

23 There were two main ways to latinize a name. The easier one consisted of simply adding a Latin-sounding ending that would render the name as a noun of the first, second, or third declension. Thus, Leibniz becomes Leibnitius. The second, more ingenious, way attempted to translate the supposed meaning of the name. Thus, the Dutch Gerard de Cremer (or, in German, Gerhard von Kremer) became Gerardus Mercator, while Johannes von Königsberg became Ioannes Regiomontanus. Bauer in German means *farmer*.

it derives legitimately from the classical verb **fodio, fodere, fodi, fossum** *to dig*). He never uses the later term **minera, -ae** (f), as Andreas Libavius does. Many of Agricola's observations and prescriptions were of a strictly chemical nature and influenced Libavius, author of the first systematic chemical treatise.

De Re Metallica was translated into English early in the twentieth century by Herbert and Lou Henry Hoover, the future President and First Lady of the United States. The couple had a combined expertise in mining, geology, and Latin.[24]

---

24 It is appropriate to remember that Lou Henry Hoover (1874–1944), First Lady (1929–1933) of the United States, who graduated as a geologist from Stanford in 1898, was also a gifted polyglot. During her stay in China with her husband she became fluent in spoken Mandarin and taught herself Latin. She also had a working knowledge of French, German, Italian, and Spanish. An interesting account of this remarkable personality is given in K. A. Clements, "The New Era and the New Woman," *Pacific Historical Review* 73, no. 3 (2004): 425–462.

GEORGII AGRICOLAE

DE RE METALLICA LIBRI XII▸ QVI=
bus Officia, Inſtrumenta, Machinæ, ac omnia deniꝗ ad Metalli=
cam ſpectantia, non modo luculentiſſimè deſcribuntur, ſed & per
effigies, ſuis locis inſertas, adiunctis Latinis, Germanicisꝗ appel=
lationibus ita ob oculos ponuntur, ut clarius tradi non poſſint.

EIVSDEM

DE ANIMANTIBVS SVBTERRANEIS Liber, ab Autore re=
cognitus: cum Indicibus diuerſis, quicquid in opere tractatum eſt,
pulchrè demonſtrantibus.

FRO BEN

ΒASILEAE M▸ D◂ LVI▸

Cum Priuilegio Imperatoris in annos v.
& Galliarum Regis ad Sexennium.

Georgii Agricolae De re metallica libri XII, Froben, Basel, 1556. Property of the National Central Library of Rome. Facsimile courtesy of archive.org.

GEORGII AGRICO-
LAE DE RE METALLICA
LIBER PRIMVS.

VLTI habent hanc opinionem, rem metallicam
fortuitum quiddam esse, & sordidum opus, atq;
omnino eiusmodi negotiũ quod non tam artis
indigeat quàm laboris. Sed mihi, cum singulas
eius partes animo, & cogitatione percurro, res
uidetur longe aliter se habere. Siquidem metallicus sit oportet suæ artis peritissimus, ut pri
mo sciat, qui mons, qui collis, quæue uallestris
aut campestris positio utiliter fodi possit, aut recuset fossionem. Deinde u-næ, fibræ, commissuræq; saxorum ipsi pateant. Mox pernoscat mult plices uariasq; species terrarũ, succorum, gemmarum, lapidum, marmorũ, saxorum, metallorum, mistorum: tum habeat cognitam omnem omnis operis sub terra faciendi rationem. Nota deniq; ipsi sint artificia materiæ experiendæ, & parandæ ad excoctionem,
quæ etiam ipsa est admodum diuersa. Nam aliam exigit aurũ & argentũ,
aliam æs, aliam argentum uiuũ, aliam ferrum, aliam plumbũ, & in eo ipso
dissimilem candidum ac cinereũ uel nigrum. Quamuis autem ars succos
liquidos coquendi ad spissitudinem esse secreta à metallica possit uideri,
tamen quia ijdem succi effodiuntur etiam in terra densati, aut excoquuntur ex quibusdam terrarũ lapidũmue generibus, quæ metallici effodiunt,
& quorum quædam metallis non carent, ab ea separari non debet, quæ
excoctio iterũ non est simplex, etenim alia est salis, alia nitri, alia aluminis,
alia atramenti sutorij, alia sulfuris, alia bituminis. Metallicus præterea sit
oportet multarum artiũ & disciplinarum non ignarus: Primo Philoso-
phiæ, ut subterraneorũ ortus & causas, naturasq; noscat: Nam ad fodiendas uenas faciliore & cõmodiore uia perueniet, & ex effossis uberiores capiet fructus. Secundo Medicinæ, ut fossoribus & alijs operarijs proui-
dere possit, ne in morbos, quibus præ cæteris urgentur, incidant: aut si
inciderint, uel ipse eis curationes adhibere, uel ut medici adhibeant curare. Tertio Astronomiæ, ut cognoscat cœli partes, atq; ex eis uenarũ extensiones iudicet. Quarto Mensurarũ disciplinæ, ut et metiri queat, quàm
alte fodiendus sit puteus, ut pertineat ad cuniculũ usq; qui eò agitur, &
certos cuiq; fodinæ, præsertim in profundo, cõstituere fines terminosq;.
Tum numerorũ disciplinæ sit intelligens, ut sumptus, qui in machinas &
fossiones habendi sunt, ad calculos reuocare possit. Deinde Architecturæ, ut diuersas machinas substructionesq; ipse fabricari, uel magis fabricandi rationem alijs explicare queat. Postea Picturæ, ut machinarũ exempla deformare possit. Postremo Iuris, maxime metallici sit peritus, ut
& alteri nihil surripiat, & sibi petat non iniquũ, munusq; alijs de iure respondendi sustineat. Itaq; necesse est ut is, cui placent certæ rationes &

a   præce-

præcepta rei metallicæ hos aliosq3 nostros libros studiose diligenterq3 le
gat, aut de quaq3 re consulat experientes metallicos, sed paucos inueni‐
ci gnaros totius artis. Etenim plerunq3 alius fodiendi rationē tenet: alius
percepit scientiam lauandi, alius arte excoquendi confidit : alius discipli‐
nam terræ metiendæ occultat : alius artificiose fabricatur machinas : alius
deniq3 iuris metallici peritus est. At nos ut inueniendorū & cōficiendo‐
rum metallorum scientiam non perfecerimus, hominibus certè studiosis
ad eam percipiēdam magnum afferemus adiumentū. Verum accedamus
ad institutam rationem.

Cvm semper fuerit inter homines summa de metallis dissensio,quod
alij eis præconiū tribuerent,alij ea grauiter uituperarent,uisum mihi
est, antequam metallica præcepta tradam, ueritatis inuestigandæ causa
rem ipsam diligenter expendere. Ordiar autem ab utilitatis quæstione,
quæ duplex est, aut enim quæritur, utilis nec ne sit ars metallica his qui
uersantur in eius studio : aut reliquis hominibus utilis ne sit, an inutilis.
Qui metallicam censent inutilem esse his,qui suum studium in ipsa collo‐
cant, aiunt primo uix centesimū quemq3 fodientem metalla, uel id genus
alia, fructus ex ea re capere. Sed metallicos, quia omnes suas opes certas
& bene constitutas committūt dubiæ & lubricæ fortunæ, plerunq3 spe
falli, sumptibusq3 & iacturis exhaustos amarissimā tandem uitam, & mi‐
serrimam degere. Verum isti non uident quantū distet doctus & usu pe‐
ritus metallicus ab artis ignaro atq3 imperito, hic sine ullo delectu & dis‐
crimine fodit uenas, ille eas experitur atq3 tentat: Sed quia inuenit uel ni‐
mis angustas & duras, uel laxas & putres, ex eo colligit ipsas utiliter fodi
non posse : itaq3 fodit selectas tantum:quid igitur mirum? rerum metalli‐
carū imperitum damnum facere? peritum uero fructus ex fossione cape‐
re uberrimos? Contingit idem agricolis. Nam qui terram arant, siccā pa
riter & densam & macram, eiq3 mandant semina, tantā non faciunt mes‐
sem, quantam hi qui solum pingue ac putre colunt, & in eo faciunt semē‐
tem. Cum autem multo plures metallici sint artis imperiti quàm periti,fit
ut metallorum fossio perpaucis emolumento sit, detrimentū afferat mul‐
tis. Siquidem uulgus metallicorū,quod est cognitionis uenarum rude ig
narumq3, non raro & operam & oleū perdit. Id enim magna ex parte so‐
let accurrere ad metalla, cum uel propter magnū & graue æs alienū, quo
se obstrinxit,mercaturā deposuerit,uel laboris cōmutandi gratia relique‐
rit falcem & aratrum. Quamobrem si quando incidit in uenas metalloru
aliorūmue fossilium fœcundas, id bona magis fortuna accidit, quàm ali‐
qua subtili animaduersione. Quod autem metallica multos auxerit diui‐
tijs ex historijs intelligimus, etenim inter scriptores antiquos constat ali‐
quot respub. florentes, nonnullos reges, plurimos homines priuatos ex
metallis eorūmue ramentis diuites esse factos. Quam rem multis claris &
illustribus exemplis usus, in primo libro De ueteribus & nouis metallis
inscripto dilataui atq3 explicaui, ex quibus exemplis apparet metallicam
suis cultoribus esse utilissimam. Deinde ijdem reprehensores dicunt me‐
tallicæ quæstū minime esse stabilem,magnisq3 laudibus efferunt agricul‐
                                                                    turam

De Re Metallica

Liber Primus.

Multi habent hanc opinionem, rem metallicam fortuitum quiddam
esse, et sordidum opus, atque omnino eiusmodi negotium quod
non tam artis indigeat quam laboris. Sed mihi, cum singulas eius
5   partes animo, et cogitatione percurro, res videtur longe aliter se
habere. Siquidem metallicus sit oportet suae artis peritissimus, ut
primo sciat, qui mons, qui collis, quaeve vallestris aut campestris
positio utiliter fodi possit, aut recuset fossionem. Deinde venae,
fibrae, commissuraeque saxorum ipsi pateant. Mox pernoscat
10   multiplices variasque species terrarum, succorum, gemmarum,
lapidum, marmorum, saxorum, metallorum, mistorum: tum
habeat cognitam omnem omnis operis sub terra faciendi rationem.
Nota denique ipsi sint artificia materiae experiendae, et parandae
ad excoctionem, quae etiam ipsa est admodum diversa. Nam aliam
15   exigit aurum et argentum, aliam aes, aliam argentum vivum, aliam
ferrum, aliam plumbum, et in eo ipso dissimilem candidum ac
cinereum vel nigrum. Quamvis autem ars succos liquidos coquendi
ad spissitudinem esse secreta a metallica possit videri, tamen quia
iidem succi effodiuntur etiam in terra densati, aut excoquuntur ex
20   quibusdam terrarum lapidumve generibus, quae metallici effodiunt,
et quorum quaedam metallis non carent, ab ea separari non debet,
quae excoctio iterum non est simplex, etenim alia est salis, alia nitri,
alia aluminis, alia atramenti sutorii, alia sulfuris, alia bituminis.
Metallicus praetera sit oportet multarum artium et disciplinarum
25   non ignarus: Primo Philosophiae, ut subterraneorum ortus et
causas, naturasque noscat: Nam ad fodiendas venas faciliore et
commodiore via perveniet, et ex effosis uberiores capiet fructus.
Secundo Medicinae, ut fossoribus et aliis operariis providere
possit, ne in morbos, quibus prae caeteris urgentur, incidant:
30   aut si inciderint, vel ipse eis curationes adhibere, vel ut medici

adhibeant curare. Tertio Astronomiae, ut cognoscat coeli partes,
atque ex eis venarum extensiones iudicet. Quarto Mensurarum
disciplinae, ut et metiri queat, quam alte fodiendus sit puteus,
ut pertineat ad cuniculum usque qui eo agitur, et certos cuique
35   fodinae, praesertim in profundo, constituere fines terminosque.
Tum numerorum disciplinae sit intelligens, ut sumptus, qui in
machinas et fossiones habendi sunt, ad calculos revocare possit.
Deinde Architecturae, ut diversas machinas substructionesque ipse
fabricare, vel magis fabricandi rationem aliis explicare queat. Postea
40   Picturae, ut machinarum exempla deformare possit. Postremo
Iuris, maxime metallici sit peritus, ut et alteri nihil surripiat, et sibi
petat non iniquum, munusque aliis de iure respondendi sustineat.
Itaque necesse est ut is, cui placent certae rationes et praecepta rei
metallicae hos aliosque nostros libros studiose diligenterque legat,
45   aut de quaque re consulat experientes metallicos, sed paucos
inveniet gnaros totius artis. Etenim plerunque alius fodiendi
rationem tenet: alius percepit scientiam lavandi, alius arte
excoquendi confidit: alius disciplinam terrae metiendae occultat:
alius artificiose fabricatur machinas: alius denique iuris metallici
50   peritus est. At nos ut inveniendorum et conficiendorum metallorum
scientiam non perfecerimus, hominibus certe studiosis ad eam
percipiendam magnum afferemus adiumentum. Verum accedamus
ad institutam rationem.

• Notes •

2   **rem metallicam: Res metallica** is, literally, *the metallic thing*,
namely, *the metal industry.*

3   **omnino:** *entirely.*

4   **tam . . . quam . . .:** *so much . . . as . . .*

5–6   **se habere:** *to be.*

6   **metallicus:** *a metallurgist, a miner, a prospector.*

oportet: impersonal verb. *It is proper that,* usually in combination with an accusative or dative, but here Agricola keeps the nominative **metallicus** with **sit:** *It is necessary that the miner be . . .*

peritissimus: peritus, -a, -um takes a genitive or an ablative.

7 **qui:** interrogative adjective in indirect question.

quaeve: et quae, vel quae.

vallestris: vallester, vallestris, derived from **valles,** similar to **campester, campestris,** derived from **campus.**

8 **fodi:** passive infinitive of **fodio, fodere, fodi, fossum.**

9 **commissurae:** The expression **commissurae saxorum,** *the joints of the rocks,* is almost the same as the one used by Seneca (**commissurae lapidis**) in our selection from his *Naturales Quaestiones (Natural Questions).*

ipsi pateant: *be evident, open, clear to him.*

Mox: The common meaning of **mox** is *soon.* It can also mean *then.* We encountered this usage also in de Soto's *De Iustitia et Iure.* There we had **primum, mox,** and **deinde,** namely, three stages: *firstly, then,* and *finally* (or *thereafter*). Here we have them in the order **primo, deinde,** and **mox.**

10 **succorum:** succus (or **sucus**), -i (m), literally, *juice;* more generally, *a fluid.*

11 **mistorum:** alternative spelling for **mixtorum,** from **misceo, miscere, miscui, mixtum.** The intention here is to distinguish between pure minerals and compounds, i.e., mixtures.

12 **habeat . . . rationem:** The following is a reordered version of the Latin: **Habeat cognitam omnem rationem omnis operis faciendi sub terra.** The gerundive **omnis operis faciendi** can be replaced by **faciendi omnia opera. Ratio** means *reason, method, system.* **Habeat cognitam omnem rationem** refers to the complete knowledge of the method that a miner ought to have.

13 **materiae experiendiae:** gerundive, *of trying* or *assaying a substance.*

14   **excoctionem: excoctio, -onis** (f) from **excoquo, excoquere, excoxi, excoctum** *to boil down*.

    ipsa: referring to **artificia**.

15   **argentum vivum:** *quicksilver*, that is, *mercury* (or *hydrargyrum*).

16–17   **candidum ac cinereum vel nigrum:** modifying **plumbum**, *lead*, of which he distinguishes two further varieties. According to Hoover, the white (**candidum**) variety is "tin" and the ashen or the black (**cinereum vel nigrum**) variety is "bismuth."

17   **ars succos liquidos coquendi:** The gerund could also be expressed with the gerundive as **ars succorum liquidorum coquendorum**.

18   **secreta a metallica:** *separate from the metallurgical* [*art*]. **Secretus, -a, -um** is the perfect passive participle of **secerno, secernere, secrevi, secretum**.

19   **iidem: eidem.**

21   **carent: careo, carere, carui** *to be lacking of, to be without*, takes the ablative.

22   **quae excoctio:** This can be considered the beginning of a new sentence, or separated from the previous one by a semicolon— *which smelting, again, is not simple . . .*

23   **aluminis: alumen, aluminis** (n) *a bitter salt* (today identified with an aluminum compound).

    atramenti sutorii: Atramentum from **ater, atra, atrum** means *black fluid*. **Sutor, sutoris** (m) is *a shoemaker*. The shoemaker's ink is, according to Hoover, vitriol (sulfuric acid).

24–25   **Metallicus . . . ignarus:** After bombarding us with rather bombastic technical terms, Agricola starts a new topic (although not a new paragraph). Following Vitruvius's style, he will tell us that metallurgy is not an isolated science. It is interconnected with other arts and sciences. Notice that the various disciplines are in the genitive case as objects of **ignarus**, since the miner must not be ignorant of them.

25   **ut:** first of a series of purpose clauses.

27   **uberiores:** comparative of **uber, uberis** *rich*.

29   **quibus prae caeteris urgentur:** *by which (diseases) they are oppressed before (or more than) others.*

32   **venarum extensiones iudicet:** *that he may judge the extension of the veins.*

32–33   **Mensurarum disciplinae:** *the discipline of surveying.* In other languages a surveyor is called a "geometer," an "agrimensor," or a "measurer." In modern engineering schools the term "geomatics" is used to encompass all of the above nuances.

33   **metiri: metior, metiri, mensus sum.**

      queat: Queo, quire, quivi, quitum is a synonym of **possum, posse, potui.** Its opposite is **nequeo.**

      quam: *how*; **quam alte** *how deeply.*

34   **ad cuniculum usque: usque ad cuniculum.**

34–35   **certos . . . terminosque:** governed by **queat.** A possible reordering: **Constituere certos fines terminosque cuique fodinae, praesertim in profundo. Cuique** is dative singular of **quisque, quaeque, quodque; fodina, -ae** (f) *mine, a pit.*

36   **numerorum disciplinae:** *the science of numbers,* that is, arithmetic.

      sumptus: sumptus, -us (m) *cost, expense.*

40   **deformare:** *to delineate, to draw, to shape.*

43   **is, cui placent certae rationes et praecepta:** literally, *he to whom the true methods and precepts are pleasing.*

44   **legat:** *Let him read,* jussive subjunctive.

46   **plerunque:** used as an adverb, *mostly.* Note spelling.

46–49   **alius . . . alius . . . alius . . .:** *one . . . another . . . another . . .*

50–51   **ut . . . scientiam non perfecerimus:** *as (or although) we have not completely achieved the knowledge of . . .*

52   **accedamus:** hortatory subjunctive.

Andreas Libavius

Andreas Libavius (ca. 1555–1616) was a medical doctor and humanist. Although a believer in the possibility of transmutation of base metals into gold, he was a rationalist, in the Aristotelian sense, and also inclined to apply a strict scientific method based on empirical evidence. He profoundly disliked Paracelsus, with his mixture of science and magic, but he did adopt Paracelsian methods of research.

Although entitled *Alchemia* (*Alchemy*), his magnum opus can be considered as the first systematic textbook of chemistry. In style, Libavius owes much to Agricola in terms of the clarity of the exposition and the demarcation of various areas within the discipline. His division of chemistry into the technical part (*encheria*, or instrumentation) pertaining to the organization of a laboratory and the use of instruments, on the one hand, and a part pertaining to the actual objectives of the science, on the other hand, is particularly resounding to modern ears. It is noteworthy that he reserved the term *Chymia* for the second, more theoretical, component. The term "alchemy," as many other terms borrowed from Arabic, incorporates the Arabic definite article "al." This linguistic misunderstanding is prevalent in Spanish. What is left after eliminating the article is "chemy" or, more precisely, "chymia." Originally a Greek term, borrowed by Muslim scientists from Hellenistic sources, it may in turn have been borrowed into Greek from Ancient Egyptian to designate earth, or from Coptic to designate Egypt. Other possible etymologies have been suggested. Be that as it may, once deprived of the definite article, alchemy is chemistry, a term definitively adopted in English after Robert Boyle's publication (1661) of his book *The Sceptical Chymist*.

The influence of Libavius's work was widespread and quotations from the book were borrowed freely immediately after publication and over the succeeding centuries. An example is John Woodall's (1570–1643) treatise *The Surgeon's Mate, Military and Domestic Surgery*. The title page of the first edition of Libavius's *Alchemy* (1597) starts with the acronym D. O. M. A. (*Deo maximo optimo aeterno*). In the second, corrected and augmented, edition (1606), the Hebrew Tetragrammaton (the four-lettered name of God, which in Jewish tradition is never to be pronounced) is added above the acronym. In spite of his criticisms of Paracelsus, it seems that Libavius too had a penchant for the mystic. Paracelsus was at the same time a scientist and a mystic, whereas Libavius adhered to a stricter scientific approach. Having said that, the separation between the provable and the magical was quite fuzzy in those days.

Alchymia Andreae Libauii, recognita, emendata, et aucta, tum dogmatibus & experimentis nonnullis, Joannes Saurius, Frankfurt, 1606. By permission of the Linda Hall Library of Science, Engineering and Technology. Facsimile courtesty of archive.org.

An earlier edition (at the Bayerische Staatsbibliothek München) dates from 1597.

I

ALCHEMIÆ LIBER
PRIMVS
DE ENCHERIA

CAPVT I.

Quid Alchemia?

ALCHEMIA est ars perficiendi magisteria, & essentias puras è mistis separato corpore, extrahendi.

Quæ duo officia, quia voce laborandi vulgò comprehenduntur, euenit, vt etiam ars bene laborandi queat nominari, aut segregationis puri ab impuro, per succi formam, & fusionis modum seu solutionis, ob partis huius excellentiam, vnde & nomen arti natum iudicatur.

Exordium habet à natura, quam imitari industria primi studuerunt artifices, idq; maxime initio in succis mineralibus extrahendis è vena, & depurandis, quo pacto ipsa natura pura puta metalla, & succos è mineris profundit, vt etiam in die è venis suis extantes conspiciantur. Itaque olim in metallurgia plurimum valuit. Nunc medicinæ ministrat potius, & non in mineralibus elaborat tantum, sed & animalibus & vegetabilibus, ad vsus humanos, & salutem defendendam, quanquam etiam ornamenta vitæ conferat plurima.

(Primus inuentor eius creditur Tubalcain ille in sacris notus, quem Vulcanum nominant. Is enim primus in metallurgia, quæ pars est Alchymiæ, elaborasse scribitur. In AEgyto eius celebrator extitit Hermes, seu Mercurius Trismegistus, inuento transmutationis nobilis, à quo res quædam artis adhuc nomen habent, vt vas Hermetis seu pelicanus, nues Hermetis, sigillum Hermeticum, &c. Ita apud Mesuen sunt pil. Hermetis, hiera Hermetis, &c. Ab hoc etiam ars ipsa Hermetis nuncupatur, & intelligitur transmutatoria, quam præceptis comprehendit Gebrus Mauritanus. Ad medicinam eam accommodasse, & liquores stillatitios fecisse leguntur primi Arabes & Persæ. Vnde Auicenna à Sorsano dicitur Alchymiæ studuisse, ipseq; nominatim facit mentionem corrigendæ aquæ per sublimationem & destillationem. Hunc sequuntur Rhazes, Mesue, Bulcasis & alij, apud quos Chymica multa à reperiuntur: & nominatim Mesue Alchymistis tribuit etiam oleorum resolutorum confectionem. Nostro tempore eius fiducia Paracelsus summa inis miscuit, & peculiarem factionem Paracelsistarum genuit. Vnde Paracelsia est monstrosa quædam iactantia, ex ruditate & scientia temeritateq; conflata, miscens medicinam Alchemiæ, & hinc omnes scientias peruertens.)

Non desunt se Iudaica genti notitiam huius, am forte indicio est aqua illa nardina preciosaquæ persusus est Saluator.

CAP. II.

De partibus Alchemiæ.

ALchemiæ partes sunt duæ: Encheria & Chymia.

Encheria est prima pars Alchemiæ, de operationum modis.

Itaque hæc pars generaliter species operationum describit, quæ postea singulis magisteriis & essentiis elaborandis accommodantur. Et quia manus industria hic plurimum valet; etiam nomen inde sortita est, ut ἐγχειρησις, quasi manus artificiosè admonendæ descriptionem nomines, dicatur, cum tamen non solius sit manus, sed omnium sensuum solertiam attentionemque & ingenij acumen requirat singulare.

Inseruiunt Encheriæ, Ergalia, & Pyronomia, quarum tanta est in Alchemiæ exercitio necessitas, vt is demum artifex absolutus censeatur, qui earum notitiam & vsum habet perfectum. Debetur enim operationibus singulis, quin & fere vnius eiusdemque diuersis interuallis, suum instrumentum & ignis, vt sine illis nihil possit laudabiliter & accuratè fieri.

CAP. III.

De Ergalia, & primum de lutandis & obstruendis vasis.

ERgalia est instrumentorum alchemicorum explicatio.

Ad quam cum duo pertineant, noticia, & vsus: fundamentum huius est illa. Qui enim instrumenta chymica benè cognouit, & non tantum simplicia inspexit, sed & ea componere ad operationes certas didiceit: in vtendi rationem vnà ducitur, quam tamen perfectè exponit ipsa Encheria.

Instrumenta sunt duplicia, vasa & suppellex tumultuaria.

Vasa sunt instrumenta capiendis rebus idonea. Itaq; & capacitatem habent in se, & sua orificia.

Vasa

Alchemia

Alchemiae Liber Primus De Encheria.

Caput I.
Quid Alchemia.

Alchemia est ars perficiendi magisteria, et essentias puras e mistis
5 separato corpore, extrahendi. Quae duo officia, quia voce laborandi
vulgo comprehenduntur, evenit, ut etiam ars bene laborandi queat
nominari, aut segregationis puri ab impuro, per succi formam, et
fusionis modum seu solutionis, ob partis huius excellentiam, unde et
nomen arti natum iudicatur.

10   Exordium habet a natura, quam imitari industria primi
studuerunt artifices, idque maxime initio in succis mineralibus
extrahendis e vena, et depurandis, quo pacto ipsa natura pura puta
metalla, et succos e mineris profundit, ut etiam in die e venis suis
extantes conspiciantur. Itaque olim in metallurgia plurimum valuit.
15 Nunc medicinae ministrat potius, et non in mineralibus elaborat
tantum, sed et animalibus et vegetabilibus, ad usus humanos, et
salutem defendendam, quanquam etiam ornamenta vitae conferat
plurima.

        (Primus inventor eius creditur Tubalcain ille in sacris notus,
20 quem Vulcanum nominant. Is enim primus in metallurgia, quae
pars est Alchymiae, elaborasse scribitur. In Aegypto eius celebrator
extitit Hermes, seu Mercurius Trismegistus, invento transmutationis
nobilis, a quo res quaedam artis adhuc nomen habent, ut vas
Hermetis seu pelicanus, aves Hermetis, sigillum Hermeticum, etc.
25 Ita apud Mesuen sunt pilula Hermetis, hiera hermetis, etc. Ab hoc
etiam ars ipsa Hermetis nuncupatur, et intelligitur transmutatoria,
quam praeceptis comprehendit Gebrus Mauritanus. Ad medicinam
eam accommodasse, et liquores stillatitios fecisse leguntur primi
Arabes et Persae. Unde Avicenna a Sorsano dicitur Alchymiae
30 studuisse, ipseque nominatim facit mentionem corrigenda aquae per

sublimatione salvater et destillationem. Hunc sequuntur Rhazes,
Mesue, Bulcasis, et alii, apud quos Chymica multa reperiuntur: et
nominatim Mesue Alchymistis tribuit etiam oleorum resolutorum
confectionem. Nostro tempore eius fiducia Paracelsus summa imis
35   miscuit, et peculiarem factionem Paracelsistarum genuit. Unde
Paracelsia est monstrosa quaedam iactantia, ex ruditate et scientia
temeritateque conflata, miscens medicinam Alcemiae, et hinc omnes
scientias pervertens.)

Caput II.

40   **De partibus Alchemiae.**

Alchemiae partes sunt duae: Encheria, et Chymia. Encheria est
prima pars Alchemiae, de operationum modis. Itaque haec pars
generaliter species operationum describit, quae postea singulis
magisterijs et essentijs elaborandis accommodantur. Et quia manus
45   industria hic plurimum valet; etiam nomen inde sortita est, ut
encheiresis, quasi manus artificiose admovendae descriptionem
nomines, dicatur, cum tamen non solius sit manus, sed omnium
sensuum sollertiam attentionemque et ingenij acumen requirat
singulare.

50   Inserviunt Encheriae, Ergalia, et Pyronomia, quarum tanta est
in Alchemiae exercitio necessitas, ut is demum artifex absolutus
censeatur, qui earum notitiam et usum habet perfectum. Debetur
enim operationibus singulis, quin et fere unius eiusdemque diversis
intervallis, suum instrumentum et ignis, ut sine illis nihil possit
55   laudabiliter et accurate fieri.

• Notes •

Caput I.

1   **Encheria:** Greek word meaning *in hand*. As Libavius explains
below, this is one of the two parts of alchemy. It deals with
the various instruments and techniques used in chemical
experiments.

3   **Quid Alchemia:** Supply **sit.**

4   **magisteria:** The alchemical vocabulary is not entirely
comprehensible or expressible in terms of modern chemistry.
The concept of **magisterium** entails the attainment of the
purest form of a substance, free from all imperfections. The term
magisterium, however, is also used in a more generic way to
mean *attribute.*

       mistis: mixtis from **misceo, miscere, miscui, mixtum** *to mix,
to mingle, to combine.*

5   **separato corpore:** ablative of place where as the object of **e
mistis.**

       duo officia: These two duties are the gerunds **perficiendi** and
extrahendi. According to Libavius, they are both encompassed
in the common parlance by the single word **laborandi.**

       voce: *word,* in this case.

6   **vulgo:** adverb, *commonly.*

       evenit: impersonal.

       queat: synonym of **possit.** Subjunctive of purpose.

7   **segregationis:** The genitive is connected with **ars bene
laborandi,** clarifying **laborandi.**

9   **nomen arti natum iudicatur:** *The name of an art is considered
to be innate.* In other words, because of its striving for excellence,
alchemy can be naturally considered an art.

10   **industria:** ablative of manner; supply **cum.** It may also be
translated as *by means of diligence.*

11–12 **in succis mineralibus extrahendis e vena:** gerundive equivalent
of **in extrahendo succos minerales e vena.** The similarity of
terminology with Agricola's indicates that Libavius was familiar
with Agricola's work on the mining of minerals.

12   **quo pacto:** *in which way.* **Quo pacto** is a classical idiom meaning
in which way or *in the same way as.* It is derived from the verb
paciscor *to make a contract, to agree.* Notice that the verb
pango has the same participle. These two verbs are cognate via a
common ancestor **paco.**

12   **puta:** imperative of **puto, -are**; often used to mean *for example*. Cf. Newton's *Lectiones Opticae*.

13   **mineris: minera, -ae** (f) *a mine*; not a classical Latin word.

        in die: The expression literally means *in the day*. So, this can also be translated as *in the light of day*.

14   **extantes: exstantes** from **exsto, exstare, exstiti** *to stand out, to project, to remain in existence*. Also, **exsisto, exsistere, exstiti, exstitum**. Although our verb *to exist* clearly derives from it, **exsisto** is rarely to be translated as *I exist*. Its original meaning is *to appear, to spring forth, to come into existence*.

15   **potius:** *rather, rather more.*

17   **quanquam: quamquam,** *although, so, for . . .*

19   **Tubalcain ille:** *that famous Tubalcain.* Tubalcain is mentioned in the Scriptures (**in sacris libris**). According to Genesis 4, Tubalcain was a direct descendant of Cain, just six generations removed from his notorious ancestor. Tubalcain was "an instructor of every artificer in brass and iron." In Greek mythology, Libavius says, he corresponds to Vulcan.

21   **elaborasse:** alternative, contracted form of **elaboravisse.**

        elaborasse scribitur: When the passive voice is used in indirect statement/oratio obliqua, the subject of the infinitive is in the nominative case.

22   **extitit: existitit.** See note on line 14 above.

        Hermes, seu Mercurius Trismegistus: This mythical figure, known in Latin also as **Mercurius ter Maximus,** *the thrice greatest Mercury*, has mixed Greek and Egyptian origins. He was considered to be the author and initiator of the Hermetic corpus of literature, dealing with magic, astrology, and alchemy.

        invento: inventor. The manuscript reads **invento** where **inventor** should be understood. The **nobilis transmutatio** is the main goal and dream of alchemy, namely, the transmutation of lead, or other common metals, into gold. In a wider sense, spiritual transmutation is also considered as part of the Hermetic tradition.

23 **res quaedam ... nomen habent:** Libavius reminds us that the noun **hermes, hermetis** (m) and the adjective **hermeticus, -a, -um** are used to designate several objects and living beings, such as the vessel of Hermes, the pelican of Hermes, the various birds of Hermes, the hermetic seal, and so on.

ut: followed by the indicative here, *such as, namely.*

25 **apud:** *in the opinion of* or *in the works of.*

Mesuen: Yuhanna ibn Masawaih (777–857) or Joanis Mesue was a Nestorian physician active in Baghdad and author of several important books on medicine and physiology. He was a pioneer in ophthamology. Written originally in Arabic or Syriac, his works were translated into Latin and printed in the sixteenth century. Libavius tells us that in Mesue's works the terms **pil(leus) hermetis** and **hiera hermetis** are used. The Hiera of Hermes is a purgative concoction.

27 **Gebrus** (or Geber) **Mauritanus:** This is most probably Abu Mūsā Jābir ibn Hayyān (721–815), a Persian pioneer of modern chemistry.

28 **stillatitios:** *falling in drops.* Libavius attributes the technique of distillation to Arab and Persian doctors. In the marginal note, Libavius tells us that the Jews knew about the aqua nardina, namely, a liquid distilled from the aromatic nardus plant, as witnessed in the New Testament (John 12:3).

29 **Avicenna:** Ibn Sina (980–1037), one of the greatest philosophers and scientists in the Islamic (Persian) tradition. Libavius gives Sorsan, Persia, today's Rajashthan, India, as the birthplace of Avicenna.

31 **Rhazes:** Abū Bakr Muhammad ibn Zakariyyā Rāzī (854–925), Persian physician and chemist.

32 **Bulcasis:** *Abulcasis.* Latin for Abū al-Qāsim Khalaf ibn al-'Abbās az-Zahrāwī (936–1013), Arab surgeon born and active in Spain (al-Andalus).

34 **Paracelsus:** After naming with clear admiration some of the great pioneers of medicine and chemistry, Libavius comes to his nemesis: Paracelsus, or Philippus Bombastus von Hohenheim (1493–1541). While accepting and adopting many of Paracelsus's

contributions, Libavius had an intense dislike for his supposed arrogance and his use of magical symbols. According to Libavius, **Paracelsus miscuit summa imis**, that is, *he mixed the highest with the lowest*. Libavius is not very specific here. He declares Paracelsism a monstruous boast and a perversion of science.

Caput II.

47   **solius:** genitive singular of **solus, -a, -um**. Construe **manus** in the genitive.

50   **Ergalia, et Pyronomia:** These two terms, of Greek origin, are explained more fully in chapters 3 and 14. **Ergalia** is *the explanation of the alchemic instruments*, both their makeup and their use. **Pyronomia** teaches the proper use of fire.

50–51   **tanta ... ut ...:** *so much ... that ...*; **tanta** sets up the **ut** result clause.

Appendix I

The Pronunciation of Latin

Reading Aloud

Although present interest in Latin is mostly directed toward reading and understanding, rather than speaking, the practice of reading aloud is highly recommended. It is advisable to read a paragraph in its entirety before any attempt at translation has been made, and to try to give some intonation as if one understood the meaning of the passage at first reading. This technique, even when producing comic results, ends up developing the ability of extracting the main intuitive clues for understanding a passage. After the passage has been carefully translated and understood, it is recommended that one read it aloud once more, this time with the correct intonation.

Latin pronunciation has varied significantly, both in time and in space. Scholars have been able to determine with relative accuracy the sounds of the letters in the classical period. This "restituted" pronunciation is today used in the classics departments at most universities. More difficult is to know how exactly the Roman speech sounded in terms of intonation, that musical quality of the spoken word, and how this intonation varied with region and with social class. Another difficulty for the modern speaker may be the distinction between short and long vowels, which curiously has all but disappeared in the Romance languages—particularly in those closer to Latin, such as Italian and Spanish. But even the purest classical pronunciation would not necessarily be the correct one for reading, say, medieval or modern texts. There existed already in the Middle Ages a number of regional variations affecting mainly the sounds of certain consonants. With the passage of time, the tendency to pronounce Latin in each country using the sounds of the letters in the national language grew beyond control. Thus, the letter *c* before *e* or *i* sounded like our *k* in ancient Rome, but later like our *ss* in England, like *ts* in Poland, and like *tch* in Italy and in ecclesiastical Latin.

The Consonants

There is general agreement about the sound of the following consonants:

b, d, f, (k), l, m, n, p, q, r, x, (y), (z).

The pronunciation of these consonants is identical to their sounds in modern Italian or Spanish. Notice in particular that the *d* and the *l* are more dental than their English counterparts, and that the *r* is slightly trilled. The bracketed letters are seldom used. The *k* was used in certain proper names, and the *y* and the *z* are additions of the first century BCE to render foreign (e.g., Greek) words. In Latin the letter *y* is considered as a vowel, so it will be discussed later as such. Doubling a consonant simply doubles its duration. The letter *q* appears always in the combination *qu* followed by a vowel. The *u* is always pronounced.

For the letter *c*, there is no disagreement as to its sound (like the English *k*) before the vowels *a*, *o*, and *u*. In classical Latin this sound was also produced before the remaining vowels *e* and *i*, whereas medieval and Church Latin tended to pronounce it as a soft *tch*.

A similar situation can be observed with regard to the consonant *g*. Before *a*, *o*, and *u* it is pronounced like the English hard *g*, as in "golf" or "greed." Classical Latin used the same hard sound before the remaining vowels, but the later tendency was to pronounce the soft English *g*, as in "general" or "gin."

The letter *h* was aspirated (like in the English word "her") during the classical period, particularly at the beginning of a word. Between vowels, *h* started to lose its sound and eventually became mute in all cases (just as in modern Spanish).

In classical Latin the letter *j* does not exist. Nevertheless, it is used in some editions of Latin texts to replace *i* as a consonant (e.g., **jam = iam**, **juxta = iuxta**). It is always pronounced like a strong *i* or like the English consonant *y*.

The *s* should always be pronounced as in the English word "set," although the softer pronunciation, as in the English word "rose," can be tolerated.

The letter *t* is pronounced placing the tongue at the front teeth, as in modern Italian and Spanish. Nevertheless, in the particular combination "*ti* + vowel," in later Latin the alternative pronunciation *tsi* became widespread. Many Latin words are affected by this variant, such as those that correspond to the English words ending in *-tion* (**institutio, relatio**, etc.).

The letter *v* was pronounced originally as the English *w* in *was*. The norm in later Latin was to pronounce it as the *v* of modern English. In writing, the *v* is interchangeable with the letter *u*. The letter *w* does not exist in Latin.

A few consonant pairs deserve special treatment. In the classical period, an *h* placed after another consonant (*c, p, t*) simply represented the successive pronunciation of each individual sound, namely, the addition of an aspiration after the first consonant. Later, however, the group *ch* would be pronounced as *k*, while *ph* and *th* would be pronounced as in modern English (in words such as "philosophy" and "theology"). These combinations are typical in Latin transcription of Greek words. The group *gn* is more problematic, but one can reasonably assume that it was originally pronounced as the succession of the individual sounds (as in the English word "magnification"). An acceptable later variant is as in modern Italian (as in "gnocchi" or "signora," a sound more or less equivalent to the Spanish ñ, the Portuguese *nh*, or roughly the combination "*n* + *y*").

Vowels and Diphthongs

The original vowel characters in Latin are five: *a, e, i, o, u*. As already mentioned, the extra letter *y* was added later to represent the Greek letter u (upsilon), whose original sound is similar to the German ü or the French *u*. Eventually, the sound of this letter would become indistinguishable from that of the vowel *i*. Each of the five basic vowels can be short or long, the long vowel having the same sound as its short counterpart but lasting roughly twice as long. The sound of the vowels is captured by Spanish and Italian, although these languages do not make a systematic distinction between short and long vowels. In Italian, for example, the vowel in the stressed syllable of a word tends to be longer than in an unstressed syllable. There are enough Italian words incorporated into English, so that we don't need to resort to approximate English equivalents. Good examples are *pizza, spaghetti, cappuccino, numero uno, tutti*, etc. The length of vowels is never indicated in original Latin texts, except possibly in grammars, which use a superimposed bar called a macron to indicate a long vowel, e.g., ā, and a cup for a short vowel, e.g., ă.[25] Although, as far as scientific texts are concerned, the exact pronunciation of the length of vowels is not important in itself, knowing the length of a vowel may be important in determining where the stress of a word falls.

A minor point to be made is a gentle warning about the occasional interchangeability of the vowels *i* and *u*. This anomaly seems to have its origin in the existence of an "intermediate sound" (**sonus medius**) between the two vowels, which ended up corrupting the spelling of some words. Thus, one may sometimes find **optumus** for **optimus** and, conversely, **monimentum** for **monumentum** in classical literature.

A diphthong is a combination of two vowels pronounced in a single syllable. The Latin diphthongs are *ae, au, ei, eu*, and *oe*. The combination *ui* is pronounced as two syllables, except in a few special words: *huius, cuius, huic, cui*. Any combination of vowels not mentioned above is to be considered and voiced as two separate syllables. There is some evidence to suggest that in classical times the diphthong *au* tended to be pronounced as *o* by many people, but this practice was not necessarily entrenched in medieval times. On the other hand, the diphthong *ae* tended to be pronounced as *e*, and this practice managed to affect even the spelling of words. It is not infrequent to find the substitution of *e* for *ae* in scientific Latin, a fact that can cause some confusion to the punctilious translator.

Perhaps this is the right moment to mention other such anomalies to be found in facsimile reproductions of manuscripts and original editions. It is not uncommon to find that many words have been severely contracted by, for instance, replacing an *n* or an *m* by an over-bar or a tilde. Modern editions, on the other hand, never yield to such temptations. For specifics encountered in the facsimiles of the original Latin texts, see appendix III.

---

25 In this book, we only indicate long vowels in the glossary and the grammar appendix.

Syllabification and Accentuation

The division of a word into its component syllables is a relatively easy task in Latin. Every syllable has just one vowel or diphthong. If a consonant separates two vowels, it belongs to the syllable of the second vowel or diphthong. The case of two or more consonants between vowels is only slightly more complicated. In the general case, it is only the last consonant of the group that goes with the second vowel, while the other consonants are attached to the preceding vowel. Nevertheless, the combination of any of the consonants *b*, *c*, *d*, *g*, *p*, or *t* with a following *l* or *r* counts as a single consonant, for phonetic reasons. The same is true for the combinations *ch*, *ph*, *th*, and *qu*. In this last combination, the symbol *u* does not count as a vowel, although it is pronounced as such. Finally, the letter *x* counts as two consonants: *k* + *s*.

Every polysyllabic word in Latin has a stressed syllable.[26] The stress or accent is never indicated graphically. Nevertheless, the rules for determining the stressed syllable are very simple, provided one knows the length of the vowels involved. A syllable in Latin can be long on two accounts. It can be long "by nature" if it contains a long vowel or a diphthong. And it can be long "by position" if, having a short vowel, it ends in a consonant (according to the rules of syllabification). A syllable that is not long either by nature or by position is to be considered a short syllable. Having established the rules for determining the length of a syllable, the rules for the accent of a polysyllabic word are as follows: (1) the stress never falls on the last syllable ("ultima"); (2) if the word has just two syllables, the accent falls necessarily on the first syllable; (3) if the one-but-last syllable ("penultima") is long, it carries the accent. Otherwise, the accent falls on the preceding syllable ("antepenultima"). The accent cannot go any further back.

---

26 The importance of stressing the correct syllable is illustrated in a comic episode involving Luis XVIII and his ministers in 1821. It is said that at a cabinet meeting the king, who knew Latin, exhorted the ministers with the words *macte animo*, which is more or less equivalent to "bravo!" Naturally, he followed the French practice of stressing the last syllable of every word. The shocked ministers, thinking the king was speaking French, understood *"marchez animaux"*—"go, animals"! (cited in A. Traina, *L'alfabeto e la pronunzia del latino*, 3rd ed. [Bologna: Pàtron, 1967], p. 36.)

Common Contractions

a (or ā) + ō = ō (vowel contraction)
e + ō = ō (or iō)
ē + ō = eō (vowel shortening)
ī + ō = iō (vowel shortening)
ā + t = at (vowel shortening)
ē + t = et (vowel shortening)
ī + t = it (vowel shortening)
ā + nt = ant (vowel shortening)
ē + nt = ent (vowel shortening)
e + s = is (vowel change)
e + t = it
e + mus = imus
e + tis = itis
e + nt = unt (or iunt)
i + nt = iunt

In short, the consonant endings tend to reduce the length of the vowel, the short e tends to change to a short i, and the ō ending either absorbs or shortens the preceding vowel. The alternative endings indicated in parentheses correspond to verbs of the third declension whose first person singular ends in iō, such as **faciō**. But because a verb is designated by the principal parts, there is no cause for confusion. Thus, since we say **dīcō, dīcere** we know that the third person plural will be **dīcunt**, while for the verb **capiō, capere** the third person plural will be **capiunt**. Both verbs belong to the third conjugation.

Appendix II

Compendium of Latin Grammar

Chapter I

Sentence Structure in Latin and Present Indicative of the Verb *Esse* (To Be)

The *conjugation* of Latin verbs abides by fairly regular patterns, consisting of adding (personal) suffixes to an invariable *stem*. The verb **esse**, *to be*, is (like in English) somewhat of an anomaly, with the stem exhibiting an erratic behavior. Because of its importance and ubiquity, it is best to memorize this verb, at least in the *present tense* of the *indicative mood* (or *mode*).

Number	Person	Form	Meaning
Singular	1	**sum**	I am
	2	**es**	you are
	3	**est**	he, she, it is
Plural	1	**sumus**	we are
	2	**estis**	you (pl.) are
	3	**sunt**	they are

The *infinitive* (*to be*) is **esse**. Note that, because of the unambiguousness of the personal endings, the *personal pronouns* (**ego** *I*, **tu** *you*, etc.) need not be (and usually are not) used in Latin. To make some sentences with this verb we need *nouns* and *adjectives*. Fortunately, so many nouns and adjectives in English derive from Latin (particularly in the sciences) that you should have no trouble at all translating the following sentences:

> Circulus est figura plana.
>
> Physica et biologia scientiae sunt.
>
> Philosophus esse difficile est.
>
> Sunt circuli.

The Article

Even in these simple examples you may have noticed a few of the peculiarities of Latin.

Firstly, there are no *articles*, whether definite (*the*) or indefinite (*a*, *an*). Thus, the first sentence could be translated: "A circle is a plane figure," or "The circle is a plane figure," both translations being correct. When the context is insufficient to establish the degree of definiteness, Latin adds *demonstrative* or *possessive adjectives* (**Hic circulus** . . . *This circle* . . ., **Noster circulus** *Our circle* . . ., etc.), a practice followed in some modern languages, such as the Slavic languages. The last sentence, moreover, can be translated as "They are circles," or "There are circles," or "Circles exist."

Flexible Word Order

A second feature of Latin is one that makes its style at once so beautiful and, sometimes, so difficult to translate: words in a sentence can be juggled or rearranged without altering the meaning of the sentence. The heavily *inflected* character of verbs, nouns, and adjectives allows for this degree of freedom without causing (almost) any ambiguities. Notice, as an example, that the verb was placed at the end in the last two sentences, but in the middle of the first. The following are some of the equivalent combinations:

> Circulus plana est figura.
>
> Circulus figura plana est.
>
> Difficile philosophus esse est.
>
> Difficile est philosophus esse.

In more complex sentences the possibilities multiply, and some of the classical authors seem to have experienced a perverse delight in pushing the limits of such freedom. Fortunately for us, most scientific writings do not go so far, whether in the interest of clarity or, sometimes, because their authors' mastery of Latin leaves something to be desired.

Conjunctions

The *conjunction* **et** (*and*) in an enumeration can be replaced by the *suffix* **–que** appended to the word that would follow **et**. Thus, we could have said:

> Medicina biologia**que** scientiae sunt = Medicina et biologia scientiae sunt.
>
> Medicine and biology are sciences.

Et . . . et . . . in the same clause may express *both . . . and . . .*

> Medicina et scientia et ars est.
>
> Medicine is both a science and an art.

The *adversative conjunction* "but" is rendered in Latin by **sed**.

> Natura magna sed mala est.
>
> Nature is great but evil.

Negation

To negate the action of a verb, the negative *adverb* **non** is placed before the verb.

> Artes **non** sunt scientiae.
>
> The arts are not sciences.

The term *nothing* is rendered by the noun **nihil**.

> Nihil sumus.
>
> We are nothing.

The compound **neque** means *and not*. It can be abbreviated as **nec**. *Neither ... nor...* is rendered as **nec ... nec ...** or **neque ... neque ...**

> Medicina nec ars nec scientia est.
> Medicine is neither an art nor a science.

> Neque philosophus neque medicus es.
> You are neither a philosopher nor a doctor.

Interrogation

One may indicate a question by raising the voice, by placing the verb at the beginning of the sentence, or by some other rhetorical device. Nevertheless, if more precision is desired, the *enclitic particle* **–ne** is usually appended to the first word of the sentence to indicate a legitimate question whose answer is not known or not expected to be bluntly "yes" or "no."

> Estne philosophia scientia?
> Is philosophy a science? (I would like to know)

If the answer is expected to be "no," the word **num** is used as an introduction:

> Num est philosophia scientia?
> Is perchance philosophy a science? (Certainly not!)

If the expected answer is "yes," the compound **nonne** can be used:

> Nonne est philosophia scientia?
> Is it not the case that philosophy is a science? (Of course it is!)

Particles of Affirmation and Negation

Latin does not reserve a specific word for *yes*. Instead, **ita** (*thus*), **sic** (*so*), and **maxime** (*most of all*) are commonly used. (**Maxime** may convey emphatic assent along the lines of *certainly!*)

Latin also expresses *no* in multiple ways: **non, minime. Minime** is also an adverb expressing "least."

Nonne est philosophia scientia? Ita, philosophia scientia est.

Is it not the case that philosophy is a science? Yes, philosophy is a science.

Num architectura scientia est? Minime, architectura ars est.

Is perchance architecture a science? No, architecture is an art.

Principal Parts of Verbs

Every Latin verb is designated by its principal parts, a device that helps to avoid any confusion that might otherwise arise as to how the verb should be conjugated. In English, verbs have three principal parts, such as *go, went, gone* or *do, did, done*. In Latin, there are as many as four principal parts, because the infinitive differs from the first person present indicative. (An example in English is the verb "to be," which differs from "I am"). Latin dictionaries always list verbs by their principal parts. Provisionally, until the remaining two principal parts are introduced, we shall list verbs by the first two principal parts, namely the first person singular and the infinitive of the present indicative active. Thus, the verb "to be" is, so far, **sum, esse, . . .**

It is a recommended policy to learn verbs by memorizing their principal parts.

The Verb "To Be Able": Possum, Posse, . . .

Another very important verb that follows the conjugation of **sum, esse, . . .** is **possum, posse, . . .** *to be able*, formed by prefixing the particle **pot-**, which carries the meaning of *able*, to forms of **sum**. Thus, we obtain:

pot + sum = **possum** (I can, I am able)

pot + es = **potes** (you can, you are able)

pot + est = **potest** (he/she/it can, is able)

pot + sumus = **possumus** (we are able)

pot + estis = **potestis** (you are able)

pot + sunt = **possunt** (they are able)

We (again) observe a typical phonetic change to avoid the clash between two incompatible consonants:

t + s = **ss**

The infinitive is further contracted to **posse** (rather than "potesse").

Prefixes and Derived Verbs

In English, the verbs *defer, confer, infer, refer, transfer, prefer, proffer, offer,* and *differ* are all derived from the basic Latin verb **fero, ferre, . . .** whose primary meaning is *to carry, to bear.* The derived English verbs are obtained by placing before the basic verb a short *prefix* conveying the added nuances of meaning. Some phonetic and orthographic changes may take place, such as doubling of a consonant. As we shall learn later (see pp. 260–262), many of the prefixes can also be used as independent *prepositions* with nouns. In the examples below we use the prefixes **ab-** (*away*), **ad-** (*near, at*), **de-** (*away, off*), **inter-** (*between*), **in-** (*in, into*), **prae-** (*before*), **super-** (*above*).

In the case of the verb **sum, esse, . . .** there are a few derived verbs, whose conjugation follows that of the parent verb:

> **absum, abesse, . . .** = not to be there, to be absent, to be away
>
> **assum (adsum), adesse, . . .** = to be near, to be present
>
> **desum, deesse, . . .** = to be less, to be in defect, to be missing
>
> **intersum, interesse, . . .** = to be between or involved, there to be a difference
>
> **insum, inesse** = to be in/on, to be involved in or with
>
> **praesum, praeesse** = to be in charge of, to preside
>
> **supersum, superesse, . . .** = to be above, to survive

A Challenge

Practically every Latin root has found its way into English, either directly, or through French, or through the use of scientific terminology. The open challenge is, therefore, to find for every Latin word you encounter a related English word.

Chapter II
Present Infinitive and Indicative Active

Grammarians classify Latin verbs into four groups according to their *conjugation* patterns. In the *present indicative active*, as well as in many other tenses, the differences among the patterns are so minor that it may be best to study them all at once.

One way to characterize each of the four conjugation groups consists of recognizing a "dominant" vowel, as follows:

Conjugation	Dominant Vowel
1st	ā or a
2nd	ē
3rd	e
4th	ī

All present active *infinitives* end in the syllable **–re,** preceded by the characteristic vowel.

Examples:

1st:	**cōgitō, cōgitāre, . . .**	to think
	dō, dare, . . .	to give
2nd:	**habeō, habēre, . . .**	to have (in possession)
	dēbeō, dēbēre, . . .	must, to have to, to owe
	videō, vidēre, . . .	to see
3rd:	**dīcō, dīcere, . . .**	to say, to tell
	trahō, trahere, . . .	to draw, to pull
	faciō, facere, . . .	to do, to make
	capiō, capere, . . .	to seize, to take
4th:	**audiō, audīre, . . .**	to hear, to listen
	inveniō, invenīre, . . .	to find, to invent

The present indicative stem is obtained by deleting the last syllable (–re) from the infinitive. The conjugation of the present indicative is then obtained by adding the *personal endings* to the stem. The personal endings are as follows:

Number	Person	Personal Ending
Singular	1	–ō
	2	–s
	3	–t
Plural	1	–mus
	2	–tis
	3	–nt

You have probably recognized most of these endings from the conjugation of **sum, esse**. The exception is the first person singular, where we have now –ō instead of **–m**.

Following are full paradigms of the present indicative of verbs in all conjugations. It is always beneficial to read aloud, remembering the rules for accentuation (see appendix I). Notice some minor variations: The fall of a stem vowel in some cases in the first person, the alterations of a stem vowel in 3a and 3b and in the third person plural for 3a, 3b, 4. The third conjugation splits into two patterns (3a, b) according to whether the first person does not have or has, respectively, an *i* before the final *o*. (Please see appendix I for a description of vowel changes and contractions that occur when adding the endings to the present stem.)

Because a verb is designated by its principal parts, there is no cause for confusion regarding how verbs are conjugated. Thus, since we say **dīcō, dīcere,** we know that the third person plural will be **dīcunt**, while for the verb **capiō, capere** the third person plural will be **capiunt**. Both verbs belong to the third conjugation.

		1	2	3a	3b	4
Singular	1	cōgitō	habeō	dīcō	faciō	audiō
	2	cōgitās	habēs	dīcis	facis	audīs
	3	cōgitat	habet	dīcit	facit	audit
Plural	1	cōgitāmus	habēmus	dīcimus	facimus	audīmus
	2	cōgitātis	habētis	dīcitis	facitis	audītis
	3	cōgitant	habent	dīcunt	faciunt	audiunt
Infinitive		cōgitāre	habēre	dīcere	facere	audīre

In Latin, the present indicative active can also convey the meaning of continued action (*you are thinking*, as opposed to *you think*), for which there is no separate verbal form.

Examples:

Non cogitas sed dicis.

You don't think, but you speak. (Or: you are not thinking, but speaking).

Non dicere sed audire possum.

I am not able to speak, but I am able to hear.

Philosophus magnus dicit, "Cogito ergo sum."

The great philosopher says, "I think therefore I am."

Verb Entries in the Dictionary

Verbs in the dictionary are listed under their first person singular present active indicative form, namely their first principal part. The dictionary also provides the present active infinitive (second principal part), and the other two principal parts, which will be explained in chapters VI and VII of this compendium.

Examples:

Dīcō, dīcere, dīxī, dictum = *to say*.

Some dictionaries do not repeat the stem in the infinitive form, for example, **habeō, -ēre, . . .** in place of **habeō, habēre, . . .**

In addition, some dictionaries also abbreviate the third and fourth principal parts, which we will discuss in chapters VI and VII of this compendium.

A Challenge

Formulate criteria to deduce, from the first two principal parts, the conjugation group to which a verb belongs. These criteria should not be based on the length of vowels, since lengths are never indicated in actual texts. You could write a computer program or a flow chart that would produce the full conjugation of the present indicative, given the first two principal parts of any verb.

Chapter III
First and Second Declension Nouns and Adjectives

L atin nouns and adjectives are highly *inflected*—their endings change based on various factors. In their different inflections they display *number* (singular or plural), *grammatical gender* (feminine, masculine, neuter), and *case*.

What Is a Case?

The case of a noun indicates the noun's function in a clause, namely whether it is functioning as a subject, a direct object, an indirect object, or other. Whereas verbs are *conjugated* to express person, number, tense, voice, and mood or mode, Latin nouns are *declined* to express case, gender, and number.

What Is a Declension?

Grammarians classify nouns into *five* groups according to their *declension* patterns, that is, according to the way they stray or "incline" away (de-cline, hence *declension*) from the basic form as the case changes. Adjectives, on the other hand, never belong to the fourth or fifth declensions.

It would be tempting to present all declension patterns at once, as we did with the verb conjugations. Unfortunately, though, the commonality between the declensions is less apparent than their differences. The first two declensions, however, are so similar that they warrant a common presentation in this chapter. The vast majority of Latin nouns and all adjectives belong to one of the first three declensions. The fourth and fifth declensions need to be studied too, since a few very common Latin words such as **motus** (*motion*) and **res** (*thing*) belong to them.

Latin Cases

Latin recognizes six cases: ***Nominative, Genitive, Dative, Accusative, Ablative,*** and ***Vocative.*** Their main (though by no means only) functions are as follows:

1. **Nominative:** subject of a sentence.

2. **Genitive:** possession (the possessor goes in the genitive case), and a few other functions commonly expressed in English by the word *of* preceding the noun. A remnant of the genitive case in English is the "'s" possessive construction.

3. **Dative:** indirect object of a verb. Verbs implying giving, transferring, saying, etc., tend to be accompanied by a dative to indicate the person (or thing) <u>to</u> whom or <u>for</u> whom something has been transmitted.

4. **Accusative:** direct object of a verb. In addition, certain prepositions of motion and time require a noun in the accusative case (to indicate motion <u>into</u>, <u>toward</u>, or <u>through</u>, and time or place <u>after</u>, <u>during</u>, etc.).

5. **Ablative:** practically everything else falls under this rubric. Most prepositions require the ablative case (to indicate place or time <u>in</u>, <u>at</u>, or <u>from</u> which, the means <u>by</u> which, the thing [or person] <u>with</u> or <u>without</u> which, <u>how</u> an action takes place).

6. **Vocative:** addressing a person (or thing). This is the least important of all the cases, particularly in scientific literature, where it is usually relegated to the opening sentence in the introduction (*dear reader* . . ., *o great prince* . . ., and so on) or to address an interlocutor in dialogues. Moreover, the vocative is identical to the nominative except in the second declension masculine nouns and adjectives.

Excluding the vocative case, one has to somehow internalize ten possibly different endings (five singular and five plural) in each declension, so it is a good policy to develop a skill for pattern recognition to serve as a useful (albeit sometimes dangerous) guide.

Nouns

Most nouns of the first declension are feminine (f), while most nouns of the second declension are either masculine (m) or neuter (n). The few exceptions to the feminine rule of the first declension are masculine words borrowed from Greek (such as **nauta** *sailor*, **poeta** *poet*, and **planeta** *planet*). We exemplify the first and second declensions with the nouns **figura** (f: *figure, shape*), **angulus** (m: *corner, angle*), and **spatium** (n: *space*).

	Stem:	Figur-	Angul-	Spati-
		1st declension	2nd declension (m)	2nd declension (n)
Singular	N	figūra	angulus	spatium
	G	figūrae	angulī	spatiī
	D	figūrae	angulō	spatiō
	Ac	figūram	angulum	spatium
	Ab	figūrā	angulō	spatiō
	V	(figūra)	(angule)	(spatium)
Plural	N	figūrae	angulī	spatia
	G	figūrārum	angulōrum	spatiōrum
	D	figūrīs	angulīs	spatiīs
	Ac	figūrās	angulōs	spatia
	Ab	figūrīs	angulīs	spatiīs
	V	(figūrae)	(angulī)	(spatia)

We see that, as with verbs, *there is an invariable stem (obtained by dropping the singular genitive ending)* to which characteristic endings (bolded in the above table) are added.

Hints for Pattern Recognition:

1. The nominative singular of the first declension always ends in –**a**. Most, but not all, masculine nouns of the second declension have a nominative singular in –**us**, while only neuter nominatives end in –**um**.

2. Except for nominative and accusative, in the second declension neuters follow exactly the masculine pattern (that is why they are grouped together).

3. The accusative singular ends in –**m** in both the first and second declensions. The accusative neuter singular and plural are <u>always</u> (and in all declensions) identical, respectively, to the nominative neuter singular and plural. Neuter plural nominatives (and, of course, accusatives) end in -**a**. Masculine and feminine plural accusatives of the first and second declensions end in –**s** (–**ōs** and –**ās**, respectively).

4. Genitive plurals of the first and second declensions end in **–rum**.

5. In both first and second declensions the plural ablatives are identical to the corresponding datives. This is true in all declensions.

6. In the first and second declensions, the plural datives and ablatives end in –īs regardless of gender.

7. Except for masculine singular, the vocative is the same as the nominative.

Noun Entries in the Dictionary

Nouns in the dictionary are listed under their nominative singular form. The dictionary also provides the genitive singular, which is essential for determining the stem and the declension group. The gender is also provided.

Examples:

> **liber, librī** (m) = book. Since the genitive ends in –ī, it can only belong to the second declension. The stem is **libr-**. The declension follows regularly: singular: liber, libri, libro, librum, libro (liber); plural: libri, librorum, libris, libros, libris, (libri).
>
> **mōtus, mōtūs** (m) = motion. Since the genitive does not end in –ī or –*ae*, it cannot belong to the first or second declension. (It belongs to the fourth declension, to be studied in chapter VII of this compendium.)

Some dictionaries do not repeat the stem in the genitive form. Examples: **rota, -ae** (f); **circulus, - ī** (m); **tēctum, -ī** (n).

NB: *As a rule, always look at the genitive to obtain the correct stem, since the nominative is sometimes modified, as in the following examples.*

Examples:

> **puer, puerī** (m) = boy. Stem: **puer-**
> **vir, virī** (m) = man, male. Stem: **vir-**
> **ager, agrī** (m) = farm. Stem: **agr-**

In all these examples, the conjugation follows regularly from the genitive on.

Adjectives

Adjectives must agree in number, gender, and case with the nouns they qualify.
Except for third declension adjectives, to be studied later, adjectives follow
the first declension for the feminine, and the second declension for masculine and neuter. It would seem logical, therefore, to list the forms of adjectives in the order: feminine, masculine, neuter. Nevertheless, dictionaries
and grammars tend to list the masculine first, followed by the feminine and
the neuter. To avoid confusion in pattern recognition and memory habits,
we will adhere to the usual order (masculine, feminine, neuter).

Example: magnus, magna, magnum (*great, large*)
Stem: magn-

		Masculine	Feminine	Neuter
Singular	N	magnus	magna	magnum
	G	magnī	magnae	magnī
	D	magnō	magnae	magnō
	Ac	magnum	magnam	magnum
	Ab	magnō	magnā	magnō
	V	(magne)	(magna)	(magnum)
Plural	N	magnī	magnae	magna
	G	magnōrum	magnārum	magnōrum
	D	magnīs	magnīs	magnīs
	Ac	magnōs	magnās	magna
	Ab	magnīs	magnīs	magnīs
	V	(magnī)	(magnae)	(magna)

Adjectives with masculine in –**er** are self-explanatory. Example: **piger,
pigra, pigrum** (*slow, lazy*). The genitive masculine is **pigrī**. Its stem is **pigr-**.

Substantive Adjectives

Substantive adjectives modify nouns that are absent. We often use substantive adjectives in English. Example: "The bold and the beautiful." The
nouns are not stated, but rather implied. The adjectives might be modifying
"people" or "women" or "things," etc. *In Latin, the substantive adjective must
agree in gender, number, and case, with its absent (implied) noun.*

Examples:

> Multi de natura vitae cogitant.
> Many (persons) think about the nature of life.

> Philosophi mala non amant.
> Philosophers do not love evil (things).
>> (Note the use of the neuter plural to express "things.")

Adjective Entries in the Dictionary

As we have already seen, dictionaries list adjectives in the order masculine, feminine, neuter. You should, therefore, search for an entry according to the masculine singular nominative form of the adjective. Most dictionaries will list the masculine singular nominative form in full, followed by the feminine and neuter endings. Example: **magnus, –a, –um.**

Prepositions

Prepositions are words placed before a noun to indicate a temporal, spatial, or causal relation to the noun. Examples of prepositions in English are *for, to, toward, from, away, after, with, without.* In Latin, prepositions invest the noun affected with a declension case: We say that a preposition *governs* a case. Some prepositions govern two different cases, and in each instance they have a slightly different meaning. Thus, the Latin preposition **in**, when governing an accusative noun, means *into*, namely, it acquires a connotation of motion toward. If, on the other hand, the noun affected is in the ablative, then **in** means *in, inside*. (A similar practice exists in modern German.)

Examples:

> Pirata in Europam navigat.
> The pirate sails into Europe (is going toward).

> Pirata in Europa navigat.
> The pirate is sailing in Europe.

Following is a list of the most common Latin prepositions together with the case (or cases) they govern and the corresponding approximate meanings. Notice that, as a rule, the accusative conveys a connotation of motion toward or through something, and the passage of time; but you should be careful not to overdo such criteria, but rather try to memorize the prepositions with their cases. Remember that since Latin writers tend to alter the order of the words of a sentence, the knowledge of the case governed by a preposition can be of great help in "disentangling the mess." For example: the preposition **de** (*about, on, from*) governs the ablative case. So, if the phrase **de figurarum natura** is to be translated, we would reason as follows: **figurarum** can only be in the genitive (plural) case, so it cannot be governed by **de**. The word **natura** (*nature*, a first declension noun) could be in the nominative singular (if the final **–a** is short), or in the ablative singular (if the final **–ā** is long). We then decide that, because of the preposition, the latter is the case and translate: "on the nature of figures." A careless analysis could have rendered "on the figures of nature" or some other incorrect possibility of combining the words at random. It is to be noted that not all situations requiring a preposition in English do so in Latin. In fact, the declensions themselves have a prepositional nuance. For example, the English "of" has no equivalent in Latin, since possession is directly indicated by the genitive case (e.g., **figurarum** = *of the figures*). Another important example along similar lines is the ablative case, which automatically carries a connotation of "means by which" (e.g., **scribo calamo** = *I am writing with a pen, I write by means of a pen*).

Preposition	Case(s)	Meaning(s)	Examples
ab (optional: ā before consonant)	abl.	from, by (agent)	**liber ā philosophō** = a book by the philosopher **ab angulō** = from the corner
ad	acc.	to (toward), up to, approximately	**ad angulum** = toward the corner
ante	acc.	in front of, before	**ante oculōs** = in front of the eyes **ante bellum** = before the war
apud	acc.	*chez*, among	**apud Rōmānōs** = among the Romans **apud Claudium** = at Claudius's house
circā	acc.	near, around	**circā stellās** = near the stars
circum	acc.	around	**circum figuram** = around the figure

contrā	acc.	against	contrā Rōmānōs = against the Romans
cum	ablative	with	cum virō = with the man
dē	ablative	about (concerning), down from	liber dē nātūrā = a book about nature
ex (optional ē before consonant)	ablative	out of, out from	ex librīs philosophī = from the philosopher's books
extrā	acc.	outside, beyond	extrā terram = beyond the earth
in	acc. ablative	into in (position)	in angulum = into the corner in angulō = in the corner
inter	acc.	between, among, during	inter virōs = among the men
intrā	acc.	within	intrā hōram = within an hour intrā murōs = within the walls
ob	acc.	because of, in front of	ob magnam formam = because of (its) great beauty
per	acc.	through, because of	per campum currit = she runs through the field
post	acc.	after, behind	post longam vītam = after a long life
prae	acc.	in front of, in preference to	officium prae otium = duty before leisure
prō	ablative	in front of, in place of, on behalf of	dīcit prō amīcō = he speaks on behalf of his friend
propter	acc.	because of, on account of	propter errata = because of mistakes
sine	ablative	without	sine dubiō = without a doubt

sub	acc. ablative	downward under, below	**sub terrās** = down to hell **sub terrīs** = underground, in hell
super	acc. ablative	above, over, on about, onto	**comēta cadit super terram** = a comet is falling on the earth **liber est super mensā** = the book is on the table
suprā	acc.	above, beyond	**suprā caelum** = beyond the sky
trans	acc.	on the other side of	**trans fluvium** = on the other side of the river
ultrā	acc.	beyond	**ultrā officium** = beyond duty

Chapter IV
Third Declension Nouns and Adjectives

I t is a characteristic of the third declension that the stem is often short-ened in the nominative singular, so that *it is imperative to remember both the nominative and the genitive singular, which contains the full stem.* Although there is no mathematical way to establish any rules for the shortened nominative, a certain ineffable quasi-musical pattern emerges with some practice and familiarity.

Third declension nouns may be of any of the three genders. The feminine and masculine nouns follow identical patterns, while neuter nouns differ in only two respects: (i) the nominative and accusative are identical (a rule never broken in Latin), and (ii) the nominative and, therefore, also the accusative, plural have the typical neuter ending –a. Otherwise, the third declension is gender-indifferent.

> **Examples:**
> **lēx, lēgis** (f, *law*)
> **mēns, mēntis** (f, *mind*)
> **quālitās, quālitātis** (f, *quality*)
> **homō, hominis** (m, *man, human being*)
> **auctor, auctōris** (m, *author, producer, originator*)
> **corpus, corporis** (n, *body*)
> **tempus, temporis** (n, *time*)

		Stem: lĕg-	Stem: auctor-	Stem: corpor-
Singular	N	lēx	auctor	corpus
	G	lēgis	auctōris	corporis
	D	lēgī	auctōrī	corporī
	Ac	lēgem	auctōrem	corpus
	Ab	lēge	auctōre	corpore
	V	(lēx)	(auctor)	(corpus)

	N	lēgēs	auctorēs	corpora
	G	lēgum	auctorum	corporum
Plural	D	lēgibus	auctoribus	corporibus
	Ac	lēgēs	auctorēs	corpora
	Ab	lēgibus	auctoribus	corporibus
	V	(lēgēs)	(auctorēs)	(corpora)

In each case, the stem is obtained by deleting the ending –is from the genitive singular. Notice that the genitive plural ending is –um (not –ōrum), so for instance, *of men* = **hominum**, *of the qualities* = **quālitātum**, etc. Note the accentuation of the genitive plurals: since the *o* in the stem of **tempus, temporis** is short the genitive plural is **témporum**, not **tempórum**. A similar remark applies to **corpus**. (See appendix I regarding accentuation.)

Pattern Recognition

As in the first and second declensions: i) masculine and feminine nouns in the accusative singular end in –**m** and in the accusative plural end in –**s**. ii) The dative and ablative plural of all nouns are identical. In the third declension, however, the typical ending for the dative and ablative plural is –**ibus**. From here we get the English word "omnibus," namely, "for all people."

Although the declension patterns themselves are quite indifferent to gender, there are some general rules for certain nominative endings that make it easy to recognize the gender in many cases. The most common are the following:

	-tās, -tātis	(English: -ty) quality, quantity
Feminine:	-tūs, -tūtis	(English: -tue) virtue
	-tūdō, -tūdinis	(English: -tude) similitude, amplitude
	-tiō, -tiōnis	(English: -tion) nation, liberation
Masculine:	-or, -ōris	(English: -or) factor, professor
	-us (with short u)	
Neuter:	-e	
	-al	(English: -al) animal
	-ar	

In the last three categories (namely neuter nouns with nominatives in –e, –al, or –ar) there is a slight irregularity in the ablative singular ending (–ī, instead of –e) and an added –i in the nominative (and accusative) and genitive plural endings (–ia, instead of –a, and –ium, instead of –um). These irregularities do not gravely impair recognition. Moreover, they become the rule for all third declension adjectives.

Examples:

Mens sana in corpore sano. (Juvenal)
A healthy mind in a healthy body.

Homo homini lupus est. (Latin proverb)
Man is a wolf to man.

Unus pro omnibus, omnes pro uno.
One for all (everyone), all (everyone) for one.

E pluribus unum.
(St. Augustine, who said "Ex pluribus unum," a motto still found today on all US coins and bills)
Out of many, one.

There is, however, one especially irregular third declension noun that must be learned: **vīs, vīs** (f, *force*; in plural it may mean *strength*):

		Stem: vī-
Singular	N	vīs
	G	vīs
	D	vī
	Ac	vim
	Ab	vī
	V	(vīs)
Plural	N	vīrēs
	G	vīrium
	D	vīribus
	Ac	vīrēs
	Ab	vīribus
	V	(vīrēs)

Note: Carefully distinguish **vīs, vīs** (a feminine third declension noun) from **vir, virī** (a masculine second declension noun). In fact, they don't have a single form in common!

A man of strength.
Vir virium.

The men have strength.
Viri vires habent.

Building Latin Vocabulary for Free!

As already suggested above, the following rules almost always apply:

1. Practically all English nouns ending in "-ty" derive from third declension feminine Latin nouns ending in "-tas, -tatis." Examples: **universitas, universitatis** = university, **immensitas, immensitatis** = immensity. About 1,500 English words fall into this category.

2. Practically all English nouns ending in "-tion" derive from third declension feminine Latin nouns ending in "-tio, -tionis." Examples: **natio, nationis** = nation, **mutatio, mutationis** = mutation. About 2,500 English words fall into this category. The same rule applies for practically all English nouns ending in "-sion."

3. Practically all English nouns ending in "-tude" derive from third declension feminine nouns ending in "-tudo, -tudinis." Examples: **magnitudo, magnitudinis** = magnitude, **amplitudo, amplitudinis** = amplitude.

4. Many English nouns ending in "-or" derive from third declension masculine Latin nouns ending in "-or, -oris." Examples: **factor, factoris** = factor, **doctor, doctoris** = doctor. About 600 English words fall into this category.

5. Most nouns ending in English "-ence" derive from *first* declension feminine nouns ending in "-entia, -entiae." Examples: **sententia, sententiae** = sentence, **malevolentia, malevolentiae** = malevolence. About 300 English words fall into this category.

With little effort, you have already acquired over 5,000 Latin words.

Third Declension Adjectives

Third declension adjectives generally have the same forms for feminine and masculine, with the neuter exhibiting similar patterns to neuter nouns. Some adjectives exhibit different forms for nominative singular in the feminine and masculine, and this is indicated in dictionaries by listing three (masculine, feminine, neuter) rather than just two (masculine-feminine, neuter) entries.

Examples: **celer, celeris, celere** (*swift*); **brevis, breve** (*short*). As already mentioned, some specific adjectival endings include an additional –*i*.

		Masculine/ Feminine	Neuter	Masculine/ Feminine	Neuter
Singular	N	brevis	breve	celer/cēleris	celere
	G	brevis	brevis	celeris	celeris
	D	brevī	brevī	celerī	celerī
	Ac	brevem	breve	celerem	celere
	Ab	brevī	brevī	celerī	celerī
	V	(brevis)	(breve)	(celer/celeris)	(celere)
Plural	N	brevēs	brevia	cēlerēs	cēleria
	G	brevium	brevium	celerium	celerium
	D	brevibus	brevibus	cēleribus	cēleribus
	Ac	brevēs	brevia	cēlerēs	cēleria
	Ab	brevibus	brevibus	cēleribus	cēleribus
	V	(brevēs)	(brevia)	(cēlerēs)	(cēleria)

All adjectives retain the forms of their particular declension, even when modifying or qualifying a noun of another declension. For example: *liber brevis est* = the book is short.

Examples:

Magnum opus scribit. (opus, operis, n)
He writes a great work.

Non magna virtute ducit tyrannus, sed magna vi.

The tyrant does not lead by means of great virtue, but by
means of great force.

Ars longa, vita brevis. (Hippocrates)
Art is long, life is short.

Many adjectives of the third declension can be seen as *present participles*
(see chapter IX of this compendium). Their nominative singular in the masculine, feminine, and neuter ends in **–ens** (e.g., **potens**, powerful).

Chapter V
The Relative Pronoun and the "Q" Words

The "*Q*" Words

M any of the English "*w*" words (*who, what, which, why, when*), relative pronouns (*that*), and adverbs (*how*) and other important "little" words of very frequent use start in Latin with a *q*.

The Relative Pronoun

The dominant element to master the "*q*" words is the *relative pronoun* (*that, which, who*), used prevalently in *subordinate clauses*. Surprisingly perhaps, English has preserved declined forms for the relative pronoun:

N who

G whose

D to whom, for whom

Ac whom

Ab (in, from, by means of. . .) whom

The declension of the Latin relative pronoun (**quī, quae, quod**) is a peculiar mixture of the first, second, and third declensions. The following table shows the full declension. Notice the highlighted common forms for the genitive and dative singular and, as usual, for the dative and ablative plural.

		Masculine	Feminine	Neuter
Singular	N	quī	quae	quod
	G	cuius	cuius	cuius
	D	cui	cui	cui
	Ac	quem	quam	quod
	Ab	quō	quā	quō
Plural	N	quī	quae	quae
	G	quōrum	quārum	quōrum
	D	quibus	quibus	quibus
	Ac	quōs	quās	quae
	Ab	quibus	quibus	quibus

In a subordinate clause, as in English, the relative pronoun acquires the case dictated by its function in the clause (subject, direct object, etc.). The gender and number, naturally, are dictated by the gender and number of the thing represented by the pronoun (the *antecedent* or *anchor*).

Examples:

Circulus est figura plana, in cuius mediō centrum est.

A circle is a plane figure, in whose middle (in the middle of which) is the center.

Circulus est figura plana, quae in mediō centrum habet.

A circle is a plane figure, which has the center in the middle.

The Interrogative Pronoun

Based on the relative pronoun, the interrogative forms undergo some changes in the singular, but remain identical to those of the relative pronoun in the plural. The changes in the singular forms can be summarized as follows: (i) the masculine and feminine forms coalesce into the masculine ones; (ii) the nominative masculine/feminine singular and nominative neuter (and accusative) singular acquire the new forms **quis, quid** (instead of **quī, quod**), respectively. Thus, for example, we may say:

Quid facere possum?
What can I do?

Quis librum habet?
Who has the book?

The complete declension of the interrogative pronoun is as follows:

		Masculine Feminine	Neuter
	N	quis	quid
	G	cuius	cuius
Singular	D	cui	cui
	Ac	quem	quid
	Ab	quō	quō

Plural	N	quī	quae	quae
	G	quōrum	quārum	quōrum
	D	quibus	quibus	quibus
	Ac	quōs	quās	quae
	Ab	quibus	quibus	quibus

There is a subtlety with the interrogative pronoun: it has to be distinguished grammatically from the *interrogative adjective*. In context, it is not difficult to tell the difference between the two. A pronoun, literally, stands for a noun, whereas an adjective is attached to a noun. In the case of the interrogative adjective, therefore, the "*q*" word will usually be followed by a noun. In that case, the forms revert to those of the relative pronoun.

Examples:

Quid habes in mente?

What do you have in mind? (interrogative pronoun)

Quod punctum habes in mente?

Which point do you have in mind? (interrogative adjective)

Variants of the Relative Pronoun

A common variant of the relative (and interrogative) pronoun is obtained by adding the ending **–dam** to all declensions. This device confers an indefinite flavor to the pronoun, which can then be used as an adjective. The meaning is conveyed in English by words such as *a certain*, or *some*.

Examples:

Quaedam leges verae sunt.

Some laws are true.

Homo quidam audit quod dicis.

A certain man is hearing what you say.

Another common variant is obtained by doubling the pronoun, which conveys then the idea of *any*, or *whatever*. Upon doubling, some minor spelling changes may occur (**quidquid = quicquid**). The addition of the ending **–quam** has an effect similar to the doubling. If the syllable **–que** is appended, the connotation is *each* (**quisque** = *each one*). Note that this is different from the appending of the enclitic **–que** = *and*.

More "*Q*" Words

Following is a list of some of the most common "*q*" words and their approximate meanings. Notice that most of them are indeclinable adverbs (the exception is **quantus**, which functions as an adjective).

> **quia:** *since, because*
> **quam:** *than, as*
> **quamquam:** *however*
> **quamvis:** *however, although*
> **quando:** *when, whenever*
> **quantus, quanta, quantum:** *how much*
> **quare:** *why, because of which*
> **quasi:** *as if, like*
> **quatenus:** *as long as*
> **quemadmodum:** *how*
> **quomodo:** *how*
> **quidem:** *indeed, certainly*
> **quin:** *nay rather, that not*
> **ne . . . quidem:** *not even*
> **quod:** *because*
> **quondam:** *once*
> **quoniam:** *since* (causal)
> **quoque:** *also*
> **quot:** *how many*
> **quisque, quaeque, quodque:** *each*

Although **cur** is not a "*q*" word, it is a contracted form of **quare** in the sense of "why."

Chapter VI
More about Verbs in the Indicative
Introduction

Latin recognizes only six verbal tenses as opposed to the richer variety of English tenses. In particular *Latin does not have special forms to express present continuous or future continuous (or progressive) action.* Thus, "I read" and "I am reading" are both rendered in Latin as **lego**.

The six Latin tenses are best understood by dividing them into two groups of three tenses each, as follows:

1. The <u>present-stem</u> group, consisting of the present, imperfect, and future tenses.

2. The <u>perfect-stem</u> group, consisting of the perfect, pluperfect, and future perfect tenses.

In Latin the word **perfectus, –a, –um** means <u>complete</u>. With this in mind, we may say that the tenses in the second group denote *completed action*. These tenses, moreover, can be regarded as having a relation of temporal dependence on other tenses, as will be presently explained.

The Present-Stem Group

The <u>present tense</u>, which we have already learned, indicates present or present continuous action. Accordingly, the sentence **libros scribimus** can be translated as *we write books* or *we are writing books*. The context will decide which one is the better translation.

The <u>future tense</u> expresses simple future or future continuous action. "We will write books" and "we will be writing books" are both rendered as **libros scribemus.**

The <u>imperfect tense</u> does not have an exact equivalent in English, but can be roughly considered equivalent to the past continuous tense in expressions such as *we were writing books* or *we used to write books.*" They are both rendered by **libros scribebamus.** The implication is that the action extended over a period of time in the past without a definite date of completion.

Notice that **scribimus, scribemus,** and **scribebamus** all contain the present stem "scrib-," to which personal endings are added.

The Perfect-Stem Group

The perfect tense indicates a completed action. Its temporal dependence is subordinate to the present tense. When we say *we wrote books* or *we have written books*, the implication is that from the vantage point of today the action can be considered completed. Latin does not distinguish the subtle difference between the English simple past (*we wrote books*) and the so-called present-perfect tense (we have written books). They are both rendered as **libros scripsimus**.

The pluperfect tense, as its name indicates, refers to a "more than completed" action. It corresponds to the English past perfect (or pluperfect) tense. It is used to indicate an action that was already completed at a past time. Thus, its completion is relative to another action completed in the past. For example, we may say "Shakespeare had written many plays before James acceded to the throne of England." The coronation of James I as king of both Scotland and England took place in the year 1603. That is a definite event in the past and is thus rendered in the perfect tense. By the time of the coronation, Shakespeare was 39 years of age and a well-known playwright. He had already written some of his great tragedies. "We had written books" is rendered in Latin as **libros scripseramus**.

The future perfect tense expresses an action that will have been completed already by a definite date in the future. It corresponds exactly to the English future perfect tense. Thus we may say "by the end of this century robots will have taken over most of our manufacturing jobs." We place ourselves at a future date, such as the year 2099, and we look back in time to a future date, such as 2060, which will be obviously past with respect to 2099. An observer in 2099 will be able to say "robots took over all our manufacturing jobs more than thirty years ago." *We will have written books* is rendered in Latin as **libros scripserimus**.

Notice that **scripsimus**, **scripseramus**, and **scripserimus** all share the *perfect stem* "scrips-," to which personal endings are added.

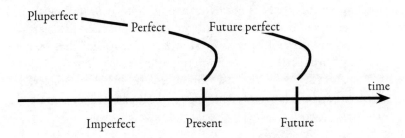

Figure 5: A Timeline of the Latin Tenses

Present-Stem Tenses: Present, Future, Imperfect

The Future Tense

We have already mastered the present tense. The *future* tense has two different systems of endings: one for the first two conjugations, and the other one for the third and fourth. The future endings for the first two conjugations are very simple as they abide by the following rule: between the stem and the present personal endings, we insert the letters **–bi–**, except in the first person singular, where the **i** disappears, and the third person plural, where it changes to a **u**. Thus we have:

First conjugation (1)	Second conjugation (2)
cōgitā**bō**	habē**bō**
cōgitā**bis**	habē**bis**
cōgitā**bit**	habē**bit**
cōgitā**bimus**	habē**bimus**
cōgitā**bitis**	habē**bitis**
cōgitā**bunt**	habē**bunt**

Note: At this point, you have internalized the concepts of person and number and, thus, labels are no longer provided.

For the remaining two conjugations, a characteristic *e* tends to replace (3a) or supplement (3b and 4) the characteristic *i* of the present tense. The first person singular ends in **–am**.

Third conjugation (3a)	Third –iō conjugation (3b)	Fourth conjugation (4)
dīc**am**	faci**am**	audi**am**
dīc**ēs**	faci**ēs**	audi**ēs**
dīc**et**	faci**et**	audi**et**
dīc**ēmus**	faci**ēmus**	audi**ēmus**
dīc**ētis**	faci**ētis**	audi**ētis**
dīc**ent**	faci**ent**	audi**ent**

The verbs **sum, esse** *to be* and **possum, posse** *to be able* have, as usual, special forms, somewhat similar to those of the first two conjugations, but with the *b* replaced by an *r*. These forms are worth memorizing, since they have other uses.

sum, esse, . . .	possum, posse, . . .
erō	poterō
eris	poteris
erit	poterit
erimus	poterimus
eritis	poteritis
erunt	poterunt

The Imperfect Tense

The imperfect is extremely regular. The endings are as follows:

-bam
-bās
-bat
-bāmus
-bātis
-bant

We obtain the stem by removing the ending **-re** from the infinitive. The fourth conjugation adds an ē after the *i*. Just as in the present tense, 3b abides by the same pattern as the fourth conjugation.

cōgitābam	habēbam	dīcēbam	faciēbam	audiēbam
cōgitābās	habēbās	dīcēbās	faciēbās	audiēbās
cōgitābat	habēbat	dīcēbat	faciēbat	audiēbat
cōgitābāmus	habēbāmus	dīcēbāmus	faciēbāmus	audiēbāmus
cōgitābātis	habēbātis	dīcēbātis	faciēbātis	audiēbātis
cōgitābant	habēbant	dīcēbant	faciēbant	audiēbant

The verbs **sum, esse** *to be* and **possum, posse** *to be able*, similarly to the future tense, exchange the *b* for an *r*:

eram	poteram
erās	poterās
erat	poterat
erāmus	poterāmus
erātis	poterātis
erant	poterant

The Perfect-Stem Tenses: Perfect, Pluperfect, Future Perfect

The Perfect Tense

As in English, there are several past tenses in Latin to convey different degrees of remoteness or simultaneity. In English, we have a *simple past* ("I thought"), a *present perfect* ("I have thought"), and a *pluperfect* ("I had thought"). In addition, we have a *continuous past* ("I was thinking, I used to think"), and combinations thereof. In Latin, the English simple past and the present perfect coalesce into one tense, called the *perfect*. The continuous past becomes the *imperfect*. The *pluperfect* remains as in English.

Latin, just as English, also has a *future perfect*. Thus we say: "By the time I arrive, you will have finished your job." This is an instance of *future perfect* in English, which exists also in Latin.

Of all the tenses, the most difficult to internalize is the perfect, because it often undergoes, literally, a radical change, that is, a change at the root. So much so, that *the first person singular of the perfect tense is the standard third principal part of the verb designation* (and there is still one more to go!). Note that in English too we have the past as one of the principal parts of a verb, e.g., "do, did, done." You may remember that so far a verb was designated by the first person singular of the present active indicative, followed by the present active infinitive (for example: **cōgitō, cōgitāre** and **audiō, audīre**). This way of designating (and remembering) verbs helps in getting the right conjugation. Now we will add the perfect, which, as we said, generally exhibits a radical change. The good news is that, once the perfect stem is known, the conjugation is completely regular and identical for all verb groups! The endings are:

-ī
-istī
-it
-imus
-istis
-ērunt

Note that the endings for all but the first two singular persons are similar to the present-tense endings.

As mentioned, the third principal part of a verb is, by convention, the first person singular of the perfect active indicative. The stem is obtained by simply removing the final -ī. Even the verbs **sum, esse, fuī** *to be* and **possum, posse, potuī** *to be able* are, in this respect, completely regular. Here are the first three principal parts of a few verbs:

> **audiō, audīre, audīvī**
> **cōgitō, cōgitāre, cōgitāvī**
> **dīcō, dīcere, dīxī**
> **faciō, facere, fēcī**
> **habeō, habēre, habuī**
> **sum, esse, fuī**
> **possum, posse, potuī**

Most verbs of the first conjugation, moreover, form their perfect stems regularly, by adding a *v* to the present stem.

cōgitāvī	dīxī	fuī
cōgitāvistī	dīxistī	fuistī
cōgitāvit	dīxit	fuit
cōgitāvimus	dīximus	fuimus
cōgitāvistis	dīxistis	fuistis
cōgitāvērunt	dīxērunt	fuērunt

The perfect stem is also used regularly to form the *perfect active infinitive*. All that has to be done is to add the ending –**isse** to the perfect stem. Examples: **cōgitāvisse** = to have thought, **dīxisse** = to have said, **fuisse** = to have been, etc. Notice that the syllable containing the letter *i* is stressed (accented) because of the double *s*.

Perfect Forms in the Dictionary

The usual rule for looking up verbs applies, namely, one must search for the entry of the first person singular, present tense, active, indicative. This might present a challenge when one encounters a verb that has undergone a radical change (literally) in its perfect form. It is recommended, therefore, to make a habit of reading and reciting the principal parts. Having said that, not all verbs undergo radical changes (as we have already seen), and most changes are not too severe. With practice, a sort of musical pattern emerges that renders the altered root recognizable in its present-tense form.

Example:
> Veni, vidi, vici (attributed to Julius Caesar).
>> Note the perfect forms of **veniō, videō, vincō** respectively.
>
> I came, I saw, I conquered.

The Future Perfect and the Pluperfect

We are left with just two tenses: the future perfect and the pluperfect. They are relatively easy, since they are formed with the perfect stem by adding, respectively, the future or the imperfect of the verb **sum, esse, fuī** *to be*.

Example:
cōgitō, cōgitāre, cōgitāvī
Perfect stem: **cōgitāv-**

Future perfect	Pluperfect
cōgitā**verō**	cōgitā**veram**
cōgitā**veris**	cōgitā**verās**
cōgitā**verit**	cōgitā**verat**
cōgitā**verimus**	cōgitā**verāmus**
cōgitā**veritis**	cōgitā**verātis**
cōgitā**verint**	cōgitā**verant**

Notice that in the third person plural of the future perfect the ending is **–erint** (rather than the expected **–erunt**) to avoid confusion with the perfect tense. The future perfect and pluperfect forms have an underlying logic that, not surprisingly, is similar to that in English. When we say "I will have heard" (future perfect), we are also combining a future of the auxiliary (*to have*) with a past of the main verb (*to hear*). In Latin, the auxiliary is a future of **sum, esse, fuī** *to be*, conveying the meaning of "I will be in the situation of having heard." A similar logic applies to the pluperfect.

Summary of the Indicative Active Mood

There are no more tenses left, so we can summarize some of the features of the whole conjugation of the indicative active system as follows:

- *A verb is characterized (so far) by three principal parts:* the first person singular of the present indicative (e.g., **dīcō**), the present infinitive (**dīcere**), and the first person singular of the perfect indicative (**dīxī**). These parts are sufficient to determine the whole conjugation pattern unambiguously.

- *The infinitive determines the conjugation group, while the first person of the present distinguishes between 3a and 3b* (e.g., **capiō, capere, cēpī,** ... must be 3b since the first principal part has an *i* before the *o*. It cannot be fourth conjugation since the infinitive does not end in **-īre**).

- *The present, imperfect, and future of the verb **sum, esse, fuī** to be are crucial for various reasons,* some of which are: (i) for themselves, as they are ubiquitous in literature of every kind; (ii) for conjugating that other ubiquitous verb **possum, posse, potuī** *to be able*, which is essentially a combination of **pot-** and **esse**; (iii) for conjugating many derived verbs, such as **absum, abesse, afuī** *to be absent*; (iv) the future perfect and the pluperfect of all verbs are formed regularly from the perfect stem (obtained by deleting the final ī from the third principal part) by adding, respectively, the future and imperfect forms of **sum, esse, fuī**; (v) some tenses of the passive voice (to be studied later) are formed regularly from forms of the auxiliary **sum, esse, fuī**.

- *The differences in conjugation between the five groups of verbs are not very severe,* and are actually quite logical considering the different characteristic vowels (*a, e, i*) and their lengths. *The only drastic departure occurs in the future tense,* where there is a rift between the first and second conjugations on the one hand, and the third and fourth, on the other.

- *The forms of the imperfect are easily recognized by the characteristic -ba-*, which appears in all persons and in all conjugations of all verbs (except **sum, esse, fuī** *to be* and its derived verbs, which exhibit a characteristic *-ra-*).

- *Many regularities are discernible, cutting along all tenses and all conjugations:* (i) the first person singular always ends in –ō or –**m** or –ī; (ii) the second person singular always ends in –**s** or –**stī**; (iii) the third person singular always ends in –**t**; (iv) the first person plural always ends in –**mus**; (v) the second person plural always ends in –**tis**; and (vi) the third person plural always ends in –**nt**. These regularities are invaluable as far as recognition is concerned.

Chapter VII
The Fourth and Fifth Declensions

The fourth and fifth declensions comprise the smallest groups of nouns. The fourth declension comprises mostly masculine nouns, a few neuters, and even fewer feminine nouns. The letter *u* prevails in most endings and one needs to be on guard not to mistake a fourth declension noun with a second declension one. It is the genitive that permits one to tell the difference most definitely. The masculine and feminine forms are identical, while the neuter forms exhibit typical discrepancies.

		motus (motion, m)	manus (hand, f)	cornū (horn, n)
Singular	N	motus	manus	cornū
	G	motūs	manūs	cornūs
	D	motuī	manuī	cornū
	Ac	motum	manum	cornū
	Ab	motū	manū	cornū
	V	(motus)	(manus)	(cornū)
Plural	N	motūs	manūs	cornua
	G	motuum	manuum	cornuum
	D	motibus	manibus	cornibus
	Ac	motūs	manūs	cornua
	Ab	motibus	manibus	cornibus
	V	(motūs)	(manūs)	(cornua)

Compared with the third declension, the similarities are many, taking into consideration that the *u* takes over in almost all endings.

If *u* is the vowel of choice for the fourth declension, *e* is for the fifth. There aren't many nouns in this group, but at least one of them is very common, so it is best to have familiarity with this declension. As in the fourth, there is a third declension flavor throughout. Only one noun (**diēs, diēī**) is masculine or feminine; the rest are feminine.

		diēs (day, m or f)	rēs (thing, f)
Singular	N	diēs	rēs
	G	diēī	reī
	D	diēī	reī
	Ac	diem	rem
	Ab	diē	rē
	V	(diēs)	(rēs)
Plural	N	diēs	rēs
	G	diērum	rērum
	D	diēbus	rēbus
	Ac	diēs	rēs
	Ab	diēbus	rēbus
	V	(diēs)	(rēs)

The Demonstrative Pronouns and Adjectives

There are three different demonstrative pronouns (and adjectives) in Latin to signify a person's or a thing's distance from the speaker: **hic, haec, hoc** *this one here*, **ille, illa, illud** *that one there*, and **iste, ista, istud** *that one over there by you*. They follow basically the pattern of first and second declension adjectives, with similar irregularities to those of the relative pronoun (**quī, quae, quod**) discussed in chapter V of this compendium.

hic, haec, hoc ("this one here")

		Masculine	Feminine	Neuter
Singular	N	hic	haec	hoc
	G	huius	huius	huius
	D	huic	huic	huic
	Ac	hunc	hanc	hoc
	Ab	hōc	hāc	hōc
Plural	N	hī	hae	haec
	G	hōrum	hārum	hōrum
	D	hīs	hīs	hīs
	Ac	hōs	hās	haec
	Ab	hīs	hīs	hīs

ille, illa, illud ("that one there")

		Masculine	Feminine	Neuter
Singular	N	ille	illa	illud
	G	illīus	illīus	illīus
	D	illī	illī	illī
	Ac	illum	illam	illud
	Ab	illō	illā	illō
Plural	N	illī	illae	illa
	G	illōrum	illārum	illōrum
	D	illīs	illīs	illīs
	Ac	illōs	illās	illa
	Ab	illīs	illīs	illīs

Another usage of **hic/haec/hoc** and **ille/illa/illud** is *the latter* and *the former*, respectively.

Iste, ista, istud (*that one over there by you*) follows exactly the same pattern as **ille, illa, illud**.

Examples:

Notiones illius scriptoris semper magnae erant.

The ideas of that writer were always great.

Poteritne pax post hanc victoriam perseverare?

Will peace be able to persevere after this victory?
 (pax, pācis [f] = *peace*)

Hae de virtute rei publicae cogitabant.

These women were thinking about the virtue of the republic.
 (rēs pūblica [f] = *republic, public affair*)

Irregular Adjectives (and Pronouns)

A few very important and common adjectives (and pronouns) of the first/second declension exhibit the following irregularity: *in the genitive and dative singular they are declined as the demonstrative pronouns (and adjectives) we have just learned.* Otherwise, they are completely regular. These adjectives are the following:

ūnus, ūna, ūnum (*one*)

alius, alia, aliud (*other*; notice the neuter form in the nominative singular)

alter, altera, alterum (*the other one of two*)

ipse, ipsa, ipsum (*-self*)

tōtus, tōta, tōtum (*all, whole*)

ūllus, ūlla, ūllum (*some, any*)

nūllus, nūlla, nūllum (*no, not any*)

sōlus, sōla, sōlum (*alone*)

Examples:

Quis custodiet ipsos custodes? (Juvenal)
Who will guard the guards themselves?

Cave hominem unius libri. (Thomas Aquinas)
Beware the man of one book.

Vox unius, vox nullius. (Legal expression)
The voice of one is the voice of nobody.

Haec dixit alteri.
He said these things to the other person.

The Personal Pronouns

For the first and second persons, the personal pronouns are completely gender indifferent.

First-Person Personal Pronouns			
ego	(I)	**nōs**	(we)
meī	(of me)	**nostrum/nostrī**	(of us)
mihī	(to me)	**nōbīs**	(to us)
mē	(me)	**nōs**	(us)
mē	(by, with, etc., me)	**nōbīs**	(by, with, etc., us)

Second-Person Personal Pronouns			
tū	(you)	**vōs**	(you)
tuī	(of you)	**vestrum/vestrī**	(of you)
tibi	(to you)	**vōbīs**	(to you)
tē	(you)	**vōs**	(you)
tē	(by, with, etc., you)	**vōbīs**	(by, with, etc., you)

We note that the genitive forms of the first- and second-person personal pronouns are not to be used to indicate possession, but only reference. Example: "your recollection" indicates possession, whereas "the recollection of you by the witness" indicates reference. In one case we are answering the question "whose recollection?" and in the other the question "the recollection of whom?," and these are two very different things. **Vestrum** and **nostrum** are used as *partitive genitives*, e.g., "Some of us are here." For possession, we must use the *possessive adjectives* discussed later in this chapter.

Examples:

Quis nostrum hoc scribet?
Who of us (among us) will write this?

Qui sine peccato est vestrum, primus in illam lapidem mittat. (John 8:7) (**Mittat** is in the subjunctive mood, to be studied in chapter X of this compendium.)
He that is without sin among you, let him first cast a stone at her.

Propter timorem vestri, discessi.
On account of the fear of you, I departed.

Hodie mihi, cras tibi. (Latin proverb)
(hodie = *today*, cras = *tomorrow*)
Today for me, tomorrow for you, i.e., What is for me today (my lot) will be for you tomorrow.

Third-Person Personal Pronouns

The third-person personal pronoun is **is, ea, id** (*he, she, it*). It is also used to express a lighter form of "this" or "that." *It follows the pattern of the demonstrative pronouns with the addition of an initial* e *to most forms.*

is, ea, id ("he, she, it")

		Masculine	Feminine	Neuter
Singular	N	is	ea	id
	G	eius	eius	eius
	D	eī	eī	eī
	Ac	eum	eam	id
	Ab	eō	eā	eō
Plural	N	eī	eae	ea
	G	eōrum	eārum	eōrum
	D	eīs	eīs	eīs
	Ac	eōs	eās	ea
	Ab	eīs	eīs	eīs

Adding the suffix **–dem**, we obtain an emphasis in the sense of "the very same." Some small orthographical irregularities occur (is + dem = īdem, id + dem = idem, eum + dem = eundem, etc.).

Examples:

id est

That is. We often see this as the abbreviation "i.e."

Non omnes eadem amant aut easdem cupiditates
studiaque habent. (Horace) (studium, studiī (n) = *study, zeal, desire, pursuit*)

Not all people love the same things or have the same desires and pursuits.

Is mihi eundem librum legit.

He read the same book to me.

Is mihi dedit librum eius

He gave me the book (of him/her; not his own).

The Reflexive Pronouns

Reflexive pronouns refer back to the subject. The first- and second-person singular and plural personal pronoun forms are used also as reflexive forms (*myself, yourself, ourselves, yourselves*).

Examples:

Nos rogamus, "Quis est iste homo stultus?"
We are asking ourselves, "Who is that foolish man?"

Te laudas propter superbiam.
You praise yourself on account of conceit.

Nisi pro me sum, quis pro me erit? Sed si pro me tantum
sum, quid sum? (Hillel the Elder)
If I am not for myself, who will be for me? But if I am
only for myself, what am I? (nisi = *if . . . not*)

For the third person (*himself, herself, itself, themselves*), the reflexive pronoun can be obtained from the second person by substituting *s* for *t* in the singular forms. The plural forms of the third-person personal pronoun are identical to the singular counterparts:

	Singular/Plural
N	n/a
G	**suī**
D	**sibi**
Ac	**sē**
Ab	**sē**

Examples:

Per se
Through itself/by itself

Bellum se ipsum alet. (Cato the Elder quoted in Livy)
(alo, alere, alui, altum [*or* alitum] = *nourish*)
War feeds itself.

Sibi magnam laudem dant.
They give themselves great praise.

The Possessive Adjectives

The first- and second-person possessive adjectives are regular first/second declension adjectives:

> **meus, mea, meum** (*my*)
>
> **noster, nostra, nostrum** (*our*)
>
> **tuus, tua, tuum** (*your*)
>
> **vester, vestra, vestrum** (*your*, pl.)

Note that, as with all adjectives, the gender, number, and case of the possessive adjective agrees with the noun it modifies, regardless of the gender of the possessor.

Examples:

> Ille vir dixit: "amo matrem meam."
> That man said: "I love my mother."

> Illa femina patrem nostrum amat.
> That woman loves our father.

For *his own, her own, its own, their own*, Latin uses a regular first/second declension adjective:

> **suus, sua, suum** (*his own, her own, its own, their own*)

To indicate possession by someone other than the subject, the genitive forms of the possessive pronoun are used:

> **eius, eius, eius** (*his, her, its*)
>
> **eōrum, eārum, eōrum** (*their*)

Examples:

> Nero suam matrem amabat.
> Nero loved his (own) mother.

> Nero matrem eius amabat.
> Nero loved his/her (i.e., someone else's) mother.

Note the important distinction!

Chapter VIII
The Passive Voice and Deponent Verbs

I n English, the passive voice of a verb is formed by a combination of some form of the auxiliary verb *to be* and the past participle of the main verb. Thus, for example, we have:

Present:	The lesson is learned
(Present continuous):	The lesson is being learned
Past:	The law was formulated
(Present perfect):	The law has been formulated
(Past continuous):	The law was being formulated
Pluperfect:	The city had already been taken (when the reinforcement arrived)
Future:	The command will be obeyed
Future perfect:	The child will have been delivered (by the time the sailor returns)

Latin follows a similar idea of a compound with **sum, esse, fuī** only for the perfect, the pluperfect, and the future perfect. The present, imperfect, and future, on the other hand, have special one-word forms characterized by an *r* in most of the endings. These passive endings are as follows:

-r

-ris

-tur

-mur

-minī

-ntur

To form the passive voice for the present, imperfect, or future, the technique is the following: simply take the present, imperfect, or future conjugations, and replace their active endings with the passive ones. Exceptions to this rule: a) The first person singular present passive, in which the *o* ending is not dropped, b) The second-person singular forms of groups 3a and 3b in the present tense drop the *i* and add *e* before **–ris**.

Example:

agō, agere, ēgī (*to do, to lead*)

Present Passive	Future Passive	Imerfect Passive
agor	agar	agēbar
ageris	agēris	agēbāris
agitur	agētur	agēbātur
agimur	agēmur	agēbāmur
agiminī	agēminī	agēbāminī
aguntur	agentur	agēbantur

Some examples:

cōgitātur	(it is thought)
faciēbāntur	(they were being done)
dicētur	(it will be said)
audiēris	(you will be heard)

Note that what was the direct object of the verb in the active voice is now the subject of the passive verb.

Liber scribitur.

The book is written. (**Liber** is the subject of the passive verb.
It is, therefore, in the nominative).

The Perfect Passive System and the Ablative Of Agent

To form the perfect, the future perfect, and the pluperfect in the passive voice we need, as in English, the passive perfect participle. *In Latin, this is precisely the fourth and last principal part of a verb.* Note that in English too the third principal part of the verb is the *perfect passive participle* (PPP). E.g., "do, did, done." In Latin, the fourth principal part is combined with **sum** (perfect), **erō** (future perfect), and **eram** (pluperfect) to form the passives of the perfect system.

The fourth principal part is usually given in the neuter singular nominative. Very often, the passive perfect participle is obtained by adding **–tum** to the present stem, or a slight variation thereof. Many English words derive from the fourth principal part: *dictum* (dīcō, dīcere, dīxī, dictum), *script* (scrībō, scrībere, scrīpsī, scrīptum), *fact* (faciō, facere, fēcī, factum), *act* (agō, agere, ēgī, actum), *captive* (capiō, capere, cēpī, captum), *tactile* (tangō, tangere, tetigī, tactum).

cōgitō, cōgitāre, cōgitāvī, cōgitātum

The meaning of **cōgitātum** is roughly: "in the state of having been thought."

Examples:
 dīcō, dīcere, dixī, dictum
  (dictum = *having been said*)
 faciō, facere, fēcī, factum
  (factum = *having been done*)
 audiō, audīre, audīvī, audītum
  (audītum = *having been heard*)

To form the passive compound tenses, i.e., perfect, future perfect, and pluperfect, one must combine a form of the fourth principal part with the present, future, or imperfect form of **sum, esse, fuī** respectively. Example: **fēmina audīta est** (*a woman was heard/has been heard*), **fēmina audīta erit** (*a woman will have been heard*), **fēmina audīta erat** (*a woman had been heard*). You may have noticed that the participle **audīta** also functions as a predicate adjective modifying **fēmina**. The perfect participle declines in the same pattern as adjectives of the first and second declension and, logically, agrees with its subject in gender, number, and case.

Example:
 Perfect passive of **audīre**

Masculine	Feminine	Neuter
audītus sum	audīta sum	audītum sum
audītus es	audīta es	audītum es
audītus est	audīta est	audītum est
audītī sumus	audītae sumus	audīta sumus
audītī estis	audītae estis	audīta estis
audītī sunt	audītae sunt	audīta sunt

Notice that the perfect passive (*I was heard* or *I have been heard*) is formed with the *present* form of **sum, esse, fuī**. This is, in a way, very logical, since the "past" connotation is already implied in the participle:

Audītus sum.

I was heard (I am in the state of having been heard).
> *The speaker is masculine, singular.*
>
> [Note: To express "I am heard," you must use the present passive: **audior**.]

Verba audīta sunt.

The words have been heard (The words are in the state of having been heard).

Fēminae audītae sunt.

The women have been heard.

For the pluperfect, one uses the imperfect of **sum, esse, fuī***:*

audītus, -a, -um + eram, erās, erat

audītī, -ae, -a + erāmus, erātis, erant

Examples:

audītus eram

I had been heard. *The speaker is masculine, singular.*

audītae eramus

We had been heard. *The speakers are feminine, plural.*
> A remote-pluperfect is sometimes encountered
> (**audītus fuī**).

For the future perfect, the future of **sum, esse, fuī** *is used:*

audītus, -a, -um + erō, eris, erit

audītī, -ae, -a + erimus, eritis, erunt

Examples:

audītus erō

I will have been heard. *The speaker is masculine, singular.*

audīta erunt

These things will have been heard. [as opposed to
audientur = *they will be heard*]

Ablative of Agent

We have seen that when we use a passive verb, the subject does not perform the action, but rather receives it. In the sentence **Fēminae audītae erant**, fēminae is the subject of **audītae erant**, even though **fēminae** is not performing the action. The doer or agent, if needed, goes in the ablative case preceded by the preposition **ab** (or **ā**, before consonants). The preposition **ab** may be omitted for inanimate objects, but is usually employed with people. This is similar to the English "by" or "at the hands of." Let's hear Isaac Newton in his *Principia*:

> Projectilia perseverant in motibus suis nisi quatenus a resistentia aeris retardantur.
>
> Projectiles persevere in their motions except to the extent that they are slowed down by the resistance of the air.

> Laudatur ab his; culpatur ab illis. (Horace)
> He is praised by these men; he is blamed by those men.

Passive Infinitives

The present passive infinitive is obtained from the active infinitive by changing the final –**e** to –**ī**, except for verbs of the third conjugation, where the whole ending –**ere** is changed to –**ī**.

Examples:

cōgitāre = *to think*	**cōgitārī** = *to be thought*
vidēre = *to see*	**vidērī** = *to be seen, to seem*
dīcere = *to say*	**dīcī** = *to be said*
capere = *to seize*	**capī** = *to be seized*
audīre = *to hear*	**audīrī** = *to be heard*

> Amor misceri cum timore non potest. (Publilius Syrus)
>   (misceō, miscēre, miscuī, mixtum = to mix)
> Love cannot be mixed with fear.

The perfect passive infinitive is formed, naturally, with the perfect participle and the infinitive **esse**.

Examples:

> **cōgitātus esse** = to have been thought (masculine singular)
>
> **visum esse** = to have been seen (neuter singular)
>
> **facta esse** = to have been done (neuter plural or feminine singular).

Notice that even in the infinitive the participle has a gender and a number.

Deponent Verbs

Many verbs in Latin do not have active forms. They are known as "deponent verbs." They are conjugated only in the passive forms, but have an active meaning. Only three principal parts are valid for deponent verbs.

Examples:

> **arbitror, arbitrārī, arbitrātus sum** = *to judge, to deem, to think*
>
> **sequor, sequī, secūtus sum** = *to follow*
>
> **experior, experīrī, expertus sum** = *to try*
>
> **conor, conārī, conātus sum** = *to attempt*
>
> **morior, morī, mortuus sum** = *to die*

The conjugation group of each verb can be deduced from the form of the infinitive.

Examples:

> Non sequitur.
>
> It does not follow.
>
> Homo stultus! Postquam divitias habere coepit mortuus est! (Cicero)
>
> Foolish man! He died after he began to have riches!

Dictionary Entries for Deponent Verbs

The same rule regarding dictionary entries applies as for all verbs. You must search according to the verb's first person singular present tense indicative form. If the verb is deponent, you will notice the *r* ending of the first person singular. The perfect is usually listed in the masculine singular form of the participle + **sum**. Deponent verbs have only three principal parts listed in the dictionary. Remember that all three forms of the deponent verbs are active in meaning. There are a few exceptions to this rule in the cruel form of "semi-deponent" verbs, but you need not worry much about them.

Chapter IX
Participles, Gerundive, and Gerund

The word "participle" comes from the Latin **participō, participāre, participāvī, participātum**, which means *to partake*, or *to share*. A participle is a hybrid entity: It is an adjective formed from a verb stem. *As an adjective it agrees in number, gender, and case with the word it modifies. As a verb, it has tense and voice, and it may take objects.*

In English, participles appear in the present active and in the past (or perfect) passive forms. For example:

> The *writing* hand (present active)
>
> The *written* word (past passive)

Latin has two participles in the active voice (present and future), and two in the passive voice (perfect and future). (The future active participle would be roughly translated as: "about to write," and the future passive participle as: "about to be written," or "that must be written.")

The Present Participle

The present participle is declined as an *adjective of the third declension* and is formed by adding **–ns** to the present (active) stem of the verb. The genitive is in **–ntis** and its stem is its genitive minus **–is**. The ablative singular ends in **–ntī** or **–nte**. It may help to think of the word "prese**nt**" to recognize the persistent **–nt** in the declension pattern of the present participle, except for the nominative singular. For verbs of the conjugations 3b and 4, the characteristic *i* is preserved. Thus we have:

cōgitāns, cōgitantis	*(thinking)*
vidēns, videntis	*(seeing)*
capiēns, capientis	*(seizing)*
audiēns, audientis	*(hearing)*

Only the present participle is declined as an adjective of the third declension. As we shall see, the remaining participles are declined in the pattern of first/second declension adjectives.

Present participle of **agō, agere, ēgī, actum**, *doing, leading*...

	Masculine and Feminine	Neuter
	agēns	agēns
	agentis	agentis
Singular	agentī	agentī
	agentem	agēns
	agentī, agente	agentī, agente
	agentēs	agentia
	agentium	agentium
Plural	agentibus	agentibus
	agentēs	agentia
	agentibus	agentibus

Examples:

Galileus, lunam videns, de forma eius scripsit.

Galileus, seeing the moon, wrote about its beauty/form.

Galileus audientibus discipulis de forma lunae dixit.

Galileo spoke about the beauty/form of the moon to the listening students.

Many English nouns (and adjectives) are derived from Latin present participles. They normally end (in English) in **–nt**.

Examples:

agens, agentis *agent*; **sentiens, sentientis** *sentient*; **vigilans, vigilantis** *vigilant*; **gradiens, gradientis** *gradient*; **continens, continentis** *continent*; **dependens, dependentis** *dependent*.

The Future Active Participle

The future active participle is declined as *an adjective of the first/second declension*. It is obtained by adding **–ūrus, –ūra, –ūrum** to the stem obtained by deleting the ending **–um** from the fourth principal part (i.e., from the passive perfect participle).

Example:
videō, vidēre, vīdī, vīsum

The stem of the passive perfect participle is, therefore, **vīs-**. Thus we obtain:

vīsūrus, vīsūra, vīsūrum (*about to see*)

Femina, cogitatura magnam notionem, tacet.
The woman, about to think a great idea, keeps silent.

Another important use of the future active participle is its role in the regular formation of the future infinitive, by adding the infinitive **esse**. For example:

cōgitātūrus (-a, -um) esse = *to be about to think.*

Translating Participles

When translating participles, you should feel free to provide extra explanatory words such as *while, since, although, when*, etc. Just as in English, the tense of a participle is not absolute, but rather is relative to that of a main verb. In other words, regardless of the tense of a verb in the main clause, a present participle is contemporaneous to the main verb, a perfect participle is prior to the main verb, and a future participle is subsequent to the main verb.

Examples:
Caesar, Brutum videns, dicit/dixit/dicet "Et tu?"
Caesar, seeing Brutus, says/said/will say, "You too?"
Upon seeing Brutus, Caesar says/said/will say, "You too?"

Caesar, visus a Bruto, dicit/dixit/dicet, "Et tu?"
Caesar, having been seen by Brutus, says/said/will say, "You too?"

Caesar, Brutum visurus, dicit/dixit/dicet, "Et tu?"
Caesar, about to see Brutus, says/said/will say, "Et tu?"
   (In this example, Caesar has prophetic prowess!)

Passive Perfect Participle

The passive perfect participle is nothing but the fourth principal part of a verb, covered in chapter VIII of this appendix.

Examples:

Acta (n pl)
The things done

Pirata captus nunquam timet
A captured pirate never fears

Passive Future Participle: The Gerundive

The passive future participle (also called the *gerundive*) is formed, like the present active participle, *from the present active stem.* The endings are –**ndus, –nda, –ndum.**

Examples:

Agenda (n pl)
The things (about) to be done.

Addendum (n sing)
The thing to be added.

Referendum (n sing)
The thing to be referred.

Caesar, a piratis capiendus, nunquam timebat.
Caesar, about to be captured by pirates, never feared.

The passive future participle + a form of **esse** conveys a sense of obligation or necessity. This construction is called the ***passive periphrastic.*** Its name is terrifying, but its construction is rather simple.

Examples:

Haec agenda sunt.
These things must be done.

Hoc addendum est.
This must be added.

Delenda est Carthago. (Cato the Elder)
Carthage must be destroyed.

Quod erat demonstrandum.
That which had to be demonstrated. Often abbreviated as
"QED" at the end of a mathematical or philosophical proof.

Quod erit demonstrandum.
That which will have to be demonstrated.

A *dative of agent* is used with the passive periphrastic, rather than the ablative. The use of the dative is logical, because the intended meaning is "It is for us to do these things."

Examples:

Hic liber mihi scribendus erat.
This book was for me to be written. (I had to write this book)

Haec nobis agenda sunt.
These things are for us to be done. (We must do these things).

We have now covered the formations of participles in their declensions, tenses, and voices.

	Active	Passive
Present	Present stem + –ns (**agēns, agentis**)	n/a
Perfect	n/a	4th principal part stem + –**us**, –**a**, –**um** (**actus, acta, actum**)
Future	4th principal part stem + –**ūrus**, –**ūra**, –**ūrum** (**actūrus, actūra, actūrum**)	Present stem + –**ndus**, –**nda**, –**ndum** (**agendus, agenda, agendum**)

Participles as Substantive Adjectives

Participles, like adjectives, may modify an absent (implied) noun. They must agree in number, gender, and case with the unexpressed noun. These types of participles often come to function as nouns themselves.

Examples:

Amans de amore scripsit.

The lover (i.e., the loving man/woman) wrote about love.

Sapiens de vita cogitat.

The wise person (i.e., the man/woman who knows) thinks about life.

Participles of Deponent Verbs

When it comes to participles, deponent verbs retain an active meaning in all but the future passive. Thus:

arbitrans = *judging*
arbitrātus = *having judged*
arbitratūrus = *about to judge*
arbitrandus = *about to be judged*

So, in the case of deponent verbs, we have three active participles (rather than two) and one passive participle (rather than two).

Ave, Imperator, morituri te salutant. (Suetonius)

Hail, Emperor, those who are about to die salute you.

Deponent Infinitives

As we have already seen, the present infinitive of deponent verbs is passive in form but active in meaning: **arbitrari** = *to judge*.

This is also true of the perfect infinitive: (**arbitratus, –a, –um + esse** = *to have judged*.)

The future infinitive takes an active form with active meaning. Thus, **arbitraturus, –a, –um + esse** = *to be about to judge*.

The Gerund: A Verbal Noun

The gerund is a commonly used device, whereby the future passive participle's meaning becomes that of an active noun. *Its forms are identical to those of the gerundive (future passive participle) in all cases, but the gerund does not have a nominative case and it is always a neuter singular noun.* Its meaning corresponds to the English gerund, a verbal noun whose ending is *–ing*. Like all participles, the gerund can take an object.

Examples:

> Cogitando intellegimus.
> By thinking we understand.

> Ars cogitandi
> The art of thinking

> Modus operandi
> The way of operating/working

> Philosophus scit artem cogitandi antiquas notiones novo modo.
> The philosopher knows the art of learning ancient notions in a
> new way.

Since the gerund, having no nominative case, may not be used as a subject, the infinitive (another verbal noun) is used instead. The infinitive used as a noun is construed in the neuter gender.

Example:

> Errare est humanum.
> To err is human.

Gerundive Phrases

We have already seen the gerundive as a future passive participle. It functions as a simple adjective in all genders, numbers, and cases with the endings **–ndus, –nda, –ndum**. We have also seen that the gerundive + **esse** conveys a sense of obligation, a construction also known as "passive periphrastic."

Often the gerundive is preferred over the gerund where a direct object in the accusative case is involved.

For example, using the gerund we could say:

> Philosophus scit artem cogitandi notiones.
> The philosopher knows the art of thinking ideas.

But, using the gerundive, we could also say, with the same meaning:

> Philosophus scit artem notionum cogitandarum.
> Literally: The philosopher knows the art of the ideas to be thought.

We see that the former direct object ("notiones") steals the case and place of the gerund (the genitive case), and the gerundive then acts as an adjective with a passive meaning.

Another common construction of the gerundive is genitive + **causā** to express purpose:

> Librorum legendorum causa venit.
> He came for the sake of books to be read/for the sake of reading books.

Similarly, **ad** + the accusative of the gerundive is used to express purpose:

> Ad libros scribendos venit.
> He came for the sake of writing books/He came to write books.

Alternatively, the gerund (instead of the gerundive) may also be used to express purpose with **ad**:

> Ad scribendum libros venit.
> He came for the purpose of writing books.

Both the gerundive and gerund phrases in the above examples are grammatically correct, but Latin tends to prefer the gerundive construction.

Chapter X
The Subjunctive and Its Uses

T he basic uses of the subjunctive mood are two: (i) the expression of wishes, hopes, fears, and other types of ideas involving some measure of uncertainty; (ii) the expression of different types of conditional statements. In fact, (ii) can be seen as a particular case of (i), but it is best to treat them separately.

In English, the subjunctive mood is expressed by the use of forms that mostly coincide with indicative ones. Not so in Latin. Examples of English subjunctive:

> Let there <u>be</u> a line . . .
>
> It is expected that he <u>write</u> a test . . .
>
> If I <u>were</u> more thoughtful . . .

We see that in (proper) English the subjunctive forms manifest themselves through indicative forms used somewhat "strangely": sometimes the infinitive is used ("it is necessary that the triangle <u>be</u> equilateral"), sometimes "were" appears instead of "was," and so on. Although it may be possible to somehow manage in English without a conscious knowledge of the subjunctive, this would be unthinkable in Latin or in any of the modern Romance languages. Even young children in, say, Spain or Latin America become aware of the right constructions and the need to use them if they are to get what they want (e.g., in Spanish: "quiero que me compr<u>es</u> un regalo" = literally "I want that you buy me a present"). In scientific Latin, the subjunctive is used extensively for conditional sentences. For those learning the forms of Latin verbs, it is quite fortunate that Latin did not develop a separate form for the "conditional" or "potential" mood, which English introduces through the use of "should" or "would":

> If I had more money, I would buy a new car.

This is a case of a "contrary-to-fact" condition, further discussed below in this chapter. In the example above, the unspoken implication is: "but I don't, so I won't." For this kind of sentence, Latin uses the subjunctive twice.

Scientific Latin frequently uses the subjunctive mood to express an assumption, such as: *sit AC linea*, the English translation for which is the familiar "let AC be a line."

Present Subjunctive

If you have mastered the present of the indicative mood, your memory will not be overly taxed by the present subjunctive forms. The rule of thumb is as follows: the **a** of the first conjugation changes to an **e**, whereas the other conjugations (that did not have an **a** in the indicative) acquire an **a**. The first person singular requires a special treatment consisting in adding an **–m**.

Indicative		Subunctive	
cōgitō	(I think)	cōgitem	(that I think, let me think)
cōgitās		cōgitēs	
cōgitat		cōgitet	
cōgitāmus		cōgitēmus	
cōgitātis		cōgitētis	
cōgitant		cōgitent	

And so:

> dīcam, dīcās, dīcat, . . .
> faciam, faciās, faciat, . . .
> audiam, audiās, audiat, . . .

The same substitutions are applicable to the passive forms and to deponents:

> cōgiter, cōgitēris, cōgitētur, . . .
> sequar, sequāris, sequātur, . . .

The verbs **sum, esse, fuī** *to be* and **possum, posse, potuī** *to be able,* as usual, have special forms:

sim	possim
sīs	possīs
sit	possit
sīmus	possīmus
sītis	possītis
sint	possint

The subjunctive often expresses a wish or a gentle command, namely "the jussive" from the Latin **iubeō, iubēre, iūssī, iūssum** = *to command.*

Examples:

audiamus

let us hear

hoc cogitent

let them think this

sit linea recta

let there be a straight line/let the line be straight

sit vis vobiscum!

may the force be with you!

Imperfect Subjunctive

The imperfect subjunctive is often used in purpose, result, and conditional clauses (to be studied below in this chapter). We form the imperfect subjunctive by simply adding the personal endings (active or passive) to the present active infinitive (i.e., the second principal part). Thus:

cōgitārem	**essem**
cōgitārēs	**essēs**
cōgitāret	**esset**
cōgitārēmus	**essēmus**
cōgitārētis	**essētis**
cōgitārent	**essent**

We form the passive voice of the imperfect subjunctive by adding the personal endings to the present active infinitive, rather than to the passive infinitive.

vidērer

vidērēris

vidērētur

vidērēmur

vidērēminī

vidērentur

Purpose Clauses

In English we often use an infinitive to indicate the purpose of an action in the main clause. Example: Galileo built a telescope in order to look at the stars, *or* . . . so that he could look . . . Latin almost always uses a subjunctive clause to indicate purpose, which is introduced by **ut**. To introduce a negative purpose (*so that not, lest . . .*) Latin uses **nē**.

> Hoc dico ut audias
> I say this (so) that you may hear

> Hoc dicam ut audias
> I will say this (so) that you may hear

> Hoc dixi ut audires
> I said this (so) that you might hear

> Hoc dicebam ne audires
> I was saying this lest you might hear/so that you would not hear

Result Clauses

A result clause indicates the outcome of an action in the main clause. In both English and Latin the main clause often contains an adverb or adjective modifying the degree (quality or quantity) of a noun or a verb. Examples: Archimedes was *so excited* that he shouted, "Eureka! Eureka!" Cicero spoke *so eloquently* that all in the courthouse were riveted.

In English, result clauses are introduced by "that" followed by the indicative mood, while Latin result clauses are set off by **ut** and a subjunctive verb. When the clause contains a negative result, it is set off by **ut** and a negation word, such as **nōn, nihil, nēmō, numquam,** or **nūllus.** (Purpose clauses with negation are introduced by **nē**, as we have already seen.)

Here are some commonly employed adverbs and adjectives in the main clause, which indicate that a result clause is to follow:

> **ita, tam, sīc** (*so, in such a way*)
> **tantus, –a, –um** (*so much, so great*)

Examples:
> Newton tanta scripsit ut ab omnibus laudaretur.
> Newton wrote things so great that he was praised by all.

Newton tanta scripsit ut non ab omnibus intellegeretur.

Newton wrote things so great that he was not understood by all.

Cicero tam bene loquitur ut omnes taceant.

Cicero speaks so well that all are silent. (**taceō, tacēre, tacuī, tacitum** = *to be silent*)

Translating Purpose Clauses and Result Clauses

Since purpose clauses convey the desire for an outcome rather than an actual outcome, often it is best to add "might" or "may" prior to the verb in the subjunctive clause. In a result clause it is often best to translate the verb in the subjunctive clause as an indicative.

Examples:

Purpose: Dixi ut audires.

I spoke so that you might hear.

Result: Tam bene dixi ut audires.

I spoke so well that you heard. (**bene** = *well*)

Purpose: Galileus stellas spectat ut mundum intellegat.

Galileo observes the stars so that he may understand the universe.

Result: Galileus tam strenue stellas spectat ut mundum intellegat.

Galileo observes the stars so actively that he understands the universe.

The difference between purpose and result clauses is also reflected in the negation:

Purpose: Monui te ne errares.

I warned you so that you might not err.

Result: Tam monui te ut non errares.

I warned you so much that you did not err (as a result of my admonitions).

There are only two tenses of the subjunctive left: perfect and pluperfect. The rules of formation are simple. *In the active system, the perfect is formed by appending –eri to the perfect stem and then adding the personal endings.* Note that, except for the first person singular, its forms are identical to the indicative active future perfect (except for the length of some vowels). In conditional clauses (to be studied later in this chapter), the use of the future perfect is more frequent than the perfect subjunctive.

Perfect Active Subjunctive

The perfect active is formed from the perfect stem followed by eri + *the personal endings:*

> **cōgitāverim, cōgitāveris, cōgitāverit, cōgitāverīmus, cōgitāveristis, cōgitāverint**

Pluperfect Active Subjunctive

The pluperfect active is formed from the perfect active infinitive followed by the personal endings:

> **cōgitāvissem, cōgitāvissēs, cōgitāvisset . . .**

The passive system, on the other hand, follows the usual rules for compound tenses. In other words, the passive system consists of the perfect passive participle plus the present subjunctive of **sum, esse, fuī** (for the perfect passive subjunctive) or plus the imperfect subjunctive of **sum, esse, fuī** (for the pluperfect passive subjunctive). Note that the perfect passive participle matches the subject in gender and number.

> Perfect passive: **cōgitātus sim, cōgitātus sīs, cōgitātus sit . . .**
>
> Pluperfect passive: **cōgitātus essem, cōgitātus essēs, cōgitātus esset . . .**

Use of the Subjunctive in Indirect Questions

An indirect question reports a question asked, rather than a direct quotation. Example: They ask what Galileo is observing (indirect); They asked, "What is Galileo observing?" (direct). In Latin, the subjunctive is used in indirect questions and is introduced by an interrogative adjective, adverb, or pronoun.

Examples:

Rogant quid Galileus spectet.

They ask what Galileo is observing.

Rogant quid a Galileo spectatum sit.

They ask what has been observed by Galileo.

Conditional Sentences

Conditions in Latin are introduced by **si** (= *if*). There are many different kinds of conditions, and some of them may require just the indicative mood, while others require the subjunctive.

Example:

Si studes discis.

If you study, you learn.

In this statement there is no implication as to whether or not you are studying. It is just a statement of cause and effect ("if A then B"). But we could also cast a shadow of scepticism by saying:

Si studeas discas.

If you should study, you would learn.

Minus saepe erres, si scias quid nescias. (Cicero)

You should err less often, if you would know what you do not know.

The subjunctive has been used to convey the should/would combination, but still without a clear implication as to the real present or future state of affairs. A much more technical construction is the so-called *contrary-to-fact* condition. When we say in English "If I studied I would learn," the implication is clear: but I don't study, so actually I won't learn. Or in the past: If I had studied, I would have learned (but I didn't, so I haven't).

These sentences consist always of two parts: the condition not fulfilled and the outcome not achieved. Latin, mercifully, uses the subjunctive for both. For the present condition, the imperfect subjunctive is used. For the past condition, the pluperfect subjunctive is used. Notice how similar to English this policy really is! Our last two examples would be translated, respectively, as:

Si studerem, discerem.
If I studied, I would learn.

Si studuissem, didicissem.
If I had studied, I would have learned.

In mathematical proof, this is the kind of statement that would be typically used in the so-called *reductio ad absurdum*, such as in Euclid's proof of the infinity of prime numbers.

More examples:

"Heu" dixisses si te in speculo vidisses. (adapted from Horace)
You would have said "alas!" if you had seen yourself in the
   mirror.

Id faceres si adesses. (adapted from Cicero)
You would do it if you were here.

The conjunction **nisi** is used to express *if not*, *unless*, or *except*. It often takes the subjunctive.

Example:

Actus non facit reum nisi mens sit rea (from a Latin legal phrase
   expressing the common-law test of criminal liability). (**reus,
   –a, –um** = *guilty*)
The act does not make one guilty unless the mind be guilty.

Cum Clauses + Subjunctive

Cum as a preposition means *with*, but it can also be used as a conjunction, meaning *when*, or *since*, or *although*. In those cases, often the subjunctive is used.

Examples:

Cum librum legisset, multa intellexisset.
When he had read the book, he had understood many things.
Since he had read the book, he had understood many things.

Cum librum legisset, multa non intellexisset.
Although he had read the book, he had not understood many
   things.

Chapter XI
Some Special Verbs

T here are a few Latin verbs that exhibit significant irregularities. They are, on the other hand, so important that they cannot be ignored. Their importance derives not just from their intrinsic meanings (*to carry, to go*, etc.), but also from the fact that they are used to form many derived verbs, some of which you will recognize from their English versions.

The first such verb is **ferō** (= *to carry*). Its principal parts are **ferō, ferre, tulī, lātum**. Notice the missing *e* in the infinitive (**ferere > ferre**) as well as the surprisingly different forms for the third and fourth principal parts. The main irregularity in conjugation is the sometimes missing *e* in some forms of the present indicative. Otherwise, the conjugation is regular.

> Present Active: **ferō, fers, fert, ferimus, fertis, ferunt**
>
> Present Passive: **feror, ferris, fertur, ferimur, feriminī, feruntur**

Ferō is used in many figurative meanings: *to bear, to tolerate, to endure*, etc. As already mentioned, it is the basis for many derivatives, such as:

> **conferō, conferre, contulī, collātum**
> (*to bring together, to compare*) (note: n + l = ll) *
> **offerō, offerre, obtulī, oblātum**
> (*to offer*) (b + f = ff)*

Many other derivatives are used (**refero, defero, infero, transfero, af-fero***, etc.).

(*Note: The prefixes **ad, cum,** and **ob** undergo some changes when used in compound verbs.)

Next in importance is **fīō** (*I am made, I become*). This verb is active in form but passive in meaning (effectively, the passive of **faciō**). Consider the biblical "fiat lux," *let light come into existence.* This passive character is obvious in the principal parts:

> **fīō, fierī, factus sum**

which betray what is going on, and show that the only thing that is irregular is the present stem, i.e., **fīō** (instead of **facior**), **fīam** (instead of **faciar**), and so on.

Indicative: fīō, fīs, fit, fīmus, fītis, fīunt
fīēbam, fīēbās, fīēbat, . . .

Subjunctive: fīam, fīās, fīat, . . .
fierem, fierēs, fieret, . . .

Examples:

Ex nihilo nihil fit.
Nothing comes/is made from nothing. (Lucretius)

Fiat lux! (Genesis)
Let there be light!

To go is expressed by **eō, īre, iī** or **īvī, itum**. From the infinitive it is clear that this is a fourth conjugation verb. Its irregularities derive from the brevity of its stem (just one vowel), which, in conjugation, wavers between *e* and *i*. Some of the derived verbs are:

abeō = *I depart*
pereō = *I die*
exeō = *I go out* ("exit")
ineō = *I go into*

The final three verbs we will deal with are all mutually related:

volō, velle, voluī	(*I wish, I want*)
nōlō, nōlle, nōluī	(*I don't wish, I am not willing*)
mālō, mālle, māluī	(*I prefer, I rather wish*)

Note: do not confuse **volō, velle, voluī** with the regular first conjugation verb **volō, volāre** = *to fly*.
Some of the forms of **volō, velle, voluī** are as follows:

Present indicative:	**volō, vīs, vult, volumus, vultis, volunt**
Present subjunctive:	**velim, velīs, velit, velīmus, velītis, velint**
Imperfect subjunctive:	**vellem, vellēs, vellet, vellēmus, vellētis, vellent**

Nōlō, nōlle, nōluī (a compound of **ne** + **volō**) and **mālō, mālle, māluī** (a compound of **magis** + **volō**) both have irregularities in the present indicative:

nōlō, nōn vīs, nōn vult, nōlumus, nōn vultis, nōlunt
mālō, māvīs, māvult, mālumus, māvultis, mālunt.

Chapter XII
Comparison of Adjectives and Adverbs

I n Latin, as in English, there are three degrees of intensity to any adjective:

Examples:

big	bigger	biggest
good	better	best
important	more important	most important

We refer to the first degree as *positive*, the second degree as *comparative* (A is bigger than B, etc.), and to the third degree as *superlative* (A is the biggest of all, etc.). From the three English examples, we can appreciate that there is sometimes a *regular* form of comparative and superlative (ending in *–er* and *–est*, respectively), sometimes an *irregular* form (*good, better, best*; *bad, worse, worst*; etc.), and a *generic* form (making use of the auxiliary words *more, most*). The same is true in Latin.

The regular forms in Latin are obtained as follows: to the adjective stem (which is best seen in the genitive singular) the comparative endings **–ior, –ior, –ius**, and the superlative endings **–issimus, –issima, –issimum** are added to the genitive stem. The comparative is then declined in the third declension, and the superlative in the first/second (regardless of the declension group of the original adjective).

Examples:

longus, longa, longum	(= *long*)
longior, longior, longius	(= *longer*)
longissimus, longissima, longissimum	(= *longest*)

brevis, brevis, breve	(= *short*)
brevior, brevior, brevius	(= *shorter*)
brevissimus, brevissima, brevissimum	(= *shortest*)

The declension of the comparative follows the rule of nouns of the third declension, rather than that of adjectives (that is, it lacks the characteristic *i* in some forms). For example, the full declension of **longior** is **longior, longiōris, longiōrī, longiōrem longiōre; longiōrēs, longiōrum, longiōribus, longiōrēs, longiōribus.**

Examples:

Scripsistisne epistulam dulcissimae puellae?
Did you (pl) write a letter to the sweetest girl?

Narrat fabulam de homine fortiore.
She tells a story about a braver man.

As for irregular comparatives and superlatives, here are some of the commonest:

bonus, melior, optimus = *good, better, best*
magnus, maior, maximus = *great, greater, greatest*
malus, peior, pessimus = *bad, worse, worst*
multus, plūs, plūrimus = *much, more, most*
parvus, minor, minimus = *small, smaller, smallest*

The comparative conjunction is **quam** (= *than*). Because it places two objects in a state of comparison, the two sides being compared must go in the same case.

Examples:

Haec linea longior quam illa est.
This line is longer than that one.

Melius est nomen bonum quam divitiae multae. (Proverbs 22:1)
A good name is better than many riches.

Ablative of Comparison

When the first part of the comparison is in the nominative or accusative case, **quam** may be omitted and the second part of the comparison may be expressed in the ablative.

Example:

Sunt facta verbis difficiliora. (Cicero)
Deeds are more difficult than words.

Adverbs

Adverbs modify (or qualify) adjectives, verbs, or other adverbs. They are not declined. In English, there are regular adverbs (formed by adding –*ly* to the adjective, e.g., *important, importantly*), and irregular adverbs (e.g., *well*). The same is true in Latin. The regular endings are as follows:

–ē, for the first/second declension adjectives,

–iter, for the third declension adjectives.

Thus we have:

longus > longē

brevis > brev**iter**

Many common adverbs do not follow these rules, including, naturally, those that do not directly derive from adjectives (**ita, tam, semper**, etc.). They have to be learned or found in the dictionary.

Adverbs, as adjectives, can also appear in comparative and superlative degrees. The comparative is usually identical with the neuter nominative singular of the comparative form of the adjective (it ends, therefore, in –**ius**). The superlative is formed by the ending –ē added to the superlative stem of the adjective.

Examples:

breviter, brevius, brevissimē (*brief, more briefly, most briefly*)

bene, melius, optimē (*well, better, best*)

male, peius, pessimē (*badly, worse, worst*)

multum, plūs, plūrimum (*much, more quantity, most quantity*)

magnopere, magis, maximē (*greatly, more, most/especially*)

Examples:

Bonus orator breviter dicit.

A good orator speaks briefly.

Hic orator brevius dicit quam tu.

This orator speaks more briefly than you.

Hic orator brevissime dicit.

This orator speaks most briefly.

Chapter XIII
Special Constructions

H aving presented a considerable part of Latin grammar, we need now to describe a few very common constructions used to convey ideas in an aesthetically pleasing and economic way. The first such construction we will tackle is the so-called ***accusative-infinitive construction,*** which is used for indirect statement/oratio obliqua (or, less accurately, reported speech). Consider the following examples of direct and indirect statements:

> They think: "he is right."
> They think that he is right.
> They think him to be right.

The first sentence is a *direct statement.* The second is an *indirect statement,* and so is the third. The accusative-infinitive construction closely resembles the third option: the subject of the reported sentence ("he is right") becomes the direct object ("him") of the main verb (a verb of thinking, in this case), while the verb of the reported sentence ("is") moves to the infinitive ("to be").

Consider the following examples:

> Magister dicit: "lex vera est."
> The teacher says: "The law is true."

> Magister dicit legem veram esse.
> The teacher says the law to be true. (The teacher says that the law is true.)

> Magister dixit: "lex vera fuit."
> The teacher said: "The law was true."

> Magister dixit legem veram fuisse.
> The teacher said the law to have been true. (The teacher said that the law had been true.)

The tense of the infinitive indicates (i) contemporaneity with the tense of the main verb if the infinitive is present; (ii) precedence, if it is perfect; (iii) subsequence, if it is future. The accusative-infinitive construction (with verbs of thinking, believing, saying, understanding, etc.) is so strong that sometimes the main verb is not even mentioned. Thus, Newton starts his chapter on the laws of motion as follows:

> Lex 1. Corpus omne <u>perseverare</u> in statu suo quiescendi vel movendi uniformiter in directum, nisi quatenus a viribus impressis cogitur statum illum mutare.

In this example, the main verb (**dico**, perhaps) is absent. In English, we could render this as: "First Law: That every body perseveres in its state. . . ."

The second important construction is the ***ablative absolute***. The ablative absolute is a *participial phrase* that contains both a noun and a modifying participle in the ablative case. Ablative absolute phrases describe a circumstance related to the main clause, but do not involve the subject or the object of the main statement. Often the ablative absolute is separated from the main clause by commas.

> Lege scriptā, philosophus ex urbe discessit.

This can be translated as:

> Once the law had been written,
> Because the law had been written,
> The law having been written,
> Although the law had been written,
> With the law having been written,
> } the philosopher departed from the city.

The ablative absolute is self-contained and never relates back to a subject or object of another clause.

Example:
> Legem scribens, philosophus ex urbe discessit. – not an ablative absolute!
> Writing the law, the philosopher departed from the city.

(In this example the participle **scribens** modifies the subject of the next clause **philosophus**, so it cannot be an ablative absolute).

Common Adverbial Expressions

Non modo . . . sed etiam *or* **non solum . . . sed etiam**

Not only . . . but also

Example:

Illi non solum pecuniam sed etiam vitam pro patria
profuderunt. (Cicero)

They poured forth not only money but also (their) life for the
fatherland.

Appendix III

Manuscript and Original Source Quirks

O rganized by author and work, this list provides a key to the abbreviations, alternate spellings, idiosyncrasies, and quirks of the original Latin manuscripts and early printings. These notes assist those working with the Latin found in the facsimiles of the original texts.

It is not uncommon to find that many words have been severely contracted by, for instance, replacing an *n* or an *m* by an over-bar or a tilde.

Isidore

Etymologiae

e.q: est quod, est quia.

pceptis: praeceptis.

que: quae.

Qn: quando.

eloquétie: eloquentiae.

sue maxīe: suae, maxime.

Q: quae.

Septīa: septima.

Existimat́: Existimatur is an impersonal *they*, namely, *everybody*.

Francis Bacon

Novum Organum Scientiarum

poβint: possint.

Vitruvius

De Architectura

Note that punctuation did not exist in ancient literature. You may occasionally find that paragraphs can be broken up into sentences differently than suggested by modern editions. In particular, watch for commas and semicolons, which sometimes are more a hindrance than a help in the translation. Sometimes (as in the case of **pro portione** in our selection), even the separation into words can be questioned. In this version, many letters *m* and *n* are missing, often replaced with an accent over the preceding letter. In addition, the letter *p* at the beginning of a word usually stands for **per**.

pficiútur: perficiuntur.

ratiocinatióe: ratiocinatione.

cuiuscunq;: cuiuscunque.

atq;: atque.

pót: potest.

itaq;: itaque.

contenderút: contenderunt.

nó: non.

vident': videntur.

quiutrúque: qui utrumque.

pdidicerút: perdidicerunt.

utraq;: utraque.

neq;: neque.

q: quod.

pcontátibus: percontantibus.

Pelopónesi: Peloponensis.

ducerent': ducerentur.

caryatiú: caryatium.

traderet': traderetur.

Alberti
De Re Aedificatoria
quibusve: Notice that the word has been split between two lines.

Isidore
Etymologiae

que: quae.

omis: omnis.

etates: aetates.

Maimonides
De Regimine Sanitatis

One can practically read the text without any help. The printing in this first edition is extremely clear. Notice, however, that sometimes words are arbitrarily split or joined together and that a bar (or tilde) over a vowel signifies a missing *n* or *m* (not only at the end of a word). Some endings are abbreviated, such as *-9* for *-us* or *-ibus*, and an apostrophe for the passive ending *-ur*. The diphthong *ae* is often contracted to *e*.

conbuste compositionis: Misprint for **robustae compositionis,** as can be seen in another printed version (1518) available at https://archive.org/details/tractatusrabbimo00maim.

De bilitabit: debilitabitur.

aliquodqd: aliquod quod.

letificat: laetificat

optinuerunt: obtinuerunt.

maifeste: manifeste.

abeatur: Misprint for **habeatur.**

f: scilicet.

aialis: animalis,

Si militer: similiter.

in huius: Probably a misprint for **in huiusmodi**

Harvey

Exercitatio Anatomica de Motu Cordis et Sanguinis in Animalibus

sed revera: sed re vera.

Euclid

Elements

In this version, as in many medieval Latin manuscripts and books, the diphthong *ae* is usually collapsed into the single vowel *e*. Thus **aequales** becomes **equales** and **lineae** becomes **linee**. One has to be constantly mindful of this feature, particularly when it comes to the identification of singular genitive and dative or plural nominative of nouns and adjectives of the first declension. When reading directly from the facsimile, do bear in mind the typical abbreviations (such as a tilde over a vowel to indicate a missing letter, usually but not always an *m*, or the letter *q*, followed by some symbol, to stand for **que**). A symbol that looks somewhat like the lower case Greek letter tau stands for the conjunction **et**.

que sunt: quae sunt.

due superficies quadrate: duae superficies quadratae.

extracte: extractae.

line: lineae.

directe iuncte: directae iunctae.

plures q' due: plures quam duae

linee ducte: lineae ductae.

pono éc equales: pono esse aequales

c.b.τ.d.c.τ: *cb* et *dc* et.

dividã vtrãq3 eaꝗ p eqlia: dividam utramque earum per equalia.

circũferentie: circumferentiae.

qui sunt.a.d.e.: This must be a misprint. Construe as **qui sunt ad** *e*.

igit': igitur.

p.13: per 13.

sitr: This cannot be read clearly. Assume what is meant is **sunt**.

per correlariũ prime huius: per corollarium primae huius

circulum fecet: What appears to be an *f* is in fact an *s*. **seco, secare:** *to cut.*

eaꝗ: earum, but this should probably be **eorum** (*of them, i.e., of the circles*).

intra vl' extra: intra vel extra.

p.20.pmi: per 20 primi.

due linee.e.b.т.b.a longiores.e.a: duae lineae *eb* et *ba* longiores *ea*.

qre: quare.

qṁ: quoniam.

qᵈ: quod.

Copernicus

De Revolutionibus Orbium Coelestium

coelestium: Notice that this is a single word, split between two lines without any indication that this is the case.

ꞇj: This symbol is equivalent to a double *i* (**ii**).

utrunq': utrunque

imò: immo

Motuũ: motuum.

&: et.

inno tescere: as in other cases, a word **innotescere** has been split between two lines without any indication.

ingen temque: Again a word has been split without notice.

que at: One word, namely, **queat.**

ijs: iis.

Alhazen

Opticae Thesaurus

operatione: operationem.

Latin-English Glossary

ā, ab (*prep.* + *abl.*), from, away from, at the hands of, by

abdūcō, abdūcere, abdūxī, abductum, to lead away, to take away

abeō, abīre, abiī, abitum, to go away

aberrātiō, aberratiōnis (*f.*), aberration, deviation, escape, relief

abrādo, abrādere, abrāsī, abrāsum, to scrape off, to rub, to abrade

abrumpō, abrumpere, abrūpī, abruptum, to break off, to tear away

abscindō, abscindere, abscīdī, abscīssum, to tear off, to cut out

abscīssa, abscīssae (*f.*), abscissa (*math.*)

absolūtus, absolūta, absolūtum, complete, absolute

absolvō, absolvere, absolvī, absolūtum, to free, to release, to complete, to pay off, to absolve

absorbeō, absorbēre, absorbuī, absorptum, to swallow, to absorb

absum, abesse, āfuī, āfutūrum, to be away, to be absent

absurdus, absurda, absurdum, discordant, absurd, foolish

abundō, abundāre, abundāvī, abundātum, to overflow, to abound, to be rich in (+ *abl.*)

ac (*contracted form of* **atque**)

accedō, accēdere, accessī, accessum, to approach

accelerō, accelerāre, accelerāvī, accelerātum, to accelerate, to hasten

accessiō, accessiōnis (*f.*), an approach, addition, appendage

accidō, accidere, accidī, to fall, to befall, to happen, to come to pass

accipiō, accipere, accēpī, acceptum, to receive, to get, to take (*rarely:* to accept)

accommodō, accommodāre, accommodāvī, accommodātum, to fit, to apply, to adjust, to put on

accrēscō, accrēscere, accrēvī,
accrētum, to grow, to increase

accumbō, accumbere, accubuī,
accubitum, to lie down

accūrātus, accūrāta, accūrātum,
careful, precise, accurate

aciēs, aciēī (f.), sharp edge, line of
battle

ācta, āctōrum (n. pl.), deeds,
actions, proceedings, records
(from agō)

āctiō, āctiōnis (f.), action

acūmen, acūminis (n.), sharpness,
acuteness, cunning

acūtus, acūta, acūtum, sharp,
acute, pointed

ad (prep. + acc.), to, up to, until, at

adaptō, adaptāre, adaptāvī,
adaptātum, to fit, to adapt, to
adjust

additiō, additiōnis (f.), addition

addō, addere, addidī, additum,
to add, to bring

adeō (adv.), so far, to such an
extent, so much so, so

adhibeō, adhibēre, adhibuī,
adhibitum, to apply, to bring
to bear, to use

adhūc (adv.), thus far, up to now,
to this point

adiaceō, adiacēre, adiacuī, to lie
by the side of, to be adjacent

adiciō, adicere, adiēcī, adiectum,
to throw to, to add

adinveniō, adinvenīre, adinvēnī,
adinventum, to come upon, to
discover, to invent, to find out

aditus, aditūs (m.), entrance,
access

adiūmentum, adiūmentī (n.),
help, assistance

adiungō, adiungere, adiunxī,
adiunctum, to join, to attach

admētior, admētīrī, admensus
sum, to measure out to

admīrābilis, admīrābile,
wonderful, admirable

admīrātiō, admīrātiōnis (f.),
wonder, admiration

admīror, admīrārī, admīrātus
sum, to wonder at, to admire

admisceō, admiscēre, admiscuī,
admixtum, to mix, to admix

admodum (adv.), entirely, wholly,
quite

admoneō, admonēre, admonuī,
admonitum, to admonish, to
remind, to urge

admoveō, admovēre, admōvī,
admōtum, to move something
to, to move something

adnotō, adnotāre, adnotāvī,
adnotātum, to note, to remark,
to comment on, to distinguish
(alt. spel.: annotō)

adōrō, adōrāre, adōrāvī,
adōrātum, to speak to, to
worship, to ask, to pray to, to
admire

adsequor, adsequī, adsecūtus
sum, to pursue, to obtain, to
attain, to comprehend (alt.
spel.: assequor)

adsum, adesse, adfuī, to be
present, to arrive (+ dat.)

advehō, advehere, advexī,
advectum, to bring to, to
import, to convey to

adversus, adversum (*adv. or prep. + acc.*), against, opposite, opposed to

advertō, advertere, advertī, adversum, to turn toward (*alt. spel.:* **advortō**)

aedificātiō, aedificātiōnis (*f.*), structure, instructing, act of constructing

aedificatōrius, aedificatōria, aedificatōrium, pertaining to construction

aedificium, aedificiī (*n.*), building, edifice

aedificō, aedificāre, aedificāvī, aedificātum, to build

aeger, aegra, aegrum, sick, ill

aegritūdō, aegritūdinis (*f.*), sickness

Aegyptus, Aegyptī (*f.*), Egypt

aequābilis, aequābilis, aequābile, similar, equal, equable, impartial

aequālis, aequālis, aequāle, equal

aequālitās, aequālitātis (*f.*), equality

aequātiō, aequātiōnis (*f.*), equation

aequitās, aequitātis (*f.*), equity, evenness, impartiality

aequus, aequa, aequum, equal, uniform; even, balanced, fair

āēr, āeris (*m.*), air, atmosphere

aes, aeris (*n.*), copper, bronze, money

aestimātiō, aestimātiōnis (*f.*), estimation, valuation, appraisal

aestimō, aestimāre, aestimāvī, aestimātum, to esteem, to deem, to appraise, to estimate

aestīvus, aestīva, aestīvum, pertaining to summer, estival

aetās, aetātis (*f.*), age

aeternus, aeterna, aeternum, eternal, everlasting, immortal

aevum, aevī (*n.*), eternity, age

affectus, affectūs (*m.*), condition, disposition, feeling, affection (*alt. spel.:* **adfectus, adfectūs**)

afferō, afferre, attulī, allātum, to carry, to bring to, to report (*alt. spel.:* **adferō, adferre, adtulī, adlātum**)

affirmatīvus, affirmatīva, affirmatīvum, affirmative, positive

Āfricānus, Āfricāna, Āfricānum, belonging to Africa

aggredior, aggredī, aggressus sum, to approach, to attack (*alt. spel.:* **adgredior, adgredī, adgressus sum**)

aggregō, aggregāre, aggregāvī, aggregātum, to add, to join, to attach (*alt. spel.:* **adgregō, adgregāre, adgregāvī, adgregātum**)

agitō, agitāre, agitāvī, agitātum, to agitate, to incite, to set in constant motion, to consider, to treat a subject

agō, agere, ēgī, actum, to drive, to lead, to set in motion, to do, to treat

agricola, agricolae (*m.*), farmer, agriculturist

āiō, to say, to affirm (*defective verb; most common forms:* **ait, aiunt**)

āla, ālae (*f.*), wing

albus, alba, album, white

alchēmia, alchēmiae (*f.*), alchemy, chemistry (*alt. spel.:* **alcēmia, alcēmiae; alchymia, alchymiae**)

alchēmista, alchēmistac (*m.*), alchemist

alibī (*adv.*), elsewhere, at another place

aliēnus, aliēna, aliēnum, belonging to another, foreign to

aliōquīn (*adv.*), otherwise, in other respects, moreover

aliquantus, aliquanta, aliquantum, some, of some size, moderate

aliquī, aliqua(e), aliquod (*adj.*), some

aliquis, aliqua (aliquis), aliquid (*pron.*), someone, something, anyone, anything

aliquōmodō (*adv.*), somehow, in some manner

aliquot, some, several, a few

aliter (*adv.*), otherwise

aliunde (*adv.*), from elsewhere

alius, alia, aliud, other, another

allātum (*perf. passive participle of* **afferō**)

allēgō, allēgāre, allēgāvī, allēgātum, to commission, to send on business, to allege (*alt. spel.:* **adlēgō, adlēgāre, adlēgāvī, adlēgātum**)

alligō, alligāre, alligāvī, alligātum, to tie, to bind (*alt. spel.:* **adligō, adligāre, adligāvī, adligātum**)

alter, altera, alterum, one of two, the other one

altus, alta, altum, high, elevated, deep

alūmen, alūminis (*n.*), a salt of variously identified composition

ambō, ambae, ambō, both (*irregular adj., pl. only*)

amnis, amnis (*m.*), river, stream

amoenus, amoena, amoenum, pleasant, charming

amor, amōris (*m.*), love

āmoveō, āmovēre, āmōvī, āmōtum, to move away, to remove

ampliō, ampliāre, ampliāvī, ampliātum, to enlarge, to amplify

amplius (*adv.*), further, in a higher degree

amplus, ampla, amplum, ample, spacious

an (*conj.*), whether

analogia, analogiae (*f.*), analogy, similarity, ratio, proportion

angulus, angulī (*m.*), angle, corner

anima, animae (*f.*), soul, breath of life

animadvertō, animadvertere, animadvertī, animadversum, to pay attention, to notice, to blame (*alt. spel.:* **animadvortō, animadvortere, animadvortī, animadvorsum**)

animal, animālis (*n.*), animal,
living creature

animālis, animālis, animāle,
belonging to life, animate

animus, animī (*m.*), soul, mind,
spirit, character, intellect

anniversārius, anniversāria,
anniversārium, yearly,
recurring every year

annuō, annuere, annuī, annūtum,
to nod in assent, to agree (*alt.
spel.:* adnuō, adnuere, adnuī,
adnūtum)

annus, annī (*m.*), year

ante (*adv. or prep. + acc.*), before,
in front

anteā (*adv.*), formerly, before

antequam (*conj.*), before

antidotum, antidotī (*n.*),
antidote

aorta, aortae (*f.*), aorta

aperiō, aperīre, aperuī, apertum,
to open, to uncover

apertus, aperta, apertum, open

apogēus, apogēa, apogēum,
blowing from the land (*used
in the neuter as a noun for the
astronomical apogee*)

Apollō, Apollinis (*m.*), Apollo

appārentia, appārentiae (*f.*),
appearance

appāreō, appārēre, appāruī,
appāritum, to appear, to
become manifest

appellō, appellāre, apellāvī,
appellātum, to call, to call by
name, to summon, to address

appetītus, appetītūs (*m.*),
appetite, desire, longing

appetō, appetere, appetīvī,
appetītum, to desire, to seek,
to strive for

applicō, applicāre, applicāvī,
applicātum, to apply, to
place, to attach (*alt. forms:
applicō, applicāre, applicuī,
applicitum*)

appōnō, appōnere, apposuī,
appositum, to place at, to place
by, to add to

aptus, apta, aptum, fitting,
appropriate, suitable

apud (*prep. + acc.*), at, in the house
of, in the presence of, in the
opinion of

aqua, aquae (*f.*), water

Arabs, Arabis (*m.*), Arab

arbiter, arbitrī (*m.*), judge, arbiter,
witness

arbitramentum, arbitramentī
(*n.*), judgment, decision,
opinion

arbitrārius, arbitrāria,
arbitrārium, arbitrary, matter
of opinion

arbitrium, arbitriī (*n.*), judgment,
decision

arceō, arcēre, arcuī, (arcitum),
to defend, to protect, to
enclose

Archimēdēs, Archimēdis (*m.*),
Archimedes

architectonicus, architectonica,
architectonicum, architectural

architectūra, architectūrae (*f.*),
architecture

architectus, architectī (*m.*),
architect, builder

arcus, arcūs (*m.*), arc, arc of a
circle, arc of an orbit, arch,
bow
ārea, āreae (*f.*), area
argentum, argentī (*n.*), silver,
money
argumentum, argumentī (*n.*),
argument, theme, subject, plot
of a story
arguō, arguere, arguī, argūtum,
to argue, to declare, to prove, to
accuse
Aristotelēs, Aristotelis (*m.*),
Aristotle
arithmetica, arithmeticae (*f.*),
arithmetic
arithmeticus, arithmetica,
arithmeticum, arithmetical,
arithmetic
arma, armōrum (*n. pl.*), weapons,
arms, tools
arō, arāre, arāvī, arātum, to
plough, to till, to farm
arripiō, arripere, arripuī,
arreptum, to snatch, to seize
(*alt. spel.:* **adripiō, adripere,**
adripuī, adreptum)
arrogāns, arrogantis, arrogant,
haughty (*alt. spel.:* **adrogāns,**
adrogantis)
ars, artis (*f.*), art, skill, practice,
knowledge
Artaxerxēs, Artaxerxis (*m.*),
Artaxerxes
artēria, artēriae (*f.*), artery
arteriola, arteriolae (*f.*), small
artery, arteriole
articulus, articulī (*m.*), article,
part, joint

artifex, artificis (*m./f.*), maker,
artificer, craftsman, skilled
worker
artificiālis, artificiālis, artificiāle,
artificial
artificiōsus, artificiōsa,
artificiōsum, artistic, skillful
artificium, artificiī (*n.*), skill, art,
trick, work of art
artus, artūs (*m.*), joint, limb
ascendō, ascendere, ascendī,
ascēnsum, to ascend, to rise
Asclepiodotus, Asclepiodotī (*m.*),
Asclepiodotus
Asclepius, Asclepiī (*m.*),
Asclepius, Aesculapius, Greek
god of medicine (*alt. spel.:*
Aesculāpius, Aesculāpiī)
aspectus, aspectūs (*m.*), glance, a
looking at, appearance, aspect
asper, aspera, asperum, rough,
uneven, harsh (*alt. spel.:* **asper,**
aspra, asprum)
aspiciō, aspicere, aspexī,
aspectum, to look at, to
behold, to consider
assequor, assequī, assecūtus sum,
to follow after, to attain, to
comprehend (*alt. spel.:* **adsequor,**
adsequī, adsecūtus sum)
asserō, asserere, asseruī, assertum,
to assert, to allege, to set free, to
join to oneself (*alt. spel.:* **adserō,**
adserere, adseruī, adsertum)
assiduus, assidua, assiduum,
constant, persistent, assiduous,
always in the same place (*alt.*
spel.: **adsiduus, adsidua,**
adsiduum)

assignō, assignāre, assignāvī, assignātum, to assign, to attribute, to ascribe (*alt. spel.:* **adsignō, adsignāre, adsignāvī, adsignātum**)

assūmō, assūmere, assumpsī, assumptum, to take, to claim, to assume (*alt. spel.:* **adsūmō, adsūmere, adsumpsī, adsumptum**)

astrologia, astrologiae (*f.*), astrology, astronomy

astronomia, astronomiae (*f.*), astronomy

astronomicus, astronomica, astronomicum, astronomical, astronomic

astronomus, astronomī (*m.*), astronomer

astrum, astrī (*n.*), star, celestial body

at (*conj.*), but, but on the other hand, yet

atque (*conj.*), and, and also, and even (*alt. spel.:* **ac**, *before consonants*)

atquī (*conj.*), nevertheless, however, indeed, but now

ātrāmentum, ātrāmentī (*n.*), black liquid, ink

attamen (*conj.*), but nevertheless, but yet

attendō, attendere, attendī, attentum, to stretch toward, to direct one's attention to

attentiō, attentiōnis (*f.*), attention, attentiveness

atterō, atterere, attrīvī, attrītum, to rub away, to waste

attineō, attinēre, attinuī, attentum, to concern, to pertain to, to keep

attingō, attingere, attigī, attāctum, to reach, to arrive at, to touch

attollō, attollere, to rise, to raise, to appear

attrahō, attrahere, attraxī, attractum, to attract, to draw to, to drag

attribuō, attribuere, attribuī, attribūtum, to attribute, to assign, to impute

auctor, auctōris (*m.*), author, producer, originator (*alt. spel.:* **authōr, authōris**)

auctōritās, auctōritātis (*f.*), authority (*alt. spel.:* **authōritās, authōritātis**)

audiō, audīre, audīvī, audītum, to hear, to listen

auferō, auferre, abstulī, ablātum, to take away, to carry off, to remove

augeō, augēre, auxī, auctum, to increase, to augment, to enlarge

Augustīnus, Augustīnī (*m.*), Augustine

aura, aurae (*f.*), air, breeze, aura

auricula, auriculae (*f.*), auricle, auricula, earlobe

aurum, aurī (*n.*), gold

auscultō, auscultāre, auscultāvī, auscultātum, to listen, to hear

auster, austrī (*m.*), south, south wind

aut (*conj.*), or

autem (*conj.*), however, on the other hand, but

autumnālis, autumnālis, autumnāle, autumnal, pertaining to the fall season

avāritia, avāritiae (*f.*), avarice, greed

āvertō, āvertere, āvertī, āversum, to turn away, to avert, to avoid, to keep off (*alt. spel.*: āvortō, āvortere, āvortī, āvorsum)

Avicenna, Avicennae (*m.*), Avicenna, Ibn Sina

avis, avis (*f.*), bird

axiōma, axiōmatis (*n.*), axiom, principle

axis, axis (*m.*), axis, axle

bellum, bellī (*n.*), war

bene (*adv.*), well

bibliothēca, bibliothēcae (*f.*), library

bibō, bibere, bibī, bibitum, to drink

bitūmen, bitūminis (*n.*), asphalt, bitumen

bonus, bona, bonum, good

brevis, brevis, breve, short, brief

cadō, cadere, cecidī, cāsum, to fall, to fall down

caelum, caelī (*n.*), sky, heavens. (*alt. m. pl.*: caelī, caelōrum; *alt. spel.*: coelum, coelī)

caeruleus, caerulea, caeruleum, blue, sky-blue

Caesar, Caesaris (*m.*), Caesar

calculō, calculāre, calculāvī, calculātum, to compute, to reckon, to calculate

calculus, calculī (*m.*), pebble, small stone, counting pebble, calculus (*math.*)

calefaciō, calefacere, calefēcī, calefactum, to heat, to make warm (*passive*: calefiō, calefierī, calefactus sum)

Calendae, Calendārum (*f. pl.*), the first day of the Roman month (*alt. spel.*: Kalendae, Kalendārum)

calidus, calida, calidum, warm, hot, fiery

calleō, callēre, calluī, to be callous, hardened, experienced

calor, calōris (*m.*), heat, warmth

campester, campestris, campestre, pertaining to the field

candidus, candida, candidum, white, bright, honest, candid

Canōpus, Canōpī (*m.*), Canopus (the star or the Egyptian city)

cantus, cantūs (*m.*), song, chant, melody, incantation

capāx, capācis, roomy, capacious, ample, capable

capiō, capere, cēpī, captum, to take, to grasp, to seize, to comprehend

captus, captūs (*m.*), grasping, taking; capacity, potentiality

Capuanus, Capuana, Capuanum, a resident of Capua

caput, capitis (*n.*), head

cardinal, cardinālis (*m.*), a cardinal of the church

careō, carēre, caruī, (caritum), to be without, to be free from, to be lacking in

carmen, carminis (*n.*), song, poem, incantation

carō, carnis (*f.*), flesh

Caryae, Caryatārum (*f. pl.*), Caria, a city in the Greek Peloponnese (*alt. spel.:* **Caria, Cariae**)

caryātes, caryātium (*m. pl.*), inhabitants of Caria

Caryātis, Caryātidis (*f.*), the goddess Diana

castitās, castitātis (*f.*), chastity, moral purity

cāsus, cāsūs (*m.*), fall, destruction, mishap, case, occurrence

causa, causae (*f.*), cause, lawsuit

cautiō, cautiōnis (*f.*), precaution, care, legal obligation

cautus, cauta, cautum, cautious, wary

caveō, cavēre, cāvī, cautum, to guard against, to be aware of, to caution

caverna, cavernae (*f.*), cave, cavern

cavō, cavāre, cavāvī, cavātum, to excavate, to make hollow

celeber, celebris, celebre, well-attended, renowned, celebrated

celebrātor, celebrātōris (*m.*), praiser, one who celebrates

celebrātus, celebrāta, celebrātum, renowned, celebrated

celer, celeris, celere, fast, swift, speedy

celeritās, celeritātis (*f.*), speed, swiftness

celeriter (*adv.*), quickly, swiftly, speedily

cēnseō, cēnsēre, cēnsuī, cēnsum, to think, to deem, to express an opinion; to consider

centripetus, centripeta, centripetum, centripetal, seeking the center

centrum, centrī (*n.*), center

cernō, cernere, crēvī, crētum, to distinguish, to discern, to perceive, to decide, to resolve

certificātiō, certificātiōnis (*f.*), certification, a making certain

certus, certa, certum, certain, determined, definite, assured

cessō, cessāre, cessāvī, cessātum, to cease, to stop, to delay

cēterus, cētera, cēterum, the other, the rest (*alt. spel.:* **caeterus, caetera, caeterum**)

chalybs, chalybis (*m.*), steel, iron, a steel piece

Choos, (Chous, Choī) (*m.*), Kos, a Greek island in the Aegean Sea (not to be confused with the nearby island of Chios)

chronologia, chronologiae (*f.*), chronology, the keeping of times of events

chymia, chymiae (*f.*), chemistry

chymicus, chymica, chymicum, chemical

cibus, cibī (*m.*), food, nourishment

cinereus, cinerea, cinereum,
ashen, ashy

cingō, cingere, cinxī, cinctum, to
gird, to surround, to enclose

circā (*adv. and prep.* + *acc.*), about,
around

circinus, circinī (*m.*), compass for
drawing circles

circuitiō, circuitiōnis (*f.*), a going
around

circulāris, circulāris, circulāre,
circular

circulus, circulī (*m.*), circle

circum (*adv. and prep.* + *acc.*),
about, around

circumferentia, circumferentiae
(*f.*), circumference

circumlātiō, circumlātiōnis (*f.*),
circuit, revolution

circumspargō, circumspargere,
circumsparsī, circumsparsum,
to scatter around, to strew
(*alt. spel.:* circumspergō,
circumspergere, circumspersī,
circumspersum)

cisterna, cisternae (*f.*), cistern,
reservoir

citius (*adv.*), sooner, more quickly

citō, citāre, citāvī, citātum, to
cite, to quote

citrā (*adv. and prep.* + *acc.*), on this
side

cīvīlis, cīvīlis, cīvīle, civil,
pertaining to citizens or to
public life

cīvitās, cīvitātis (*f.*), city, state,
citizenship

clādēs, clādis (*f.*), damage, injury,
disaster

clārus, clāra, clārum, clear,
evident, illustrious, famous

claudō, claudere, clausī,
clausum, to close, to shut, to
conclude

coaptō, coaptāre, coaptāvī,
coaptātum, to fit together, to
adjust

coelestis, coelestis, coeleste,
heavenly, celestial (*alt. spel.:*
caelestis, caelestis, caeleste)

coelitus (*adv.*), heavenly, from
heaven (*alt. spel.:* caelitus)

coelum, coelī: see caelum, caelī

(coepiō, coepere), coepī,
coeptum, (to begin), to have
begun (defective verb–only in
perfect)

cogitātiō, cogitātiōnis (*f.*),
thought, thinking, meditation

cogitō, cogitāre, cogitāvī,
cogitātum, to think, to
consider, to reflect

cognātiō, cognātiōnis (*f.*),
relationship, kinship,
resemblance

cognitus, cognita, cognitum,
known

cognomentum, cognomentī (*n.*),
name, nickname, surname

cognōscō, cognōscere, cognōvī,
cognitum, to become
acquainted with

cōgō, cōgere, coēgī, coactum,
to bring together, to force, to
coerce

cohaereō, cohaerere, cohaesī,
cohaesum, to hold together, to
adhere, to be consistent

collābor, collābī, collāpsus
sum, to collapse, to fall down
(*alt. spel.*: conlābor, conlābī,
conlāpsus sum)

colligō, colligere, collēgī,
collēctum, to collect, to
gather, to consider (*alt. spel.*:
conligō, conligere, conlēgī,
conlēctum)

collis, collis (*m.*), hill

collocātiō, collocātiōnis (*f.*),
arrangement, placement
(*alt. spel.*: conlocātiō,
conlocātiōnis)

collocō, collocāre, collocāvī,
collocātum, to place, to
arrange, to set (*alt. spel.*:
conlocō, conlocāre,
conlocāvī, conlocātum)

collūdō, collūdere, collūsī,
collūsum, to play together, to
conspire, to collude (*alt. spel.*:
conlūdō, conlūdere, conlūsī,
conlūsum)

colō, colere, coluī, cultum, to
cultivate, to till, to tend, to
dwell, to care

color, colōris (*m.*), color

colōrō, colōrāre, colōrāvī,
colōrātum, to color, to dye

columna, columnae (*f.*), column,
pillar

combūrō, combūrere, combussī,
combustum, to burn up, to
consume (*alt. spel.*: conbūrō,
conbūrere, conbussī,
conbustum)

comēta, comētae (*m.*), comet (*alt.
spel.*: comētēs, comētae)

commendātiō, commendātiōnis
(*f.*), commendation,
recommendation

commentārium, commentāriī
(*n.*), note, notebook, diary
(*alt. spel.*: commentārius,
commentāriī [*m.*])

commentum, commentī (*n.*),
fabrication, invention

commeō, commeāre, commeāvī,
commeātum, to come and go,
to visit frequently

commercium, commerciī
(*n.*), trade, commerce,
correspondence, intercourse

commissūra, commissūrae (*f.*),
joint, junction, connection

committō, committere,
commīsī, commissum, to
bring together, to entrust, to
commit

commodō, commodāre,
commodāvī, commodātum,
to accommodate, to adapt, to
suit, to furnish

commodus, commoda,
commodum, proper, fit,
convenient

commoveō, commovēre,
commōvī, commōtum, to
shake, to excite, to influence

commūnicō, commūnicāre,
commūnicāvī,
commūnicātum, to
communicate, to share, to
inform

commūnis, commūnis,
commūne, common, general,
shared, ordinary

commūtātiō, commūtātiōnis (*f.*),
change, alteration

compāgō, compāginis (*f.*),
assembly of parts, structure

compendium, compendiī (*n.*),
abridgment

comperiō, comperīre, comperī,
compertum, to find out, to
discover

compertus, comperta,
compertum, known, certain

competō, competere, competīvī,
competītum, to agree, to
coincide, to match, to pertain,
to be competent

complector, complectī,
complexus sum, to embrace, to
encompass

compleō, complēre, complēvī,
complētum, to fill up, to
complete, to accomplish, to
fulfill

complūrēs, complūrēs, complūra
(complūria), several, many

compōnō, compōnere,
composuī, compositum, to
put together, to arrange, to
compose

compositiō, compositiōnis (*f.*),
composition, arrangement

comprehendō, comprehendere,
comprehendī, comprehēnsum,
to comprise, to comprehend, to
grasp (*alt. spel.:* compraehendō,
compraehendere,
compraehendī,
compraehēnsum *and*
comprendō, comprendere,
comprendī, comprēnsum)

comprehensiō,
comprehensiōnis (*f.*),
comprehension

compressiō, compressiōnis (*f.*),
compression

cōnātus, cōnātūs (*m.*), effort,
attempt, undertaking

concinnō, concinnāre,
concinnāvī, concinnātum,
to put together, to produce

concipiō, concipere, concēpī,
conceptum, to hold together,
to take in, to conceive

conclūdō, conclūdere, conclūsī,
conclūsum, to include, to
conclude

conclūsiō, conclūsiōnis (*f.*),
conclusion

concussiō, concussiōnis (*f.*),
concussion, shaking

concutiō, concutere, concussī,
concussum, to shake together,
to agitate

condūcō, condūcere, condūxī,
conductum, to bring together,
to lead

conductor, conductōris (*m.*),
conductor (electrical),
contractor, hirer

cōnfectiō, cōnfectiōnis (*f.*),
production, completion

cōnferō, cōnferre, cōntulī,
collātum (conlātum), to
bring together, to collate, to
apply, to confer, to discuss, to
compare

cōnficiō, cōnficere, cōnfēcī,
cōnfectum, to make, to get,
to obtain, to accomplish

cōnfīdō, cōnfīdere, cōnfīsus sum (*semi-deponent verb*), to trust, to believe

cōnfingō, cōnfingere, cōnfinxī, cōnfictum, to invent, to form, to fabricate, to feign

cōnflō, cōnflāre, cōnflāvī, cōnflātum, to conflate, to blow together, to kindle, to melt, to forge

cōnfōrmātiō, cōnfōrmātiōnis (*f.*), form, shape, conformation, arrangement

congressus, congressūs (*m.*), meeting, encounter, fight

congruō, congruere, congruī, to come together, to coincide, to agree

coniciō, conicere, coniēcī, coniectum, to throw together, to hurl

coniectūra, coniectūrae (*f.*), conjecture, guess

connexiō, connexiōnis, connection, logical conclusion (*alt. spel.*: cōnexiō, cōnexiōnis)

cōnor, cōnārī, cōnātus sum, to attempt, to try, to undertake

conquiēscō, conquiēscere, conquiēvī, conquiētum, to rest, to be still

cōnscendō, cōnscendere, cōnscendī, cōnscensum, to go up, to ascend, to mount

cōnscrībō, cōnscrībere, cōnscrīpsī, cōnscrīptum, to enroll, to enlist, to write

cōnsecūtiō, cōnsecūtiōnis (*f.*), sequence, order, consequence, attainment

cōnsentiō, cōnsentīre, cōnsensī, cōnsensum, to agree, to assent

cōnsequor, cōnsequī, cōnsecūtus sum, to follow, to be a consequence, to reach, to attain

cōnservō, cōnservāre, cōnservāvī, cōnservātum, to keep, to preserve, to maintain, to save

cōnsīderātiō, cōnsīderātiōnis (*f.*), consideration, reflection

cōnsīderō, cōnsīderāre, cōnsīderāvī, cōnsīderātum, to look at, to consider, to regard

cōnsilium, cōnsiliī (*n.*), consultation, deliberation, assembly, council, advice

cōnsistō, cōnsistere, cōnstitī, (cōnstitum), to consist, to stand, to stop, to exist

cōnsortium, cōnsortiī (*n.*), companionship, partnership

cōnspiciō, cōnspicere, cōnspexī, cōnspectum, to look, to behold, to perceive, to look with attention, to attract attention

cōnspīrō, cōnspīrāre, cōnspīrāvī, cōnspīrātum, to breathe together, to agree, to conspire

cōnstituō, cōnstituere, cōnstituī, cōnstitūtum, to cause to stand, to organize, to constitute, to determine, to decide

cōnstitūtiō, cōnstitūtiōnis (*f.*), constitution, condition, disposition, nature

cōnstō, cōnstāre, cōnstitī,
(cōnstātum), to stand together,
to consist, to correspond, to
stand firm, to be constant

cōnsuēscō, cōnsuēscere,
cōnsuēvī, cōnsuētum, to
accustom, to be accustomed, to
habituate

cōnsul, cōnsulis (m.), consul

cōnsulō, cōnsulere, cōnsuluī,
cōnsultum, to deliberate, to
consult, to consider, to ask the
advice of

cōnsultor, cōnsultōris (m.),
adviser, one who asks for advice

cōnsūmō, cōnsūmere,
cōnsumpsī, cōnsumptum, to
consume, to use, to spend

cōnsummo, cōnsummāre,
cōnsummāvī, cōnsummātum,
to sum up, to accomplish, to
complete

contāctus, contāctūs (m.),
contact, touch, contagion

contendō, contendere, contendī,
contentum, to strain, to
stretch, to strive, to contend

contentus, contenta, contentum
(perfect passive participle of
contendō and of contineō)

continenter (adv.), continuously,
uninterruptedly, immediately

contineō, continēre, continuī,
contentum, to hold together,
to contain, to restrain

contingō, contingere, contigī,
contāctum, to touch, to border
on, to concern, to happen, to
befall

continuō (adv.), at once, directly,
continuously

continuō, continuāre,
continuāvī, continuātum, to
unite, to make continuous, to
extend

continuus, continua,
continuum, continuous,
unbroken

contorqueō, contorquēre,
contorsī, contortum, to twist,
to contort

contrā (adv. and prep. + acc.),
opposite, against

contractiō, contractiōnis (f.),
contraction, abbreviation,
anxiety

contractus, contractūs (m.),
contraction, contract,
agreement

contradistinctus,
contradistincta,
contradistinctum,
contradistinct, distinct by way
of contrast

contrahō, contrahere, contraxī,
contractum, to draw together,
to contract, to transact

contrārius, contrāria,
contrārium, contrary,
opposite

contrīstō, contrīstāre,
contrīstāvī, contrīstātum, to
sadden, to make gloomy

contrōversia, contrōversiae (f.),
dispute, quarrel, controversy

contumēlia, contumēliae
(f.), outrage, insult, affront,
contumely

**conveniō, convenīre, convēnī,
conventum,** to come together,
to meet, to assemble, to
convene, to agree, to be
suitable

conversātiō, conversātiōnis (*f.*),
frequent use, frequent dealings

conversō, ē conversō, on the
contrary, on the other hand,
vice versa

**convertō, convertere, convertī,
conversum,** to turn around, to
turn in another direction, to
alter

convulsiō, convulsiōnis (*f.*),
convulsion, dislocation

coopertōrium, coopertōriī (*n.*),
covering, garment

Copernicus, Copernicī (*m.*),
Copernicus

cōpia, cōpiae (*f.*), plenty,
multitude, wealth, troops

coquō, coquere, coxī, coctum, to
cook, to bake

cor, cordis (*n.*), heart, mind

corōllārium, corōllāriī (*n.*),
garland of flowers, corollary
(*math.*)

corōna, corōnae (*f.*), crown,
garland, wreath

**corporālis, corporālis,
corporāle,** corporeal, of the
body

corpus, corporis (*n.*), body

corrēctiō, corrēctiōnis (*f.*),
correction, amendment

**corrigō, corrigere, corrēxī,
corrēctum,** to set straight, to
correct, to amend

**corripiō, corripere, corripuī,
correptum,** to seize violently,
to snatch away, to catch

**corrumpō, corrumpere, corrūpī,
corruptum,** to destroy, to spoil,
to corrupt

crēdibilis, crēdibilis, crēdibile,
credible, deserving belief

**crēdō, crēdere, crēdidī,
crēditum,** to believe, to think,
to trust, to entrust

crūrālis, crūrālis, crūrāle, crural,
pertaining to the legs

cubiculum, cubiculī (*n.*),
bedroom

cum (*prep. + abl.*), with; (*conj.*)
when, while, as, since

cūnctus, cūncta, cūnctum, all, all
together, the whole

cunīculus, cunīculī (*m.*), mine,
underground passage

cupiditās, cupiditātis (*f.*), desire,
longing, lust, ambition

cupidus, cupida, cupidum,
desirous, covetous, lustful,
eager, ambitious

**cupiō, cupere, cupīvī (cupiī),
cupītum,** to desire, to wish for,
to want

cūr (*adv.*), why

cūra, cūrae (*f.*), care, attention,
trouble, administration

cūrātiō, cūrātiōnis (*f.*), attention,
cure, healing, care

cūrō, cūrāre, cūrāvī, cūrātum,
to care for, to attend to, to
administer

currō, currere, cucurrī, cursum,
to run

currus, currūs (*m.*), chariot

cursus, cursūs (*m.*), course, voyage, flow, trajectory

curva, curvae (*f.*), curve (*math.*)

curvō, curvāre, curvāvī, curvātum, to bend, to curve

cuspis, cuspidis (*f.*), pointed edge, sting, spear

cutis, cutis (*f.*), skin

dē (*prep. + abl.*), down from, away from; about, concerning

dēbeō, dēbēre, dēbuī, dēbitum, to owe, to be indebted, to have the obligation to, to have to

dēbilis, dēbilis, dēbile, weak, feeble

dēbilitās, dēbilitātis (*f.*), weakness

dēbilitō, dēbilitāre, dēbilitāvī, dēbilitātum, to weaken

decem, ten

dēceptiō, dēceptiōnis (*f.*), deception, deceit

decet, decēre, decuit, it is proper, it is fitting

dēcidō, dēcidere, dēcidī, to fall down

dēclārātiō, dēclārātiōnis (*f.*), declaration, clarification

dēclārō, dēclārāre, dēclārāvī, dēclārātum, to declare, to proclaim, to make clear

dēclīnō, dēclīnāre, dēclīnāvī, dēclīnātum, to deflect, to turn away, to deviate, to incline

decor, decōris (*m.*), elegance, grace

decus, decoris (*n.*), ornament, beauty, glory

dēdūcō, dēdūcere, dēdūxī, dēductum, to lead down, to bring down, to subtract, to reduce

dēfectus, dēfectūs (*m.*), failure, defect, absence, desertion

dēfendō, dēfendere, dēfendī, dēfensum, to defend, to protect, to reject, to ward off

dēfēnsiō, dēfēnsiōnis (*f.*), defense, protection, warding off

dēferō, dēferre, dētulī, dēlātum, to carry down, to bring to an appropriate place, to report, to transfer

dēficiō, dēficere, dēfēcī, dēfectum, to abandon, to fail, to cease

dēfīniō, dēfīnīre, dēfīnīvī, dēfīnītum, to set a limit, to define

dēfīnītiō, dēfīnītiōnis (*f.*), definition

dēflectō, dēflectere, dēflexī, dēflexum, to bend down, to turn aside

dēfōrmātiō, dēfōrmātiōnis (*f.*), deformation, reshaping

dēfōrmō, dēfōrmāre, dēfōrmāvī, dēfōrmātum, to form, to fashion, to give shape, to deform

dēglūtiō, dēglūtīre, dēglūtīvī, dēglūtītum, to swallow down

dēglūtītiō, dēglūtītiōnis (*f.*), swallowing, deglutition

deinde (*adv.*), then, next, thereafter, from there

dēlectō, dēlectāre, dēlectāvī,
dēlectātum, to delight, to
please

dēmittō, dēmittere, dēmīsī,
dēmissum, to send down, to
bring down

dēmōnstrātiō, dēmōnstrātiōnis
(*f.*), demonstration, indication,
proof (*math.*)

dēmōnstrō, dēmōnstrāre,
dēmōnstrāvī, dēmōnstrātum,
to show, to explain, to indicate,
to demonstrate, to prove
(*math.*)

dēmum (*adv.*), finally, at last, in
short

dēnique (*adv.*), finally, further, in
short

dēnsō, dēnsāre, dēnsāvī,
dēnsātum, to thicken, to
condense, to crowd together

dēnsus, dēnsa, dēnsum, thick,
dense, condensed, frequent

deorsum (*adv.*), downward

dēpendeō, dēpendēre, dēpendī,
to hang from, to depend upon

dēpōnō, dēpōnere, dēposuī,
dēpositum, to put down, to
deposit, to lay aside

dēprimō, dēprimere, dēpressī,
dēpressum, to press down, to
sink, to depress, to oppress

dēpurō, dēpurāre, dēpurāvī,
dēpurātum, to purify, to refine

dēscendō, dēscendere, dēscendī,
dēscensum, to descend, to
climb down, to go down

dēscensus, dēscensūs (*m.*),
descent

dēscrībō, dēscrībere, dēscrīpsī,
dēscrīptum, to describe, to
trace, to explain, to delineate, to
copy, to transcribe

dēscrīptiō, dēscrīptiōnis
(*f.*), description, copy,
representation

dēsīderium, dēsīderiī (*n.*), desire,
yearning

dēsignō, dēsignāre, dēsignāvī,
dēsignātum, to designate, to
mark, to indicate, to nominate,
to name

dēsinō, dēsinere, dēsiī, dēsitum,
to desist, to cease, to stop

dēstillātiō, dēstillātiōnis (*f.*),
dripping, distillation

dēsum, dēesse, dēfuī, to fall
short, to be wanting, to fail

dētegō, dētegere, dētexī,
dētectum, to uncover, to
disclose

dēterior, dēterior, dēterius
(*comparative adj.*), worse,
inferior, poorer

dēterminātiō, dēterminātiōnis
(*f.*), boundary, limit,
determination

dēterminō, dētermināre,
dētermināvī, dēterminātum,
to limit, to determine

dētineō, dētinēre, dētinuī,
dētentum, to hold back, to
withhold, to keep, to occupy

dēturbō, dēturbāre, dēturbāvī,
dēturbātum, to dislodge, to
force away, to eject

deus, deī (*m.*), god, deity (*alt. nom.
pl.*: diī)

dexter, dextera, dexterum, right, right-hand, dexterous, skillful (*alt. spel.*: **dexter, dextra, dextrum**)

dialectica, dialecticae (*f.*), dialectics, logic

dialecticus, dialectica, dialecticum, dialectic, pertaining to discussion

diametrum, diametrī (*n.*), diameter (*math.*)

dīcō, dīcere, dīxī, dictum, to say, to speak, to express, to tell, to appoint

diēs, diēī (*m. and f.*), day

differentia, differentiae (*f.*), difference

differentiālis, differentiālis, differentiāle, differential (*math.*)

differō, diferre, distulī, dīlātum, to differ, to delay, to postpone, to scatter

difficilis, difficilis, difficile, difficult

difficultās, difficultātis (*f.*), difficulty, distress

digitus, digitī (*m.*), finger

dignitās, dignitātis (*f.*), dignity, esteem, merit, rank

dignus, digna, dignum, worthy, suitable

diiūdicō, diiūdicāre, diiūdicāvī, diiūdicātum, to decide, to distinguish, to judge between opposing parties

dīlātō, dīlātāre, dīlātāvī, dīlātātum, to expand, to dilate, to spread out

dīligēns, dīligēntis, diligent, careful

dīligentia, dīligentiae (*f.*), diligence, care, economy

dīmēnsiō, dīmēnsiōnis (*f.*), measurement, dimension

dīminūtiō, dīminūtiōnis (*f.*), diminution, lessening (*alt. spel.*: **dēminūtiō, dēminūtiōnis**)

dīnumerō, dīnumerāre, dīnumerāvī, dīnumerātum, to enumerate, to count

dīrēctiō, dīrēctiōnis (*f.*), direction

dīrēctus, dīrēcta, dīrēctum, straight, direct

dīrigō, dīrigere, dīrēxī, dīrēctum, to direct, to aim, to arrange

discēdō, discēdere, discessī, discessum, to depart, to separate, to go away

disciplīna, disciplīnae (*f.*), discipline, learning, body of knowledge, education

discō, discere, didicī, to learn, to get to know

discooperiō, discooperīre, discooperuī, discoopertum, to uncover, to lay bare

discutiō, discutere, discussī, discussum, to break apart, to disperse, to scatter, to destroy (*medieval*: **discutō, discutere,** to discuss, to examine)

disertus, diserta, disertum, eloquent, clever, well thought

displōdō, displōdere, displōsī, displōsum, to burst, to explode

dispōnō, dispōnere, disposuī, dispositum, to arrange, to dispose

dispositiō, dispositiōnis (*f.*), disposition, orderly arrangement

disputatiō, disputatiōnis (*f.*), argument, dispute, discussion

dissecō, dissecāre, dissecuī, dissectum, to cut up, to dissect, to dismember

dissectiō, dissectiōnis (*f.*), dissection, dismemberment

disserō, disserere, disseruī, dissertum, to discuss, to examine, to expound

disserō, disserere, dissēvī, dissitum, to spread

dissimilis, dissimilis, dissimile, dissimilar, unlike

distantia, distantiae (*f.*), distance

distendō, distendere, distendī, distentum, to stretch, to distend

distinctiō, distinctiōnis (*f.*), distinction, difference

distinguō, distinguere, distinxī, distinctum, to separate, to distinguish

distō, distāre, distitī, to stand apart, to be at some distance from

distorqueō, distorquēre, distorsī, distortum, to distort, to twist

distribūtiō, distribūtiōnis (*f.*), distribution, division

diū (*adv.*), for a long time

diurnus, diurna, diurnum, daily, pertaining to a day

diutius (*adv.*), longer, for a longer time

dīvergō, dīvergere, to diverge (*neol.*)

dīversificō, dīversificāre, dīversificāvī, dīversificātum, to diversify, to become many

dīversitās, dīversitātis (*f.*), diversity, difference

dīversus, dīversa, dīversum, diverse, turned into different directions

dīvidō, dīvidere, dīvīsī, dīvīsum, to divide, to separate

dīvīnitus (*adv.*), by divine influence, admirably

dīvīsibilis, dīvīsibilis, dīvīsibile, divisible

dīvīsiō, dīvīsiōnis (*f.*), division

dīvitiae, dīvitiārum (*f. pl.*), wealth, riches

dō, dare, dedī, datum, to give

doceō, docēre, docuī, doctum, to teach

docilis, docilis, docile, docile, teachable

docilitās, docilitātis (*f.*), docility, teachability

doctor, doctōris (*m.*), teacher, doctor

doctrīna, doctrīnae (*f.*), teaching, knowledge, learning, science, doctrine

doctus, docta, doctum, learned person, experienced

dogma, dogmatis (*n.*), philosophical doctrine, dogma

doleō, dolēre, doluī, to suffer pain, to cause pain

dolus, dolī (*m.*), deception, fraud

domesticus, domestica, domesticum, belonging to the house, domestic

dominium, dominiī (*n.*), ownership

dominus, dominī (*m.*), master

domus, domūs (*f., irregular declensions*), house, home

dubitō, dubitāre, dubitāvī, dubitātum, to doubt, to hesitate, to waver

dūcō, dūcere, dūxī, ductum, to lead, to draw, to draw out

ductiō, ductiōnis (*f.*), leading away, drawing away

dum (*conj.*), while, as long as

dumtaxat (*adv.*), exactly, at least, at most

duo, duae, duo (*adj., irregular declension*), two

duplex, duplicis (*adj.*), double, twofold

duplus, dupla, duplum, double, twice as much

dūrus, dūra, dūrum, hard, tough

ē, ex (*prep. + abl.*), out of, from, since

eccentricitās, eccentricitātis (*f.*), eccentricity

eccentricus, eccentrica, eccentricum, eccentric

ēdō, ēdere, ēdidī, ēditum, to emit, to give out, to produce

ēducātiō, ēducātiōnis (*f.*), education, training

ēdūcō, ēdūcere, ēdūxī, ēductum, to draw out, to lead out, to raise up

efficiō, efficere, effēcī, effectum, to produce, to bring about, to effect, to make

effodiō, effodere, effodī, effossum, to dig out

efformō, efformāre, efformāvī, efformātum, to form, to fashion, to shape

egeō, egēre, eguī, to be in need, to want, to be without

ego (*pers. pron.*), I

ēgregiē (*adv.*), excellently, very well

ēiusmodī, of this kind, such

ēlabōrō, ēlabōrāre, ēlabōrāvī, ēlabōrātum, to strive, to elaborate, to work out

ēlectricitās, ēlectricitātis (*f.*), electricity

ēlectricus, ēlectrica, ēlectricum, electrical, amber-like

ēlegans, ēlegantis, fine, tasteful, choice

elementum, elementī (*n.*), first principle, rudiments, element (*chem.*)

elenchus, elenchī (*m.*), pearl, Socratic method of logical refutation

elephantus, elephantī (*m.*), elephant

elephās, elephantis (*m.*), elephant

ēlevātiō, ēlevātiōnis (*f.*), elevation

ēlevō, ēlevāre, ēlevāvī, ēlevātum, to raise, to elevate, to alleviate

ēliciō, ēlicere, ēlicuī, ēlicitum, to entice, to elicit

ēloquentia, ēloquentiae (*f.*), eloquence

emō, emere, ēmī, ēmptum, to buy

ēmolumentum, ēmolumentī (*n.*), profit

empīricus, empīrica, empīricum, empirical, based on practical experience

ēmptiō, ēmptiōnis (*f.*), purchase

ēmptor, ēmptōris (*m.*), buyer

ēnārrō, ēnārrāre, ēnārrāvī, ēnārrātum, to narrate, to explain in full

encheria, encheriae (*f.*), the part of chemistry dealing with experimental instrumentation (*from the Greek "in hand"*)

enim (*conj.*), indeed, truly, for, because, in fact

eō (*adv.*), to that point, so much

eō, īre, īvī (iī), itum, to go, to walk, to pass

eōdem (*adv.*), to the same place

epicyclium, epicyclī (*n.*), epicycle (*astr.*)

epiglōttis, epiglōttidis (*f.*), epiglottis (*anat.*)

epitomē, epitomēs (*f.*), epitome, abridgment (*irr. Greek declension*)

equidem (*adv.*), indeed, truly, certainly

equus, equī (*m.*), horse

ergalia, ergaliae (*f.*), alchemic discipline dealing with experimental instruments

ergō (*adv.*), therefore, consequently

ērigō, ērigere, ērēxī, ērēctum, to erect, to build, to raise up

errāticus, errātica, errāticum, wandering, straying

errō, errāre, errāvī, errātum, to wander, to stray, to err, to be mistaken

error, errōris (*m.*), error, mistake

ērudītiō, ērudītiōnis (*f.*), erudition, knowledge

ērudītus, ērudīta, ērudītum, learned, educated, trained

Escolāpius, Escolāpiī (*m.*), Aesculapius, the Greek god of medicine (*classical spelling:* Aesculāpius, Aesculāpiī)

essentia, essentiae (*f.*), essence

et (*conj. and adv.*), and, also

etenim (*conj. and adv.*), for indeed

ethica, ethicae (*f.*), ethics, moral philosophy

etiam (*conj.*), and yet, even, still, also

etiamsī (*conj.*), even if, although

etsī (*conj.*), even if, although, and yet, notwithstanding

euthygrammon, euthygrammī (*n.*), ruler, straightedge, rectilinear figure

ēvādō, ēvādere, ēvāsī, ēvāsum, to come out, to turn out, to become, to escape, to evade

ēveniō, ēvenīre, ēvēnī, ēventum, to come out, to turn out, to result, to befall, to happen

ēventus, ēventūs (*m.*), result, outcome, consequence, event, success

ēvidēns, ēvidēntis, clear, evident

ēvincō, ēvincere, ēvīcī, ēvictum, to prevail, to conquer completely ēvolō, ēvolāre, ēvolāvī, ēvolātum, to fly away, to rush forth, to escape

ex, ē (*prep.* + *abl.*), out of, from, since

exāctē (*adv.*), exactly, accurately

exaudiō, exaudīre, exaudīvī, exaudītum, to hear, to listen

excellentia, excellentiae (*f.*), excellence, distinction, merit

excelsitās, excelsitātis (*f.*), elevation, loftiness

excelsus, excelsa, excelsum, elevated, lofty, eminent

excessus, excessūs (*m.*), departure, deviation, compensation (*medieval*)

excitatiō, excitatiōnis (*f.*), rousing, excitation

excitō, excitāre, excitāvī, excitātum, to arouse, to awaken, to excite, to kindle

excoctiō, excoctiōnis (*f.*), boiling

excōgitō, excōgitāre, excōgitāvī, excōgitātum, to think thoroughly, to conceive, to devise, to contrive

excoquō, excoquere, excoxī, excoctum, to boil down, to cook

excrēscō, excrēscere, excrēvī, excrētum, to grow up, to increase

excutiō, excutere, excussī, excussum, to shake out, to examine, to investigate

exemplar, exemplāris (*n.*), model, copy

exemplificō, exemplificāre, exemplificāvī, exemplificātum, to exemplify, to make an example

exemplum, exemplī (*n.*), example, sample, copy

exercitātiō, exercitātiōnis (*f.*), exercise

exercitium, exercitiī (*n.*), exercise, practice

exercitō, exercitāre, exercitāvī, exercitātum, to exercise, to practice, to keep at work

exhibeō, exhibēre, exhibuī, exhibitum, to hold out, to show, to present, to display, to exhibit, to produce

exigō, exigere, exēgī, exāctum, to demand, to require, to complete, to force out

existimātiō, existimātiōnis (*f.*), judgment, opinion, reputation, consideration

exīstimō, exīstimāre, exīstimāvī, exīstimātum, to value, to judge, to consider

existō, existere, extitī, (existitus), to appear, to come into existence, to become, to be, to exist (*alt. spel.*: exsistō, exsistere, exstitī)

exōrdium, exōrdiī (*n.*), beginning, introduction

expectō, expectāre, expectāvī, expectātum, to wait, to expect, to look out for, to hope (*alt. spel.*: exspectō, exspectāre, exspectāvī, exspectātum)

expediō, expedīre, expedīvī,
expedītum, to be useful or
expedient, to release

experientia, experientiae (*f.*),
experience, trial, test

experientissimus, experientissima,
experientissimum,
most enterprising, most
knowledgeable, most active

experimentum, experimentī (*n.*),
experiment, test, experience

experior, experīrī, expertus sum,
to try, to test, to attempt, to
learn by experience, to assay

expertus, experta, expertum,
experienced, expert, tried

expleō, explēre, explēvī,
explētum, to fill out, to
complete, to fulfill

explicātiō, explicātiōnis (*f.*),
explanation, unrolling,
unfolding

explicō, explicāre, explicāvī,
explicātum, to explain, to
unroll, to expand

explōrō, explōrāre, explōrāvī,
explōrātum, to investigate, to
explore, to examine

expressiō, expressiōnis (*f.*),
expression, pressing out,
expulsion

exsistō, exsistere, exstitī,
exstitum, to appear, to spring
forth, to come into existence

extensiō, extensiōnis (*f.*),
extension, stretching, swelling

extenuō, extenuāre, extenuāvī,
extenuātum, to make thin, to
weaken

exter, extera, exterum, outward,
outer, foreign

externus, externa, externum,
external

extō, extāre, extitī, to stand out,
to be still in existence (*alt. spel.*:
exstō, exstāre, exstitī)

extorqueō, extorquēre, extorsī,
extortum, to twist out, to
extort

extrā (*adv. and prep.* + *acc.*),
outside, beyond

extrahō, extrahere, extraxī,
extractum, to draw out, to drag
out, to extract, to extricate, to
prolong

extrēmum, extrēmī (*n.*), limit, end

extrēmus, extrēma, extrēmum,
outermost (*superlative of* exter)

exultātiō, exultātiōnis (*f.*),
exultation, great joy (*alt. spel.*:
exsultātiō, exsultātiōnis)

fabrica, fabricae (*f.*), production,
work, device, workshop, fabric,
structure

fabricō, fabricāre, fabricāvī,
fabricātum, to make, to form,
to forge

fabricor, fabricārī, fabricātus
sum (*alternative deponent form
of* fabricō, fabricāre, fabricāvī,
fabricātum)

fabula, fabulae (*f.*), tale, story,
fable, conversation

faciēs, faciēī (*f.*), face,
countenance, appearance,
aspect

facilis, facilis, facile, easy, affable

facillimus, facillima, facillimum, most easy (*superlative of* **facilis**)

faciō, facere, fēcī, factum, to make, to do

factiō, factiōnis (*f.*), faction, group of interest, political party

facultās, facultātis (*f.*), faculty, ability, opportunity, means, power

facundia, facundiae (*f.*), eloquence, expressivity, facundity

falcidius, falcidia, falcidium, relating to Publius Falcidius, a tribune of the plebs in 40 BCE

falsus, falsa, falsum, false, untrue

fāma, fāmae (*f.*), report, rumor, public opinion, fame, repute

famēs, famis (*f.*), hunger

fatīgō, fatīgāre, fatīgāvī, fatīgātus, to tire, to weary, to fatigue, to vex, to harass

faucēs, faucium (*f. pl.*), throat, gullet, narrow passage, chasm

fax, facis (*f.*), torch, light, flame

fenestra, fenestrae (*f.*), window

ferē (*adv.*), almost, nearly, quite

feriō, ferīre, ferīvī, ferītum, to hit, to strike, to cut

ferō, ferre, tulī, lātum, to bear, to bring, to carry, to report, to tell, to say

ferrum, ferrī (*n.*), sword, weapon, iron, iron implement

fessus, fessa, fessum, weary, tired

fibra, fibrae (*f.*), fiber, filament

fictītius, fictītia, fictītium, counterfeit, fictitious, feigned

fidēs, fideī (*f.*), faith, confidence, trust, confirmation, proof

fidūcia, fidūciae (*f.*), trust, assurance, deposit, pledge

figūra, figūrae (*f.*), figure, shape

fīlius, fīliī (*m.*), son

fingō, fingere, finxī, fictum, to form, to fashion, to feign, to invent

fīnis, fīnis (*m. and f.*), end, border, limit, boundary, aim

fīō, fierī, factus sum, to become, to happen, to come into existence

firmus, firma, firmum, firm, strong

fīxus, fīxa, fīxum, fixed

flātus, flātūs (*m.*), wind, breath, arrogance

flāvus, flāva, flāvum, yellow, golden-yellow

flōreō, flōrēre, flōruī, to bloom, to flourish, to prosper

flūmen, flūminis (*n.*), stream, river

fluō, fluere, fluxī, fluxum, to flow, to stream

fluvius, fluviī (*m.*), river

fodīna, fodīnae (*f.*), mine, pit

fodiō, fodere, fōdī, fossum, to dig, to excavate

fons, fontis (*m.*), fountain, source

forāmen, forāminis (*n.*), hole, aperture

fore, forem (*alternative forms for* **futurum esse** *and* **essem**)

fōrma, fōrmae (*f.*), form, shape, image, beauty

fōrmula, fōrmulae (*f.*), rule, prescription, formula (*math.*)

forsan (*adv.*), perhaps
forsitan (*adv.*), perhaps
fortasse (*adv.*), perhaps
fortassis (*adv.*), perhaps
forte (*adv.*), by chance,
accidentally, perhaps
fortis, fortis, forte, strong
fortiter (*adv.*), strongly
fortuītus, fortuīta, fortuītum,
accidental, fortuitous
fortūna, fortūnae (*f.*), fortune,
property, fate, luck
forum, forī (*n.*), forum,
marketplace
fossiō, fossiōnis (*f.*), excavation
fossor, fossōris (*m.*), digger,
excavator
frangō, frangere, frēgī, fractum,_
to break, to shatter
fraus, fraudis (*f.*), deceit, fraud,
crime
frequentia, frequentiae (*f.*), large
number, abundance
frīgidus, frīgida, frīgidum, cold,
chilly
frūctus, frūctūs (*m.*), fruit,
produce, enjoyment, profit
frūmentum, frūmentī (*n.*), grain,
corn, wheat
fulmen, fulminis (*n.*),
thunderbolt, lightning
fūnctiō, fūnctiōnis (*f.*),
performance, execution,
functioning, function (*math.*)
fundāmentum, fundāmentī (*n.*),
base, foundation
fundō, fundāre, fundāvī,
fundātum, to found, to
establish, to lay a foundation

fūnis, fūnis (*m.*), rope, cord
fūsiō, fūsiōnis (*f.*), outpouring,
fusion (*chem.*)
fūsus, fūsa, fūsum, poured out,
flowing, full, broad
futūrus, futūra, futūrum, about
to be (*future partic. of* **sum,**
esse, fuī)

gaudeō, gaudēre, gāvīsus sum, to
rejoice, to delight in
gemma, gemmae (*f.*), precious
stone, jewel, gem
generāliter (*adv.*), generally, in
general
generātrīx, generātrīcis (*f.*),
begetter, producer,
generator (*m.*: **generātor,**
generātōris)
generō, generāre, generāvī,
generātum, to beget, to
engender, to generate
gēns, gēntis (*f.*), clan, family, tribe,
nation
genū, genūs (*n.*), knee
genus, generis (*n.*), kind, sort,
gender, family
geōgraphia, geōgraphiae (*f.*),
geography
geōmetrēs, geōmetrae (*m.*),
geometer
geōmetria, geōmetriae (*f.*),
geometry
geōmetricus, geōmetrica,
geōmetricum, geometrical
germānicus, germānica,
germānicum, German
gerō, gerere, gessī, gestum, to
carry on, to conduct, to wage

gignō, gignere, genuī, genitum,
to beget, to give rise to, to bring
forth, to produce
gladiātōrius, gladiātōria,
gladiātōrium, gladiatorial,
pertaining to gladiators
globōsus, globōsa, globōsum,
spherical
globulus, globulī (*m.*), small
sphere, small ball, globule
glōria, glōriae (*f.*), glory, fame
glōriōsē (*adv.*), gloriously,
boastingly
gnārus, gnāra, gnārum, skilled,
known
gradātim, gradually, by degrees,
step by step
gradus, gradūs (*m.*), step, stair,
stage, degree (*math.*)
graecē (*adv.*), in Greek
Graecia, Graeciae (*f.*), Greece
graecus, graeca, graecum,
Greek
grammatica, grammaticae (*f.*),
grammar
grandis, grandis, grande,
great, large, tall, full-grown,
important
grāphis, grāphīdis (*f.*), drawing
instrument, sketch, drawing
grātia, grātiae (*f.*), grace, charm,
favor, regard, service, thanks
grātulor, grātulārī, grātulātus
sum, to congratulate, to give
thanks, to rejoice
grātus, grāta, grātum, pleasing,
agreeable
gravis, gravis, grave, heavy,
important

gravitās, gravitātis (*f.*), weight,
importance, dignity, gravity
(*phys.*)
gravō, gravāre, gravāvī,
gravātum, to load, to burden,
to oppress
grex, gregis (*m.*), flock, herd,
company, community
gubernātor, gubernātōris (*m.*),
pilot, ruler, governor (*f.*:
gubernātrīx, gubernātrīcis)
gula, gulae (*f.*), appetite, gluttony,
throat
gutta, guttae (*f.*), drop, small
quantity
gȳrus, gȳrī (*m.*), circuit, circle,
ring

habeō, habēre, habuī, habitum,
to have, to possess
hāctenus (*adv.*), so far, up to this
point, hitherto
haereō, haerēre, haesī, haesum,
to stick, to adhere to, to stop, to
be at a loss
haeresis, haeresis (*f.*), sect, school
of thought
harmonia, harmoniae (*f.*),
concord, consonance,
harmony
haud (*adv.*), not, not at all, by no
means
Hēraclītus, Hēraclītī (*m.*),
Heraclitus
herba, herbae (*f.*), herb, grass,
weed, blade of grass
herculānensis, herculānensis,
herculānense, from the town
of Herculaneum

Hermēs, Hermētis (*m.*), Hermes (the Roman god Mercury)

hermēticus, hermētica, hermēticum, relating to Hermes

hībernus, hīberna, hībernum, wintry, of winter (*alt. spel.*: **hybernus, hyberna, hybernum**)

hīc (*adv.*), here

hic, haec, hoc (*pron. and adj.*), this

hice, haece, hoce (*adv.*), here (*emphatic form of* **hic, haec, hoc**)

hiera, hierae (*f.*), a consecrated garland, a prize in a race

hinc (*adv.*), from here, hence

historia, historiae (*f.*), history, inquiry

historicus, historica, historicum, historical

homō, hominis (*m.*), human being, person, man

honestus, honesta, honestum, honorable, respectable, virtuous, honest

honus, honeris (*n.*), load, burden (*alt. medieval spel. of* **onus, oneris**)

hōra, hōrae (*f.*), hour, time

hostis, hostis (*m. and f.*), stranger, enemy, foe

hūiusmodī, of this kind

hūmānus, hūmāna, hūmānum, human, pertaining to human beings

hūmidus, hūmida, hūmidum, humid, moist, wet (*alt. spel.*: **ūmidus, ūmida, ūmidum**)

humilis, humilis, humile, lowly, humble, poor

hūmor, hūmōris (*m.*), fluid, dew, moisture (*alt. spel.*: **ūmor, ūmōris**)

hydrographia, hydrographiae (*f.*), hydrography

hypothesis, hypothesis (*f.*), hypothesis, supposition

iaceō, iacēre, iacuī, to lie down, to lie at rest

iaciō, iacere, iēcī, iactum, to throw, to cast, to hurl

iactantia, iactantiae (*f.*), boasting, bragging, arrogance

iam (*adv.*), already, now, immediately

iānua, iānuae (*f.*), door, entrance

ibī (*adv.*), there, at that place, at that time

ibīdem (*adv.*), in the same place, at that moment

ictus, ictūs (*m.*), stroke, blow

īdem, eadem, idem (*pron.*), the same

ideō (*adv.*), for that reason, therefore, on that account

īdōlon, īdōlī (*n.*), image, specter, idol

idōneus, idōnea, idōneum, suitable, appropriate, fit, apt

igitur (*adv.*), therefore, consequently, so, then

īgnārus, īgnāra, īgnārum, ignorant, unknown

igniō, ignīre, ignīvī, ignītum, to ignite, set on fire

ignis, ignis (*m.*), fire

īgnōrō, īgnōrāre, īgnōrāvī, īgnōrātum, to be ignorant of, not to know

ille, illa, illud (*pron. and adj.*), that, that yonder, that famous, the former

illūminō, illūmināre, illūminavī, illūminātum, to illuminate, to light

illūstrātiō, illūstrātiōnis (*f.*), illustration, illumination

imāgō, imāginis (*f.*), image, representation, likeness, figure, portrait

imitor, imitārī, imitātus sum, to imitate, to copy

immediātus, immediāta, immediātum, not mediated, immediate

immigrō, immigrāre, immigrāvī, immigrātum, to migrate, to move into

immisceō, immiscēre, immiscuī, immixtum, to mix in

immittō, immittere, immīsī, immissum, to send in, to let in, to release

immō (*adv.*), nay rather, on the contrary

immōbilis, immōbilis, immōbile, immovable, unchangeable

immōtus, immōta, immōtum, unmoved, firm, motionless (*alt. spel.*: **inmōtus, inmōta, inmōtum**)

impediō, impedīre, impedīvī, impedītum, to ensnare, to hinder, to impede

impellō, impellere, impullī, impulsum, to set in motion, to push, to impel

impendeō, impendēre, to overhang, to impend

imperium, imperiī (*n.*), command, order, empire

impingō, impingere, impēgī, impāctum, to drive against, to strike, to impinge on (*phys.*)

impleō, implēre, implēvī, implētum, to fill in, to fill up

impōnō, impōnere, impōsuī, impōsitum, to put into, to lay upon, to impose

impositiō, impositiōnis (*f.*), application, imposition

impossibilis, impossibilis, impossibile, impossible

impressiō, impressiōnis (*f.*), impression

imprimō, imprimere, impressī, impressum, to press, to imprint, to apply

impulsus, impulsūs (*m.*), push, impulse (*phys.*)

impūrus, impūra, impūrum, unclean, impure

īmus, īma, īmum, lowest (*superlative of* **inferus**)

in (*prep. + abl.*), in, at; (*prep. + acc.*) into, toward

inaequālis, inaequālis, inaequāle, unequal

inānis, inānis, ināne, empty, useless, worthless

incendō, incendere, incendī, incēnsum, to set on fire, to inflame

incessō, incessere, incessīvī, to step, to walk, to assail

inchoō, inchoāre, inchoāvī, inchoātum, to begin (*alt. spel.*: **incohō, incohāre, incohāvī, incohātum**)

incidentia, incidentiae (*f.*), occurrence, incidence (*phys.*)

incidō, incidere, incidī, incāssum, to fall upon, to incur, to occur, to happen

incīdō, incīdere, incīdī, incīssum, to cut into, to engrave, to cut off (to make an incision)

incipiō, incipere, incēpī, inceptum, to begin, to commence (*alt. spel.*: **incipiō, incipere, incoepī, incoeptum**)

incitō, incitāre, incitāvī, incitātum, to incite, to urge, to set in motion, to excite

inclīnātiō, inclīnātiōnis (*f.*), leaning, bending, inclination

inclīnō, inclīnāre, inclīnāvī, inclīnātum, to bend, to incline, to turn

inclūdō, inclūdere, inclūsī, inclūsum, to shut in, to enclose, to include

inconditus, incondita, inconditum, disorderly, confused

incrēdibilis, incrēdibilis, incrēdibile, incredible, extraordinary

indāgō, indāgāre, indāgāvī, indāgātum, to explore, to investigate

inde (*adv.*), thence, from there

indēfīnītē (*adv.*), indefinitely

indēterminātus, indētermināta, indēterminātum, unbounded, indeterminate, unspecified

India, Indiae (*f.*), India

indicātiō, indicātiōnis (*f.*), assignment of a value, indication

indicium, indiciī (*n.*), information, evidence, disclosure, clue, symptom, indication, sign

indicō, indicāre, indicāvī, indicātum, to point out, to indicate, to make known, to put a price on

indīcō, indīcere, indīxī, indictum, to announce, to proclaim, to declare

indigentia, indigentiae (*f.*), need, lack, indigence

indigeō, indigēre, indiguī, to need, to require, to long for

indīviduus, indīvidua, indīviduum, indivisible, inseparable, individual

indīvisibilis, indīvisibilis, indīvisibile, indivisible

indūcō, indūcere, indūxī, inductum, to lead in, to bring in, to introduce, to induce, to put on, to draw over

inductiō, inductiōnis (*f.*), introduction, induction (*logic*)

Indus, Inda, Indum, Indian

industria, industriae (*f.*),
industry, diligence, zeal

ineō, inīre, iniī (inīvī), initum, to
go in, to enter

ineptus, inepta, ineptum,
unsuitable, silly, clumsy, inept

īnfestō, īnfestāre, īnfestāvī,
īnfestātum, to trouble, to
harass, to infest

īnficiō, īnficere, īnfēcī,
īnfectum, to dye, to taint, to
corrupt, to infect, to color, to
poison

īnfirmitās, īnfirmitātis
(*f.*), infirmity, weakness,
unsteadiness, instability

īnfirmō, īnfirmāre, īnfirmāvī,
īnfirmātum, to weaken, to
impair, to refute, to cancel

īnfrīgidō, īnfrīgidāre,
īnfrīgidāvī, īnfrīgidātum, to
chill, to cool

ingeniōsus, ingeniōsa,
ingeniōsum, ingenious, clever,
talented

ingenium, ingeniī (*n.*), character,
nature, temperament, innate
quality, cleverness, talent

ingēns, ingentis, huge, monstrous,
enormous

ingredior, ingredī, ingressus
sum, to walk in, to enter

inhabitō, inhabitāre, inhabitāvī,
inhabitātum, to dwell in, to
inhabit

inīquus, inīqua, inīquum, unfair,
unjust, uneven, unequal

initium, initiī (*n.*), beginning, first
principle

iniūria, iniūriae (*f.*), injustice,
wrong, injury

inmoderātiō, inmoderātiōnis
(*f.*), lack of moderation, excess
(*alt. spel.*: **immoderātiō,**
immoderātiōnis)

innītor, innītī, innixus sum, to
lean on, to depend upon, to
support oneself by

innōtēscō, innōtēscere, innōtuī,
to become known

innūmerus, innūmera,
innūmerum, countless,
numberless

inopia, inopiae (*f.*), poverty, lack,
need

inquīrō, inquīrere, inquīsīvī,
inquīsītum, to investigate, to
inquire, to look for

īnscrībō, īnscrībere, īnscrīpsī,
īnscrīptum, to inscribe, to
impress, to ascribe

īnserviō, īnservīre, īnservīvī,
īnservītum, to serve, to be of
service, to look after, to be a
slave, to be devoted to

īnsitus, īnsita, īnsitum, inserted,
implanted, innate, intrinsic

īnspiciō, īnspicere, īnspexī,
īnspectum, to look into, to
examine, to inspect

īnstar (*n. indecl.*), image, likeness,
in the form of, like

īnstituō, īnstituere, īnstituī,
īnstitūtum, to establish, to
found, to place, to educate

īnstitūtiō, īnstitūtiōnis (*f.*),
arrangement, method,
education, institution

īnstrūmentum, īnstrūmentī
(*n.*), instrument, apparatus,
implement, means
īnstruō, īnstruere, īnstruxī,
īnstructum, to build, to
prepare, to equip, to teach, to
instruct
īnsula, īnsulae (*f.*), island,
tenement building
īnsum, īnesse, īnfuī, to be in, to
belong to, to be contained in
integrus, integra, integrum,
entire, whole
intellēctus, intellēctūs (*m.*),
perception, understanding,
intellect
intellegō, intellegere,
intellēxī, intellēctum, to
understand, to comprehend,
to perceive (*alt. spel.:*
intelligō, intelligere,
intellixī, intellictum)
intendō, intendere, intendī,
intentum, to stretch, to direct
oneself toward, to intend, to
strive
inter (*prep. + acc.*), between,
among, amid, during
interdīcō, interdīcere, interdīxī,
interdictum, to prohibit, to
forbid, to decree
interdum (*adv.*), sometimes
intereō, interīre, interiī,
interitum, to perish, to die
interficiō, interficere, interfēcī,
interfectum, to kill
interior, interior, interius
(*comparative adj.*), inner,
interior, nearer

intermedius, intermedia,
intermedium, intermediate,
in between
internus, interna, internum,
internal
interpretātiō, interpretātiōnis
(*f.*), explanation,
interpretation, translation
intervallum, intervallī (*n.*),
interval, distance
intrā (*adv. and prep. + acc.*),
within
intueor, intuērī, intuitus sum,
to look at, to consider, to
contemplate
inundātiō, inundātiōnis (*f.*),
flood, inundation
invalēscō, invalēscere, invaluī, to
become strong, to prevail
inveniō, invenīre, invēnī,
inventum, to find, to discover,
to come upon, to invent
inventiō, inventiōnis (*f.*),
invention, ingenuity
inventor, inventōris (*m.*),
inventor, discoverer
investīgō, investīgāre,
investīgāvī, investīgātum, to
investigate, to search out
invicem (*adv.*), mutually,
alternately
invītō, invītāre, invītāvī,
invītātum, to invite
Ippōcratēs, Ippōcratis (*m.*),
Hippocrates (*alt. spel.:*
Hippōcratēs, Hippōcratis)
ipse, ipsa, ipsum (*pron. and adj.*),
self, himself, herself, itself
īris, īridis (*f.*), the rainbow

irratiōnālis, irratiōnālis, irratiōnāle, irrational

is, ea, id (*pron.*), he, she, it, this, that

iste, ista, istud (*pron.*), that by you

isthic, isthaec, isthoc (*pron.*), that by you (*alt. spel.*: **istic, istaec, istoc**)

istīc (*adv.*), there, here, over there

ita (*adv.*), thus, so

Ītalia, Ītaliae (*f.*), Italy

itaque (*adv.*), and so, therefore

item (*adv.*), likewise, also, besides, moreover

iterō, iterāre, iterāvī, iterātum, to repeat, to do a second time

iterum (*adv.*), again, a second time

itidem (*adv.*), likewise

iubeō, iubēre, iussī, iussum, to command, to order, to bid, to prescribe

iūcundus, iūcunda, iūcundum, pleasant, agreeable, delightful

iūdicium, iūdiciī (*n.*), judgment, trial, opinion, sentence, consideration

iūdicō, iūdicāre, iūdicāvī, iūdicātum, to judge, to decide, to consider

iungō, iungere, iūnxī, iūnctum, to yoke, to join, to unite, to attach

iūrisconsultus, iūrisconsultī (*m.*), lawyer, expert in the law, jurist

iūs, iūris (*n.*), right, legal right, law

iūsiūrandum, iūrisiūrandī (*n.*), oath

Iustīnus, Iustīnī (*m.*), Justin, Justinus

iūstitia, iūstitiae (*f.*), justice

iūstus, iūsta, iūstum, just, fair, rightful, lawful

j (*j = i*)

labor, labōris (*m.*), work, toil, labor, exertion, hardship

labōrō, labōrāre, labōrāvī, labōrātum, to toil, to work, to strive, to suffer

laetificātiō, laetificātiōnis (*f.*), rejoicing

laetificō, laetificāre, laetificāvī, laetificātum, to cheer, to delight, to gladden, to fertilize

laetitia, laetitiae (*f.*), joy, delight

lāna, lānae (*f.*), wool

lapis, lapidis (*m.*), stone

larinx, laringis (*f.*), larynx, voice box (*alt. spel.*: **larynx, laryngis**)

lascīviō, lascīvīre, lascīvīvī, lascīvītum, to be licentious, to be wanton, to run riot, to frolic, to sport, to be playful

lateō, latēre, latuī, to lie hidden, to be concealed

laterālis, laterālis, laterāle, lateral, belonging to the side

lātitūdō, lātitūdinis (*f.*), width, breadth, extent, latitude

lātus, lāta, lātum, broad, ample, wide

latus, lateris (*n.*), side, flank

laudābiliter (*adv.*), laudably, in a praiseworthy manner

laus, laudis (*f.*), praise, commendation

lavō, lavāre, lāvī, lautum (lavātum), to wash, to bathe

laxus, laxa, laxum, loose, relaxed

lectīca, lectīcae (*f.*), litter (sedan chair)

lēctiō, lēctiōnis (*f.*), reading, perusal, lecture

lēctor, lēctōris (*m.*), reader

lectus, lectī (*m.*), bed, dining couch

lēgitimus, lēgitima, lēgitimum, lawful, legitimate

legō, legere, lēgī, lēctum, to read, to peruse, to pick, to choose

levis, levis, leve, light, not heavy

leviter (*adv.*), lightly, softly

lēx, lēgis (*f.*), law, statute, precept

līber, lībera, līberum, free

liber, librī (*m.*), book

līberālis, līberālis, līberāle, liberal, worthy of a free man

līberē (*adv.*), freely

līberō, līberāre, līberāvī, līberātum, to free, to liberate, to release

libet, libēre, libitum est (libuit) (*impersonal vb.*), it pleases, it is agreeable

lībrātiō, lībrātiōnis (*f.*), levelling, libration (*astr.*)

lībrō, lībrāre, lībrāvī, lībrātum, to balance, to keep in equilibrium

licet, licēre, licitum est (licuit) (*impersonal vb.*), it is allowed, one may

licitus, licita, licitum, permitted, licit

ligula, ligulae (*f.*), small tongue, spoon, shoe strap, shoe buckle, trigger (*alt. spel.*: lingula, lingulae)

līnea, līneae (*f.*), line

līneāmentum, līneāmentī (*n.*), drawing, sketch

lingua, linguae (*f.*), tongue, language

liquidus, liquida, liquidum, liquid, fluid

liquor, liquōris (*m.*), liquor, liquid

littera, litterae (*f.*), letter of the alphabet, character, epistle (*alt. spel.*: litera, literae)

litterātus, litterāta, litterātum, learned, literate, lettered

lītus, lītoris (*n.*), shore, seashore (*alt. spel.*: littus, littoris)

loca, locōrum (*n. pl.*), connected places, region, locality

locus, locī (*m.*), place, spot, literary passage

logica, logicae (*f.*), logic

logicus, logica, logicum, logical

longē (*adv.*), a long way off, far away

longitūdō, longitūdinis (*f.*), length, longitude

longus, longa, longum, long

loquor, loquī, locūtus sum, to speak

Lūcīlius, Lūcīliī (*m.*), Lucilius

lucrum, lucrī (*n.*), profit, gain

lūcubrātiō, lūcubrātiōnis (*f.*), working by night, nocturnal study, lucubration, meditation

lūmen, lūminis (*n.*), light, eye

lūminōsus, lūminōsa,
lūminōsum, bright, luminous,
full of light
lūna, lūnae (*f.*), moon
lūx, lūcis (*f.*), light, daylight

māchina, māchinae (*f.*), machine,
device, artifice
māchinātiō, māchinātiōnis
(*f.*), contrivance, mechanism,
machinery, machination
madidus, madida, madidum,
wet, moist
magis (*adv.*), more, in a higher
degree
magisterium, magisteriī (*n.*),
directorship, magistracy,
mastership, pure substance (*alch.*)
magnificō, magnificāre,
magnificāvī, magnificātum,
to esteem highly, to praise
magnus, magna, magnum, great,
large, big
māior, māior, māius, larger,
greater, older
mālō, mālle, māluī, to prefer, to
rather choose
malus, mala, malum, bad, evil
mandō, mandāre, mandāvī,
mandātum, to order, to
command, to entrust, to
commission
maneō, manēre, mānsī, mānsum,
to remain, to stay
manifestē (*adv.*), evidently, plainly
manifestō, manifestāre,
manifestāvī, manifestātum,
to reveal, to manifest, to show
clearly

manifestus, manifesta,
manifestum, evident,
palpable, clear, manifest,
obvious
manus, manūs (*f.*), hand
mare, maris (*n.*), sea, ocean
marmor, marmoris (*n.*), marble
marmoreus, marmorea,
marmoreum, marble-like,
made of marble
Mars, Martis (*m.*), Mars (*astr.*)
māteria, māteriae (*f.*), matter,
material, subject matter
mathēmatica, mathēmaticae (*f.*),
mathematics
mathēmaticus, mathēmatica,
mathēmaticum, mathematical
mathēmaticus, mathēmaticī (*m.*),
mathematician
mātrōna, mātrōnae (*f.*), matron,
wife, lady
mātrōnālis, mātrōnālis,
mātrōnāle, pertaining to a
matron
mātūtīnus, mātūtīna,
mātūtīnum, pertaining to the
morning
Maurītānia, Maurītāniae (*f.*),
Mauritania
Maurītānus, Maurītāna,
Maurītānum, of Mauritania,
African, Moor
maximē (*adv.*), most of all,
absolutely, indeed
maximum, maximī (*n.*),
maximum (*math.*)
maximus, maxima, maximum,
largest, greatest, eldest,
maximal

mēchanica, mēchanicae (*f.*), mechanics

mēchanicus, mēchanica, mēchanicum, mechanical

mēchanicus, mēchanicī (*m.*), mechanic, engineer

medeor, medērī, to heal, to cure

medicīna, medicīnae (*f.*), medicine

medicus, medica, medicum, medical

medicus, medicī (*m.*), physician, doctor

mediō, mediāre, mediāvī, mediātum, to place in the middle, to intercede, to intermediate

mediocris, mediocris, mediocre, moderate, ordinary

mediocriter (*adv.*), moderately, in moderation

meditātiō, meditātiōnis (*f.*), meditation, contemplation, exercise, practice

medium, mediī (*n.*), the middle

medius, media, medium, middle

melinconicus, melinconica, melinconicum, melancholic, having black bile (*classical spel.*: **melancholicus, melancholica, melancholicum**)

melior, melior, melius, better

membrum, membrī (*n.*), member, limb

memoria, memoriae (*f.*), memory, remembrance

memorō, memorāre, memorāvī, memorātum, to mention, to recount, to call to mind

mēns, mēntis (*f.*), mind, intellect

mensūra, mensūrae (*f.*), measure, extent

mentiō, mentiōnis (*f.*), mention

mercātor, mercātōris (*m.*), merchant, trader

mercor, mercārī, mercātus sum, to trade, to buy and sell

Mercurius, Mercuriī (*m.*), Mercury

mereor, merērī, meritus sum, to deserve, to merit, to earn

meritum, meritī (*n.*), merit, desert, benefit

merx, mercis (*f.*), merchandise, goods

mēta, mētae (*f.*), target, end, turning post

metallicus, metallica, metallicum, metallic, pertaining to a mine

metallicus, metallicī (*m.*), metallurgist, miner, prospector

metallum, metallī (*n.*), metal, mine

metallurgia, metallurgiae (*f.*), metallurgy

meteōrologia, meteōrologiae (*f.*), meteorology

methodus, methodī (*f.*), method

mētior, mētīrī, mēnsus sum, to measure, to distribute

metodicus, metodica, metodicum, methodical (*classical spel.*: **methodicus, methodica, methodicum**)

metuō, metuere, metuī, metūtum, to fear

metus, metūs (*m.*), fear

meus, mea, meum, my, mine
(*gender agrees with thing
possessed*)

minera, minerae (*f.*), mine

minerālis, minerālis, minerāle,
mineral

minimē (*adv.*), least of all,
minimally, not at all

minimum, minimī (*n.*),
minimum (*math.*)

minimus, minima, minimum,
smallest, least, minimal

**ministrō, ministrāre, ministrāvī,
ministrātum,** to serve, to take
care, to wait upon

minor, minor, minus, smaller,
lesser, younger

**minōrō, minōrāre, minōrāvī,
minōrātum,** to diminish, to
lessen

minu (*adv.*), less

minūtus, minūta, minūtum, very
small, little, minute

mīror, mīrārī, mīrātus sum, to be
astonished at, to admire

mīrus, mīra, mīrum, astonishing,
wonderful, admirable

**misceō, miscēre, miscuī,
mixtum,** to mix, to mingle, to
combine (*alt. spel. of* **mixtum:
mistum**)

mistus, mista, mistum, mixed,
tempered (*alt. spel.:* **mixtus,
mixta, mixtum**)

mittō, mittere, mīsī, missum, to
send, to dispatch, to let go, to
release

mōbilis, mōbilis, mōbile,
movable, mobile, changeable

moderātor, moderātōris (*m.*),
controller, manager, ruler,
moderator

**moderātus, moderāta,
moderātum,** moderate,
temperate, restrained

modius, modiī (*m.*), a capacity
measure of about eight liters

modo (*adv.*), only, just, merely, just
now

modus, modī (*m.*), measure,
standard, meter, manner, mode

mōlēs, mōlis (*f.*), large mass, rock

molestus, molesta, molestum,
troublesome, annoying, labored

mōlior, mōlīrī, mōlītus sum, to
toil, to strive, to labor, to stir, to
displace

mōmentum, mōmentī (*n.*),
movement, importance,
momentum (*phys.*)

monēta, monētae (*f.*), mint for
coin making, coin, money

mōns, montis (*m.*), mountain

**monstrōsus, monstrōsa,
monstrōsum,** monstrous,
strange (*alt. spel.:*
**monstruōsus, monstruōsa,
monstruōsum**)

mora, morae (*f.*), delay, stay,
tarrying, space of time

morbus, morbī (*m.*), sickness,
disease

morior, morī, mortuus sum, to die

moror, morārī, morātus sum, to
delay, to hinder, to linger, to
tarry, to stay

mortālis, mortālis, mortāle,
mortal

mōs, mōris (*m.*), habit, custom, fashion, character

mōtiō, mōtiōnis (*f.*), motion, movement

mōtrix, mōtrīcis (*f.*), a (feminine) mover, a cause of motion

mōtus, mōtūs (*m.*), motion, movement

moveō, movēre, mōvī, mōtum, to move something, to set in motion

mox (*adv.*), soon, presently

muliebris, muliebris, muliebre, womanly, feminine

multiplex, multiplicis, manifold

multiplicātiō, multiplicātiōnis (*f.*), multiplying, multiplication (*math.*)

multiplicō, multiplicāre, multiplicāvī, multiplicātum, to multiply, to increase

multus, multa, multum, much, many

mundānus, mundānī (*m.*), of the world, cosmopolitan, worldly (used as adjective only in *Latin of Science* in Kepler texts)

mundus, munda, mundum, elegant, neat, clean

mundus, mundī (*m.*), cosmos, universe, world

mūniō, mūnīre, mūnīvī, mūnītum, to fortify, to protect, to build, to wall

mūnītiō, mūnītiōnis (*f.*), fortification, protection

mūnus, mūneris (*n.*), spectacle, public show, gladiatorial show, gift, office, function, duty

mūs, mūris (*m.*), mouse, rat

mūsculāris, mūsculāris, mūsculāre, pertaining to muscles

mūsculus, mūsculī (*m.*), muscle

mūsica, mūsicae (*f.*), music, poetry

mūsicus, mūsica, mūsicum, musical, poetic

mūtātiō, mūtātiōnis (*f.*), change, alteration

mūtō, mūtāre, mūtāvī, mūtātum, to change, to alter, to exchange, to move

mūtulus, mūtulī (*m.*), projecting bracket, cornice, overhang (*arch.*)

mūtuō (*adv.*), mutually, reciprocally

mūtuus, mūtua, mūtuum, mutual, reciprocal

nam (*conj.*), because, for, in fact, actually

nārrātiō, nārrātiōnis (*f.*), narration, telling

nārrō, nārrāre, nārrāvī, nārrātum, to narrate, to tell, to say

nāscor, nāscī, nātus sum, to be born

nātūra, nātūrae (*f.*), nature, character, essence

nātūrālis, nātūrālis, nātūrāle, natural

nātūrāliter (*adv.*), naturally

nauticus, nautica, nauticum, nautical, naval

nāvigium, nāvigiī (*n.*), ship, vessel

nāvis, nāvis (*f.*), ship, boat

nē (*adv. and conj.*), not, lest, that not

Neāpolis, Neāpolis (*f.*), Naples

nec (*conj.*), and not, neither

necessāriō (*adv.*), necessarily

necessārius, necessāria, necessārium, necessary, unavoidable

necesse esse, to be necessary, to be unavoidable

necessitās, necessitātis (*f.*), necessity, inevitability

neglēctus, neglēctūs (*m.*), disregard, neglect

neglegō, neglegere, neglēxī, neglēctum, to neglect, to disregard (*alt. spel.:* negligō, negligere, neglixī, neglictum)

negō, negāre, negāvī, negātum, to deny, to say no, to refuse

negōtiātiō, negōtiātiōnis (*f.*), business, buying and selling

negōtium, negōtiī (*n.*), occupation, employment, affair, trouble, trade, matter

nēmō, nēminis (*m.*), no one, nobody

nempe (*adv.*), indeed, truly, of course

nēquāquam (*adv.*), by no means, in no wise, not at all

neque (*conj.*), and not, neither

nequeō, nequīre, nequīvī, nequitum, to be unable

nervus, nervī (*m.*), sinew, tendon, nerve, cord, string

neuter, neutra, neutrum, neither of the two, neuter

Nīcolāus, Nīcolāī (*m.*), Nicolaus

nictus, nictūs (*m.*), wink, twinkling

niger, nigra, nigrum, black, dark

nihil (*n. indecl.*), nothing (*alt. spel.:* nīl, nichil)

nihilōminus (*adv.*), nevertheless, notwithstanding

nihilum, nihilī (*n.*), nothing

nīmīrum (*adv.*), undoubtedly, certainly

nimius, nimia, nimium, too much, excessive

nisi (*conj.*), if not, unless, except if, except that

nīsus, nīsūs (*m.*), strain, pressure, push (*alt. spel.:* nīxus, nīxūs)

nitēscō, nitēscere, nituī, to glitter, to begin to shine

nītor, nītī, nīxus sum (nīsus sum), to lean on, to strive

nitor, nitōris (*m.*), brilliance, brightness, elegance

nitrum, nitrī (*n.*), natron, soda carbonate

nōbilis, nōbilis, nōbile, renowned, noble

nocīvus, nocīva, nocīvum, harmful, injurious

nocumentum, nocumentī (*n.*), harm, injury

nōmen, nōminis (*n.*), name

nōminātim (*adv.*), by name, explicitly

nōminō, nōmināre, nōmināvī, nōminātum, to name, to call, to appoint, to nominate, to mention

nōn (*adv.*), not

nōnnūllus, nōnnūlla,
nōnnūllum, some, a few,
several

nōnnunquam (*adv.*), sometimes

norma, normae (*f.*), carpenter's
square, rule, standard, norm

normālis, normālis, normāle,
normal, perpendicular (*math.*)

nōscō, nōscere, nōvī, nōtum,
to come to know, to become
acquainted with

noster, nostra, nostrum, our, ours

notābilis, notābilis, notābile,
noteworthy, remarkable

nothus, notha, nothum, mixed
breed, hybrid, spurious,
counterfeit

nōtiō, nōtiōnis (*f.*), notion, idea

nōtitia, nōtitiae (*f.*), knowledge,
acquaintance, notion

notō, notāre, notāvī, notātum,
to mark, to write, to remark, to
indicate, to observe

novem (*indecl.*), nine

november, novembris, novembre,
relating to the month of
November

novitās, novitātis (*f.*), newness,
novelty

novus, nova, novum, new

noxius, noxia, noxium, harmful,
hurtful, noxious, criminal

nūllus, nūlla, nūllum, none, not
any, no, nobody

numerus, numerī (*m.*), number,
measure

numquam (*adv.*), never (*alt. spel.:*
nunquam)

nunc (*adv.*), now, at this moment

nuncupō, nuncupāre,
nuncupāvī, nuncupātum,
to name, to call by name, to
nominate

nūtō, nūtāre, nūtāvī, nūtātum, to
nod, to waver, to move up and
down

ob (*prep.* + *acc.*), on account of,
because of, for the sake of, in
front of

obedientia, obedientiae
(*f.*), obedience (*alt. spel.:*
oboedientia, oboedientiae)

ōbiciō, ōbicere, ōbiēcī,
ōbiectum, to throw against,
to place before, to expose (*alt.
spel.:* ōbiiciō, ōbiicere, ōbiēcī,
ōbiectum)

oblīquē (*adv.*), obliquely, at a slant,
sideways

oblīquus, oblīqua, oblīquum,
oblique, slanting, to one side

oblongus, oblonga, oblongum,
oblong, elongated, ovoidal

obnoxius, obnoxia, obnoxium,
liable to punishment, exposed to

obolus, obolī (*m.*), obol, coin, a
unit of weight

obscūrātiō, obscūrātiōnis (*f.*),
darkening

obscūrus, obscūra, obscūrum,
dark, obscure, hidden,
indistinct, unknown

observātiō, observātiōnis (*f.*),
observation

observō, observāre, observāvī,
observātum, to observe, to
watch, to keep, to respect

obsideō, obsidēre, obsēdī,
obsessum, to sit by, to beset, to
besiege

obtineō, obtinēre, obtinuī,
obtentum, to hold, to possess,
to obtain, to occupy (*alt. spel.*:
optineō, optinēre, optinuī,
optentum)

obtūrō, obtūrāre, obtūrāvī,
obtūrātum, to stop, to block,
to close

obvius, obvia, obvium, in the
way, exposed to, ready at hand

occāsiō, occāsiōnis (*f.*),
opportunity, occasion, favorable
moment

occidō, occidere, occidī, to go
down, to set, to fall

occultō, occultāre, occultāvī,
occultātum, to hide, to conceal

occultus, occulta, occultum,
hidden, secret

occupātus, occupāta,
occupātum, occupied, busy

occurrō, occurrere, ocucurrī
(occurrī), occursum, to run to
meet, to fall upon

ōceanus, ōceanī (*m.*), ocean

octāvus, octāva, octāvum, eighth

octō (*indecl.*), eight

oculus, oculī (*m.*), eye

oeconomia, oeconomiae (*f.*),
economy, management of the
household

offendō, offendere, offendī,
offēnsum, to offend, to shock,
to strike

offēnsiō, offēnsiōnis (*f.*), offense,
strike, dislike

offerō, offerre, obtulī, oblātum,
to offer, to bring forward, to
inflict

officium, officiī (*n.*), duty, office,
service, function

oleum, oleī (*n.*), oil

ōlim (*adv.*), once, formerly, once
upon a time

omnimodus, omnimoda,
omnimodum, of every kind

omnīnō (*adv.*), entirely, altogether,
wholly, absolutely

omnis, omnis, omne, all, every

onus, oneris (*n.*), weight, burden,
load, expense

opera, operae (*f.*), effort, exertion,
work

operārius, operāriī (*m.*), worker,
laborer

operātiō, operātiōnis (*f.*),
operation, activity, effect

operiō, operīre, operuī,
opertum, to cover, to shut, to
close

operor, operārī, operātus sum, to
work, to be busy

opīnābilis, opīnābilis, opīnābile,
conjectural, subject to opinion

opīniō, opīniōnis (*f.*), opinion,
repute

opīnor, opīnārī, opīnātus sum,
to suppose, to think, to believe

oportet, oportere, oportuit
(*impersonal*), it is proper, it is
fitting, it behooves

oppidum, oppidī (*n.*), town

oppōnō, oppōnere, oppōsuī,
oppōsitum, to place opposite
to, to oppose

optica, opticae (*f.*), optics
opticē, opticēs (*f.*), optics
opticus, optica, opticum, optical
optimē (*adv.*), very well, excellently
optimus, optima, optimum, best, excellent
optō, optāre, optāvī, optātum, to choose, to wish, to desire
opus, operis (*n.*), work, deed
ōrātiō, ōrātiōnis (*f.*), speech, speaking, oration
orbiculāris, orbiculāris, orbiculāre, circular
orbis, orbis (*m.*), circle, sphere, world
orbita, orbitae (*f.*), orbit (*astr.*)
ōrdināta, ōrdinātae (*f.*), ordinate (*math.*)
ōrdinātiō, ōrdinātiōnis (*f.*), arrangement
ōrdinō, ōrdināre, ōrdināvī, ōrdinātum, to arrange, to set in order
ōrdior, ōrdīrī, ōrsus sum, to begin
ōrdō, ōrdinis (*m.*), array, line, row, series, order
organum, organī (*n.*), instrument, implement, organ (*anat.*)
orīgō, orīginis (*f.*), beginning, origin, source
orior, orīrī, ortus sum, to arise, to rise, to appear, to originate
ōrnāmentum, ōrnāmentī (*n.*), equipment, furniture, ornament, decoration
ōrnō, ōrnāre, ōrnāvī, ōrnātum, to equip, to adorn, to furnish, to embellish

ōrō, ōrāre, ōrāvī, ōrātum, to speak, to pray, to beseech
orthogōnaliter (*adv.*), orthogonally, perpendicularly (*math.*)
ōs, ōris (*n.*), mouth, face
ōtium, ōtiī (*n.*), leisure, idleness
ovis, ovis (*f.*), sheep

pactum, pactī (*n.*), agreement, contract (*in ablative*: means, way)
paedonomus, paedonomī (*m.*), institutor, superintendent for the education of children
pallidus, pallida, pallidum, pale, wan, sickly
pallor, pallōris (*m.*), paleness, pallor
palpebra, palpebrae (*f.*), eyelid
pānis, pānis (*m.*), bread
pannus, pannī (*m.*), piece of cloth, garment, rag
paracelsista, paracelsistae (*m.*), follower of the doctrines of Paracelsus
paracelsius, paracelsia, paracelsium, relating to Paracelsus
Paracelsus, Paracelsī (*m.*), Paracelsus
parallēlus, parallēla, parallēlum, parallel (*math.*)
pariēs, parietis (*m.*), wall of a house
pariō, parīre, peperī, partum, to bring forth, to bear, to give birth to
pariter (*adv.*), equally, at the same time

parō, parāre, parāvī, parātum, to prepare

pars, partis (*f.*), part, portion

particula, particulae (*f.*), particle, small part

partim (*adv.*), partly, in part

parum (*adv.*), too little, not enough, very little

passim (*adv.*), here and there, far and wide

passiō, passiōnis (*f.*), suffering, enduring, experience

pateō, patēre, patuī, to be open, to lie open, to be manifest, be evident

pater, patris (*m.*), father

patior, patī, passus sum, to suffer, to undergo, to endure, to experience, to permit

patrius, patria, patrium, pertaining to a father, of the native country

paucus, pauca, paucum, few, little

paulātim (*adv.*), gradually, little by little

peccātum, peccātī (*n.*), sin, transgression, error

pectus, pectoris (*n.*), breast

pecūliāris, pecūliāris, pecūliāre, private, one's own, special, peculiar

pecūnia, pecūniae (*f.*), property, wealth, money

pelicānus, pelicānī (*m.*), pelican

peloponnensis, peloponnensis, peloponnense, Peloponnesian

pena, penae (*f.*), penalty, fine (*classical spel.*: **poena, poenae**)

pendō, pendere, pependī, pēnsum, to suspend, to weigh, to pay a penalty

pene (*adv.*), almost, nearly (*classical spel.*: **paene**)

penes (*prep.* + *acc.*), in the possession of, in the power of

penetrō, penetrāre, penetrāvī, penetrātum, to penetrate, to enter

penitus (*adv.*), deeply, wholly

pēnsō, pēnsāre, pēnsāvī, pēnsātum, to weigh, to balance, to ponder, to consider, to pay

per (*prep.* + *acc.*), through, throughout, during, for the sake of, by

peragō, peragere, perēgī, peractum, to go through, to carry through, to complete

perceptiō, perceptiōnis (*f.*), perception, grasping, comprehension

percipiō, percipere, percēpī, perceptum, to take in, to feel , to perceive, to grasp, to understand

percunctor, percunctārī, percunctātus sum, to ask, to inquire (*alt. spel.*; **percontor, percontārī, percontātus sum**)

percurrō, percurrere, percucurrī (percurrī), percursum, to run through, to traverse, to run over

percutiō, percutere, percussī, percussum, to strike, to beat, to pierce

perdiscō, perdiscere, perdidicī, to learn thoroughly

perdō, perdere, perdidī, perditum, to lose, to waste, to ruin

perdūcō, perdūcere, perdūxī, perductum, to lead through, to lead to, to bring to

pereō, perīre, periī (perīvī), perītum, to perish, to pass away, to vanish

perexiguus, perexigua, perexiguum, very small

perfectē, perfectly, completely

perfectus, perfecta, perfectum, perfect, complete, finished

perficiō, perficere, perfēcī, perfectum, to accomplish, to bring about, to complete, to obtain

perfunctōriē (*adv.*), perfunctorily, carelessly

perfundō, perfundere, perfūdī, perfūsum, to steep in, to fill with

pergō, pergere, perrēxī, perrēctum, to continue, to proceed, to go on

perhibeō, perhibēre, perhibuī, perhibitum, to hold, to consider, to adduce

perīculum, perīculī (*n.*), danger, peril, hazard, trial, test

perīgaeum, perīgaeī (*n.*), perigee (*astr.*)

perinde (*adv.*), in like manner, just as if

periodicus, periodica, periodicum, periodic, taking place at regular intervals

perītia, perītiae (*f.*), expertise, skill

perītus, perīta, perītum, expert, skilled

permūtātiō, permūtātiōnis (*f.*), exchange, permutation

permūtō, permūtāre, permūtāvī, permūtātum, to change completely, to exchange

perniciōsus, perniciōsa, perniciōsum, destructive, ruinous, pernicious

pernōscō, pernōscere, pernōvī, pernōtum, to become thoroughly acquainted with

perpendiculāris, perpendiculāris, perpendiculāre, perpendicular (*math.*)

perpendō, perpendere, perpendī, perpēnsum, to weigh carefully, to consider, to examine

perpetuō (*adv.*), continuously, uninterrupted, forever

perscrūtor, perscrūtārī, perscrūtātus sum, to examine, to investigate

persequor, persequī, persecūtus sum, to pursue, to follow constantly, to continue, to proceed, to execute

persēs, persae (*m.*), Persian

persevērō, persevērāre, persevērāvī, persevērātum, to persevere, to persist

persuādeō, persuādēre, persuāsī, persuāsum, to persuade, to convince, to prevail upon

perterritus, perterrita,
perterritum, terrified

pertineō, pertinēre, pertinuī, to
belong, to relate to, to pertain,
to be applicable

perturbō, perturbāre,
perturbāvī, perturbātum, to
confuse, to disturb, to perturb

pervagor, pervagārī, pervagātus
sum, to wander, to roam, to
pervade, to be widely spread

perveniō, pervenīre, pervēnī,
perventum, to reach, to arrive
at, to attain to, to come to

perversus, perversa, perversum,
perverse, wrong, askew,
crooked

pervertō, pervertere, pervertī,
perversum, to turn upside
down, to subvert, to pervert

pervestīgō, pervestīgāre,
pervestīgāvī, pervestīgātum,
to investigate, to search into

petō, petere, petīvī, petītum, to
seek, to pursue, to demand, to
solicit

petra, petrae (f.), rock, stone

phaenomenon, phanomenī (n.),
phenomenon, appearance

philosophia, philosophiae (f.),
philosophy

philosophicus, philosophica,
philosophicum, philosophical

philosophus, philosophī (m.),
philosopher

physica, physicae (f.), physics,
natural science

physicē, physicēs (f.), physics,
natural science

physicus, physica, physicum,
physical, relating to physics

physiologia, physiologiae (f.),
science, natural philosophy,
physiology

pictūra, pictūrae (f.), picture,
painting

pigmentum, pigmentī (n.),
pigment, paint, color

pingō, pingere, pinxī, pictum, to
paint, to color, to depict

pius, pia, pium, dutiful, pious,
honest; merciful

placeō, placēre, placuī, placitum,
to please, to be acceptable to

plaga, plagae (f.), zone, region,
district

plāga, plāgae (f.), blow,
misfortune, disaster

plānē (adv.), certainly, obviously,
directly, wholly, distinctly

planēta, planētae (m.), planet

plānitia, plānitiae (f.), level
surface, plain

plānum, plānī (n.), plane (math.)

plānus, plāna, plānum, flat, even,
level

Platō, Platōnis (m.), Plato

plēnus, plēna, plēnum, full

plērunquē (adv.), mostly (alt. spel.:
plērumquē)

pleurēsis, pleurīdis (f.), pleurisy

plumbum, plumbī (n.), lead,
leaden object

plūrēs, plūrēs, plūra (pl.), more
numerous, several, many

plūrimus, plūrima, plūrimum,
most, very many

plūs (adv.), more, in a higher degree

poēta, poētae (*m.*), poet

polīticus, polītica, polīticum, political, civil

Polliō, Polliōnis (*m.*), Vitruvius (Marcus Vitruvius Pollio)

Pompēius, Pompēiī (*m.*), Pompey

pondus, ponderis (*n.*), weight, burden

pōnō, pōnere, posuī, positum, to put, to place, to lay

populus, populī (*m.*), nation, people, community

porrigō, porrigere, porrēgī, porrēctum, to extend, to stretch out, to reach out

porrō (*adv.*), forward, further, moreover

porta, portae (*f.*), gate, door, entrance

portiō, portiōnis (*f.*), portion, share, part

Posīdōnius, Posīdōniī (*m.*), Posidonius

positiō, positiōnis (*f.*), position, placement

possessiō, possessiōnis (*f.*), possession, property

possibilis, possibilis, possibile, possible

possum, posse, potuī, to be able, can

post (*prep.* + *acc.*), after, behind

posteā, after that, afterward

posterior, posterior, posterius, next, following after, posterior

posterus, postera, posterum, subsequent

postquam (*conj.*), after, when

postrēmō (*adv.*), finally

postrēmus, postrēma, postrēmum, last, final, hindmost

postulō, postulāre, postulāvī, postulātum, to demand, to request, to claim, to accuse

potestās, potestātis (*f.*), power, control, authority, capacity

potior, potior, potius, better, preferable

potissimus, potissima, potissimum, best of all, most important

potius (*adv.*), rather, preferably

pōtō, pōtāre, pōtāvī, pōtātum, to drink

pōtus, pōtūs (*m.*), drink

prae (*adv. and prep.* + *acc.*), before, in front of

praecēdō, praecēdere, praecessī, praecessum, to go before, to precede, to surpass

praeceptum, praeceptī (*n.*), precept, order, rule

praecipitō, praecipitāre, praecipitāvī, praecipitātum, to cast down headlong, to throw oneself down, to rush, to destroy

praecipuus, praecipua, praecipuum, special, peculiar

praedīcō, praedīcere, praedīxī, praedictum, to mention before, to foretell, to predict

praedispositus, praedisposita, praedispositum, prepared in advance, predisposed

praeferō, praeferre, praetulī, praelātum, to carry before, to bring to light, to prefer

praefīniō, praefīnīre, praefīnīvī,
praefīnītum, to predetermine,
to fix, to limit, to prescribe

praeoccupātus, praeoccupāta,
praeoccupātum, anticipated,
preoccupied

praeparō, praeparāre,
praeparāvī, praeparātum, to
prepare

praescrībō, praescrībere,
praescrīpsī, praescrīptum,
to prescribe, to prefix (alt.
spel.: prescrībō, prescrībere,
prescrīpsī, prescrīptum)

praescrīptiō, praescrīptiōnis (f.),
introduction, pretext, precept,
prescription

praesēns, praesēntis, present, at
hand, for the moment

praesentārius, praesentāria,
praesentārium, present, at
hand, for the moment

praesertim (adv.), especially,
particularly

praesidium, praesidiī (n.),
protection, defense, support

praestō, praestāre, praestitī,
praestitum, to stand out, to
excel, to exhibit, to offer; to
confer, to grant, to lend

praesūmō, praesūmere,
praesumpsī, praesumptum, to
take for granted, to suppose, to
presume, to anticipate

praeter (adv. and prep. + acc.),
except, beyond

praetereā (adv.), besides, moreover

praeteritus, praeterita,
praeteritum, gone by, past

prāxis, prāxeōs (f.), praxis,
practice (acc. sing.: prāxin)

premō, premere, pressī, pressum,
to press, to squeeze, to
compress, to keep down

pressiō, pressiōnis (f.), means of
leverage, pressure (phys.)

pretiōsus, pretiōsa, pretiōsum,
valuable, precious, costly

pretium, pretiī (n.), worth, value,
price

prex, precis (f.), request, entreaty,
wish, prayer

prīmōrdium, prīmōrdiī (n.),
origin, first beginning, original
element

prīmus, prīma, prīmum, first,
foremost

prīnceps, prīncipis (m.), prince,
ruler

prīncipāliter (adv.), primarily,
principally

prīncipium, prīncipiī (n.),
beginning, principle,
foundation

prior, prior, prius, former,
previous, superior

prisma, prismatis (n.), prism

prīvātus, prīvāta, prīvātum,
private, for private use

prīvilēgium, prīvilēgiī (n.),
privilege, private law, special law

prō (prep. + abl.), for, on behalf of,
in front of

probitās, probitātis (f.), honesty,
probity

probō, probāre, probāvī,
probātum, to approve, to
prove, to judge, to test

prōcēdō, prōcēdere, prōcessī, prōcessum, to go forth, to proceed, to make progress

Procilius, Prociliī (m.), Procilius (Lucius Procilius)

prōdeō, prōdīre, prōdiī, prōditum, to go forth, to appear

prōdūcō, prōdūcere, prōdūxī, prōductum, to lead forth, to bring forward, to produce, to advance, to draw

prōductiō, prōductiōnis (f.), prolongation, production

prōferō, prōferre, prōtūlī, prōlātum, to bring forth, to offer, to publish, to utter, to lengthen

prōficiō, prōficere, prōfēcī, prōfectum, to make progress, to gain

prōficīscor, prōficīscī, prōfectus sum, to set out, to start, to proceed

prōfiteor, prōfitērī, prōfessus sum, to avow, to own up, to confess, to profess, to declare

prōfundō, prōfundere, prōfūdī, prōfūsum, to pour forth, to cause to flow

profundus, profunda, profundum, deep, profound

prōgressīvus, prōgressīva, prōgressīvum, progressive, moving forward

prōgressus, prōgressūs (m.), advance, progress

prōiectīlis, prōiectīlis, prōiectīle, projectile

prōlixitās, prōlixitātis (f.), extension, extent

prōlogus, prōlogī (m.), prologue, preface

prōmittō, prōmittere, prōmīsī, prōmissum, to promise, to send forth

prōmoveō, prōmovēre, prōmōvī, prōmōtum, to move forward, to improve, to promote

promptuārium, promptuāriī (n.), repository, storeroom

prōpellō, prōpellere, prōpulī, prōpulsum, to push forward, to propel, to impel, to drive away

properō, properāre, properāvī, properātum, to hasten, to accelerate

prōpōnō, prōpōnere, prōposuī, prōpositum, to put forward, to propose, to publish

prōportiō, prōportiōnis (f.), proportion

prōportiōnālis, prōportiōnālis, prōportiōnāle, proportional (math.)

prōpositiō, prōpositiōnis (f.), proposition

propriē (adv.), properly, in a proper sense, especially

proprius, propria, proprium, one's own, special, proper

propter (prep. + acc.), on account of, because of, near at hand

proptereā (adv.), on that account, therefore

prōpulsiō, prōpulsiōnis (f.), driving forward, repelling, propulsion prōrēpō, prōrēpere, prōrepsī, (prōrēptum), to creep forward, to crawl

prorsus (adv.), directly, truly

prōtrūdō, prōtrūdere, prōtrūsī, prōtrūsum, to push forward, to defer

prout (conj.), just as, according as

prōvideō, prōvidēre, prōvīdī, prōvīsum, to foresee, to take precautions for, to make preparations for

proximus, proxima, proximum, nearest, closest

prūdēns, prūdentis, prudent, wise, knowing, foreseeing

prūdentia, prūdentiae (f.), prudence, discretion, foresight

pūblicē (adv.), publicly, for the people

pūblicus, pūblica, pūblicum, public, common, belonging to the people

puer, puerī (m.), child, boy

puerpera, puerperae (f.), woman in childbirth or labor

pulcher, pulchra, pulchrum, beautiful (alt. spel.: pulcer, pulcra, pulcrum)

pulmō, pulmōnis (m.), lung

pulsus, pulsūs (m.), beating, pulse

pulvis, pulveris (f.), dust, powder

punctim (adv.), by stabbing, by thrusting

punctum, punctī (n.), point

pūrificō, pūrificāre, pūrificāvī, pūrificātum, to purify, to clean

purpureus, purpurea, purpureum, purple colored

pūrus, pūra, pūrum, pure, clean

puteus, puteī (m.), pit, well

putō, putāre, putāvī, putātum, to think, to consider, to suppose

pyronomia, pyronomiae (f.), the art of managing the fire (alch.)

pyrrhichē, pyrrhichēs (f.), a war dance

quadrāgintā (indecl.), forty

quadruplex, quadruplicis (adj.), fourfold, quadruple (as noun)

quadruplus, quadrupla, quadruplum, fourfold, four times as much

quaerō, quaerere, quaesīvī, quaesītum, to seek, to search for, to inquire, to require

quaestiō, quaestiōnis (f.), inquiry, question

quāliscumque, quāliscumque, quālecumque, of whatever kind, any whatever (alt. spel.: quāliscunque, quāliscunque, quālecunque)

quālitās, quālitātis (f.), quality, property

quam, than (after comparative)

quamobrem (adv.), wherefore, for which reason, on which account

quamplūrimus, quamplūrima, quamplūrimum, very much, very many

quamvīs (adv.), as you will, although

quandō (adv.), when

quandōque (adv.), whenever

quandōquidem (conj.), since, because

quanquam (*conj.*), although, however (*alt. spel.:* **quamquam**)

quantitās, quantitātis (*f.*), quantity

quantus, quanta, quantum, how great, how much, how many, as great as

quantuslibet, quantalibet, quantumlibet, as great as you will, however much

quāpropter (*adv.*), on which account, wherefore

quārē (*adv.*), why, on which account

quārtus, quārta, quārtum, fourth

quasi (*adv.*), as if, just as, almost

quātenus (*adv.*), how far, as far as

quaternī, quaternae, quaterna, four each, four at a time

quatiō, quatere, (quasī), quassum, to shake, to shatter

quattuor (*indecl.*), four (*alt. spel.:* **quatuor**)

quemadmodum (*adv.*), in what manner, how

queō, quīre, quīvī, quītum, to be able

quī, quae, quod (*rel. pron.*), who, which, what, that

quia (*conj.*), because, why, that

quīcumque, quaecumque, quodcumque, whoever, whatever, whichever (*alt. spel.:* **quīcunque, quaecunque, quodcunque**)

quid (*interr.*), what

quīdam, quaedam, quoddam (quiddam), a certain, somebody, a kind of, so to speak

quidem (*adv.*), indeed, certainly

quidnam (*adv.*), why in the world

quiēscō, quiēscere, quiēvī, quiētum, to rest, to repose

quīlibet, quaelibet, quodlibet, any one you will, anything

quīn (*adv.*), why not, rather, nay

quīnam, quaenam, quodnam (*interr.*), which, what

quīngentī, quīngentae, quīngenta, five hundred

quīnque (*indecl.*), five

quīntus, quīnta, quīntum, fifth

quippe (*adv.*), of course, indeed

quisquam, quaequam, quidquam (quicquam), anybody, anyone, anything

quisque, quaeque, quidque, each, every

quisquis, quaequae, quidquid (quicquid), whoever, whichever, whatever

quīvīs, quaevīs, quodvīs, whoever you will, whatever you will, any one

quoad (*adv.*), how far, as long as, as far as

quōdammodo (*adv.*), in a certain manner

quōmodo (*adv.*), how

quōmodocunque (*adv.*), in whatever way (*alt. spel.:* **quōmodocumque**)

quoniam (*adv.*), since, seeing that

quoque (*adv.*), also, too

quot, how many

quotīdiē (*adv.*), daily, every day

quotuplex, quotuplicis (*adj.*), how many fold

quum (*conj.*), when, as, since, whereas (*alt. spel.*: cum)

radius, radiī (*m.*), spoke of a wheel, ray of light, radius (*math.*)

rādīx, rādīcis (*f.*), root, base

rāna, rānae (*f.*), frog

rārus, rāra, rārum, rare, sparse, thin

ratiō, ratiōnis (*f.*), reason, motive, reasoning, principle, computation, method, theory, ratio (*math.*)

ratiōcinātiō, ratiōcinātiōnis (*f.*), reasoning, logical argument, syllogism

ratiōnālis, ratiōnālis, ratiōnāle, rational, reasonable

ratiōnābiliter (*adv.*), reasonably, according to reason

raucus, rauca, raucum, hoarse, harsh-sounding

reāctiō, reāctiōnis (*f.*), reaction

recēdō, recēdere, recessī, recessum, to recede, to go back, to withdraw

recēnseō, recēnsēre, recēnsuī, recēnsum (recēnsitum), to count, to survey, to consider

recipiō, recipere, recēpī, receptum, to take back, to receive, to accept

reciprocē (*adv.*), reciprocally, mutually, returning

recondō, recondere, recondidī, reconditum, to hide, to store, to close again

rēctē (*adv.*), correctly, rightly

rectificō, rectificāre, rectificāvī, rectificātum, to rectify, to make straight

rectilineus, rectilinea, rectilineum, rectilinear (*math.*)

rēctor, rēctōris (*m.*), ruler, director, controller

rēctus, rēcta, rēctum, straight, correct, right (*math.*)

recūsō, recūsāre, recūsāvī, recūsātum, to refuse, to object, to refute, to take exception

reddō, reddere, reddidī, redditum, to give back, to bring back, to repay, to provide, to render

reditus, reditūs (*m.*), return, coming back

referō, referre, rettulī, relātum, to carry back, to bring back, to refer, to report

rēfert, rēferre, rētulit, it matters, it concerns, it makes a difference

reflectō, reflectere, reflexī, reflexum, to bend back, to reflect (*phys.*)

refractiō, refractiōnis (*f.*), refraction (*phys.*)

refrāgor, refrāgārī, refrāgātus sum, to oppose

refrangibilitās, refrangibilitātis (*f.*), refringency, refractability (*phys.*) (*neol.; classical spelling would have been* refringibilitās)

refringō, refringere, refrēgī, refrāctum, to break up, to break back, to refract (*phys.*)

regimen, regiminis (*n.*), guidance, direction

regiō, regiōnis (*f.*), region, territory, district, direction

rēgnum, rēgnī (*n.*), kingdom, royal power

regō, regere, rēxī, rēctum, to rule, to govern

regressus, regressūs (*m.*), return, retreat, going back

rēgula, rēgulae (*f.*), rule, model, ruler

relaxō, relaxāre, relaxāvī, relaxātum, to loosen, to relax

religiō, religiōnis (*f.*), religion, worship

religō, religāre, religāvī, religātum, to fasten, to bind, to tie

relinquō, relinquere, relīquī, relictum, to leave behind, to abandon, to neglect

reliquus, reliqua, reliquum, left behind, remaining

remedium, remediī (*n.*), remedy, medicine, cure

removeō, removēre, remōvī, remōtum, to move back, to withdraw, to remove

repente (*adv.*), suddenly

repercutiō, repercutere, repercussī, repercussum, to strike back, to cause to rebound, to reverberate

reperiō, reperīre, repperī, repertum, to find, to discover

repertor, repertōris (*m.*), discoverer, inventor, finder

repleō, replēre, replēvī, replētum, to fill up

reprehendō, reprehendere, reprehendī, reprehēsum, to blame, to censure, to restrain

requīrō, requīrere, requīsīvī, requīsītum, to demand, to require, to ask for

rēs, reī (*f.*), thing, matter, affair

resideō, residēre, resēdī, resessum, to remain sitting, to stay, to reside

resīdō, resīdere, resēdī, resessum, to settle, to subside

resistentia, resistentiae (*f.*), resistance, opposition

resistō, resistere, restitī, to stay, to oppose, to resist

resolvō, resolvere, resolvī, resolūtum, to untie, to loosen, to release, to dissolve, to melt, to dilute

respectivē (*adv.*), respectively

respondeō, respondēre, respondī, respōnsum, to answer, to reply, to respond, to correspond

respōnsum, respōnsī (*n.*), reply, answer

rēspūblica, rēspūblicae (*f.*), republic, state, commonwealth, public interest

restaurō, restaurāre, restaurāvī, restaurātum, to restore, to rebuild

restituō, restituere, restituī, restitūtum, to replace, to reinstate

restitutiō, restitutiōnis (*f.*), restoration, reinstatement, restitution

restō, restāre, restitī, to stay back,
to withstand, to remain

retardō, retardāre, retardāvī,
retardātum, to delay, to retard,
to hinder, to impede, to slow
down

retrahō, retrahere, retrāxī,
retractum, to draw back, to
drag, to prevent

revēlō, revēlāre, revēlāvī,
revēlātum, to unveil, to reveal,
to uncover

revertor (revertō), revertere
(revertī), revertī (reversus
sum), to turn back, to return,
to revert

revocātiō, revocātiōnis (f.),
calling back, revocation,
recalling

revocō, revocāre, revocāvī,
revocātum, to call back, to call
off, to revoke

revolūtiō, revolūtiōnis (f.),
revolution, act of revolving

rēx, rēgis (m.), king

rhētorica, rhētoricae (f.), oratory,
rhetoric

rhythmus, rhythmī (m.), rhythm
(alt. spel.: rhytmus, rhytmī)

rigēns, rigentis, rigid, stiff

rigidus, rigida, rigidum, rigid,
rough

rōbustus, rōbusta, rōbustum,
strong, hard, powerful

Rōma, Rōmae (f.), Rome

rota, rotae (f.), wheel

rotō, rotāre, rotāvī, rotātum, to
make something turn, to cause
rotation

rotunditās, rotunditātis (f.),
roundness

rubeō, rubēre, rubuī, to become
red, to blush

ruber, rubra, rubrum, red

rudis, rudis, rude, raw, rough,
rude

ruditās, ruditātis (f.), rudeness,
ignorance, roughness

ruīna, ruīnae (f.), ruin, fall,
collapse, disaster

ruō, ruere, ruī, rutum, to fall
down, to collapse, to hurl down

rūpēs, rūpis (f.), rock, cliff

rūrsus (adv.), back, again

saccus, saccī (m.), sack, bag

sacer, sacra, sacrum, holy, sacred

saepe (adv.), often

sāl, salis (f.), salt

salebra, salebrae (f.), rough road

saltem (adv.), at least

saltō, saltāre, saltāvī, saltātum,
to dance

saltus, saltūs (m.), forest,
mountain pass, ravine

salūbris (salūber), salūbris,
salūbre, healthy, salubrious,
vigorous

salūs, salūtis (f.), health, welfare,
safety

salūtō, salūtāre, salūtāvī,
salūtātum, to greet, to salute

salvātor, salvātōris (m.), savior

sānātiō, sānātiōnis (f.), cure,
healing

sānē (adv.), reasonably, really,
indeed, certainly

sanguis, sanguinis (m.), blood

sānitās, sānitātis (*f.*), health, sanity

sānus, sāna, sānum, healthy, sane

satis (*adv.*), sufficiently, enough

satisfaciō, satisfacere, satisfēcī, satisfactum, to satisfy, to pay, to make amends

saxum, saxī (*n.*), rock, stone

scalpellum, scalpellī (*n.*), scalpel, surgical knife

scenicus, scenica, scenicum, pertaining to the stage, theatrical (*alt. spel.*: scaenicus, scaenica, scaenicum)

scientia, scientiae (*f.*), science, knowledge

scīlicet (*adv.*), certainly, of course, to be sure, namely

scintilla, scintillae (*f.*), spark, glimmer

scintillō, scintillāre, scintillāvī, scintillātum, to sparkle, to glitter

sciō, scīre, scīvī, scītum, to know, to understand

sclopētum, sclopētī (*n.*), firearm, rifle (*cf. Spanish* escopeta = *shotgun*)

scrībō, scrībere, scrīpsī, scrīptum, to write, to engrave

scrūpulus, scrūpulī (*m.*), scruple, anxiety, doubt, worry

sēcernō, sēcernere, sēcrēvī, sēcrētum, to sever, to separate, to discern, to distinguish

sēclūdō, sēclūdere, sēclūsī, sēclūsum, to shut off, to seclude, to separate

secō, secāre, secuī, sectum, to cut

secta, sectae (*f.*), sect, school, faction, party

sectiō, sectiōnis (*f.*), cutting, section

sector, sectārī, sectātus sum, to follow continually

secundō (*adv.*), secondly

secundum (*prep. + acc.*), after, in accordance with

secundus, secunda, secundum, second, following, favorable

sēcūrus, sēcūra, sēcūrum, unconcerned, carefree, safe, secure

sed (*conj.*), but

sedecuplus, sedecupla, sedecuplum, sixteenfold

sēdēs, sēdis (*f.*), dwelling, residence, seat

sēdō, sēdāre, sēdāvī, sēdātum, to soothe, to calm, to allay

sēgregātiō, sēgregātiōnis (*f.*), separation, segregation

sējungō, sējungere, sējunxī, sējunctum, to separate, to disjoin (*alt. spel.*: sēiungō)

semel (*adv.*), once, a single time

semper (*adv.*), always

senātor, senātōris (*m.*), senator

senātus, senātūs (*m.*), senate, council of elders

sēnsus, sēnsūs (*m.*), sense, sensation, perception, feeling, meaning

sententia, sententiae (*f.*), opinion, sentence

sentiō, sentīre, sēnsī, sēnsum, to feel, to perceive

sēparō, sēparāre, sēparāvī, sēparātum, to separate

septem (*indecl.*), seven

septentriō, septentriōnis (*m.*), north, the north wind

septentriōnes, septentriōnum (*m. pl.*), north, the seven stars of the Great or Little Bear constellation

septimus, septima, septimum, seventh

sequor, sequī, secūtus sum, to follow

sermō, sermōnis (*m.*), conversation, talk, speech, language

servitūs, servitūtis (*f.*), servitude, slavery

servō, servāre, servāvī, servātum, to keep, to observe, to preserve, to retain

servus, servī (*m.*), slave

seu (*conj.*), or, or if, or rather

sexāgintā (*indecl.*), sixty

sextus, sexta, sextum, sixth

sī (*conj.*), if

sīc (*adv.*), so, thus

sīcut (sīcutī) (*adv.*), just as, as for example

sīdus, sīderis (*n.*), star, constellation

sigillum, sigillī (*n.*), seal

significō, significāre, significāvī, significātum, to signify, to mean, to give a sign, to indicate

signō, signāre, signāvī, signātum, to engrave, to inscribe, to indicate, to assign

signum, signī (*n.*), sign, mark, indication, signal

silex, silicis (*m.*), rock, stone, flint

silva, silvae (*f.*), forest

similiter (*adv.*), similarly, in like manner

similitūdō, similitūdinis (*f.*), likeness, similarity, resemblance, analogy

simmētria, simmētriae (*f.*), symmetry (*classical spel.:* **symmētria, symmētriae**)

simplex, simplicis, simple, uncomplicated

simpliciter (*adv.*), simply

simul (*adv.*), at the same time, together

sīn (*conj.*), if however

sine (*prep.* + *abl.*), without

singulāris, singulāris, singulāre, single, individual, singular

singulus, singula, singulum, single, separate, one each, one at a time

sinister, sinistra, sinistrum, left-hand, awkward, unlucky, unfavorable

sinō, sinere, sīvī, situm, to permit, to allow, to let, to place

sīquidem (*conj.*), if indeed, since

sīquis, sīqua, sīquid (sīquod), if anyone, if someone

situs, sita, situm, placed, located

situs, sitūs (*m.*), site, situation, location

sīve (*conj.*), or, or if, or rather

societās, societātis (*f.*), society, association, partnership

sociō, sociāre, socāvī, sociātum, to join, to associate, to unite, to combine

sōl, sōlis (*m.*), sun

sōlāris, sōlāris, sōlāre, solar, of
the sun

solemniter (*adv.*), solemnly,
religiously (*alt. spels.*:
sollemniter, solenniter)

soleō, solēre, solitus sum, to be
accustomed to

sōlicitūdō, sōlicitūdinis (*f.*),
solicitude, care, anxiety,
uneasiness (*alt. spel.*:
sollicitūdō, sollicitūdinis)

solitus, solita, solitum,
accustomed, usual, habitual,
customary

sollertia, sollertiae (*f.*),
cleverness, skill

sōlstitiālis, sōlstitiālis,
sōlstitiāle, relating to the
summer solstice

solum, solī (*n.*), floor, ground,
foundation

solus, sola, solum, alone, only

solūtiō, solūtiōnis (*f.*), loosening,
payment, dissolution, solution
(*chem.*)

sonitus, sonitūs (*m.*), sound,
noise

sonus, sonī (*m.*), sound, voice,
tone

sophisticus, sophistica,
sophisticum, sophistical

sordidus, sordida, sordidum,
dirty, vile, base

Sorsanus, Sorsanī (*m.*), Sorsanus
(*latinized name of a disciple of
Avicenna*)

sortītus, sortīta, sortītum,
obtained by lot or by chance

spatium, spatiī (*n.*), space, extent

speciēs, speciēī (*f.*), appearance,
look, likeness, species, sort,
particular case

spectō, spectāre, spectāvī,
spectātum, to look, to
observe, to watch, to tend
toward

speculātiō, speculātiōnis (*f.*),
inspection, consideration,
speculation

speculor, speculārī, speculātus
sum, to look out, to watch, to
observe, to explore

speculum, speculī (*n.*), mirror

specus, specūs (*m.*), cave, cavern

sphaera, sphaerae (*f.*), sphere,
globe

sphaericus, sphaerica,
sphaericum, spherical

spīritus, spīritūs (*m.*), breath,
breeze, breath of life, spirit

spīrō, spīrāre, spīrāvī, spīrātum,
to breathe, to blow, to exhale

spissitūdō, spissitūdinis (*f.*),
density, thickness

splendidus, splendida,
splendidum, bright, shining,
splendid, magnificent

splendor, splendōris (*m.*),
brilliance, splendor, brightness

statim (*adv.*), immediately, at once,
firmly

statua, statuae (*f.*), statue, image

statuō, statuere, statuī,
statūtum, to place, to establish,
to determine, to decide, to
ordain

statūra, statūrae (*f.*), height,
stature

status, statūs (*m.*), standing,
position, situation, state,
condition

stēlla, stēllae (*f.*), star, planet,
constellation

sternō, sternere, strāvī, strātum,
to stretch out, to extend, to
pave a road

stillātītius, stillātītia,
stillātītium, falling in drops,
stillatitious

stimulus, stimulī (*m.*), goad,
incentive, stimulus, pointed
stake

stō, stāre, stetī, statum, to stand,
to be at a place

stola, stolae (*f.*), gown, woman's
robe, matron

stolātus, stolāta, stolātum,
wearing a stola

strāgēs, strāgis (*f.*), overthrowing,
debris, carnage, slaughter,
massacre

structūra, structūrae (*f.*),
structure, building

studeō, studēre, studuī, to be
eager, to apply oneself to, to
strive after

studiōsē (*adv.*), eagerly, zealously

studiōsus, studiōsa, studiōsum,
zealous, eager, studious,
anxious

studium, studiī (*n.*), eagerness,
zeal, enthusiasm, study

stultior, stultior, stultius, more
foolish

stupefactiō, stupefactiōnis (*f.*),
stupefaction, astonishment,
numbness

sub (*prep. + acc. or abl.*), up under,
underneath

subdūcō, subdūcere, subdūxī,
subductum, to draw away, to
remove, to draw up, to subtract
(*math.*)

subeō, subīre, subīvī, subitum,
to go up from under, to pass
under, to undergo

subiaceō, subiacēre, subiacuī, to
lie under

sūbiciō, sūbicere, sūbiēcī,
sūbiectum, to place under,
to throw up from below, to
subject

sūbiectum, sūbiectī (*n.*), theme,
subject matter

sūbiectus, sūbiecta, sūbiectum,
subject

subinde (*adv.*), immediately,
thereupon, often

sublīmātiō, sublīmātiōnis (*f.*),
sublimation (*chem.*)

sublūnāris, sublūnāris,
sublūnāre, sublunar (*astr.,*
meteor.)

submittō, submittere, submīsī,
submissum, to submit, to
send under, to bring down,
to send up from below (*alt.*
spel.: **summittō, summittere,**
summīsī, summissum)

subōrdinātus, subōrdināta,
subōrdinātum, subordinate,
arranged under

substantia, substantiae (*f.*),
substance, essence

substructiō, substructiōnis (*f.*),
substructure, foundation

subsum, subesse, subfuī, to be near, to be close at hand, to be under, to exist

subterrāneus, subterrānea, subterrāneum, underground, subterranean

subtīlis, subtīlis, subtīle, fine, thin, refined, subtle

subtilisātus, subtilisāta, subtilisātum, subtilized, made finer, made thinner

subtīlitās, subtīlitātis (*f.*), fineness, thinness, subtlety, exactness

subtractiō, subtractiōnis (*f.*), subtraction (*math.*)

subveniō, subvenīre, subvēnī, subventum, to come to help, to relieve

successīvē (*adv.*), successively

successīvus, successīva, successīvum, successive

succinctus, succincta, succinctum, succinct, concise

succurrō, succurrere, succurrī, succursum, to run to help, to come up from below, to come to mind

succus, succī (*m.*), juice, liquid, drink (*alt. spel.*: **sūcus, sūcī**)

succussiō, succussiōnis (*f.*), earthquake, shaking from below

succutiō, succutere, succussī, succussum, to shake from below

sufficiō, sufficere, suffēcī, suffectum, to be sufficient, to afford

sulfur, sulfuris (*m.*), sulfur (*alt. spels.*: **sulphur, sulphuris; sulpur, sulpuris**)

sum, esse, fuī, to be, to exist, to live, to happen, to be there

summitās, summitātis (*f.*), highest part, summit

summoveō, summovēre, summōvī, summōtum, to move up from below, to remove, to banish

summus, summa, summum, highest, uppermost

sūmptus, sūmptūs (*m.*), cost, expense

super (*adv. and prep.* + *acc. or abl.*), over, above

superabundō, superabundāre, superabundāvī, superabundātum, to be very abundant, to superabound

superficiēs, superficiēī (*f.*), surface, area (*math.*)

superior, superior, superius, higher, superior, previous

superveniō, supervenīre, supervēnī, superventum, to appear, to arrive unexpectedly, to happen suddenly

supīnus, supīna, supīnum, lying on one's back, face upward

suppetō, suppetere, suppetīvī, suppetītum, to be enough, to be in store, to be available

suppōnō, suppōnere, suppōsuī, suppōsitum, to place under, to lay down, to substitute, to add

suprā (*adv. and prep.* + *acc.*), above, over

suprādictus, suprādicta,
suprādictum, mentioned
above, spoken of before

surrentinus, surrentina,
surrentinum, from Surrentum
(modern Sorrento)

surripiō, surripere, surripuī,
surrpetum, to pilfer, to take
away secretly or surreptitiously

sūrsum (adv.), upward

sustineō, sustinēre, sustinuī,
sustentum, to support, to
sustain, to keep up

sūtor, sūtōris (m.), shoemaker,
cobbler

sūtōrius, sūtōria, sūtōrium, of a
shoemaker

suus, sua, suum, his own, her
own, its own (gender agrees
with thing possessed)

tabula, tabulae (f.), table

tālis, tālis, tāle, of such a kind,
such

tam (adv.), so, so far, to such a
degree

tamen (conj.), however, yet,
nevertheless

tametsī (conj.), even if, although

tandem (adv.), finally, at last

tangēns, tangentis (f.), tangent
(math.)

tangō, tangere, tetigī, tactum, to
touch

tanquam (adv.), just as, as if (alt.
spel.: tamquam)

tantum (adv.), so much, only

tantus, tanta, tantum, so great, so
much, of such a size

tantusdem, tantadem, tantundem,
just so much, just so great

taxō, taxāre, taxāvī, taxātum,
to reproach, to estimate, to
appraise

tēctum, tēctī (n.), roof

tegimen, tegiminis (n.),
cover, protection (alt. spels.:
tegmen, tegminis; tegumen,
teguminis)

tegō, tegere, tēxī, tēctum, to
cover, to protect

tellūs, tellūris (f.), earth, soil, the
Earth

temere (adv.), by chance, blindly,
carelessly

temeritās, temeritātis (f.),
rashness, thoughtlessness,
chance

temperāmentum, temperāmentī
(n.), moderation, right
proportion

tempus, temporis (n.), time

tendō, tendere, tetendī, tentum
(tēnsum), to stretch, to aim at

teneō, tenēre, tenuī, (tentum), to
hold, to possess, to keep on

tentō, tentāre, tentāvī, tentātum,
to try, to attempt, to undertake,
to tempt (alt. spel.: temptō,
temptāre, temptāvī,
temptātum)

tenuis, tenuis, tenue, thin,
slender, subtle, tenuous

tepidus, tepida, tepidum,
lukewarm, tepid

tergeō, tergēre, tersī, tersum, to
wipe, to clean, to polish (alt.
spel.: tergō, tergere)

terminō, termināre, termināvī, terminātum, to bound, to confine, to limit, to determine

terminus, terminī (*m.*), limit, boundary

terra, terrae (*f.*), land, earth, country, region, the Earth

terrestris, terrestris, terrestre, terrestrial, earthly

tersus, tersa, tersum, clean, neat

tertiō (*adv.*), thirdly

tertius, tertia, tertium, third

testātiō, testātiōnis (*f.*), bearing witness, testifying

tetanus, tetanī (*m.*), cramp, tetanus (*med.*)

theatrum, theatrī (*n.*), theater

Theodoricus, Theodoricī (*m.*), Theodoric (Theoderic)

theōrēma, theōrēmatis (*n.*), theorem (*math.*)

theōria, theōriae (*f.*), theory, speculation

thēsaurus, thēsaurī (*m.*), treasure, repository

timeō, timēre, timuī, to fear, to dread

timidus, timida, timidum, fearful, timid

tonicus, tonica, tonicum, pertaining to the muscle tone (*med.*)

tot (*indecl. adj.*), so many

totidem (*indecl. adj.*), just as many

totiens (*adv.*), so often, so many times

tōtus, tōta, tōtum, whole, complete, entire

tractātus, tractātūs (*m.*), treatise, treatment

tractō, tractāre, tractāvī, tractātum, to treat, to deal with, to drag along

tractus, tractūs (*m.*), tract, dragging, drawing

trāditiō, trāditiōnis (*f.*), tradition, handing over

trādō, trādere, trādidī, trāditum, to hand over, to report

trāductiō, trāductiōnis (*f.*), transfer

trahō, trahere, traxī, tractum, to drag, to draw, to pull

trāiciō, trāicere, trāiēcī, trāiectum, to throw across, to cross, to pierce

trānseō, trānsīre, trānsiī, trānsitum, to go over, to pass by

trānsferō, trānsferre, trānstulī, trānslātum, to carry across, to transfer, to transport, to transcribe

trānsfūsiō, trānsfūsiōnis (*f.*), pouring out, transfusion (*med.*)

trānsiens, transeuntis, passing by

trānsmūtātiō, trānsmūtātiōnis (*f.*), transposition, change, transmutation (*alch.*)

trānsmūtātōrius, trānsmūtātōria, trānsmūtātōrium, of transmutation

trānsportātiō, trānsportātiōnis (*f.*), removal, conveying over, transport

trānsversus, trānsversa,
trānsversum, transverse,
running across, oblique

tremō, tremere, tremuī,
(tremitum), to tremble, to
quake

tremor, tremōris (m.), tremor,
quaking, trembling

trēs, tria, trium, three

triangulāris, triangulāris,
triangulāre, triangular

triangulum, triangulī (n.),
triangle

triangulus, triangula,
triangulum, triangular

tribuō, tribuere, tribuī,
tribūtum, to distribute, to
attribute, to assign

tribus, tribūs (f.), tribe, a division
of people

trīclīnium, trīclīniī (m.), dining
room, couch for reclining,
triclinium (arch.)

triplex, triplicis, threefold

triplus, tripla, triplum, triple,
threefold

Trismegistus, Trismegistī
(m.), Hermes Trismegistus,
Mercurius

trīticum, trīticī (n.), wheat

triumphāns, triumphantis,
triumphant, exulting

triumphus, triumphī (m.),
triumph, triumphal procession

trochus, trochī (m.), hoop

tueor, tuērī, tuitus (tūtus) sum,
to look at, to behold, to protect,
to look after

tum (adv.), then, at that time

tunc (adv.), then, at that time

turbō, turbāre, turbāvī,
turbātum, to disturb, to throw
into confusion

tūtius (adv.), more safely

tuus, tua, tuum, your, thine
(gender agrees with thing
possessed)

ūberior, ūberior, ūberius, more
fruitful

ubī (interr. and rel. adv.), where,
when

ubīque (adv.), everywhere

ūllus, ūlla, ūllum, anyone,
anything

ulna, ulnae (f.), elbow, arm, cubit

ultimus, ultima, ultimum, last,
final, farthest

ultrā (adv. and prep. + acc.),
beyond, farther, above

umbra, umbrae (f.), shadow, shade

ūnā (adv.), together, at the same
time, in one

undātiō, undātiōnis (f.),
undulation

unde (adv.), whence, from where

ūndecim (indecl.), eleven

undequaque (adv.), from
everywhere, everywhere (alt.
spel.: undique)

ūnicus, ūnica, ūnicum, singular,
unique, alone of its kind

ūniformiter (adv.), uniformly,
equally, in one form

ūniversālis, ūniversālis,
ūniversāle, general, universal

ūniversum, ūniversī (n.), universe,
world

ūniversus, ūniversa, ūniversum, whole, entire

ūnus, ūna, ūnum, one

ūnusquisque, ūnaquaeque, ūnumquodque, each one

urbānus, urbāna, urbānum, urban, of the city

urbs, urbis (*f.*), city

urgeō, urgēre, ursī, to urge, to press, to insist

usque (*adv.*), up to, all the way, until

usqueadeō, to such a point

ūsus, ūsūs (*m.*), use, practice, usufruct, exercise

ut (*adv.*), so that, in order that, how (*alt. spel.*: utī)

uter, utra, utrum, which of two, either

uterque, utraque, utrumque, each of two, both

ūtilitās, ūtilitātis (*f.*), usefulness, profit, advantage

ūtiliter (*adv.*), usefully, profitably

ūtor, ūtī, ūsus sum, to use, to employ

utrinque (*adv.*), from both sides

utrobīque (*adv.*), on both sides, on either hand

vacō, vacāre, vacāvī, vacātum, to be vacant, to be at leisure, to have time

vādō, vādere, vāsī, to go, to walk

vaeniō, vaenīre, vaeniī, vaenitum, to be sold, to be worth, to go for sale (*alt. spel.*: vēneō, vēnīre, vēniī, vēnitum)

valdē (*adv.*), very much, greatly

valeō, valēre, valuī, to be well, to be strong; to have value

vallester, vallestris, vallestre, of the valley

vallis (vallēs), vallis (*f.*), valley

variō, variāre, variāvī, variātum, to vary; to affect, to alter

varius, varia, varium, diverse, various, manifold

vās, vāsis (*n.*), vessel, receptacle, utensil

vastō, vastāre, vastāvī, vastātum, to lay waste, to ravage, to devastate, to empty

vastus, vasta, vastum, empty, desolate, vast, enormous

vegetābilis, vegetābilis, vegetābile, vegetal

vehemēns, vehementis, vehement, violent, strong, powerful

vehementer (*adv.*), vehemently, strongly

vehementior, vehementior, vehementius, more vehement

vehementius (*adv.*), more vehemently

vehiculum, vehiculī (*n.*), vehicle, conveyance

vel (*conj.*), or, or rather

vēlōcitās, vēlōcitātis (*f.*), speed, velocity

velutī (*adv.*), as, even as, just as, just as if

vēna, vēnae (*f.*), blood vessel, vein, streak

venditiō, venditiōnis (*f.*), sale

venditor, venditōris (*m.*), seller, vendor

vendō, vendere, vendidī, venditum, to sell

venerātiō, venerātiōnis (f.), reverence, respect, veneration

veniālis, veniālis, veniāle, gracious, pardonable, venial

veniō, venīre, vēnī, ventum, to come

ventriculus, ventriculī (m.), belly, ventricle (anat.)

ventus, ventī (m.), wind

Venus, Veneris (f.), Venus

venustās, venustātis (f.), beauty, charm, elegance

venustus, venusta, venustum, charming, beautiful, lovely

verbum, verbī (n.), word

vērē (adv.), truly

vērisimilior, vērisimilior, vērisimilius, more likely

vērisimilis, vērisimilis, vērisimile, probable, likely

vēritās, vēritātis (f.), truth

vernus, verna, vernum, spring-like, vernal, relating to spring

vērō (adv.), truly, really, but, but in fact

versō, versāre, versāvī, versātum, to turn, to bend (in passive: to be about, to treat, to be engaged in)

versus (adv.), toward, in the direction of

vertex, verticis (m.), whirl, eddy, summit, pole

vērum (conj.), but, but in fact

vērus, vēra, vērum, true, real, genuine

vespertīnus, vespertīna, vespertīnum, of the evening, western

vestīgium, vestīgiī (n.), trace, footmark, footstep

vetus, veteris, old

vexō, vexāre, vexāvī, vexātum, to harass, to disturb, to annoy, to abuse, to damage

via, viae (f.), way, road

vibrō, vibrāre, vibrāvī, vibrātum, to shake, to quiver, to cause to vibrate

vīcīnus, vīcīna, vīcīnum, near, neighboring

vicis, vicis (f.), change, alternation, succession, turn

vicissim (adv.), in turn

vicissitūdō, vicissitūdinis (f.), change, vicissitude

victor, victōris (m.), victor, conqueror

victōria, victōriae (f.), victory, conquest

vidēlicet (adv.), clearly, manifestly, of course

videō, vidēre, vīdī, vīsum, to see

vigor, vigōris (m.), vigor, energy

vigorōsus, vigorōsa, vigorōsum, strong, vigorous

vīlla, vīllae (f.), country house, estate, farm

vincō, vincere, vīcī, victum, to conquer, to overcome, to defeat

vindicō, vindicāre, vindicāvī, vindicātum, to vindicate, to avenge, to claim, to liberate, to spare

vīnum, vīnī *(n.)*, wine, grape, grapevine

vir, virī *(m.)*, man, hero, husband

Virgilius, Virgiliī *(m.)*, Virgil *(alt. spel.*: Vergilius, Vergiliī)

viridārium, viridāriī *(n.)*, pleasure garden

viridis, viridis, viride, green

viror, virōris *(m.)*, greenness, verdure

virtūs, virtūtis *(f.)*, virtue, courage, character, excellence, manliness

vīs, vīs *(f.)*, force, power, strength, violence, energy *(pl.*: vīrēs, vīrium)

vīsibilis, vīsibilis, vīsibile, visible, apparent, that can be seen, that can see

vīsiō, vīsiōnis *(f.)*, seeing, sight, vision, view

vīsitātiō, vīsitātiōnis *(f.)*, visit, sight, visitation

vīsīvus, vīsīva, vīsīvum, visual

vīsus, vīsa, vīsum, having been seen, having been observed, having been understood

vīsus, vīsūs *(m.)*, the action of looking, the power of sight, a vision, appearance

vīta, vītae *(f.)*, life, subsistence, a way of life

Vitellius, Vitelliī *(m.)*, Vitellius (Witelo)

vītō, vītāre, vītāvī, vītātum, to avoid, to evade, to shun

vitreus, vitrea, vitreum, glassy, vitreous

Vitruvius, Vitruviī *(m.)*, Vitruvius (Marcus Vitruvius Pollio)

vitulus, vitulī *(m.)*, calf, bull calf

vīvēns, vīventis, living

vīvus, vīva, vīvum, live, alive, living, lively

vix *(adv.)*, barely, with difficulty, hardly

vocābulum, vocābulī *(n.)*, name, designation, expression, term

vocō, vocāre, vocāvī, vocātum, to call, to beckon, to name, to designate

volō, velle, voluī, to be willing, to wish, to want, to mean

voluptās, voluptātis *(f.)*, pleasure

vōtum, vōtī *(n.)*, vow, desire, will, prayer

vōx, vōcis *(f.)*, voice, speech, expression

Vulcānus, Vulcānī *(m.)*, Vulcan

vulgāris, vulgāre, common, plain, simple

vulgō *(adv.)*, generally, commonly, publicly

vulgō, vulgāre, vulgāvī, vulgātum, to publish, to broadcast, to divulge, to make known among the people

vulgus, vulgī *(m.)*, the common people, the public, the crowd

vulnus, vulneris *(n.)*, wound, injury

Printed and bound by PG in the USA

USA2019PGIL